FAST TRACK TO A 5

Preparing for the **AP***
Microeconomics and
Macroeconomics Examination

To Accompany
Principles of Economics
5th and 6th Editions
by N.Gregory Mankiw

Aster Chin
Lakeside School, Seattle, Washington

Matt Romano
Marist School, Atlanta, Georgia

SOUTH-WESTERN
CENGAGE Learning™

Australia • Brazil • Japan • Korea • Mexico • Singapore • Spain • United Kingdom • United States

*AP and Advanced Placement Program are registered trademarks of the College Entrance Examination Board, which was not involved in the production of, and does not endorse, this product.

ISBN-13: 978-0-538-48040-6
ISBN-10: 0-538-48040-8

South-Western
5191 Natorp Boulevard
Mason, OH 45040
USA

Cengage Learning is a leading provider of customized learning solutions with office locations around the globe, including Singapore, the United Kingdom, Australia, Mexico, Brazil, and Japan. Locate your local office at: **international.cengage.com/region**.

Cengage Learning products are represented in Canada by Nelson Education, Ltd.

For your course and learning solutions, visit **www.cengage.com/school**.

Visit our company website at **www.cengage.com**.

Printed in the United States of America
1 2 3 4 5 6 7   15 14 13 12

CONTENTS

ABOUT THE AUTHORS

ASTER CHIN has taught AP Microeconomics and AP Macroeconomics at Lowell High School in San Francisco, California, International Economics at Columbia University's School of Social Work in New York City, and continues to teach Microeconomics and Development Economics at Lakeside School in Seattle, Washington. She received her bachelor's degree in Economics from the University of California, Davis, a master's degree in Economics from the University of California, Berkeley, and a second master's degree in International Economic an d Political Development from Columbia University. Aster has been a reader for the AP Macro economics/Microeconomics exam since 2005.

MATT ROMANO teaches AP Microeconomics and AP Macro economics at Marist School in Atlanta, Georgia. He holds a bachelor's degree in marketing from Auburn University and a master's degree in applied economics from Georgia Southern University. He is an AP Macroeconomics reader, has been a presenter at the annual conference of the Georgia Independent Schools Association and is active with the Georgia Council on Economic Education.

PREFACE

In his landmark 1890 textbook *Principles of Economics,* economist Alfred Marshall famously declared "economics is the study of people in the ordinary business of life." While the accepted definition of the field does call for greater detail, professor Marshall was absolutely correct in his assertion that economics, while highly technical at times, truly boils down to an analysis of the everyday decision making to which we all can relate.

Aster Chin
Matt Romano

ACKNOWLEDGEMENTS

I am so incredibly grateful to have my husband Greg's support in all of life's adventures, but am particularly thankful for his support and encouragement throughout the writing of this book. A special thanks to my former students and colleagues at Lowell High School in San Francisco, California, for helping to spark my passion for teaching AP Economics. Thanks also to my current Lakeside economics students, who have continued to inspire me to hone my teaching skills. This project would not be complete without the help of our reviewers, Sarah (Skeeter) Makepeace and Sue Weaver, the editors, and the many other professionals who contributed to the publication of this work.

Aster Chin

First of all, my contribution to this book would never have occurred without the patience and support of my wife throughout the process—I am forever grateful for her calming presence. I also want to thank my colleagues in the Marist social studies department whose encouragement and input have driven me to continually improve in my knowledge of economics and my ability to communicate it. Of course, this book would not have been completed without the efforts of editor John Haley, reviewers Sarah (Skeeter) Makepeace and Sue Weaver, and countless other editors and professionals—their work is greatly appreciated. Finally, to the economics students of Marist School I owe a massive debt of gratitude for the fact that their curiosity and receptiveness to economic theory is the primary reason I look forward to going to work each and every day. Thank you.

Matt Romano

Part I

Strategies for the AP Exam

PREPARING FOR THE AP* MACROECONOMICS AND MICROECONOMICS EXAMINATIONS

Advanced Placement Economics, which includes both Microeconomics and Macroeconomics, is a practical course that is also academically rigorous. It is designed to help the student develop a thorough understanding of the principles of economics that apply both to the functions of individual decision makers, consumers, and producers within the larger economic system, and to an economic system as a whole.

As spring approaches and the Advanced Placement examination looms large on the horizon, you may start to feel intimidated. You are certainly not alone. Learning how to take all the information you have learned this year and apply it in a way that will demonstrate your expertise can be very overwhelming at times.

The best way to achieve success on any AP exam is to master it, rather than letting it master you. If you manage your time effectively, you will meet one major challenge—learning a considerable amount of material in the time remaining. In addition, if you think of these tests as a way to demonstrate how well your mind works, you will have an advantage—attitude *does* help.

This book is designed to put you on a fast track to a successful score. *Focused* review and practice time will help you master the examination so that you can walk in better prepared, more confident, and ready to do well on the test.

WHAT'S IN THIS BOOK

This book is keyed to *Principles of Economics,* 5th and 6th editions, by N. Gregory Mankiw. However, because this book follows the College Board Topic Outline for AP Macroeconomics and AP Microeconomics, it is compatible with other economics textbooks as well. We have designed this book to help students prepare for this exam irrespective of the text being used.

---

* AP and Advanced Placement Program are registered trademarks of the College Entrance Examination Board, which was not involved in the production of and does not endorse this product.

This guide is divided into three sections. Part I offers suggestions for preparing for the exam, from signing up to take the test to writing a complete response for each free-response question. Part I ends with diagnostic tests for both microeconomics and macroeconomics that will help you determine which sections you may need more focus as you prepare for the exam. The diagnostic tests are designed in the same format as the Advanced Placement Examinations, with 60 multiple-choice questions and 3 free-response questions that follow the College Board Topic Outline.

The diagnostic tests should help you identify the areas in which you need the most practice. To make this easier for you, the content areas covered by each problem are noted. In reviewing the answers to the diagnostic tests, you will be able to identify gaps in your knowledge by noting groups of questions from the same content area that give you trouble. Page references that accompany each answer allow you to go directly to the appropriate coverage in the Mankiw *Principles of Economics* textbook to review the content areas in most need of your attention. You will also be able to compare your responses to the free-response questions with the suggested answers in the book to identify weaknesses that may exist in conveying your written responses to the test readers.

Part II consists of 12 chapters that encompass all of the topics tested by both the AP Macroeconomics and AP Microeconomics examinations. Each of these chapters is listed as a key subject in the College Board content outline. The percentages below indicate the approximate proportion of exam questions in each chapter devoted to each of the overarching topic areas (microeconomics and macroeconomics).

Chapter 1	Basic Economic Concepts	Macro 8–12%
		Micro 8–14%
Chapter 2	Markets Overview	Micro 15–20%
Chapter 3	Markets and Welfare	Micro 5–10%
Chapter 4	Perfectly Competitive Markets	Micro 10–15%
Chapter 5	Imperfectly Competitive Markets	Micro 10–15%
Chapter 6	Factor Markets	Micro 10–18%
Chapter 7	Market Failures and Externalities	Micro 12–18%
Chapter 8	Macroeconomic Indicators	Macro 12–16%
Chapter 9	The Financial Sector and Monetary Policy	Macro 15–20%
Chapter 10	Inflation, Unemployment, and Stabilization Policies	Macro 20–30%
Chapter 11	Economic Growth and Productivity	Macro 5–10%
Chapter 12	Macroeconomics of the Open Economy	Macro 10–15%

The chapters are **not** intended to be a substitute for a textbook and class discussions; they offer review and help you prepare for the exam. Each chapter also has the textbook sections listed for further review if, as you prepare for the exam, you find a topic that needs more study. At the end of each chapter, you will find 15 multiple-choice and 2 free-response questions based on the content of that chapter. Again, you will find page references with each answer directing you to the appropriate discussion on each point in the 5th and 6th editions of *Principles of Economics*.

Part III offers 4 complete AP Economics examinations—2 AP Macroeconomics exams and 2 AP Microeconomics exams. At the end of each exam you will find answers, explanations, and references to the 5th and 6th editions for each of the 60 multiple-choice and 3 free-response questions.

SETTING UP A REVIEW SCHEDULE

If you have been steadily doing your homework and keeping up with the coursework, you will be in good shape. The key to preparing for the examination is to begin as early as possible; don't wait until the exam is just a week or two away to begin your studying. But even if you've done all that—or if it's too late to do all that—there are other ways to pull it all together.

To begin, read Part I of this book. You will be much more comfortable going into the test if you understand how the test questions are designed and how best to approach them. Then take the diagnostic tests and see where you stand.

Set up a schedule for yourself on a calendar. If you begin studying early, you can chip away at the review chapters in Part II. You'll be surprised—and pleased—by how much material you can cover if you study a half hour per day for a month or so before the test. Look carefully at the sections of the diagnostic test; if you missed a number of questions in one particular area, allow more time for the chapters that cover that area of the course. The practice tests in Part III will give you more experience with different kinds of multiple-choice questions and the wide range of free-response questions.

If time is short, reading the review chapters may not be your best course of action. Instead, skim through the chapter reviews to re-familiarize yourself with the main ideas. Spend the bulk of your time working on the multiple-choice and free-response questions at the end of each review. This will give you a good idea of your understanding of that particular topic. Then take the tests in Part III.

If time is really short, go straight from Part I to Part III. Taking practice tests repeatedly is one of the fastest, most practical ways to prepare.

BEFORE THE EXAM

By February, long before the exam, you should make sure that you are registered to take it. Many schools take care of the paperwork and handle the fees for their AP students, but check with your teacher or the AP coordinator to be certain that you are on the list. This is especially important if you have a documented disability and need test accommodations. If you are studying AP independently, call AP Services at the College Board for the name of an AP coordinator at a local school who will help you through the registration process.

The evening before the exam is not a great time for partying—nor is it a great time for cramming. If you like, look over class notes or skim through your textbook, concentrating on the broad outlines rather than the small details of the course. You might also want to skim through this book and read the AP Tips. This is a great time to get your things together for the next day. Sharpen a fistful of number 2 pencils with good erasers; collect several black or dark-blue ballpoint pens for the free-response questions; make sure that you bring a watch (cell phones and other electronic devices will not be allowed into the test site); pack a healthy snack for the break such as a piece of fruit, granola bar, and/or bottled water; make sure you have whatever identification is required as well as the admission ticket. Then relax and get a good night's sleep.

On the day of the examination, it is wise to eat breakfast—studies show that students who eat a healthy breakfast before testing generally do better. Be careful not to drink a lot of liquids, thereby necessitating a trip to the bathroom during the test. Breakfast will give you the energy you need to power you through the test—and more. You will spend some time waiting while everyone is seated in the right room for the right test. That's before the test has even begun. Each exam will take approximately two hours with a reading period between the multiple choice section (70 minute response period) and the free response section (10 minute reading period followed by a 50 minute writing period) If you take both the AP Microeconomics and AP Macroeconomics exams, you will have, at minimum, a one hour break between the two tests. Be prepared for a long test time. You don't want to be distracted by hunger pangs.

Be sure to wear comfortable clothes; take along a sweater in case the heating or air-conditioning is erratic. Be sure to wear clothes you like—everyone performs better when they think they look better.

You have been on the fast track. Now go get a 5!

TAKING THE AP ECONOMICS EXAMS

Both the AP Macroeconomics and AP Microeconomics exams have two sections: Section I consists of 60 multiple-choice questions; Section II contains 3 free-response questions. The exam format is the same for both AP Macroeconomics and AP Microeconomics examinations. You will have 70 minutes to complete the multiple-choice portion of the exam. You then have 60 minutes for the free-response questions (10 minutes to read the questions and 50 minutes to write your answers). You should answer all three questions. Some AP exams allow you to choose among the free-response questions, but economics is **not** one of them. Keep an eye on your watch and devote about 20 minutes to question 1 and about 15 minutes on questions 2 and 3. Since question 1 carries more weight on your overall score for each exam, you want to be sure to at least try the first couple of parts of this question. Please note that watch alarms are *not* allowed.

Below is a chart to help you visualize the breakdown of the exam:

Section	Multiple-Choice Questions	Free-Response Questions	
Weight	66.6% of the exam	33.3% of the exam (weighted as follows)	
		~15%	~7.5%
Number of Questions	60	Question 1	Questions 2-3
Time Allowed	70 minutes	50 minutes plus 10 minutes to read the questions	
Suggested Pace	1 minute per question	20 minutes for this question	15 minutes per question

STRATEGIES FOR THE MULTIPLE-CHOICE SECTION

Here are some rules of thumb to help you work your way through the multiple-choice questions:

SCORING OF MULTIPLE CHOICE There are five possible answers for each question. As of June 2010, there is no longer a penalty on the AP Economics exam for wrong answers. You will simply not get credit for the wrong answer. Since there is no penalty for guessing, be sure to answer every question prior to the end of the 70 minutes allotted. This means fill in a bubble for each of the 60 questions.

FIND QUESTIONS YOU KNOW FIRST Find questions you are confident of and work those first. (Generally the easier questions appear first on the exam.) Then return to the questions you skipped. Make a mark in the booklet on questions you are unsure of and return to those questions later.

READ EACH QUESTION CAREFULLY Pressed for time, many students make the mistake of reading the questions too quickly or merely skimming them. By reading each question carefully, you may already have some idea about the correct answer. You can then look for that answer in the responses. Careful reading is especially important in EXCEPT questions (see the next section that describes the types of multiple-choice questions).

ELIMINATE ANY ANSWER YOU KNOW IS WRONG You can write on the multiple-choice questions in the test book. As you read through the responses, draw a line through every answer you know is wrong. This will help you in choosing correct solutions on questions you aren't sure about.

READ EACH RESPONSE, THEN CHOOSE THE MOST ACCURATE ONE AP examinations are written to test your precise knowledge of a subject. Sometimes there are a few answers that seem correct, but one of them is more specific and therefore the correct response.

AVOID ABSOLUTE RESPONSES These answers often include the words "always" or "never."

MARK AND SKIP TOUGH QUESTIONS If you are hung up on a question, mark it in the margin of the question book. You can come back to it later if you have time. Make sure you skip that question on your answer sheet as well. In the end, however, be sure to answer ALL questions prior to the end of the 70 minutes.

WORKING BACKWARD Some students find it beneficial to glance through the exam to get an idea of how to pace their per-question time allocation. Other students find it beneficial to work backward, as they may find that some of the more difficult questions help identify questions found at the beginning. If you decide to work backward, be sure to fill in the correct ovals. If you start from the beginning of the test, be careful not to spend too much time on the early questions, since questions toward the end of the exam become more difficult. Remember, your goal is to finish the entire exam and answer all of the questions.

TYPES OF MULTIPLE-CHOICE QUESTIONS

There are various kinds of multiple-choice questions. Here are some suggestions for how to approach each one.

CLASSIC/BEST-ANSWER QUESTIONS

This is the most common type of multiple-choice question. It simply requires you to read the question and select the correct answer. For example:

1. Which of the following situations would necessarily lead to an increase in the price of apples?

    (A) Medical researchers discover that eating apples reduces the chances of a person's developing cancer.
    (B) Weather during the growing season is ideal for apple production.
    (C) A technological breakthrough enables apple farmers to use the same amount of inputs as before to produce more apples per acre.
    (D) The price of oranges fall.
    (E) There is a freeze that destroys apple crops.

Answer: **A.** This is the only correct answer as the demand for apples should increase with the discovery that apples may reduce the chance of a person developing cancer.

EXCEPT QUESTIONS

In EXCEPT style questions, you will notice all of the answer choices but one are correct. The best way to approach these questions is to treat them as true/false questions. Mark a T or an F in the margin next to each possible answer. There should be only one false answer, and that is the answer you should select. For example:

1. All of the following will shift the supply curve of kites to the right EXCEPT:
    (A) an increase in the price of kites
    (B) an improvement in the technology used to manufacture kites
    (C) a reduction in the price of material from which kites are made
    (D) an increase in the number of people who sell kites
    (E) lower wages for kite workers

Answer: **A.** Answers (B) through (E) will shift the supply curve to the right. An increase in the price of kites increases the *quantity of kites supplied,* but has no effect on the supply of kites.

ANALYSIS/APPLICATION QUESTIONS

These questions require you to apply your knowledge of economics to a given situation or problem. For example:

1. What happens to a monopolist's price, profit, and output if only its fixed costs decrease?

Price	Profit	Output
(A) No change	Increase	No change
(B) No change	Increase	Increase
(C) Decrease	Decrease	Decrease
(D) Increase	Increase	Increase
(E) Decrease	No change	No change

Answer: **A.** This is the only correct solution, since the decline in fixed costs will lower average total costs only (and will not affect marginal or other variable costs). The monopolist's profit-maximizing output and price do not change and are still where MR (marginal revenue) = MC (marginal cost).

FREE-RESPONSE QUESTIONS

There are three free-response questions that should all be answered. These three questions account for 33% of the final score you receive on the exam. The first free-response question generally consists of 67% of your free-response score. The second and third questions are relatively shorter and will account for the remaining 33% of the grade. This means the long question makes up approximately 15% of the entire test score while the two short questions each make up 7.5%. Therefore, it is important to answer all questions as completely as possible.

These questions can cover multiple content areas as well as connections between several topics. Any or all of the key topics of the AP exam may be found in the free-response section. The following hints may help you prepare for this half of the exam.

You have ten minutes to read the questions before you can even begin to answer; plan to at least skim the three questions first, since you won't know which question is on your strongest topic and they are not placed in a particular topic order. As you are reading, you may want to quickly write down your ideas about the subject of each question. Once you have done this, you should go immediately to the question you find to be the easiest of the three. To help you better focus on the question, you might underline key words and draw quick graphs.

While you do not have to answer the questions in any particular order, do consider the amount of time you spend on each. Because the first question is longer and will have the largest impact on your score, you should spend the most amount of time on it. Of your 50 minutes answering time, 20 should be spent on question 1. This leaves about 15 minutes each for questions 2 and 3. As they are designed to be shorter questions, this should be a sufficient amount of time to answer each question thoroughly and leave time for review.

As you finish, you should reread and note any key phrases or points that are made in each question. Once you have answered each question, be sure you read the prompt again to ensure you have actually answered the question asked. Examination readers comment routinely that students don't actually answer the question that was asked. While the information you give may be correct, if it doesn't answer the question, you won't get credit.

Don't assume any question is asking for a "cookie cutter" type response. The AP readers who review your answer will be reading for a correct answer in the context of the question, and not just a memorized response. In that light, also be sure to use economics vocabulary correctly. If you are not sure about the correct vocabulary, it is permissible to use a short phrase in place of the word you are unsure about. Correct notation is also important, especially when using graphs. It won't hurt to define your notation for clarity, but be sure you are using the notation correctly.

KEY POINTS TO ANSWERING FREE-RESPONSE QUESTIONS

In answering the free-response questions, it is important to note the word choices used in the questions. Focus your writing for the AP Economics Exam with these points in mind.

READ Carefully read the question and circle key phrases and comments you are to address. Watch for the specific wording and don't make assumptions about what you are being asked before completely reading the question. As stated above, be certain that you answer the question being asked of you.

CONTEXT Be sure to answer in the context of the problem. For a complete answer you are required to address the context of the question presented and make valid conclusions based on the given scenario.

DEFINE To define means to state the meaning of a word or phrase or to give a specific example. For instance, if a question asks you to define "comparative advantage," the response is "the ability to produce a good or service at a lower opportunity cost than another producer." Definitions are usually just one sentence.

LABEL Correct labeling of all graphs is essential and will earn you points. Know your graphs going into the test and be certain you can apply/interpret them in the appropriate context.

VOCABULARY Use economics vocabulary correctly. The AP readers don't want to hear fancy economics lingo, especially if you use it incorrectly. This will weaken your response.

ANSWER SEQUENTIALLY While you can answer the questions themselves in any order you like, be certain that within each individual question the answer is organized sequentially. Not only will this make it easier on the AP reader, it will also help you as you organize your thought process in addressing the question itself. Be careful to read the question though, because some questions are linked so that you have to answer some parts in sequence, whereas other parts are stand-alone.

ANSWER Did you actually answer the question? Reread to be sure you have answered what was asked, and leave it at that. There are no points for quantity, only for quality.

EXPLAIN/WHY/HOW Be ready to give a cause or reason for your answer. Explanations usually include the word "because" and allow you to make a connection between a stated cause (in the question) and its effect on a market or the economy as a whole. Follow the instructions carefully and do not assume more than the prompt states when answering the question.

SCORING FREE-RESPONSE QUESTIONS

Free-response questions are scored using a rubric that assigns points for each part of the answer. For example, if part (a) requires you to identify and explain two factors, that part of the question will likely be worth 4 points (1 point for each identification and 1 point for each explanation). If part (b) requires you to draw a graph, that part of the response will likely assign multiple points for both a correctly labeled graph as well as some interpretation of the graph and some stated change within the context of the question.

Keep in mind that both economic knowledge and verbal communication are essential in the AP Economics exam. To earn a high score, you must demonstrate that you are able to correctly illustrate economic concepts (on a graph or calculation) and properly interpret those concepts in the context of the question.

For the following free-response question, you will find a sample answer that earns full credit based on a potential rubric.

QUESTION

In an economy operating at full employment levels of output, inflation begins to rise steadily in the United States for several quarters.

(a) Describe an appropriate open market operation the central bank could implement to decrease inflationary pressures.

(b) What effect would the monetary policy action you described in part (a) have on bank reserves? Explain.

(c) Illustrate on two correctly labeled side-by-side graphs of the foreign exchange market the effect this change would have on the values of the dollar and the euro, assuming the European Central Bank makes no discretionary policy change. Be certain that your graphs clearly identify the following:

    i.   The change in demand for dollars by Europeans
    ii. Original and new exchange rates of the dollar
    iii. The change in the supply of euros on the foreign exchange market
    iv. Original and new exchange rates of the euro

(d) Describe the effects the change in part (b) would have on U.S. net exports.

(e) Illustrate on a correctly labeled aggregate demand–aggregate supply graph the effects of the change in net exports described in part (d). Clearly show on your graph the following:

    i. Original output (Y) and price level (P) at full employment
    ii. The new aggregate demand curve
    iii. The new output (Y_1) and price level (P_1)

Answer: Starting with part (a) and working sequentially; points earned from the rubric in parenthesis (11 points total).

(a) Sell securities (1 point)

(b) Bank reserves would decrease. (1 point) As the bank pays for government bonds purchased from the central bank, money is withdrawn from bank deposits, directly reducing the amount of money in circulation. (1 point)

(c)

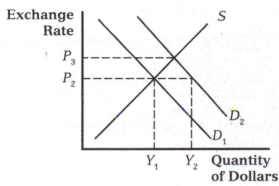 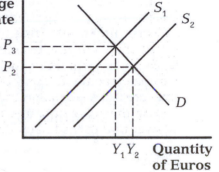

    i. The demand for dollars increases. (1 point)
    ii. New equilibrium shows that the dollar appreciates. (1 point)
    iii. The supply of Euros increases. (1 point)
    iv. New equilibrium shows that the euro depreciates. (1 point)

(d) Net exports in the U.S. would decrease. (1 point)

(e)

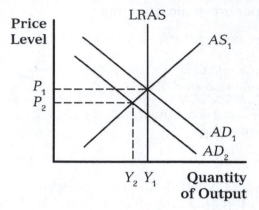

i. See correctly labeled graph. (1 point)
ii. AD shifts to the left. (1 point)
iii. Output decreases and price level increases. (1 point)

A FINAL WORD OF ADVICE

This book is designed to prepare you for the AP Economics exams, but it is also meant to create a relationship between you and the material that will last a lifetime. In order to accomplish this, you must not only memorize the terminology and basic formulas, but also apply this information to everyday experiences. The best way to ensure success on this, or any other exam, is to know the material well. Go beyond sheer memorization and use this book as a tool to expand your understanding of economics. Do so, and the test score will take care of itself.

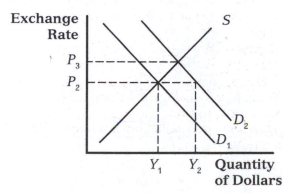

MICROECONOMICS DIAGNOSTIC TEST

This test will give you some indication of how you might score on the AP Microeconomics Exam and what topic areas you should study further. This test will help you to pinpoint strengths and weaknesses on the key content areas covered by the exam.

AP Microeconomics Examination
Section I: Multiple-Choice Questions
Time: 70 Minutes
60 Questions

Directions: Each of the following questions or incomplete statements is accompanied by five suggested answers or completions. Select the one that best answers the question or completes the statement.

1. Mr. Microeconomics left his teaching job which paid $60,000/yr and invested $50,000 of his retirement fund (which was earning 10% interest) to pay for cost of goods sold in his newly opened specialty bookstore. If he collects $150,000 in revenues from his specialty bookstore business, what is Mr. Microeconomics' economic profit?
   (A) $20,000.
   (B) $25,000.
   (C) $35,000.
   (D) $95,000.
   (E) $100,000.

2. When average variable costs are falling, what else must be true?
   (A) Average fixed costs must be rising.
   (B) Marginal costs must be rising.
   (C) Marginal costs must be falling.
   (D) Average total costs are falling.
   (E) Average total costs are rising.

3. Which of the following statements about a firm's production function are true?
   I.   Marginal product is zero when total product is at its maximum.
   II. When average product is falling, marginal product is also falling.
   III. When average product is rising, marginal product is falling.
   (A) I and II only.
   (B) II and III only.
   (C) I, II, and III.
   (D) I only.
   (E) III only.

4. During a football game, it starts to rain. Your economics class runs the concession stand at this game and raises the price of coffee from 50 cents to 75 cents per cup. They sell more coffee than ever before. Which answer explains this?
   (A) The supply of coffee increased.
   (B) The demand for coffee increased.
   (C) The demand curve for coffee was elastic.
   (D) The demand curve for coffee was inelastic.
   (E) The supply of coffee decreased.

GO ON TO NEXT PAGE 15

5. Which of the following is true in the market for a certain product if producers consistently are willing to sell more at the market price than consumers are willing to buy?
   (A) The product is inferior.
   (B) There is a price ceiling on the product.
   (C) There is a price floor on the product.
   (D) Demand is highly inelastic.
   (E) Supply is highly inelastic.

6. If an economy is being allocatively efficient, then this means that the economy is
   (A) using the least-costly production techniques.
   (B) fully employing all economic resources.
   (C) maximizing the returns to factors of production.
   (D) maximizing the difference between marginal benefit and marginal cost.
   (E) maximizing the sum of both consumer and producer surplus.

7. A perfectly competitive firm is operating where marginal revenue is greater than marginal costs. What should this firm do to increase profits?
   (A) Increase its price.
   (B) Decrease its price.
   (C) Keep production levels constant.
   (D) Increase production.
   (E) Decrease production.

8. In the short run, a firm in a perfectly competitive market will stay in business despite the fact that total revenue is less than total cost as long as
   (A) marginal revenue is increasing.
   (B) marginal costs exceed marginal revenue.
   (C) total revenue exceeds total sunk costs but not total variable costs.
   (D) total revenue equals total fixed costs.
   (E) total revenue exceeds, or is at least equal to, total variable costs.

9. In a market economy, public goods such as library services are not likely to be provided in sufficient quantities by the private sector because
   (A) Private firms are less efficient at producing public goods than the government.
   (B) The use of public goods cannot be withheld from those who do not pay for them.
   (C) The government can produce public goods at a lower cost.
   (D) There is an overuse of public goods that makes the good rival in consumption.
   (E) Private firms _do_ provide sufficient quantities of a public good in a market economy, so all of the above statements are false.

10. Labor, capital, and natural resources are all examples of which of the following?
    (A) Factors of production.
    (B) Public goods.
    (C) Inferior goods.
    (D) Outputs.
    (E) Production substitutes.

11. You must determine the long-run equilibrium output of a competitive firm. You are permitted to see only one curve. Which one would be most helpful?
    (A) Average fixed cost.
    (B) Average variable cost.
    (C) Average total cost.
    (D) Marginal cost.
    (E) Demand.

12. If a perfectly competitive firm is currently losing money in the short run, what will happen to the market supply and equilibrium price in the long run?

	Market Supply	Equilibrium Price
(A)	Increase	Decrease
(B)	Increase	Increase
(C)	No change	Decrease
(D)	Decrease	Decrease
(E)	Decrease	Increase

13. Which of the following will increase wages for workers at a car production factory?
    (A) An increase in the number of individuals certified to make cars.
    (B) An increase in the demand for cars.
    (C) An increase in the price of gasoline.
    (D) An increase in the tax on cars.
    (E) An effective price ceiling for cars.

14. Which of the following would necessarily cause an increase in the demand for computers, a normal good?
    (A) An increase in income.
    (B) An increase in online retail stores selling computers.
    (C) Consumers' expectation that the price of computers will fall in the future.
    (D) An increase in taxes on computers.
    (E) An increase in the price of computers.

15. The more substitutes a good has,
    (A) the greater its price elasticity of demand.
    (B) the lower its price elasticity of demand.
    (C) the less elastic the demand for the good.
    (D) the more inelastic the demand for the good.
    (E) the greater the product's income elasticity.

16. Which of the following statements is true for a profit-maximizing monopolist?
    (A) Its demand curve intersects the supply curve.
    (B) Its marginal cost exceeds its price.
    (C) Its price equals marginal cost.
    (D) Its price exceeds marginal revenue.
    (E) Its demand is price inelastic.

17. From an efficiency standpoint, a monopolist
    (A) Produces the allocatively efficient amount of a good.
    (B) Charges too high a price and produces too little of a good.
    (C) Charges too low a price and produces too little of a good.
    (D) Charges too high a price and produces too much of a good.
    (E) Charges too low a price and produces too much of a good.

18. A perfectly competitive firm will hire a number of laborers where
    (A) the marginal product of labor is at a maximum.
    (B) labor wages are equal to the product price.
    (C) the product price equals the marginal revenue product of labor.
    (D) the product price equals the marginal product of labor.
    (E) the marginal revenue product of labor equals to labor wages.

19. In comparison to perfectly competitive firms, monopolistically competitive firms face
    (A) less elastic demand.
    (B) a vertical demand curve.
    (C) a horizontal demand curve.
    (D) perfectly inelastic demand.
    (E) more elastic demand.

20. An effective rent control law would most likely affect the housing market in the following way
    (A) lead to a surplus of housing.
    (B) lead to a shortage of housing.
    (C) lead to market equilibrium.
    (D) lead to an increase in the supply of housing.
    (E) lead to an increase in the number of home purchases.

21. When there is a surplus in an unregulated, free market,
    (A) price will increase and the quantity demanded will also increase.
    (B) price will increase and the quantity demanded will decrease.
    (C) price will decrease and the quantity demanded will increase.
    (D) price will decrease and the quantity demanded will also decrease.
    (E) price will remain constant and the quantity demanded will increase.

22. When marginal utility is equal to zero, total utility is
    (A) also equal to zero.
    (B) at a maximum point.
    (C) negative.
    (D) increasing, but at a decreasing rate.
    (E) decreasing at a decreasing rate.

23. All of the following statements regarding costs are correct EXCEPT
    (A) average variable cost is the difference between average total cost and marginal cost.
    (B) average fixed cost is the difference between average total cost and average variable cost.
    (C) average total cost is the sum of average variable cost and average fixed cost.
    (D) marginal cost is the price of an extra variable input.
    (E) marginal cost is the additional cost for any level of output.

24. A normal profit is
    (A) the average profitability of a firm in one business cycle.
    (B) calculated by subtracting explicit costs from total revenue.
    (C) calculated by subtracting both explicit and implicit costs from total revenue.
    (D) the difference between total revenue and total cost.
    (E) the compensation for the opportunity cost of entrepreneurial talent.

25. Marginal revenue equals average revenue in a perfectly competitive firm because
    (A) the firm's demand curve is perfectly inelastic.
    (B) the market demand curve is perfectly elastic.
    (C) the firm's supply curve is elastic.
    (D) the firm's demand curve is perfectly elastic.
    (E) the market supply curve is unit elastic.

26. Marginal utility
    (A) explains why product supply curves slope upward.
    (B) typically increases as additional units of a good are consumed.
    (C) is the additional output a firm gains when it hires another unit of labor.
    (D) is the additional satisfaction from the consumption of an additional unit of a good.
    (E) is the sum of all output produced by an additional unit of labor.

27. There are negative externalities associated with the use of a freeway in major cities during rush hour because
    (A) drivers slow down other drivers because of the increased high traffic volume.
    (B) drivers value their time more.
    (C) government revenues from toll roads increase.
    (D) bus company revenues increase.
    (E) gasoline costs more.

28. The market demand curve for labor will increase when
    (A) the product price decreases.
    (B) the product price increases.
    (C) the labor supply curve increases.
    (D) the labor supply curve decreases.
    (E) the marginal product of labor decreases.

29. Use the following table to answer question 29:

Input	Total Product (output)
0	0
1	5
2	18
3	30
4	41
5	50
6	55

Based on the data in the table above, diminishing returns set in with the addition of the
(A) first unit of output.
(B) second unit of output.
(C) third unit of output.
(D) fourth unit of output.
(E) fifth unit of output.

30. All of the following are examples of price discrimination EXCEPT
(A) a theater that charges children less than adults for a movie.
(B) universities that charge higher tuition for out-of-state residents than in-state residents.
(C) school dances that are more expensive for non-students than students.
(D) a phone company charges more for long distance calls on weekdays versus weekends.
(E) tickets to a football game are more expensive than to a basketball game in the same stadium.

31. If a firm doubles all of its inputs and its output, the firm is experiencing
(A) increasing marginal returns.
(B) diminishing marginal returns.
(C) constant returns to scale.
(D) increasing returns to scale.
(E) decreasing returns to scale.

32. Under which market structure would consumer surplus be the lowest?
(A) A natural monopoly.
(B) A regulated, fair return monopoly.
(C) An unregulated, single-priced monopoly.
(D) A perfectly price discriminating monopoly.
(E) A purely competitive firm.

33. Suppose that an effective minimum wage is imposed in a labor market. Holding all else constant, if the labor supply increases, which of the following statements is true?
(A) Unemployment in the market will increase.
(B) The quantity of labor supplied will decrease.
(C) The quantity of labor demanded will increase.
(D) The market demand will increase.
(E) The market demand will decrease.

34. Suppose that a family buys all of its clothing from a discount store and treats these items as inferior goods. Under these circumstances, this family's consumption of discount store clothing will necessarily
(A) increase when a family member wins the state lottery.
(B) increase when a family member gets a raise in pay at work.
(C) remain unchanged when its income rises or falls.
(D) decrease when a family member becomes unemployed.
(E) decrease when a family member experiences an increase in income.

35. All of the following statements regarding the circular flow of economic activity between consumers and producers are true EXCEPT
    (A) households sell factor services to firms.
    (B) households buy factor services from firms.
    (C) households buy products from firms.
    (D) firms sell products to households.
    (E) firms buy factor services from households.

36. What will happen to a monopolist's price and output if the monopolist's marginal costs decrease?

	Price	Output
(A)	Increase	Increase
(B)	Increase	Decrease
(C)	Increase	No change
(D)	Decrease	Decrease
(E)	Decrease	Increase

37. Firms that work together are most likely associated with
    (A) a monopoly.
    (B) an oligopoly.
    (C) a monopolistically competitive firm.
    (D) a perfectly competitively firm.
    (E) a perfectly competitive labor market.

38. If a firm that hires two different types of resources wants to produce a certain level of output at least cost, it should hire each resource so that
    (A) the marginal product per dollar spent on each resource is equal.
    (B) the marginal product of each resource is equal.
    (C) each resource reaches its point of diminishing marginal returns.
    (D) the firm hires more of the resource with the highest marginal product.
    (E) the firm hires more of the less expensive resource.

39. In order to internalize the negative externality created by firms whose production process emits unwanted pollution, economists often recommend imposing a tax on the firms because
    (A) taxes will decrease the incentive for firms to pollute and eliminate pollution completely.
    (B) taxes will increase revenue to the government.
    (C) taxes provide an incentive for firms to increase production.
    (D) taxes will provide an incentive for firms to use the most efficient production methods to reduce pollution.
    (E) the firm will pay the pollution costs.

40. A technological advance leads to an improvement in the production technology for a certain good. This leads to
    (A) an increase in the demand for the good.
    (B) an increase in the supply of the good.
    (C) an increase in the price of the good.
    (D) a shortage of the good.
    (E) a surplus of the good.

41. The allocation of resources in a market economy is described by which of the following statements?
    I.   The government decides which goods will be produced and which consumers will have the opportunity to buy them.
    II. Buyers and sellers exchange goods and services through market interactions.
    III. Prices help producers determine whether they are producing too little or too much of a good.
    (A) I only
    (B) II only
    (C) III only
    (D) I and III only
    (E) II and III only

42. Which of the following would cause an economy's production possibilities frontier (PPF) to shift out?
    (A) An technological improvement that increases total productivity.
    (B) An increase in the number of unemployed workers.
    (C) A decline in trade with other countries.
    (D) Switching from the production of one good to another.
    (E) An increase in the number of unused machines.

43. The demand for good A falls with a decrease in the price of good B. Good A is
    (A) a complement to good B.
    (B) a substitute for good B.
    (C) a necessary good.
    (D) a luxury good.
    (E) an inferior good.

Use the following table to answer questions 44–46:

Output	Total Cost
0	$10
1	15
2	19
3	22
4	24
5	25

44. Suppose that the data above represents the production costs for a perfectly competitive firm. The firm's marginal cost of producing the 2nd unit of output is
    (A) $10.00.
    (B) $5.00.
    (C) $4.00.
    (D) $3.00.
    (E) $2.00.

45. The firm's average total cost of producing four units of output is
    (A) $15.00.
    (B) $10.00.
    (C) $5.00.
    (D) $6.00.
    (E) $7.00.

46. The firm's average fixed cost of producing four units of output is
    (A) $10.00.
    (B) $5.00.
    (C) $2.50.
    (D) $2.00.
    (E) $2.25.

47. In order to raise the most revenue, the government should impose a tax on goods where
    (A) the supply is perfectly elastic.
    (B) the supply is unit elastic.
    (C) the demand is perfectly elastic.
    (D) the demand is perfectly inelastic.
    (E) the demand is unit elastic.

48. All of the following statements regarding the differences between the long and short run of a perfectly competitive firm are true EXCEPT:
    (A) All input costs are variable in the short run.
    (B) Some input costs are fixed in the short run.
    (C) All input costs are variable in the long run.
    (D) It is possible for a firm to earn economic profits in the short run.
    (E) It is possible for a firm to incur economic losses in the short run.

49. Suppose that a production of a good results in a positive externality. How might the government encourage an efficient production of this good?
    (A) Impose a tax on producers of the good.
    (B) Grant a subsidy to producers of the good.
    (C) Establish a price floor in the market for this good.
    (D) Promote the trade of this good with other nations.
    (E) Place production limits on the good.

50. In what way is a monopolistically competitive firm more like a monopoly than a perfectly competitive firm?
    (A) A monopolistically competitive firm has long run economic profits.
    (B) A monopolistically competitive market has many firms.
    (C) A monopolistically competitive firm faces a downward sloping demand curve.
    (D) A monopolistically competitive firm chooses an output level where marginal revenue equals marginal cost.
    (E) A monopolistically competitive firm may enter or leave the market in the long run.

51. All of the following will shift the supply curve of bicycles to the right EXCEPT
    (A) an increase in the price of bicycles.
    (B) an improvement in the technology used to manufacture bicycles.
    (C) a reduction in the price of the materials from which bicycles are made.
    (D) an increase in the number of bicycle sellers.
    (E) lower wages for bicycle workers.

52. In order to maximize its use of resources, a firm hiring resources in a perfectly competitive market will hire resources where.
    (A) the marginal product of the resource is at its maximum.
    (B) the price of the resource equals the price of the product.
    (C) the price of the resource equals the marginal product of the resource.
    (D) the price of the resource equals the marginal resource cost of another resource.
    (E) the price of the resource equals the marginal revenue product of the resource.

53. The short-run supply curve of a perfectly competitive firm is
    (A) the firm's marginal cost curve.
    (B) the firm's average variable cost curve.
    (C) the firm's marginal cost curve above the average variable cost curve.
    (D) the firm's marginal cost curve above the average total cost curve.
    (E) the firm's marginal cost curve above the average fixed cost curve.

54. A perfectly competitive market in long-run equilibrium is productively efficient because.
    (A) firms produce where its product price equals marginal cost.
    (B) firms' marginal utility equals marginal cost.
    (C) firms are not earning a normal profit.
    (D) firms produce at least cost.
    (E) no new firms enter the market.

55. An increase in the demand for smart phones and an increase in the supply of smart phones will
    (A) decrease the equilibrium price and increase the equilibrium quantity of smart phones.
    (B) increase the equilibrium price and decrease the equilibrium quantity of smart phones.
    (C) increase the equilibrium price and increase the equilibrium quantity of smart phones.
    (D) increase the equilibrium quantity of smart phones, but the impact on price cannot be determined from the information provided.
    (E) increase equilibrium price of smart phones.

56. Suppose that the market price is currently below equilibrium. There is a situation of excess _____. The market will correct itself by allowing the price to _____.
    (A) demand; rise
    (B) demand; fall
    (C) supply; rise
    (D) supply; fall
    (E) supply; remain constant

57. In the short run, an increase in the demand for a product produced by a perfectly competitive industry will lead to
    (A) each firm increasing its output.
    (B) each firm decreasing its price.
    (C) each firm receiving less profit.
    (D) an increase in the average size of firms.
    (E) an increase in the number of firms.

58. Which of the following necessarily leads to a shift in the market demand for workers?
    (A) The creation of a government subsidized program to train new workers.
    (B) An increase in the supply of workers in this market.
    (C) An increase in the demand for goods produced by workers in this market.
    (D) A decrease in the rate of income taxes for workers in this market.
    (E) An increase in minimum wage requirements for workers in this market.

59. What is the most likely result if a private firm supplies a public good?
    (A) The firm will produce a less than efficient level of output because there will be a free rider problem.
    (B) The firm will produce a less than efficient level of output because there is insufficient competition in the market.
    (C) The firm will produce a more than efficient level of output because the costs are lower.
    (D) The firm will produce a more than efficient level of output because of externalities.
    (E) There will be an overuse of the good produced by the firm.

60. If there is a decrease in the demand for a good, what will most likely happen to the equilibrium price and quantity of that good?
    (A) Neither price or quantity will change.
    (B) Price and quantity will both increase.
    (C) Price and quantity will both decrease.
    (D) Price increases while quantity decreases.
    (E) Price decreases while quantity increases.

STOP
END OF SECTION I
IF YOU FINISH BEFORE TIME IS CALLED, YOU MAY CHECK YOUR WORK ON THIS SECTION. DO NOT GO ON TO SECTION II UNTIL YOU ARE TOLD TO DO SO.

Section II: Free-Response Questions
Planning Time—10 minutes
Writing Time—50 minutes

Directions: You have 50 minutes to answer all three of the following questions. It is suggested that you spend approximately half your time on the first question and divide the remaining time equally between the next two questions. In answering the questions, you should emphasize the line of reasoning that generated your results; it is not enough to list the results of your analysis. Include correctly labeled diagrams, if useful or required, in explaining your answer. A correctly labeled diagram must have all axes and curves clearly labeled and must show directional changes. Use a pen with black or dark blue ink.

1. Micro Mineral Springs, a profit-maximizing pure monopolist, has the following demand and total cost schedules for its bottled mineral water.

$Q_{(bottles)}$	Price	Total Cost
0	$10	$ 1
1	8	3
2	6	7
3	4	13
4	2	21
5	0	31

   (a) Calculate Micro Mineral Springs' total revenue and marginal revenue schedules.
   (b) How many bottles of mineral water will Micro Minerals Springs sell?
      (i) What price will Micro Mineral Springs' sell this water? Explain.
      (ii) Will Micro Mineral Springs' earn an economic profit at this level of output? If so, what is the amount of profit? Explain.
      (iii) Draw graphs using a marginal approach to confirm your answer in part ii.
   (c) If fixed costs increased by $5, how would this affect Micro Mineral Springs' output decision? Explain.
   (d) If fixed costs increased by $10, how would this affect Micro Mineral Springs' output decision? Explain.

2. A perfectly competitive farming industry is in long-run equilibrium. Fertilizer is an important variable input in the agricultural production process. The price of fertilizer increases for all firms in the industry.
   (a) Explain how and why the fertilizer price increase will affect this industry's price and output in the short run.
   (b) How will this fertilizer price increase affect the firm in this perfectly competitive industry? Explain your answer, addressing the specific impacts of this price increase on:
      (i) Price
      (ii) Output
      (iii) Profit
   (c) Based on your answer in part (b) above, will firms enter or exit this industry in the long run? Explain your answer.

3. Pollution Papers, a profit-maximizing firm, sells paper in a competitive market.
    (a) Draw a correctly labeled graph for the paper market and show each of the
        following:
        (i) Price
        (ii) Output
    (b) There is a negative externality in this paper market because the paper-producing
        firms emit pollution as a by-product of their production process. What policies
        can the government implement to internalize the externality? Explain your
        answer.
    (c) Draw a graph that shows the impact of your proposed policy, in part (b) above,
        on the paper market and identify how your policy proposal affects the following:
        (i) Price
        (ii) Output

ANSWERS FOR MICROECONOMICS DIAGNOSTIC TEST

SECTION I: MULTIPLE-CHOICE ANSWERS

Using the table below, score your test.

Determine how many questions you answered correctly and how many you answered incorrectly. You will find explanations of the answers on the following pages.

1. C	11. C	21. C	31. C	41. E	51. A
2. D	12. E	22. B	32. D	42. A	52. E
3. A	13. B	23. A	33. A	43. B	53. C
4. B	14. A	24. E	34. E	44. C	54. D
5. C	15. A	25. D	35. B	45. D	55. D
6. E	16. D	26. D	36. E	46. E	56. A
7. D	17. B	27. A	37. B	47. D	57. A
8. E	18. E	28. B	38. A	48. A	58. C
9. B	19. A	29. C	39. D	49. B	59. A
10. A	20. B	30. E	40. B	50. C	60. C

ANSWERS AND EXPLANATIONS

MULTIPLE-CHOICE ANSWERS

1. **C.** Economic Profit = Total Revenue – (Implicit + Explicit Costs), so you subtract the sum of the cost of starting the business plus the opportunity costs, the interest that could have been earned and the teaching salary, from the total revenue (*Principles of Economics* 5th ed. page 270/6th ed. page 262).

2. **D.** Any change in average variable costs (AVC) will impact average total costs (ATC) and marginal costs (MC), but not average fixed costs (AFC) because fixed costs are not dependent upon output. AVC and ATC move in the same direction, so if AVC falls, ATC also falls (*Principles of Economics* 5th ed. pages 274–279/6th ed. pages 267–271).

3. **A.** Marginal product (MP) is the additional change in output that comes with each additional resource unit hired. When MP declines, it means that each additional resource unit hired brings down the total output produced, so when MP = 0, total product (or total output) is at its maximum, so the first point is true. The second point is also true, because when average product (AP) falls, it is only because MP is falling (*Principles of Economics* 5th ed. pages 271–273/6th ed. pages 264–269).

4. **B.** The number of coffee buyers (a demand determinant) increases because of the rain and temperature drop. An increase in the number of coffee buyers increases demand, or shifts the demand to the right (*Principles of Economics* 5th ed. pages 69–71/6th ed. pages 70–72).

5. **C.** If producers are willing to produce more than consumers are willing to buy, it means that the market price is higher than the market equilibrium price. The only way that this is true is if the government placed a price floor in the market. Incidentally, a price floor leads to a market surplus (*Principles of Economics* 5th ed. page 78/6th ed. page 78).

6. **E.** An economy is **allocatively efficient**, *making what society wants*, when supply = demand, where consumer and producer surplus are maximized. This is also true when the economy is producing along its production possibilities frontier (PPF). At any point along an economy's PPF, a society is both allocatively and **productively efficient**, *producing at least cost* (*Principles of Economics* 5th ed. pages 26–27/6th ed. page 27).

7. **D.** The profit-maximizing output is where marginal revenue (MR) = marginal cost (MC). Since the MR > MC, the firm should increase output so that it is at least closer to producing at a quantity where MR = MC (*Principles of Economics* 5th ed. pages 292–295/6th ed. pages 282–285).

8. **E.** A firm should stay open as long as its total revenue (TR) > total variable costs (TVC) because while it is losing money, it is at least able to cover its variable inputs. Fixed costs are sunk, so we do not consider those in our short run marginal analysis. An alternative approach to this is to stay open as long as price (P) = average revenue (AR) > average variable cost (AVC) or P = AR = AVC (*Principles of Economics* 5th ed. pages 295–298/6th ed. pages 285–287).

9. **B.** There is no way to prevent people from consuming public goods, so private institutions have no incentive to produce the good since their profit potential is limited (*Principles of Economics* 5th ed. 227–231/6th ed. pages 218–223).

10. **A.** Labor, land, capital, and entrepreneurial ability make up the factors of production (*Principles of Economics* 5th ed. page 392/6th ed. page 376).

11. **C.** The profit-maximizing point for a perfectly competitive firm is where MR = MC. In the long run, this point also intersects minimum ATC, so if you can see the firm's ATC, you will know what the profit maximizing output should be (*Principles of Economics* 5th ed. pages 302–303/6th ed. pages 292–293).

12. **E.** If firms in a perfectly competitive market are losing money in the short run, some will exit the market, decreasing market supply

product to 18. The third input hired produces an additional 12 units of output, increasing the total product to 30. However, the third input hired produces one unit less than the second unit, which is why we experience diminishing returns with the third input (*Principles of Economics* 5th ed. page 561/6th ed. pages 541–542).

30. **E.** Price discrimination is when a firm/individual charges different prices to different customers <u>for the same product</u>. Option E is the only response that breaks this rule, since a football game is not the same product as a basketball game (*Principles of Economics* 5th ed. pages 326–331/6th ed. pages 315–318).

31. **C.** When a firm doubles its input and more than doubles its output, it experiences economies of scale. When it doubles its input and doubles its output, it experiences **constant returns to scale**, *the property whereby long-run average total cost stays the same as the quantity of output changes* (*Principles of Economics* 5th ed. page 281/6th ed. pages 272–273).

32. **D.** There is no consumer surplus with a perfectly price discriminating monopolist. A perfectly price discriminating monopolist takes all of the consumer surplus by charging different prices to different consumers and therefore, leaves no surplus for consumers (*Principles of Economics* 5th ed. pages 326–331/6th ed. pages 310–313).

33. **A.** An effective minimum wage is a price floor that is set above the market equilibrium price. This means that the quantity of labor supplied is greater than the quantity of labor demanded, which results in a surplus of labor, or unemployment (*Principles of Economics* 5th ed. pages 119–121/6th ed. pages 117–119).

34. **E.** When income increases, consumers buy more normal goods and fewer inferior goods. This is the definition of normal vs. inferior goods (*Principles of Economics* 5th ed. pages 464–465/6th ed. page 448).

35. **B.** According to the circular flow model, households sell factor services to firms while firms sell products to households (*Principles of Economics* 5th ed. page 25/6th ed. page 25).

36. **E.** The profit maximizing output level is where MR = MC. If marginal costs decline, then the monopolist's profit maximizing output level increases and the price that it charges decreases (*Principles of Economics* 5th ed. pages 292–295/6th ed. pages 306–307).

37. **B.** An **oligopoly** is a *market structure in which only a few sellers offer similar or identical products*. They must work together in order to charge a high price similar to a monopolist (*Principles of Economics* 5th ed. page 346/6th ed. pages 351–353).

38. **A.** In order to maximize the use of two resources, a firm should hire each resource so that the marginal product per dollar spent on each resource is the same. This is the resource maximization rule (*Principles of Economics* 5th ed. pages 400–405/6th ed. pages 377–380).

39. **D.** Public policy aimed at reducing pollution seeks to provide the proper incentives for firms to decrease pollution levels. A tax presents a disincentive for firms to pollute, therefore decreasing the amount of pollution in the environment (*Principles of Economics* 5th ed. page 210/6th ed. pages 203–204).

40. **B.** Technological improvements are a supply determinant, which means that, when technology improves, supply increases because more output can be produced (*Principles of Economics* 5th ed. pages 74–76/6th ed. pages 74–76).

41. **E.** A command economy is where government decides what goods firms/individuals will produce and who will produce them whereas a market economy is where the buyers and consumers decide what goods are produced and who produces them through market interaction (*Principles of Economics* 5th ed. pages 8–9/6th ed. pages 10–11).

42. **A.** Economic growth is represented by an outward shift of the PPF. Technological improvements increase production while keeping input levels constant, which is why the PPF shifts out with improved technology (*Principles of Economics* 5th ed. pages 26–28/6th ed. pages 26–28).

43. **B.** When the price of good B drops, demand for good A also drops only if the two goods are substitutes for one another (*Principles of Economics* 5th ed. page 70/6th ed. page 70).

44. **C.** Marginal cost is the change in cost associated with the production of an additional unit of output. The marginal cost is $4.00 because, since total costs are $15 for the first unit of output and $19 for the second unit of output, the difference between the TC for the first and second units of output is $4.00 (*Principles of Economics* 5th ed. page 277/6th ed. page 268).

45. **D.** The total cost for four units of output is $24, which means that the average total cost is $6.00 (*Principles of Economics* 5th ed. page 277/6th ed. page 268).

46. **E.** Fixed costs are $10. Average fixed costs for four units of output are $2.25 because AFC = TFC/Q = $10/4 (*Principles of Economics* 5th ed. page 277/6th ed. page 268).

47. **D.** If demand for a good is inelastic, then an increase in the price causes an increase in total revenue. This means that, if a government wants to maximize its tax revenue, it should impose a

tax on a good whose demand is perfectly inelastic (*Principles of Economics* 5th ed. pages 102–108/6th ed. pages 94–96).

48. **A.** Some input costs are fixed in the short run, but not all. This is the definition of the short run. A firm can expand its production in the long run, which means that all fixed short run costs eventually are variable in the long run (*Principles of Economics* 5th ed. page 295/6th ed. page 271).

49. **B.** By granting a subsidy to producers of the good, the government provides an incentive to the producers to not only continue producing the good, but to increase production as well (*Principles of Economics* 5th ed. pages 207–208/6th ed. pages 202–208).

50. **C.** A monopolistically competitive firm still faces a downward sloping demand curve, similar to a monopoly, though more elastic (*Principles of Economics* 5th ed. pages 348–352/6th ed. pages 332–336).

51. **A.** An increase in the price of bicycles increases the quantity of bicycles supplied but does not affect the supply of bicycles (*Principles of Economics* 5th ed. pages 67–69/6th ed. pages 73–74).

52. **E.** The resource maximizing rule states that a firm should hire resources where its marginal revenue product equals its marginal resource cost. The price paid for an input is the same thing as its marginal resource cost (*Principles of Economics* 5th ed. page 400/6th ed. page 384).

53. **C.** As long as the perfectly competitive firm can cover average variable costs, it will stay open in the short run. Since this is the case, the marginal cost curve above the average variable cost curve is the supply curve for the firm (*Principles of Economics* 5th ed. pages 295–296/6th ed. pages 288–289).

54. **D.** This is the definition of productive efficiency. When firms produce at minimum average total cost, they are productively efficient (*Principles of Economics* 5th ed. page 5/6th ed. page 5).

55. **D.** The increase in the demand for and supply of smartphones will definitely increase the total quantity, but, depending on the magnitude of each shift, can either increase or decrease prices. The price of smart phones in this situation is therefore indeterminate (*Principles of Economics* 5th ed. page 81/6th ed. page 81).

56. **A.** If price is below equilibrium, it means that the quantity demanded is greater than the quantity supplied; in other words, there is a shortage. The market corrects this by allowing prices to rise (*Principles of Economics* 5th ed. page 78/6th ed. pages 116–117).

57. **A.** Since the firm is a price taker, an increase in the demand in the market means that the market price also increases. The firm takes this higher price, which means that MR = MC at a higher output level. Therefore, the firm now increases its output level in order to maximize profit (*Principles of Economics* 5th ed. pages 292–294/6th ed. pages 282–284).

58. **C.** The demand for resources is a derived demand, based on the demand in the product market. When the demand for the product that these resources produce increases, there is also an increase in the demand for workers to produce the additional units of product (*Principles of Economics* 5th ed. pages 393–397/6th ed. pages 376–382).

59. **A.** Private firms have no incentive to produce public goods because they cannot prevent others from using the good. This results in a free rider problem (*Principles of Economics* 5th ed. page 228/6th ed. page 220).

60. **C.** A decrease in demand will lead to an decrease in equilibrium price and quantity (*Principles of Economics* 5th ed. pages 77–80/6th ed. pages 77–80).

SECTION II: FREE-RESPONSE ANSWERS

1. (10 points total)

(a)

Q	P	TR	MR	MC	TC	Total Profit or Loss
0	$10	—	—	—	$1	$ –1
1	8	$8	$8	$2	3	+5
2	6	12	4	4	7	+5
3	4	12	0	6	13	–1
4	2	8	-4	8	21	–13
5	0	0	-8	10	31	–31

For part (a)
    (1 pt for TR values)
    (1 pt for MR values)
(b)
    Rest of table <u>above</u> is needed for part (b)
        Q = 2 (1 pt)
    (i)   P = $6 (1 pt); this is the Q & P since MR = MC (1 pt)
    (ii) Total Profit = $5 (1 pt)

Q	TC	TFC	TVC	ATC	AVC
0	$1	$1	$0	—	—
1	3	1	2	3	2
2	7	1	6	3.5	3
3	13	1	12	4.3	4
4	21	1	20	5.25	5
5	31	1	30	6.2	6

See also table in part (a)

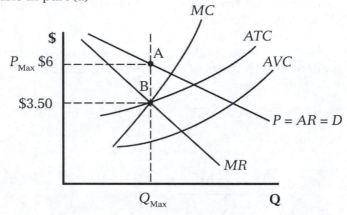

2 Bottles

(1 pt for correct labels + 1 pt for correct identification of profit maximizing P & Q)

(c) ⬆ TFC does not Δ output choice. Still MR = MC @ 2 units. (1 pt) But the firm now has TC = TR = $12 (⬆ TFC = $5) and breaks even. (1 pt)

(d) If TFC ⬆ BY $10, then firm <u>loss minimizes</u> at MR = MC @ 2 units (see table below) (1 pt)

Q	New Total Profit or Loss
0	–11
1	–5
2	–5
3	–11
4	–23
5	–41

(*Principles of Economics* 5th ed. Ch. 13/6th ed. Ch. 13)

2. A perfectly competitive farming industry is in long-run equilibrium. Fertilizer is an important variable input in the agricultural production process. The price of fertilizer increases for all firms in the industry.
    (a) The increase in the price of fertilizer will decrease industry supply (1 pt) and therefore will lead to an increased price and decreased output. (1 pt for both correct P & Q change)
    (b) Since the firm is a price-taker, the firm takes the higher price. (1 pt) A higher price means that the marginal revenue has also increased, so the profit maximizing output will increase, since MR = MC at a higher output level. (1 pt)
    However, marginal costs (MC) and average variable costs (AVC) also increase due to the increase in the price of fertilizer, which means that average total costs (ATC) increase. Profits decline as a result of this fertilizer price increase. (1 pt) It might also be the case that profits disappear altogether and that some firms incur losses. (1 pt) (*Principles of Economics* 5th ed. pages 293–300/6th ed. pages 283–290)
    (c) Assuming that some firms incur economic losses, firms will exit the industry in the long run. (1 pt) (*Principles of Economics* 5th ed. pages 302–303/6th ed. pages 292–293)

3. (6 total points)
    (a)

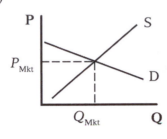

Paper

    (b) Since there is a negative externality, the market quantity is greater than the optimal, or socially acceptable, quantity. One way to provide an incentive for firms to produce less is for the government to impose a corrective tax on paper producers. (1 pt) This would encourage suppliers to supply less, thereby decreasing the total quantity of paper produced in the market. (1 pt) (*Principles of Economics* 5th ed. pages 210–214/6th ed. pages 203–207).
    (c) (1 pt for correctly labeled graph + 1 pt for correct impact on P_{tax}/Q_{opt})

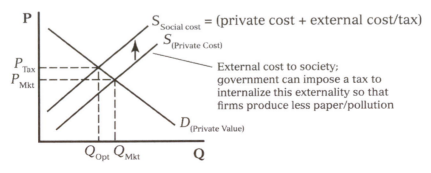

Paper Market

3. Country Z produces two finished goods, automobiles and smartphones, as illustrated on the PPC above. If production of the two goods moves from point A to point B, what might have caused the change?
   (A) Productivity increases due to new production technologies increased the quantity of smartphones.
   (B) Innovative new physical capital increased production capabilities for smartphone producers only.
   (C) Market forces shifted production from automobiles to smartphones while maintaining full employment levels of output.
   (D) Output shifted from below full employment levels up to full employment.
   (E) Rising gas prices and increased environmental consciousness provided incentive for technological gains in the automobile industry.

4. Assume contractionary monetary policies have had the effect of lowering inflation rates from a 6% annual rate down to 2%. What do economists call this drop in inflation?
   (A) Deflation.
   (B) Inflation.
   (C) Devaluation.
   (D) Depreciation.
   (E) Disinflation.

5. Country Alpha and Country Gamma are trade partners, each producing wheat and oil. Alpha is capable of producing 50 tons of wheat or 75 thousand barrels of oil in a month while Gamma can produce 10 tons of wheat or 40 thousand barrels of oil in the same month. Based on the theory of comparative advantage, which nation should produce each product?
   (A) Alpha should produce both because it has absolute advantage in both.
   (B) Alpha should produce wheat and Gamma should produce oil.
   (C) Alpha should produce oil and Gamma should produce wheat.
   (D) Gamma should produce both because it has comparative advantage for both goods.
   (E) Both nations should specialize in other products as neither has comparative advantage for either good.

6. Ceteris paribus, if consumer confidence in the market for a good were to rise, what would be the expected change in equilibrium price and quantity of that good?

	Price	Quantity
(A)	Increase	Decrease
(B)	Decrease	Indeterminate
(C)	Increase	Increase
(D)	Decrease	Decrease
(E)	Indeterminate	Increase

7. A change in consumer prices causes the CPI to increase to 175, up from its previous level of 125. Determine the percent change in consumer prices this change represents.
   (A) 25%.
   (B) 40%.
   (C) 50%.
   (D) 60%.
   (E) 75%.

8. Beta is a relatively small country with a 2010 Nominal GDP of $10,000. With 2005 as the base year and a Year 5 CPI of 125, what is Beta's Real GDP in 2005 dollars?
   (A) $4,000.
   (B) $7,500.
   (C) $8,000.
   (D) $10,000.
   (E) $12,000.

Adult population	Employed	Unemployed
200 million	60 million	20 million

9. Determine the unemployment for the nation Gamma based on the data given in the table above.
   (A) 10%.
   (B) 25%.
   (C) 30%.
   (D) 33%.
   (E) 75%.

10. Which of the following is included in GDP?
    (A) A tax refund from the federal government.
    (B) Used autos purchased by consumers.
    (C) Social security payments
    (D) A mechanic repairs his own vehicle.
    (E) Hair clippers purchased by a barber for his barber shop.

11. Which of the following would not be an example of an investment good included in GDP?
    (A) A purchase of existing Coca-Cola stock.
    (B) Renovation of McDonald's in Stonestown.
    (C) A new fax machine for a travel agency.
    (D) Increase in inventory.
    (E) A new home purchased by a family.

Answer the following questions based on the following data for a hypothetical economy. The base year for the GDP deflator is 1992 and it equaled 100 that year.

Year	Nom. GDP (billion)	Price index
1993	$4,200	120
1994	$4,300	125
1995	$4,680	130
1996	$4,958	134

12. Refer to the data above. Real GDP increased from 1995 to 1996 by approximately
    (A) $40 billion.
    (B) $100 billion.
    (C) $278 billion.
    (D) $380 billion.
    (E) $559 billion.

13. From 1992 to 1996, price rose by approximately
    (A) 5 percent.
    (B) 9 percent.
    (C) 14 percent.
    (D) 24 percent.
    (E) 34 percent.

14. As price level rises and money demand increases, nominal interest rates rise as well. Based on the interest rate effect, what is the likely outcome of this change?
    (A) Output demanded in the U.S. increases and firms increase production.
    (B) Output demanded in the U.S. decreases and firms decrease production.
    (C) Aggregate demand increases.
    (D) Aggregate demand decreases.
    (E) Long-run aggregate supply decreases.

15. GDP is an indicator of a nation's production of goods and services in a given year. Which of the following would cause an increase in a nation's GDP?
    (A) Foreign oil is purchased.
    (B) Sales of used automobiles increase dramatically.
    (C) A carpenter builds a dining room table for his daughter's apartment.
    (D) Fees are earned by a broker for the purchase of financial assets for her clients.
    (E) A mechanic restores a vintage automobile.

16. The change in aggregate demand resulting from an increase in household disposable income would affect money demand and nominal interest rates in which of the following ways?

Money Demand	Nominal Interest Rates
(A) No change	Increase
(B) Increase	Increase
(C) Increase	Decrease
(D) Decrease	No change
(E) Decrease	Indeterminate

17. Assume the economy has been operating at full employment levels of output and price level. A significant depreciation of the U.S. dollar vs. an index of foreign currencies would affect aggregate demand and equilibrium output in which of the following ways?

Aggregate Demand	Output
(A) Decrease	Decrease
(B) Decrease	Indeterminate
(C) Increase	Increase
(D) Increase	No change
(E) No change	Increase

18. If MPC equals 0.9, what is the spending multiplier?
    (A) 9.
    (B) 10.
    (C) 0.
    (D) −9.
    (E) −10.

19. Increases in output and decreases in unemployment are commonly associated with which phase of the business cycle?
    (A) Expansion.
    (B) Troughs.
    (C) Stagflation.
    (D) Depression.
    (E) Recession.

20. An increase in energy costs will most likely cause the price level and real gross domestic product to change in which of the following ways?

Price Level	Real GDP
(A) Increase	Increase
(B) Increase	Decrease
(C) Increase	No change
(D) Decrease	Increase
(E) Decrease	Decrease

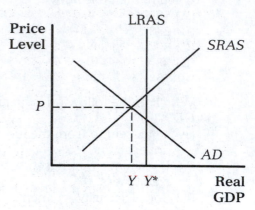

21. According to classical economic theory, which of the following describes the potential long-run self-correction of the economy depicted in the graph above?
    (A) Consumption will come out of its stagnation and shift AD to the right, bringing output back to full employment levels.
    (B) Wage rates will increase, attracting labor back to full employment levels and increasing output back to its natural rate.
    (C) Long-run aggregate supply will shift left due to decreases in spending and restore long-run equilibrium.
    (D) Nominal wages will decrease as the duration of unemployment extends, eventually shifting short-run aggregate supply to the right, bringing output back to its natural level.
    (E) Economies do not self-correct.

22. When output is below the full employment rate and unemployment is rising, this is the correct monetary policy use of open market operations.
    (A) Buying securities.
    (B) Selling securities.
    (C) Raising the discount rate.
    (D) Increasing the international value of the dollar.
    (E) Decrease the reserve ratio.

23. Which of the following would cause short-run aggregate supply to shift to the left?
    (A) An increase in subsidies for a majority of firms.
    (B) A decrease in wage rates throughout the economy.
    (C) New regulations and more strict enforcement of current regulations by OSHA regarding workplace safety conditions.
    (D) Increases in the level of technology cause structural changes in employment.
    (E) An increase in the level of human capital due to greater access to higher education.

24. The central bank is considered the lender of last resort. When commercial banks borrow money from the central bank, the interest rate charged is known as the
    (A) Prime rate.
    (B) Discount rate.
    (C) Reserve rate.
    (D) Federal funds rate.
    (E) Market rate.

25. The central bank raises the reserve ratio from 10% to 15%. Which of the following would be a potential reason for this change in policy?
    (A) Unemployment rates are rising.
    (B) Money supply is growing too slowly and holding back economic growth.
    (C) Core inflation expectations are high and the bank intends to maintain price stability by decreasing lending activity.
    (D) Banks are not lending enough money, causing stagnation in the economy.
    (E) Other central banks in the region have taken similar action.

26. If the reserve ratio is 10%, what would be the maximum effect of an open market purchase of $10,000 by the central bank?
    (A) Money supply would increase $10,000.
    (B) Money supply would increase $100,000.
    (C) Money supply would increase $1,000,000.
    (D) Money supply would decrease $100,000.
    (E) Money supply would decrease $10,000.

27. The appropriate monetary policy action meant to decrease rapid inflation would be to increase
    (A) the purchase of treasury securities.
    (B) raising marginal income tax rates.
    (C) the sale of government bonds.
    (D) money supply by reinvesting dividends.
    (E) government spending through social welfare programs.

28. Assuming velocity of money has risen 2%, what would be the result of a 4% increase in money supply when real output rises 2%?
    (A) Price level would rise 8%.
    (B) Unemployment would fall 2%.
    (C) Price level would rise 4%.
    (D) Unemployment would rise 4.5%.
    (E) Cannot be determined with the available data.

29. On a short-run Phillips Curve, high rates of inflation coincide with
    (A) high interest rates.
    (B) low interest rates.
    (C) high unemployment rates.
    (D) low unemployment rates.
    (E) low discount rates.

30. Assuming the total population is 200 million, the labor force is 100 million, and 92 million workers are employed. The unemployment rate is
    (A) 2%.
    (B) 4%.
    (C) 8%.
    (D) 10%.
    (E) indeterminate.

31. If the full employment rate of output for a nation is $15 trillion and short-run equilibrium output is $13, what course of fiscal policy action might a Keynesian economist recommend in order to return the economy to full employment levels of output?
    (A) Decrease government spending and taxes.
    (B) Buy government securities on the open market.
    (C) Increase government spending while holding taxes constant.
    (D) Raise the reserve ratio.
    (E) Keep government spending constant while increasing taxes.

32. Monetarist theory attributes inflation to
    (A) increases in government spending.
    (B) too much money being created.
    (C) decreases in taxes.
    (D) consumer expectations of future policy changes.
    (E) a lack of federal oversight in the banking industry.

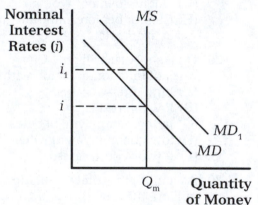

33. Assume that increasing price levels cause the above shift in money demand. If the central bank desired to keep levels of investment consistent with those prior to the shift of MD, what would be their optimal solution using open market operations?
    (A) Decrease the discount rate.
    (B) Increase the federal budget deficit.
    (C) Enforce tariffs on imported resources.
    (D) Increase money supply by purchasing securities.
    (E) Sell securities in order to increase borrowing activity.

34. The most commonly used measure for standard of living increases is an increase in the
    (A) aggregate demand.
    (B) real GDP per capita.
    (C) real GDP per worker.
    (D) real GDP per dollar of capital stock.
    (E) value of the dollar.

35. A news report claims that firms' expected rates of return are high as future business conditions are positive. What effect would this news have on the loanable funds market?

	Interest Rates	Quantity of Loanable Funds
(A)	Increase	Increase
(B)	Increase	Decrease
(C)	Decrease	Decrease
(D)	Decrease	Increase
(E)	No change	Increase

36. Which of the following is not a commonly heard argument in defense of protectionism?
    (A) Infant industries must be protected from foreign competitors.
    (B) Too much reliance on foreign producers can be dangerous in times of war.
    (C) The theory of comparative advantage.
    (D) To protect against the practice of "dumping" from foreign competitors.
    (E) Domestic manufacturers are in need of protectionist policies in order to maintain current levels of employment.

37. Assume policy changes are implemented which increase the incentive for investment in education. If this investment yields better trained and more capable labor, what will be the expected result?
    (A) An increase in potential GDP illustrated by a rightward shift of LRAS due to the increase in labor productivity.
    (B) A decrease in potential GDP due to the misallocation of funds.
    (C) A decrease in potential GDP due to a decrease in physical capital.
    (D) An increase in consumption due to increased unemployment benefits.
    (E) No change will result as resources are only being reallocated.

38. Assume a family's household disposable income increases from $50,000 one year to $55,000 the next, resulting in an increase in spending of $3,000. One may conclude that the family's
    (A) MPC equals 0.1.
    (B) MPS equals 0.4.
    (C) APC equals 0.9.
    (D) MPS equals 0.06.
    (E) APS equals 0.4.

39. The central bank announces that it expects inflation to be relatively low while unemployment rises in the following months. What would be an expected monetary policy action as a result of this forecast?
    (A) Increase government spending.
    (B) Decrease the discount rate.
    (C) Increase the reserve ration.
    (D) Sell bonds on the open market.
    (E) Decrease marginal income tax rates.

40. Compared to price in a completely closed economy, a market in an open economy with an effective quota imposed will result in
    (A) higher prices due to increased demand for the good.
    (B) lower prices due to decreased domestic demand.

    (C) increased total supply and lower prices.
    (D) increase in prices due to decreased foreign supply.
    (E) domestic demand increases leading to lower prices.

41. With an MPC of 0.8, government spending increases $20 billion while taxes decrease $10 billion. Based on this data, what is the cumulative effect on GDP?
    (A) An increase of $40 billion.
    (B) An increase of $80 billion.
    (C) An increase of $100 billion.
    (D) An increase of $140 billion.
    (E) An increase of $150 billion.

42. Which type of unemployment would increase if individuals move from full-time to part-time employment?
    (A) Cyclical.
    (B) Structural.
    (C) Annual.
    (D) Frictional.
    (E) Unemployment would not be affected by this change.

43. Assume a contractionary gap of $4 trillion. With MPC equal to 0.75, what would be the recommended fiscal policy action in order to return output to full employment levels?
    (A) Increase taxes by $4 trillion
    (B) Decrease spending by $1 trillion
    (C) Increase spending by $1 trillion
    (D) Purchase $1 trillion worth of government securities
    (E) Decrease taxes by $4 trillion

44. The natural rate of unemployment
    (A) means that the economy will always operate at its natural rate.
    (B) is equal to the total of frictional and structural employment.
    (C) means that the economy will always realize its potential output.
    (D) is a fixed unemployment rate of 5% that does not change over time.
    (E) is unattainable given an economy's existing resources.

45. Due to mainstream pessimism about labor markets, many unemployed workers end their search for jobs. What effect does this have on the labor force?
    (A) Rises because more people are now structurally unemployed.
    (B) Falls because discouraged workers are not counted in the official measurement of labor force.
    (C) Not affected because discouraged workers are not counted in the official measurement of labor force.
    (D) Falls because the amount of frictional unemployment has increased.
    (E) Rises because cyclical unemployment is increasing.

46. Assume that the world operates under a flexible exchange rate system. If the central bank of England holds money supply and interest rates steady while all other central banks increase their own money supplies, in what ways will the international value of the pound and level of English net exports change?

Int'l Value (Pound)	British Net Exports
(A) Increase	Increase
(B) No change	Increase
(C) Increase	Decrease
(D) Decrease	No change
(E) Decrease	Increase

47. The federal government implements an expansionary fiscal policy of increased spending and decreased taxes. Policy advisors predict output will increase 4% but are surprised when only 3% growth occurs. What might account for the fact that GDP increased by less than the multiplier predicted?
    (A) Policy advisors' calculation of MPS was too high.
    (B) The aggregate supply curve was perfectly elastic.
    (C) Foreign purchases of domestic goods was greater than expected due to a devalued currency.

    (D) Consumption increases more than expected because of the decrease in taxes.
    (E) Investment decreased due to rising interest rates.

48. The long-run Phillips Curve indicates that there is no relationship between inflation and unemployment in the long run. Therefore, which of the following would cause an increase in the natural rate of unemployment and shift the LRPC to the right?
    (A) An increase in unemployment benefits for the long-term unemployed.
    (B) The elimination of various social welfare programs.
    (C) A decrease in the duration of unemployment.
    (D) An increase in core inflation rates.
    (E) Expansionary monetary policies.

49. The most likely effect of an increase in the supply of loanable funds is which of the following?
    I.   Increase Interest Rates.
    II. Decrease Interest Rates.
    III. Increase Investment.
    IV. Decrease Investment.
    (A) I only.
    (B) II only.
    (C) III only.
    (D) I and IV only.
    (E) II and III only.

50. Which of the following combinations of monetary and fiscal policy would cause the greatest decrease in aggregate demand?

	Discount Rate	Gov Spending	Open Market Operations
(A)	Decrease	Increase	Buy Bonds
(B)	Decrease	Decrease	Buy Bonds
(C)	Increase	Decrease	Sell Bonds
(D)	Decrease	Increase	Sell Bonds
(E)	Increase	Decrease	Buy Bonds

51. If on receiving a checking deposit of $300 a bank's excess reserves increased by $255, the required reserve ratio must be
(A) 5%.
(B) 15%.
(C) 25%.
(D) 35%.
(E) 45%.

52. According to the Fisher effect, if firms are seeking a real return of 2% on loans and charge borrowers 5%, what is the expected rate of inflation?
(A) 10%.
(B) 7%.
(C) 5%.
(D) 3%.
(E) 2%.

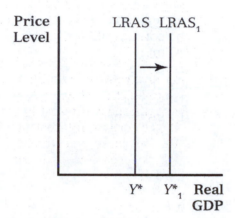

53. Which of the following is the best explanation of the above change in long-run aggregate supply in the U.S.?
(A) A decrease in the cost of imported resources.
(B) An increase in the technological capabilities of American manufacturers.
(C) Implementation of trade barriers with major industrial powers.
(D) Disposable income increases due to a major cut in marginal income tax rates.
(E) The level of physical capital declines due to overuse.

54. Assume U.S. trade is currently balanced such that total exports equal total imports. If the central bank were to pursue a policy of purchasing government bonds on the open market, what would be a likely consequence regarding the balance of trade?
(A) Exports would increase, imports would decrease and a trade surplus would result.
(B) Exports would decrease, imports would increase and a trade deficit would result.
(C) Imports and exports would increase and trade would maintain balance.
(D) Imports and exports would decrease, but the effect on the balance of trade would be indeterminate.
(E) None of the above would occur as only the credit account would be affected.

55. The Federal Reserve decides to implement a policy of buying securities on the open market while the Bank of England maintains their current monetary policy. Based on the expected change in interest rates that will occur, what will be the change in exchange rates of the U.S. dollar versus the British pound?

	Dollar	Pound
(A)	Appreciate	Depreciate
(B)	Depreciate	Appreciate
(C)	No change	Depreciate
(D)	Depreciate	No change
(E)	Appreciate	Appreciate

56. An expansionary fiscal policy will increase interest rates unless which of the following occurs?
(A) Taxes are cut instead of government expenditures increased.
(B) The money supply is increased.
(C) Wage and price controls are imposed.
(D) The exchange rate is fixed.
(E) The Fed sells government bonds.

57. The capital account on the United States' balance of payments includes all but which of the following transactions?
    (A) Changes in ownership of foreign stocks.
    (B) The sale of U.S. automobiles to German consumers.
    (C) Foreign investors construct a factory on U.S. soil.
    (D) The purchase of U.S. bonds by a foreign government.
    (E) A U.S. firm buys property in a foreign country .

58. Which of the following transactions would be included as a credit on Japan's current account?
    (A) American citizens purchase Japanese-made automobiles.
    (B) Japanese land is sold to Australian citizens.
    (C) European citizens earn interest on Japanese government bonds.
    (D) The Japanese government purchases American Treasury securities.
    (E) A Japanese firm builds a factory in the U.S.

59. Increased American imports of Japanese goods creates
    (A) an increase in demand for U.S. dollars and a decrease in demand for Japanese yen.
    (B) a decrease in demand for U.S. dollars and an increase in supply of Japanese yen.
    (C) an increase in demand for Japanese yen and a decrease in supply of U.S. dollars.
    (D) an increase in demand for Japanese yen and an increase in supply of U.S. dollars.
    (E) an increase in supply of Japanese yen and an increase in supply of U.S. dollars.

60. The fundamental problem in economics is that resources are limited; yet needs, wants, and desires are unlimited. This is summed up by the concept of
    (A) money.
    (B) power.
    (C) greed.
    (D) scarcity.
    (E) investment.

STOP
END OF SECTION I
IF YOU FINISH BEFORE TIME IS CALLED, YOU MAY CHECK YOUR WORK ON THIS SECTION. DO NOT GO ON TO SECTION II UNTIL YOU ARE TOLD TO DO SO.

Section II: Free-Response Questions
Planning Time—10 minutes
Writing Time—50 minutes

Directions: You have 50 minutes to answer all three of the following questions. It is suggested that you spend approximately half your time on the first question and divide the remaining time equally between the next two questions. In answering the questions, you should emphasize the line of reasoning that generated your results; it is not enough to list the results of your analysis. Include correctly labeled diagrams, if useful or required, in explaining your answer. A correctly labeled diagram must have all axes and curves clearly labeled and must show directional changes. Use a pen with black or dark blue ink.

1. Assume the economy has been operating a balanced budget at output levels below full employment.
   (a) Fiscal policy authorities seeking to stimulate the economy and return to the full employment rate of output enact expansionary fiscal policies. Explain how each of the following would fluctuate with an expansionary fiscal policy.
       (i)   Taxes.
       (ii) Government spending.
       (iii) The federal deficit.
   (b) Consumers are able to predict the effects of the fiscal policy. Illustrate on a correctly labeled graph of the loanable funds market the effects of the change in the deficit, being sure to show the change in interest rates.
   (c) As a result of the change in interest rates shown in part (b), explain how the value of the dollar will respond on foreign exchange markets, ceteris paribus.
   (d) Illustrate on a correctly labeled aggregate demand-aggregate supply graph the change that would occur in the U.S. economy due to the fluctuating international value of the dollar. Be sure to show on your graph the following:
       (i)   The natural rate of output, Y_f.
       (ii) The original output, Y_e, and price level, PL_e.
       (iii) The change in aggregate demand.
       (iv) The new output, Y_2, and price level, PL_2.

2. Irving Fisher was an influential American economist in the early 20th century.
   (a) Define the Fisher effect.
   (b) Assume banks have been charging 5% for money they lend. However, the actual inflation rate turns out to be 7%, higher than expected.
       (i) Use the Fisher equation to determine the real return realized by banks.
       (ii) Who benefits from this unanticipated inflation?
   (c) If consumers continue to expect this high rate of inflation, they will likely continue to demand more money.
       (i) Illustrate this concept on a correctly labeled graph of the money market.
       (ii) Explain one reason why borrowers may demand more funds.

3. Monetary policy authorities at the United States Federal Reserve attempt to maintain sustainable economic growth with low levels of inflation. Assume inflation is rising at rates higher than the central bank's goals.
   (a) Identify the open market operation the Fed will enact due to high rates of inflation.
   (b) Assume the U.S. economy had been operating at full employment levels of output and employment.

(i) Draw a graph of the short-run and long-run Phillips curves consistent with full employment. Label the long-run equilibrium point A.

(ii) Show the effects of the policy described on part (a) by labeling point B on your graph of the short-run Phillips curve.

(c) Assume that after the Fed's policy actions, Congress lifts regulations on numerous industries, expanding the capabilities of American firms. Illustrate on your graph from part (b) how this change will affect the short-run Phillips curve. Label the new long-run equilibrium point C.

ANSWERS FOR MACROECONOMICS DIAGNOSTIC TEST

SECTION I: MULTIPLE-CHOICE ANSWERS

Using the table below, score your test.

Determine how many questions you answered correctly and how many you answered incorrectly. You will find explanations of the answers on the following pages.

1. C	11. A	21. D	31. C	41. D	51. B
2. B	12. B	22. A	32. B	42. E	52. D
3. C	13. E	23. C	33. D	43. C	53. B
4. E	14. B	24. B	34. B	44. B	54. A
5. B	15. D	25. C	35. A	45. B	55. B
6. C	16. B	26. B	36. C	46. C	56. B
7. B	17. C	27. C	37. A	47. E	57. B
8. C	18. B	28. D	38. B	48. A	58. A
9. B	19. A	29. D	39. B	49. E	59. D
10. E	20. B	30. C	40. D	50. C	60. D

ANSWERS AND EXPLANATIONS

MULTIPLE-CHOICE ANSWERS

1. **C.** Productivity gains must be achieved in order to increase the maximum amount of goods produced by a nation; of the options given, only increases in physical capital will do this (*Principles of Economics* 5th ed. pages 25–28/6th ed. pages 26–28).

2. **B.** The wealth effect explains the inverse relationship between price and quantity demanded (*Principles of Economics* 5th ed. pages 67, 747/6th ed. pages 67, 727).

3. **C.** There is no increase or decrease in productivity because the PPC itself did not change. Only the combination of automobiles and smartphones changed, moving more towards smartphones and away from automobiles (*Principles of Economics* 5th ed. pages 25–28/6th ed. pages 25–28).

4. **E.** A reduction in the inflation rate is called disinflation (*Principles of Economics* 5th ed. page 819/6th ed. page 799).

5. **B.** Based on comparative advantage, Alpha should produce wheat because its opportunity cost for wheat (1.5 thousand barrels of oil) is less than Gamma's (4 thousands barrels of oil), while Gamma's opportunity cost for oil (0.25 tons of wheat) is less than Alpha's (0.67 tons of wheat) (*Principles of Economics* 5th ed. pages 54–59/6th ed. pages 54–59).

6. **C.** An increase in consumer confidence will increase demand. Ceteris paribus, the increase in demand, will increase price and quantity (*Principles of Economics* 5th ed. pages 71, 77–83/6th ed. pages 71, 77–83).

7. **B.** The percent change in CPI is ((175–125)/125) × 100. 50/125 equals 0.4, times 100 is 40 percent (*Principles of Economics* 5th ed. page 532/6th ed. page 516).

8. **C.** Real GDP equals nominal GDP divided by CPI times 100. $10,000 divided by 125 equals 80, times 100 is $8,000 (*Principles of Economics* 5th ed. pages 516–518/6th ed. pages 500–502).

9. **B.** Unemployment is the percentage of the labor force currently not working. Here, the labor force equals 80 million, 20 million of which are not working. 20 million is 25% of 80 million (*Principles of Economics* 5th ed. pages 614–616/6th ed. pages 594–596).

10. **E.** A barber purchasing clippers counts as an investment as it is a form of business spending on capital (*Principles of Economics* 5th ed. pages 512–515/6th ed. pages 496–499).

11. **A.** Stocks are not included in the calculation of GDP (*Principles of Economics* 5th ed. pages 512–515/6th ed. pages 496–499).

12. **B.** Real GDP 1995 equals $3600 ((4680/130) × 100); Real GDP 1996 equals $3700 ((4958/134) × 100) (*Principles of Economics* 5th ed. pages 516–518/6th ed. pages 500–502).

13. **E.** CPI rises from 100 in 1002 to 134 in 1996; this is a 34 percent increase (*Principles of Economics* 5th ed. pages 516–518/6th ed. pages 500–502).

14. **B.** The question describes movement along the aggregate demand curve due to an increase in price level. As a result, output demanded is decreasing and firms produce less (*Principles of Economics* 5th ed. page 747/6th ed. pages 727–728).

15. **D.** Broker fees are payment for services rendered; they would count as consumption spending in the calculation of GDP (*Principles of Economics* 5th ed. pages 512–515/6th ed. pages 496–499).

16. **B.** Increases in income will shift AD to the right, causing price level to rise. With increased price levels, money demand will increase,

causing nominal interest rates to rise as well (*Principles of Economics* 5th ed. pages 665–666/6th ed. pages 645–646).

17. **C.** Net exports increase when the currency depreciates. As a result, AD will increase and output will increase (*Principles of Economics* 5th ed. page 751/6th ed. page 728).

18. **B.** The spending multiplier is found by dividing 1 by the MPS. In this case, 1/0.1 equals 10 (*Principles of Economics* 5th ed. pages 788–790/6th ed. pages 769–770).

19. **A.** Expansion is defined as a period of positive growth in real GDP. As output increases, it is common for unemployment to decrease (*Principles of Economics* 5th ed. pages 740–742/6th ed. pages 720–722).

20. **B.** Increased energy costs cause the SRAS curve to shift left. The decrease in SRAS will drive up price level and decrease real GDP. If the situation lasts long enough, it is referred to as stagflation (*Principles of Economics* 5th ed. pages 760–761/6th ed. pages 738–740).

21. **D.** With sustained high unemployment, workers will be willing to work for less in the long run in order to gain employment. The decrease in wage rates will shift SRAS back to the right and restore full employment (*Principles of Economics* 5th ed. page 763/6th ed. page 742).

22. **A.** Buying treasury securities is the expansionary form of open market operations (*Principles of Economics* 5th ed. pages 653–656/6th ed. pages 633–634).

23. **C.** Regulations make it more difficult for firms to perform and, as a result, cause SRAS to shift to the left (*Principles of Economics* 5th ed. pages 760–761/6th ed. pages 738–740).

24. **B.** Commercial banks borrowing from the Fed must pay the money back at the discount rate (*Principles of Economics* 5th ed. pages 653–656/6th ed. pages 633–634).

25. **C.** Raising the reserve ratio is an example of contractionary monetary policy; it is intended to lower rates of inflation (*Principles of Economics* 5th ed. pages 653–656/6th ed. pages 633–634).

26. **B.** With a money multiplier of 10 (based on the equation of 1 divided by the reserve ratio, 0.1 in this case), the maximum increase in money supply would equal the $10,000 increase from the central bank times 10 (*Principles of Economics* 5th ed. pages 651–653/6th ed. pages 629–631).

27. **C.** Selling government bonds is a form of contractionary monetary policy (*Principles of Economics* 5th ed. pages 653–656/6th ed. pages 633–634).

49. **E.** As the supply of loanable funds shifts to the right, real interest rates fall, encouraging firms to spend more. Investment, therefore, also increases (*Principles of Economics* 5th ed. pages 583–591/6th ed. pages 564–572).

50. **C.** The combination of increasing discount rates, decreased government spending and the sale of bonds is the most contractionary of the five options (*Principles of Economics* 5th ed. pages 778–790/6th ed. pages 758–770).

51. **B.** Based on the data given, excess reserves increased by $255 when a $300 deposit is made. This means required reserves increased by $45. 45 is 15 percent of 300 (*Principles of Economics* 5th ed. pages 653–656/6th ed. pages 633–635).

52. **D.** The Fisher effect relates real and nominal interest rates through inflation by equating nominal interest rates to real interest rates plus inflation. With nominal rates at 5 percent and real rates at 2 percent, inflation is the difference of 3 percent (*Principles of Economics* 5th ed. pages 674–676/6th ed. pages 655–656).

53. **B.** Increased levels of technology will increase the natural rate of output, represented by the LRAS curve (*Principles of Economics* 5th ed. pages 752–756/6th ed. pages 732–735).

54. **A.** The purchase of government bonds by the Fed would result in lower interest rates. Low interest rates cause the dollar to depreciate on international markets; with a depreciated dollar, exports will rise and imports will fall, leading to a trade surplus (*Principles of Economics* 5th ed. pages 692–693/6th ed. pages 672–673).

55. **B.** High interest rates correlate with appreciated currencies on the foreign exchange market. Buying securities will lower U.S. interest rates relative to those in England; as a result, the dollar will depreciate and the pound will appreciate (*Principles of Economics* 5th ed. pages 716–721/6th ed. pages 696–701).

56. **B.** Expansionary fiscal policies may cause interest rates to rise due to increased levels of government borrowing. Central bank actions through expansionary monetary policy may keep interest rates stable (*Principles of Economics* 5th ed. pages 791–793/6th ed. pages 771–773).

57. **B.** The purchase of foreign goods and services is included on the current account (*Principles of Economics* 5th ed. pages 696–697/6th ed. pages 676–677).

58. **A.** Japan's current account is credited as foreigners are purchasing an exported good (*Principles of Economics* 5th ed. pages 692–693/6th ed. pages 672–673).

59. **D.** To purchase Japanese goods, Americans must exchange dollars for yen on the foreign exchange market. This transaction increases demand for yen and increases supply of dollars on the foreign exchange market (*Principles of Economics* 5th ed. pages 716–721/6th ed. pages 696–701).

60. **D.** Economics is the study of how scarce economic resources are allocated among unlimited needs, wants, and desires (*Principles of Economics* 5th ed. page 4/6th ed. page 4).

SECTION II: FREE-RESPONSE ANSWERS

1. **(10 points total)**
   (a) 3 points
      (i)   Taxes will decrease
      (ii) Government spending will increase
      (iii) The Federal deficit will increase
   (b) 1 point
      Supply of loanable funds will decrease or demand for loanable funds will increase (see graph). Real interest rates will increase (see graph).

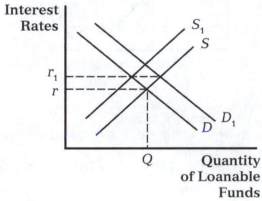

   (c) 2 points
      With nominal interest rates increasing, the dollar will appreciate internationally. Increased interest rates are an indication of higher rates of return and attract foreign investors, resulting in higher valued currencies abroad.
   (d) 4 points

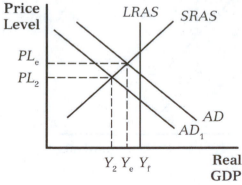

      (i) See graph, Y_f
      (ii) See graph, Y_e and PL_e

(iii) See graph, AD₁
(iv) See graph, Y₂ and PL₂
(*Principles of Economics* 5th ed. pages 716–721, 787–790/6th ed. pages 696–701, 767–770)

2. **(6 points total)**
   (a) 1 point
      The Fisher effect describes the relationship between nominal interest rates, real interest rates, and inflation.
   (b) 2 points
      (i) The real interest rate is −2%.
      (ii) Borrowers benefit from the unanticipated inflation.
   (c) 3 points

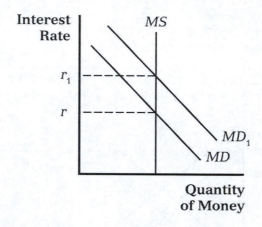

   (i) See graph, increase in money demand.
   (ii) Consumers come to expect high rates of inflation and need more liquid money as a result.

(*Principles of Economics* 5th ed. pages 674–676, 779–781/6th ed. pages 655–656, 759–761)

3. **(6 points total)**
   (a) 1 point
      Sell government securities.

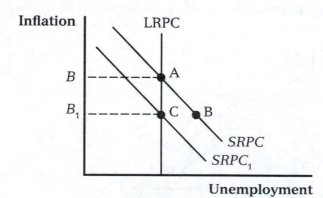

   (b) 3 points
      See graph, point A and B
   (c) 2 points
      See graph, SRPC shifts left and point C

(*Principles of Economics* 5th ed. pages 653–656, 778–787, 802–816/6th ed. pages 633–635, 758–767, 786–798)

CALCULATING YOUR SCORE

SECTION I: MULTIPLE-CHOICE QUESTIONS

[_____] × 1.25 = _____
Number Correct   Weighted Section I Score
(out of 60)   (Do not round)

SECTION II: FREE-RESPONSE QUESTIONS

Question 1 _____ × (1.2500) = _____
(out of 10)   (Do not round)

Question 2 _____ × (0.8333) = _____
(out of 6)   (Do not round)

Question 3 _____ × (0.9375) = _____
(out of 6)   (Do not round)

Sum = _____
Weighted Section II Score
(Do not round)

COMPOSITE SCORE

_____ + _____ = _____
Weighted   Weighted   Composite Score
Section I Score Section II Score (Round to nearest
whole number)

Composite Score Range	Approximate AP Grade
73–90	5
58–72	4
45–57	3
33–44	2
0–32	1

Part II

A Review of AP Economics

1

Basic Economic Concepts

Economics is *the study of how society manages its scarce resources.* You make decisions every day that capture the essence of economics. Given a limited 24-hour day, you have to make decisions regarding how to spend your time. Should you stay at home in order to study or will you go out with your friends? Similarly, given a limited budget, you have to make decisions regarding how to spend your money. Should you buy a new jacket or put your money into an interest-earning savings account? In order to make these kinds of decisions, you have to weigh the benefits and costs of each option.

Microeconomics is *the study of how households and firms make resource management decisions and how they interact in markets.* **Macroeconomics** is *the study of economy-wide phenomena resulting from resource management decisions, including inflation, unemployment, and economic growth.* These two fields are closely intertwined because overall economic changes are a result of the decisions of many people, so it is important to understand both microeconomic and macroeconomic theory. We will discuss the basic economic concepts that apply to both microeconomics and macroeconomics in this chapter.

There are costs associated with any decision made in the context of scarcity. **Scarcity** is the *limited nature of society's resources.* In this chapter, we will develop a better understanding of these economic fundamentals—scarcity, choices, and costs—and apply them to both microeconomic and macroeconomic theory.

Scarcity and Opportunity Costs

(Principles of Economics 5th ed. pages 4–6 and 49–60/6th ed. pages 4–6 and 49–60)

Like us, a society faces many decisions. Economics is the study of how a society makes decisions regarding how to use its scarce resources. Let's assume that a society's economy can only produce two goods—computers and cars. The production of computers and cars use up all of the economy's **factors of production,** *the inputs used to produce goods and services,* which means that the society faces a trade-off whenever it makes a decision regarding whether to produce more computers or cars.

Suppose that the society decides that it wants to produce more cars. In making this decision, the economy incurs a cost since it must give up the factors of production required for and any potential profit opportunities from increased computer production. Economists call these sacrifices **opportunity costs,** *whatever must be given up in order to obtain another item.* In our example, when society decides that it wants to produce more cars, the opportunity costs are the forgone computer profits and factors of production used to make computers. Society makes these decisions by weighing the costs and benefits of both choices. Although there is an opportunity cost associated with every decision, the expectation is that the decision made will provide benefits that will outweigh the costs.

MARGINAL ANALYSIS

In general, the decisions that we face are not clear cut—our decisions aren't always black or white, but typically involve shades of gray. For example, going back to our original example regarding how you would spend a 24-hour day, the decision you face is not whether you will go out with your friends or stay home to study, but whether you will stay home for an extra hour to study before going out with your friends. This type of decision making is called **marginal analysis,** *a comparison of marginal benefits and marginal costs.* A rational person will make decisions by weighing the **marginal benefits,** *the change in benefits you would receive from making the decision,* against the **marginal costs,** *the change in costs you would incur from making the decision.* With scarcity, the decision to gain the marginal benefit of an extra hour of studying must take into account the marginal cost of forgoing an hour of hanging out with friends. Every decision comes with a cost.

PRODUCTION POSSIBILITIES MODEL
(*Principles of Economics* 5th ed. pages 26–29/6th ed. pages 26–29)

Economists use the **production possibilities frontier (PPF),** *a graph that shows the combinations of output that the economy can possibly produce given the available factors of production and production technology,* to illustrate the concepts of scarcity, marginal analysis, and opportunity costs.

The figure below shows an economy's production possibilities frontier, or combinations of output that it can produce—in this case, cars and computers. Since resources are scarce, an economy cannot have an unlimited output of goods and services. Consequently, society must choose which goods and services to produce and which to forgo. If society's decision is to use all of its resources in the car industry, it produces 1,000 cars and no computers. Conversely, if it uses all of its resources in the computer industry, it produces 3,000 computers and no cars. The two endpoints of the PPF show these two extreme possibilities. The curve is a frontier because it shows the limited output potential for the economy given its scarce resources.

Realistically speaking, this society will not likely choose the production of one good over another; rather, it will conduct a marginal analysis and make an output decision that involves the production of some combination of both goods—cars *and* computers.

The economy can produce any combination of cars and computers on or inside the frontier shown in the figure below (points A, B, D, E, or F), but cannot produce outside of the PPF (at point C) because it does not have enough resources to do so. Each point *on* the PPF (points F, A, B, and E) represents the various combinations of car and computer production that is **efficient**, *where society gets the most it can from its scarce resources*, while the point lying *inside* the PPF (point D) is possible, but inefficient because society's resources are not fully utilized (due to underemployment or unemployment of resources).

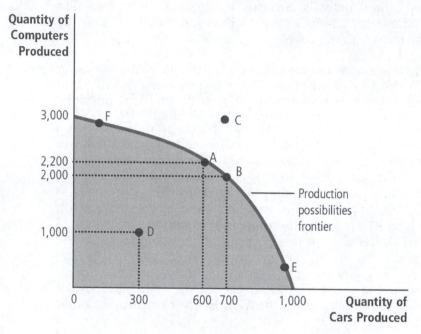

©Cengage Learning

The PPF is bowed out (not linear) because of the **law of increasing opportunity costs**, *opportunity costs increase as greater units of output are produced*. The resources needed to produce cars and computers are not perfectly adaptable to alternative uses—in other words, the inputs used to produce cars and computers are not the same, so when society decides to produce more cars, it must invest more in car production inputs and less in computer production inputs. As society chooses to increase its car production, it has to give up more computer inputs that are increasingly more valuable to computer production and therefore, incurs higher opportunity costs. Take the following simplified example.

Suppose that your high school has the option of hosting a dance or a football game in order to raise money for the school. The inputs needed to host a dance include decorations, food, and music. The inputs needed to host a football game include a game announcer, a football team, and a coach. The more dances your school wants to host, the more valuable the football game inputs your school must give up. More specifically, if your school wants to host one dance, it has to decide which of the three football game inputs it wants to give up. The rational decision is to give up the *least* valuable input first, so your school would give up the game announcer, which still enables the school to host both a dance and a football game, although the game would be without an announcer. However, if your school wants to host an additional dance, it must again decide which football game input it must give up. Let's say that your school gives up the football coach. The opportunity cost of giving up the football coach is much greater than giving up the game announcer. Without a coach, you might still be able to host both dances and football games, but the quantity and quality of football games would be sacrificed. If your school decides to host yet another dance, it must give up the football team. Without a football team, there is no possibility for your school to host a football game. With the decision to "produce" more dances comes the increasing cost of having to give up more valuable football inputs that ultimately will limit the school's production possibilities to the "production" of dances only.

This simplified example demonstrates why the law of increasing opportunity costs lead to a bowed out PPF—the more of a product that is produced, the greater its opportunity cost. Note that it is possible, although rare, to have a linear PPF if the inputs are perfectly adaptable to the production of the two goods.

AP Tip

Be sure to label your graphs on the free-response portion of the exam. On a PPF graph, all you need to do is put one good on the x-axis, put the other good on the y-axis, and draw a bowed-out curve, assuming that there are increasing opportunity costs. Points are given for labeling even if your answer is incorrect, so remember to label!

(Note that the AP does occasionally test for linear PPF graphs, so be familiar with the various PPF possibilities.)

EXPANDING THE PRODUCTION POSSIBILITIES
(*Principles of Economics* 5th ed. pages 50–59/6th ed. pages 50–59)

The PPF shows the trade-off between the outputs of different goods at a given time, but the trade-off can change over time. For example, suppose a technological advance in the computer industry raises the number of computers that a worker can produce per week. This advance enables the economy to produce more computers for any given number of cars. As a result, the PPF shifts outward for computers along the y-axis, shown by the line to the right of the original PPC in the figure below. This outward shift represents an increase in the production possibilities for the economy due to improved technology or, put more simply, this outward shift represents economic growth.

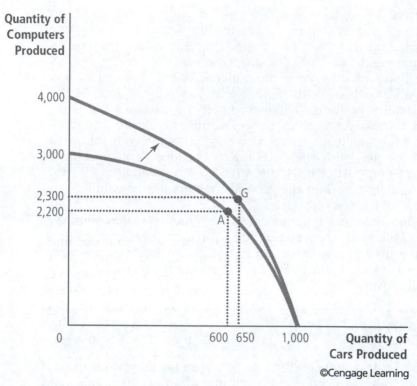

©Cengage Learning

While improved technology can expand an economy's production possibilities, a nation can experience economic growth through trade as well. To see how trade can increase an economy's production possibilities, consider the following example of a simple economy.

Assume that the world produces only two goods: meat and potatoes. Suppose that a potato farmer is also able to raise cattle and produce meat, but at a great cost because he is not very good at it. Suppose that a cattle rancher is able to grow potatoes, but also at a great cost because her land is not well suited for it. Both the farmer and rancher can benefit by specializing in the production of what he or she does best and then trading with the other person. The PPFs for both the potato farmer and cattle rancher are depicted in the next figure. Note that the PPFs are linear, which means that the law of increasing opportunity costs does not apply because the technology for producing meat and potatoes allows both the farmer and the rancher to switch between the production of the two goods at a constant rate; in other words, the resources used to produce potatoes are perfectly adaptable for meat production.

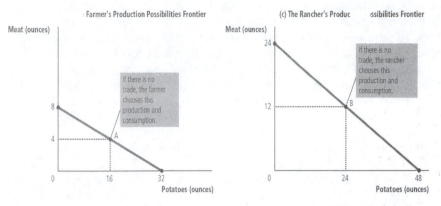

©Cengage Learning

Suppose that the farmer and rancher each work an 8-hour day and can devote this time to growing potatoes, raising cattle, or a combination of the two. If the farmer devotes all 8 hours to the production of potatoes, he can produce 32 ounces of potatoes and no meat. If he devotes all 8 hours to the production of meat, he can produce 8 ounces of meat and no potatoes. If the farmer divides his time equally (spends 4 hours on each) between the production of meat *and* potatoes, he produces 16 ounces of potatoes and 4 ounces of meat. We can draw similar conclusions based on the rancher's PPF. If the rancher devotes all 8 hours of her time to potatoes, she can produce 48 ounces of potatoes and no meat. If she devotes all 8 hours to the production of meat, she can produce 24 ounces of meat and no potatoes. The rancher can also choose to spend 4 hours each on the production of meat and potatoes, in which case she produces 24 ounces of potatoes and 12 ounces of meat. The PPF shows all of the possible production outcomes for both the farmer and the rancher.

If they do not trade with one another, then both the farmer and rancher will produce exactly what is depicted on each PPF. However, the farmer and the rancher can both expand their consumption if they each specialized in the production of meat or potatoes and traded with the other. How does this simple example relate to our discussion of economics? From a macroeconomic perspective, the farmer and the rancher can represent two different countries with a potential for increased economic growth and opportunities through international trade. From a microeconomic perspective, the farmer and the rancher can represent two individuals or firms with a potential for increased benefits through trade.

We have established that potential economic gains can be made through trade, but how do we determine whether it makes economic sense to trade and what goods to trade? How does the farmer decide if he wants to specialize in the production of one good and trade with the rancher? How does the rancher decide if she wants to specialize in the production of one good and trade with the farmer? If the farmer does specialize and trade, which of the two goods should he produce? If the rancher does specialize and trade, which of the two goods should she produce? In order to answer these questions we must consider another question: who can produce either meat or potatoes at a lower cost—the farmer or the rancher?

One approach to this question involves looking at the inputs required by the two producers. Who uses the least amount of input in the production of meat or potatoes? The producer that has the **absolute advantage**, *the ability to produce a good using fewer inputs than another producer,* in the production of meat or potatoes might consider specializing in the production of that good and trading for the other good because he or she is able to use inputs efficiently. In our example, the rancher has the absolute advantage in both the production of meat and potatoes. Does this mean that she should produce both goods herself or that she cannot gain from specialization in the production of one good and trading?

Knowing which individual has the absolute advantage does not give us the complete answer to the question regarding whether or not the rancher should engage in trade. We need to take a second approach in order to determine if it makes economic sense for the rancher to specialize and trade—we still need to determine which producer has the **comparative advantage**, *the ability to produce a good at a lower opportunity cost than another producer,* in the production of meat or potatoes. In our example, the farmer has the lower opportunity cost of producing potatoes than the rancher (see figure below). One ounce of potatoes costs the farmer ¼ ounce of meat whereas it costs the rancher ½ ounce of meat. The farmer has the comparative advantage in the production of potatoes while the rancher has the comparative advantage in the production of meat.

	Opportunity Cost of:	
	1 oz of Meat	**1 oz of Potatoes**
Farmer	4 oz potatoes	¼ oz meat
Rancher	2 oz potatoes	½ oz meat

Although it is possible for one person to have an absolute advantage in both goods, as the rancher does in this example, it is impossible for one person to have a comparative advantage in both goods because comparative advantage reflects the opportunity cost *relative* to others. So, even though the rancher has the absolute advantage in the production of both goods, she only has the comparative advantage in the production of meat and does *not* have the comparative advantage in the production of both goods. This suggests that it might be worthwhile for her to specialize and trade.

Returning to the questions we raised at the top of this page, both the farmer and rancher will choose to specialize and trade as long as they can gain from it. The gains from specialization and trade are based not on absolute advantage but on *comparative advantage,* which means that, if the farmer and rancher produce the good that he/she has the comparative advantage in, both the farmer and rancher will gain because the total quantity of meat and potatoes produced by each is *higher* with specialization and trade than if each produced both goods independently of one another. Trade can make people and countries better off. Our farmer and rancher example illustrate this point. The figure below shows these gains from a graphical and numerical perspective.

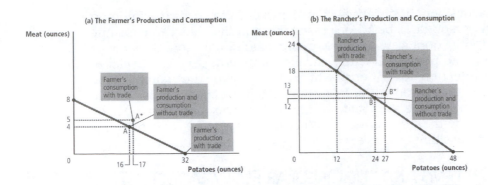

(a) The Farmer's Production and Consumption

(b) The Rancher's Production and Consumption

(c) The Gains from Trade: A Summary

	Farmer		Rancher	
	Meat	Potatoes	Meat	Potatoes
Without Trade:				
Production and Consumption	4 oz	16 oz	12 oz	24 oz
With Trade:				
Production	0 oz	32 oz	18 oz	12 oz
Trade	Gets 5 oz	Gives 15 oz	Gives 5 oz	Gets 15 oz
Consumption	5 oz	17 oz	13 oz	27 oz
GAINS FROM TRADE:				
Increase in Consumption	+1 oz	+1 oz	+1 oz	+3 oz

Without specialization and trade, both the farmer and rancher can produce at any combination of goods along their existing PPFs. In order to understand the potential gains from trade, consider the following example, as shown in the figure above.

The farmer is currently producing at point A (16 ounces of potatoes, 4 ounces of meat) and the rancher is producing at point B (24 ounces of potatoes, 12 ounces of meat). The farmer can work for 8 hours a day producing 32 ounces of potatoes in one day. If the farmer gives the rancher 15 of the 32 ounces, the rancher will give the farmer 5 ounces of meat in return. This means that, at the end of every day, the farmer will have 17 ounces of potatoes and 5 ounces of meat (point A*). By specializing in potato production and trading, the farmer has more of *both* goods. The rancher gains as well. If the rancher spends 6 hours a day raising cattle and 2 hours growing potatoes, she will produce 18 ounces of meat and 12 ounces of potatoes. After giving the farmer 5 ounces of meat in exchange for 15 ounces of potatoes, the rancher ends up with 13 ounces of meat and 27 ounces of potatoes (point B*) and will be able to consume more of both goods than she does without trade.

Both parties benefit because trade allows each to specialize in doing what each person does best. As a result, both individuals can consume more of both goods without working additional hours. From a macroeconomic perspective, this means that countries can specialize in the production of goods which they have the comparative advantage in and trade with other countries in order to increase total overall output. Trade and specialization improves opportunities for economic growth and allows producers to consume outside their production possibilities curve.

ECONOMIC SYSTEMS AND THE CIRCULAR FLOW MODEL
(*Principles of Economics* 5th ed. pages 24–25/6th ed. pages 26–29)

Every society develops its own approach to address the issue of scarcity. These different approaches can be generalized into two types of market systems—market and command. A **market system**, *an economy that allocates resources through the decentralized decisions of many firms and households as they interact in markets for goods and services*, coordinates all economic activity through **markets**, *where buyers and sellers determine what and how much to produce/consume*, and allows for the private ownership of **capital**, *the equipment and structures used to produce goods and services*. In a **command system**, *an economy that is centrally (government) planned*, government-appointed central planners decide what goods and services to produce, how much to produce and who produces and consumes these goods.

The majority of nations today use the market system, so we need to understand how this system operates. The economy consists of millions of people engaged in economic activity—buying, selling, producing, and hiring, to name a few. Economists have developed the **circular flow model**, *a visual model of the economy that shows how dollars flow through markets among households and firms*, to help simplify our thinking about economic activity within the market system. The circular flow model is depicted in the following figure.

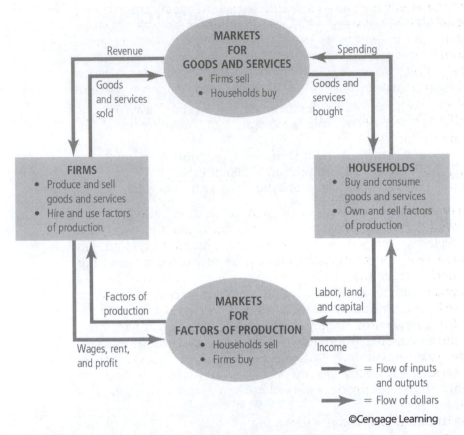

There are two types of markets within a market economy. In the market for factors of production, households provide the inputs that firms use to produce goods and services. In the market for goods and services, households buy the goods produced by the firms. The two loops connect the goods/services market to the factors of production market. The outer loop represents the flow of dollars within a market economy as households buy firm-produced goods and services and firms buy household inputs for the production of goods and services. The inner loop represents the flow of inputs and outputs. The circular flow model is useful to keep in mind when thinking about how the pieces of the economy fit together.

AP Tip

Make sure that you know the different components of the circular flow model. The circular flow model shows up often in multiple-choice questions.

BASIC ECONOMIC CONCEPTS: STUDENT OBJECTIVES FOR THE AP EXAM

You should be able to:
- define all key terms in bold.
- graph a production possibilities frontier and explain how this demonstrates the economic concepts of scarcity and opportunity cost.
- demonstrate an understanding of how economic growth occurs through graphical and written explanations.
- draw and explain all components of the circular flow model.

MULTIPLE-CHOICE QUESTIONS

1. Which of the following statements correctly describes the economic concept of scarcity?
   I.   Scarcity means that a society has limited resources.
   II. Scarcity would not exist in societies that engage in trade.
   III. Scarcity exists when society has to make a decision regarding how to allocate its resources.
   (A) I only.
   (B) II only.
   (C) III only.
   (D) I, II, and III.
   (E) I and III only.

2. All of the following regarding PPF are true EXCEPT:
   (A) The PPF indicates how much of two products a society is able to produce.
   (B) The PPF reveals how much each additional unit of one product will cost in terms of the other product.
   (C) Assuming that an economy is on its PPF, the PPF indicates that to produce more of one product society must forgo larger amounts of the other product.
   (D) The PPF specifies how much of each product society should produce.
   (E) The PPF is a model that represents options (A) through (C) above.

3. A country can produce some combination of goods outside its PPF by
   (A) specializing and engaging in international trade.
   (B) producing more capital goods and fewer consumer goods.
   (C) investing in the global economy.
   (D) using its resources sparingly.
   (E) decreasing unemployment.

4. The law of increasing opportunity costs exists because
   (A) the value of the dollar has diminished.
   (B) resources are not equally efficient in producing various goods.
   (C) wage rates invariably rise as the economy approaches full employment.
   (D) consumers tend to value any good more highly when they have little of it.
   (E) resources are scarce.

Refer to the following graph to answer Questions 5–7:

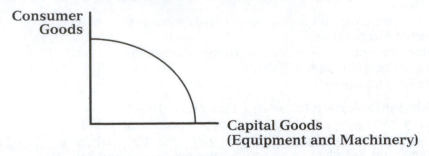

5. Assume that an economy has fully employed its productive resources. Which of the following statements about this economy's PPF is true?
   (A) The economy's current production levels are located anywhere <u>along</u> its PPF.
   (B) The economy's current production levels are located anywhere <u>inside</u> its PPF.
   (C) The economy's current production levels are located anywhere <u>outside</u> its PPF.
   (D) The economy's current production levels are located anywhere <u>along</u> or <u>inside</u> its PPF.
   (E) The economy's current production levels are located anywhere <u>inside</u> or <u>outside</u> its PPF.

6. Which of the following would cause the PPF shown above to shift outward in the long run?
   (A) Reopening capital production plants that had been closed.
   (B) Increasing the production of consumer goods.
   (C) Increasing the production of capital goods.
   (D) Switching from the production of capital goods to consumer goods.
   (E) Developing technology that allows for a more efficient equipment making process.

7. If an economy is operating <u>on</u> its PPF for consumer goods and capital goods, this means that
   (A) it is impossible to produce more consumer goods.
   (B) resources cannot be reallocated between the two goods.
   (C) it is impossible to produce more capital goods.
   (D) the economy is not producing what society wants.
   (E) more consumer goods can only be produced at the cost of fewer capital goods.

8. Which of the following must be true of a firm that is operating <u>inside</u> its PPF?
   (A) It has a market economy.
   (B) It has a command economy.
   (C) It is using its resources inefficiently.
   (D) It is using its resources efficiently.
   (E) It has an abundance of resources.

9. Trade based on comparative advantage is economically beneficial because
   (A) it promotes an efficient allocation of global resources.
   (B) it increases competition.
   (C) it provides consumers with a wider range of products.
   (D) answers (A) and (C) only.
   (E) answers (B) and (C) only.

Use the following information to answer Questions 10–12:
Assume that only two goods are produced, apples and oranges. The chart below shows the number of apples and oranges that two farmers, Farmer X and Farmer Y can produce and process in one day.

	Apples	Oranges
Farmer X	50	10
Farmer Y	80	40

10. Which of the following statements is true according to the table above?
    (A) Farmer X has the absolute advantage in the production of apples, but not in the production of oranges.
    (B) Farmer Y has the absolute advantage in the production of apples, but not in the production of oranges.
    (C) Farmer X has the absolute advantage in the production of oranges, but not in the production of apples.
    (D) Farmer X has the absolute advantage in the production of both oranges and apples.
    (E) Farmer Y has the absolute advantage in the production of both oranges and apples.

11. Based on the table above, which of the following statements is true?
    (A) Both farmers can gain from trade because Farmer X has the comparative advantage in the production of apples while Farmer Y has the comparative advantage in the production of oranges.
    (B) Both farmers can gain from trade because Farmer Y has the comparative advantage in the production of apples while Farmer X has the comparative advantage in the production of oranges.
    (C) Both farmers can gain from trade because Farmer Y has the absolute advantage in the production of oranges while Farmer X has the absolute advantage in the production of apples.
    (D) Both farmers can gain from trade because Farmer X has the absolute advantage in the production of oranges while Farmer Y has the absolute advantage in the production of apples.
    (E) Neither farmer can gain from trade because neither farmer has the comparative advantage in the production of either good.

12. Which of the following statements is true, according to the information presented in the table above?
    (A) Trade should take place, with Farmer X specializing in orange production and Farmer Y specializing in apple production.
    (B) Trade should take place, with Farmer Y specializing in orange production and Farmer X specializing in apple production.

(C) Each farmer should devote half of its inputs to apple production and half to orange production and not trade.

(D) Since Farmer X can produce both apples and oranges using fewer factors of production than Farmer Y, it cannot benefit from trade with Farmer Y.

(E) Since Farmer Y can produce both apples and oranges using fewer factors of production than Farmer X, it cannot benefit from trade with Farmer X.

13. The allocation of resources in a market economy is described by which of the following statements?

I. The government decides which goods will be produced and which consumers will have the opportunity to buy them.

II. Buyers and sellers exchange goods and services through market interactions.

III. Prices help producers determine whether they are producing too little or too much of a good.

(A) I only.

(B) II only.

(C) III only.

(D) I and III only.

(E) II and III only.

14. What interactions does the circular flow model of economic activity show between consumers and producers?

I. Firms pay households in the market for factors of production.

II. Firms sell products to households in the market for goods and services.

III. Households buy products in the market for factors of production.

IV. Households sell products to firms in the market for factors of production.

(A) I only.

(B) II only.

(C) I and II only.

(D) I, II, and IV only.

(E) III and IV only.

15. An accountant who earns $50,000 working for an accounting firm has the opportunity to start her own accounting business. It would cost $20,000 to start the business. If the accountant decides to quit her accounting job in order to start her own business, the opportunity cost of her decision is equal to
    (A) $20,000, representing the cost of starting the business.
    (B) $30,000, representing the difference between her forgone income and the cost of starting her business.
    (C) $50,000, representing her forgone income.
    (D) $70,000, representing sum of her forgone income and the cost of starting her business.
    (E) $0, because her lost wages is offset by the opportunity to start her own business.

FREE-RESPONSE QUESTIONS

1. Suppose that an economy produces two goods—bread and bicycles. Both goods are produced using labor and capital.
   (a) Draw the PPF for this economy.
   (b) What does the PPF represent and why is it likely to be bowed out from the origin?
   (c) Suppose that bicycle production technology improves. How, if at all, would this technological change affect the PPF? Explain your answer graphically and in words.
   (d) Suppose that bread factory workers are laid off. How, if at all, would this development affect the PPF? Explain your answer graphically and in words.

2. The circular flow of goods and inputs has a corresponding flow of dollar incomes and spending. What are the differences between the flow of goods and inputs with the flow of dollars? Explain in words and draw a circular flow diagram showing the dollar flows in the economy and contrast it with the circular flow of goods and inputs (factors of production).

Answers

MULTIPLE-CHOICE QUESTIONS

1. **E.** Option I is the definition of scarcity, so it is true. Even with trade, societies have limited resources, which is why option II cannot be true. Option III is true since scarcity limits the possibilities for an economy. This means that a decision must be made regarding how to use the limited resources (*Principles of Economics* 5th ed. pages 4–5/6th ed. pages 4–5).

2. **D.** Answer D is the only false statement because the PPF represents the total potential production output for an economy. It does not determine how much of each good society must produce, that is for society to decide, based on its own values and preferences (*Principles of Economics* 5th ed. pages 25–29/6th ed. pages 26–29).

3. **A.** Scarcity limits the production possibilities. Specialization and trade is one possible means to attain a point outside of a society's existing PPF because it increases the production, and subsequently, the consumption, potential (*Principles of Economics* 5th ed. pages 25–29/6th ed. pages 26–29).

4. **B.** Resources are not perfectly adaptable to the production of the goods produced by society, so when a society wants to produce of one particular good, it has to give up resources used to produce the good it is giving up. As society produces more of that good, the resources it has to give up to produce the good are increasingly more valuable, which is why there are increasing opportunity costs (*Principles of Economics* 5th ed. pages 25–29/6th ed. pages 26–29, 54–55).

5. **A.** An economy that is fully employing its resources for production has the production potential represented by any point on the PPF (*Principles of Economics* 5th ed. pages 25–29/6th ed. pages 26–29).

6. **E.** Technological improvements will enable an economy to increase its production potential over time (*Principles of Economics* 5th ed. pages 25–29/6th ed. pages 26–29).

7. **E.** The PPF represents the production potential of an economy. In order to produce more consumer goods, the economy has to give up its production of capital goods (*Principles of Economics* 5th ed. pages 25–29/6th ed. pages 26–29).

8. **C.** An economy that utilizes all of its resources will produce somewhere long its PPF. An economy that does not utilize all of its resources will produce somewhere within, inside, its PPF (*Principles of Economics* 5th ed. pages 25–29/6th ed. pages 26–29).

9. **D.** Trade based on comparative advantage increases the production potential for each country and ensures that each is using its' resources most efficiently, since it is specializing the production of a product for which it has the comparative advantage, or the lowest opportunity cost (*Principles of Economics* 5th ed. pages 54–59/6th ed. pages 50–56).

10. **E.** Farmer Y produces more apples and oranges, which is why it has the absolute advantage in the production of both goods (*Principles of Economics* 5th ed. pages 54–59/6th ed. pages 50–56).

11. **A.** Farmer X has the comparative advantage in the production of apples while Farmer Y has the comparative advantage in the production of oranges, which means that they would both benefit from specialization and trade (*Principles of Economics* 5th ed. pages 54–59/6th ed. pages 50–56).

12. **B.** See explanation to answer #11. Each farmer should specialize in the production of the good for which it has the comparative advantage, which is why B is the correct answer (*Principles of Economics* 5th ed. pages 54–59/6th ed. pages 50–56).

13. **E.** Option I cannot be true because a government dictates what a market should produce only in a command economy, not a market economy (*Principles of Economics* 5th ed. pages 8–9/6th ed. pages 10–11).

14. **C.** In the factor market, households sell resources to firms while firms buy resources from households. In the goods market, firms produce goods to sell to households while households buy the goods produced by the firms (*Principles of Economics* 5th ed. pages 24–26/6th ed. pages 24–26).

15. **D.** An opportunity cost is whatever is given up in order to attain an alternative option. The opportunity costs incurred by the accountant include not only the $20,000 for the business, but the $50,000 in salary that the accountant gives up in order to start his/her own business (*Principles of Economics* 5th ed. pages 50–51/6th ed. pages 54–55).

FREE-RESPONSE QUESTIONS

1. (a)

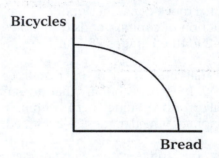

Bicycles

Bread

Note: a straight line PPF is acceptable as well, although you would have to specify that the resources to produce both were perfectly adaptable for the production of both goods. (This is not likely though, because the inputs for bicycle production are very different from the inputs for baking bread) (*Principles of Economics* 5th ed. pages 26–27/6th ed. pages 26–27).

(b) The PPF represents all of the production possibilities for this particular economy. Specifically, it represents the total output of bread and bicycles can produce given scarce resources. It is likely to be bowed out from the origin because there are increasing opportunity costs due to the fact that resources are not perfectly adaptable to the production of both goods (*Principles of Economics* 5th ed. pages 26–27/6th ed. pages 26–27).

(c) If bicycle production improves, more bicycles can be produced using the same amount of resources because bicycle production is now more efficient. This will shift the PPF to the right, illustrating an increase in the production possibilities for this country. The country experiences economic growth (*Principles of Economics* 5th ed. pages 27–29/6th ed. pages 27–29).

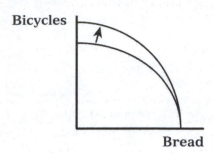

(d) It wouldn't change the frontier itself, but this means that the economy would exist somewhere inside of the PPF since resources aren't used (*Principles of Economics* 5th ed. page 26/6th ed. page 26).

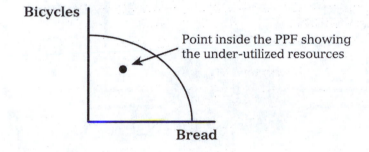

Point inside the PPF showing the under-utilized resources

2. The flow of dollars represents the flow of money that is paid by the firms to the households for use of their inputs (land, labor, capital, and entrepreneurial skills) and by the households to pay for the firm's products. The flow of goods and inputs represents the flow of the physical products and resources that are given in exchange for money by both households and firms (*Principles of Economics* 5th ed. pages 24–26/6th ed. pages 24–26).

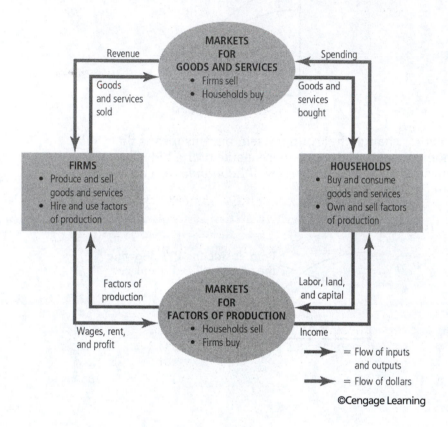

©Cengage Learning

2

HOW MARKETS WORK

Why are airfares more expensive during the summer? Why are tickets to a National Basketball Association (NBA) playoff game more expensive than a regular season game? Why are gas prices higher when there is instability in the Middle East? The answer to these questions can be found through supply and demand analysis. Supply and demand are the forces that make market economies work. They determine the quantity of each good produced and the price at which it is sold. This chapter will introduce the theory of supply and demand, as well as the concept of **elasticity**, *a measure of how much buyers and sellers respond to changes in market conditions*. A **market** is *a group of buyers and sellers of a particular good or service*. With this definition in mind, let's begin our study of markets by analyzing the behavior of both buyers and sellers.

DEMAND

(*Principles of Economics* 5th ed. pages 67–73/6th ed. pages 67–73)

Buyers demand the goods and services produced and sold by sellers in various markets. What determines buyer demand? This section will provide you with the answer to this question. Let's start with an example using the ice cream market. When the price of ice cream is high, the quantity of ice cream people are willing to buy is smaller. Conversely, when the price of ice cream is low, the quantity of ice cream people are willing to buy is greater. The economic concept here that captures this behavioral dynamic is the **law of demand**, which states that *other things equal, the quantity demanded of a good falls when the price of the good rises*. The **quantity demanded** is *the amount of a good that buyers are willing and able to purchase*.

Suppose that ice cream cones cost $3.00. At that price, I am unwilling to buy an ice cream cone, but at the price of $2.50, I am willing to buy 2 ice cream cones, which means that the quantity demanded increases from 1 to 2 when the price of ice cream decreases from $3.00 to $2.50. The figure below shows my **demand schedule** for ice cream, a table that shows the relationship between the price of a good and the quantity demanded, for ice cream cones.

Price of Ice-Cream Cone	Quantity of Cones Demanded
$0.00	12 cones
0.50	10
1.00	8
1.50	6
2.00	4
2.50	2
3.00	0

Based on the above ice cream demand schedule, we can plot the market **demand curve**, a graph of the relationships between the price of a good and the quantity demanded, as in this figure below.

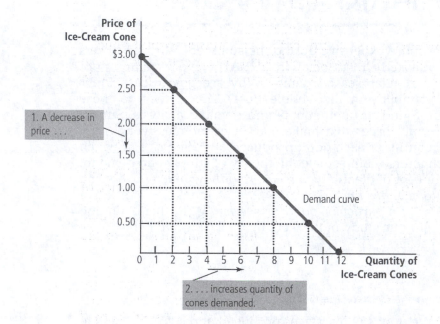

The demand curve for ice cream slopes downward since a lower price increases both consumers' willingness and ability to buy an ice cream cone. The demand curve in the figure above only represents my demand for ice cream. Since our goal is to analyze how markets work, we need to look at the **market demand** for ice cream, *which is the sum of the demand curves of everyone who is willing and able to buy* an ice cream cone. The market demand curve for ice cream follows the law of demand and, therefore, is also a downward sloping curve, as in this graph below.

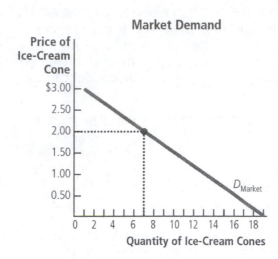

Market Demand

There are many variables that can shift the demand curve. Here are the most common variables that can **shift** the demand curve:

INCOME—Holding other things constant, if your income increases, you will have more to spend. Assuming that ice cream is a **normal good**, *a good for which, other things equal, an increase in income leads to an increase in demand*, an increase in income will lead to an increase in the demand for ice cream.

If ice cream is instead an **inferior good**, *a good for which, other things equal, an increase in income leads to a decrease in demand*, an increase in income will lead to a decrease in the demand for ice cream.

PRICE OF RELATED GOODS—The price of goods related to ice cream may affect our decision to buy ice cream. For example, suppose the price of frozen yogurt falls. You will likely buy frozen yogurt instead of ice cream since frozen yogurt and ice cream are **substitutes**, *two goods for which an increase in the price of one leads to an increase in the demand for the other*.

Alternatively, suppose that the price of ice cream cones fall. You will likely buy more ice cream because ice cream and ice cream cones are often consumed together and are therefore **complements**, *two goods for which an increase in the price of one leads to a decrease in demand for the other*.

TASTES—Obviously, if you like ice cream, you will likely buy ice cream and vice versa. Market demand can change when tastes change. Applying this to our example, when more people decide that they now like ice cream, the demand for ice cream will increase.

EXPECTATIONS—If you expect a pay raise, then you may be more likely to buy ice cream. Alternatively, if you expect the price of a good to change in the future, you may buy more or less of a good depending on the direction of the price change. For example, if you expect the price of ice cream to fall during the winter, you may choose to wait and buy your ice cream in the winter.

NUMBER OF BUYERS–If the number of ice cream buyers increase, the demand for ice cream also increases. Similarly, if the number of ice cream buyers decline, the demand for ice cream also declines. The baby-boomer generation is an interesting example of this—as baby boomers have aged through time, the demand for the goods that they buy increases.

AP Tip

A helpful pneumonic to remember these demand determinants is **S-E-P-T-I-C**: **S**ubstitutes, **E**xpectations, **P**opulation, **T**astes, **I**ncome, **C**omplements.

Any change in market demand due to changes in any of the above mentioned variables leads to a _**shift**_ in the demand curve. Refer to the following demand curves below for a better understanding of how to show a demand shift.

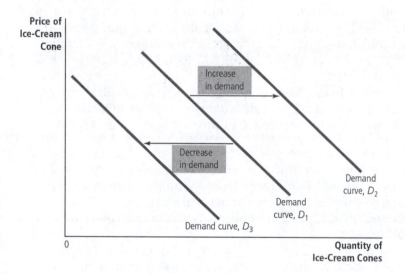

Note that, when the price of ice cream changes, the demand curve _**does not shift**_. When the price of ice cream changes, there is a _**movement along**_ the existing demand curve, meaning that there is a change in the quantity demanded (represented by a movement along the curve), not a change in demand (represented by a shift of the curve). The table below provides a good summary of the effects of the variables that influence buyers and market demand.

Variable	A Change in This Variable . . .
Price of the good itself	Represents a movement along the demand curve
Income	Shifts the demand curve
Prices of related goods	Shifts the demand curve
Tastes	Shifts the demand curve
Expectations	Shifts the demand curve
Number of buyers	Shifts the demand curve

AP Tip

The AP will test whether you know the difference between a change in the *quantity demanded* versus a change in *demand*. A change in the quantity demanded is represented by a **_movement along_** the demand curve whereas a change in demand is represented by a **_shift_** of the demand curve. The graphs here illustrate this difference graphically.

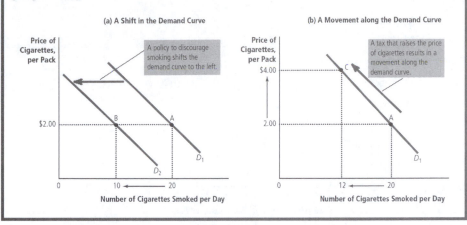

SUPPLY

(*Principles of Economics* 5th ed. pages 73–76/6th ed. pages 73–76)

We now look at the behavior of sellers in the market for ice cream. When the price of ice cream is high, producers are willing to sell more ice cream because the revenue potential is higher. Conversely, when the price of ice cream is low, ice cream producers are willing to sell less ice cream. This tells us that, as prices rise, the quantity supplied of ice cream will increase. The economic concept here that captures this behavioral dynamic is the **law of supply**, which states that *other things equal, the quantity supplied of a good rises when the price of the good rises*. The **quantity supplied** is *the amount of a good that sellers are willing and able to sell*. The law of supply is true because suppliers face increasing opportunity costs, just as in the PPF model discussed in Chapter 1.

The following table and graph show the supply schedule and supply curve.

Price of Ice-Cream Cone	Quantity of Cones Supplied
$0.00	0 cones
0.50	0
1.00	1
1.50	2
2.00	3
2.50	4
3.00	5

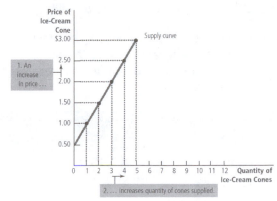

As in our demand analysis, the **market supply curve** consists of *the sum of all individual supply curves of everyone who is willing and able to sell* ice cream cones. Contrary to the demand curve, however, the market supply curve is upward sloping. The suppliers who were willing to sell at $1 are also happy to take $2 and may even provide additional units, which is one of the reasons why the quantity supplied increases as the market price increases. The following graph shows the market supply curve.

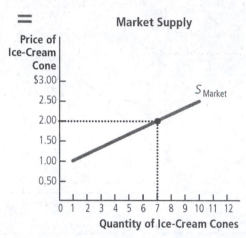

There are many variables that can shift the market supply curve. Here are the most common variables that can affect supply:

INPUT PRICES–Sellers use factors of production, or inputs, to produce goods and services. To produce ice cream, sellers may use inputs such as sugar, cream, machines, and workers. If the price of any of these inputs rises, it becomes less profitable for a seller to produce ice cream.

TECHNOLOGY–The use of technology in the production process may help to increase the overall productivity of the supplier. In our example, if the ice cream producing firm uses machinery to make ice cream, ice cream producing firms can produce and supply more ice cream to the market.

EXPECTATIONS–The amount of ice cream supplied today may depend on suppliers' expectations about the future. For example, if there is an expectation that ice cream prices will increase, ice cream producers may choose to put ice cream into storage to sell at a later date.

NUMBER OF SELLERS–Market supply depends on the number of sellers. If the number of ice cream sellers increase, the supply of ice cream also increases. Similarly, if the number of ice cream sellers decline, the supply of ice cream also declines.

AP Tip

A helpful pneumonic to remember these supply determinants is **T-I-E-S**: **T**astes, **I**nput prices, **E**xpectations, **S**ellers.

Any change in market supply due to changes in any of the above mentioned variables leads to a **_shift_** in the supply curve. Refer to the supply curves below for a better understanding of how to illustrate a supply shift. _Increases_ in supply are always to the _right_, while _decreases_ in supply are always to the _left_.

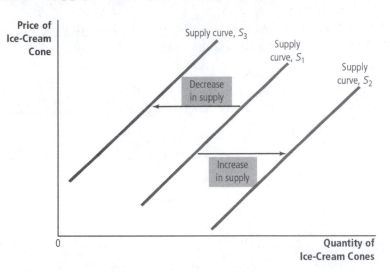

Note that, as in the case of demand, when the price of ice cream changes, the supply curve **_does not shift_**. When the price of ice cream changes, there is a **_movement along_** the existing market supply curve, meaning that there is a change in the quantity supplied (represented by a movement along the curve), not a change in supply (which is represented by a shift of the curve). The table below provides a good summary of the effects of the variables that influence sellers and market supply.

Variable	A Change in This Variable . . .
Price of the good itself	Represents a movement along the supply curve
Input prices	Shifts the supply curve
Technology	Shifts the supply curve
Expectations	Shifts the supply curve
Number of sellers	Shifts the supply curve

AP Tip

The AP will test whether you know the difference between a change in the _quantity supplied_ versus a change in _supply_.

Here's a study strategy to help you make the distinction between a shift of a curve versus a movement along a curve: all else equal, a **_change in price_** is represented by a **_movement along a curve_**, whereas a **_change in any other variable_** (either demand or supply determinant) _will lead to a_ **_shift of the curve_**.

MARKET EQUILIBRIUM: PUTTING SUPPLY & DEMAND TOGETHER

(*Principles of Economics* 5th ed. pages 77–82/6th ed. pages 77–83)

How do market supply and demand work together to determine the price and quantity of ice cream, or any good sold, in the market? Putting the supply and demand curves together, we can see that the two curves intersect. Refer to the market equilibrium graph below.

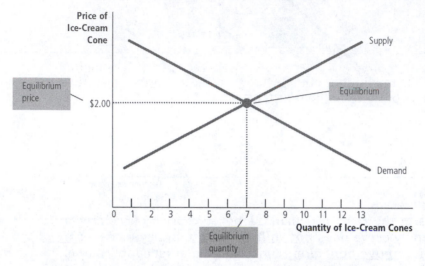

The intersection point is also known as the **market equilibrium**, *a situation where the market price has reached the level at which quantity supplied equals quantity demanded.* At this point, every buyer who is willing to pay the market price is able to find a seller who is willing to sell at that price and vice versa—in other words, all mutually beneficial trades occur at this equilibrium point. All consumer and producer surplus is maximized (refer to Chapter 3 for our discussion on consumer and producer surplus).

The equilibrium price and quantity depend on the position of the supply and demand curves—what happens when something causes a curve to shift? In order to determine what happens to market equilibrium when there is a change in either demand or supply or both, we recommend that you use the following three-step strategy identified below. Holding all else constant, suppose that there is a change that affects the market.

1. Determine whether the change affects the supply or demand curve, or both. (Use the supply and demand determinant list identified in the previous section.)

2. Decide which direction the curve shifts, if applicable.

3. Using a supply–demand market graph, draw the change to see how (or whether) it impacts market equilibrium price and quantity.

EXAMPLE 1: A CHANGE IN DEMAND

Suppose that the weather is suddenly very hot. How does this weather change affect the market price and quantity of ice cream purchased/sold? We'll use our 3-step strategy to answer this question.

1. The hot weather affects people's taste for ice cream. Taste is a demand determinant and therefore, a change in taste will shift the demand curve and will not affect the supply curve.

2. Because the hot weather causes more people to want more ice cream, the demand curve will *increase*, or *shift to the right*.

3. When market demand increases, the demand curve shifts to the right while the supply curve remains constant. This demand increase results in a higher equilibrium price and a higher quantity of ice cream sold. Refer to the figure below.

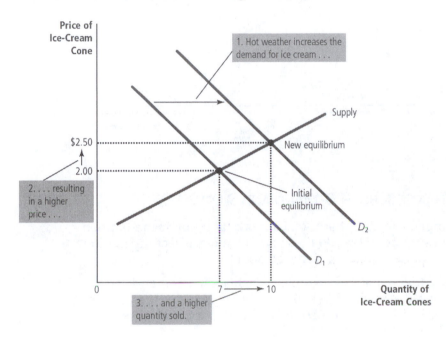

EXAMPLE 2: A CHANGE IN SUPPLY

Suppose that a hurricane destroys sugarcane crops and increases the price of sugar. Assuming that sugar is used to produce ice cream, how does this increase in the price of sugar affect the market price and quantity of ice cream purchased/sold? Again, we'll use our 3-step strategy to answer this question.

1. Sugar is an input used in the production of ice cream and therefore is a supply determinant of ice cream. An increase in the price of sugar will shift the supply curve but will not affect the demand curve.

2. Because the sugar price increase makes it more expensive for ice cream producers to make ice cream, the supply curve will *decrease*, or *shift to the left*.

3. When market supply decreases, the supply curve shifts to the left while the demand curve remains constant. This supply decrease results in a higher equilibrium price and a lower quantity of ice cream sold. Refer to the figure below.

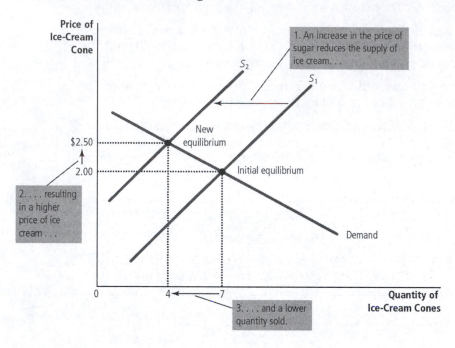

EXAMPLE 3: A CHANGE IN BOTH DEMAND AND SUPPLY

In this last example, suppose that the heat wave and hurricane happen during the same summer. How do these two changes affect the market price and quantity of ice cream purchased/sold?

1. The hot weather changes people's tastes, so demand shifts. However, supply also shifts because of the increase in the price of sugar, an input used in the production of ice cream. Here, both curves shift.

2. The demand curve will increase, or shift to the right, while the supply curve will decrease, or shift to the left.

3. When demand increases and supply decreases, the market equilibrium price increases. However, we cannot determine what happens to the market equilibrium quantity because, while we know what direction each curves shifts, we do not know the magnitude of each shift. If demand increases significantly while supply decreases by a small amount, the market equilibrium quantity increases. If, on the other hand, demand increases by a small amount while supply decreases significantly, the market equilibrium quantity decreases. Since quantity increases or decreases, depending on the magnitude of the shift, we cannot determine what happens to equilibrium quantity, although we do know for certain that the price of ice cream increases. Refer to the figure below.

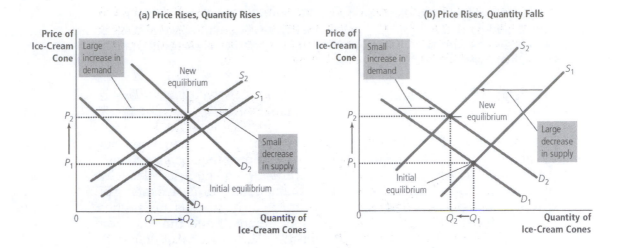

(a) Price Rises, Quantity Rises   (b) Price Rises, Quantity Falls

AP Tip

The AP multiple-choice questions will test your understanding of market analysis. Practice graphing the various market outcomes based on the following table to help you.

	No Change in Supply	An Increase in Supply	A Decrease in Supply
No Change in Demand	P same Q same	P down Q up	P up Q down
An Increase in Demand	P up Q up	P ambiguous Q up	P up Q ambiguous
A Decrease in Demand	P down Q down	P down Q ambiguous	P ambiguous Q down

ELASTICITY OF DEMAND

(*Principles of Economics* 5th ed. pages 90–98/6th ed. pages 90–98)

Economists use the concept of **elasticity**, *a measure of the responsiveness of quantity demanded or quantity supplied to a change in one of its determinants,* to measure the magnitude of changes in supply and demand. The law of demand states that an increase in the price causes a decrease in the quantity demanded. Elasticity tells us *how much* the quantity demanded changes with a change in price. The **price elasticity of demand** *measures how much the quantity demanded of a good responds to a change in the price of that good.* In other words, the price elasticity of demand is computed by:

Price elasticity of demand = $\dfrac{\text{\% change in quantity demanded}}{\text{\% change in price}}$

So if ice cream prices increase by 10% and the amount of ice cream purchased falls by 20%, the price elasticity of demand is equal to 2, which means that the change in quantity demanded is proportionately twice as large as the change in price:

$$\text{Price elasticity of demand} = \frac{\% \text{ change in quantity demanded}}{\% \text{ change in price}} = \frac{20\%}{10\%} = 2$$

Note that price elasticity of demand is always negative, but economists often drop the negative sign and report the absolute value.

The more close substitutes there are, the higher the price elasticity of demand for a good. Other factors that affect price elasticity of demand include: whether the goods are luxuries versus necessities (luxuries have a higher price elasticity of demand) and time horizon (the longer the time horizon, the higher the price elasticity of demand). The price elasticity of demand determines whether the demand curve is steep or flat. Refer to the next figure, which shows five different demand curves with varying price elasticities.

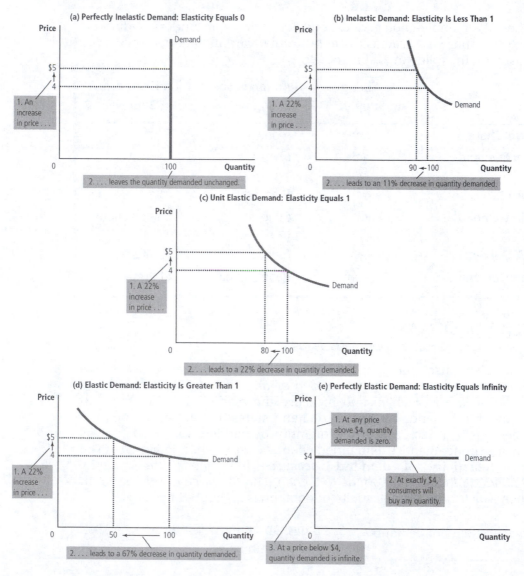

It is important to note that these five curves show the relative price elasticity of demand, but each individual curve has a portion that is inelastic and another portion that is elastic. Refer to the following diagram to see what this looks like. The top portion of the demand curve is generally the elastic portion while the bottom portion is the inelastic portion.

We are interested in studying the impact of demand elasticity on **total revenue (TR)**, *the amount paid by buyers and received by sellers of a good* (computed as TR = Price x Quantity sold). When demand is <u>inelastic</u> and the price <u>increases</u>, <u>total revenue also increases</u>. When demand is <u>elastic</u> and the price <u>increases</u>, <u>total revenue will fall</u>. Refer to the following graphs to see this.

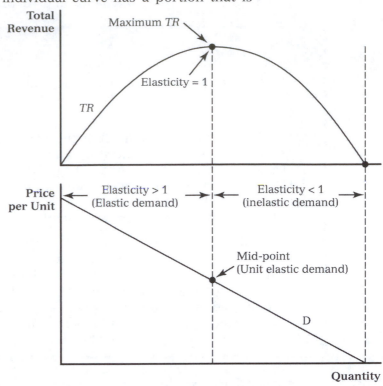

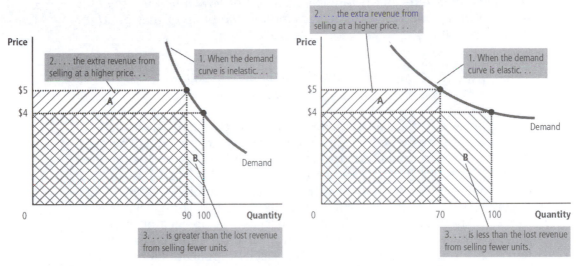

In addition to the price elasticity of demand, there are other demand elasticities. For the AP test, you should be familiar with the following:

Income elasticity $=$ % change in quantity demanded
of demand ﹍﹍﹍﹍﹍﹍﹍﹍﹍﹍﹍﹍﹍﹍﹍﹍
　　　　　　　% change in income

Cross-price elasticity $=$ % change in quantity demanded of good 1
of demand $\qquad$ % change in price of good 2

AP Tip

The AP exam generally does not require that you be able to calculate the income and cross-price elasticities, however, you do need to know the following:

■ If the value of the income elasticity of demand is positive, the good in question is a *normal good*, whereas if the income elasticity of demand is negative, the good is an *inferior good*.

■ If the cross-price elasticity is positive, the two goods in question are *substitute goods*, whereas a negative cross-price elasticity indicates that the two goods are *complementary goods*.

The AP Microeconomics exam does focus on the relationship between elasticity and total revenue and taxes. For example, if a tax increase is imposed on a good/service where there is a relatively elastic demand, total revenue will fall, but if the tax increase is imposed instead on a good/service with a relatively inelastic demand, the total revenue will increase. (Study the total revenue graphs at the bottom of the previous page that illustrate this point.)

ELASTICITY OF SUPPLY
(*Principles of Economics* 5th ed. pages 98–108/6th ed. pages 98–106)

The **price elasticity of supply** is *a measure of how much the quantity supplied of a good responds to a change in the price of that good*, or mathematically:

Price elasticity of supply $=$ % change in quantity supplied
$\qquad$ % change in price

Similar to our discussion on demand elasticity, the price elasticity of supply determines whether the supply curve is steep or flat. The main determinant of supply elasticity is length of time—the shorter the time period, the more inelastic the supply, because it is harder to get the additional inputs to increase production. Supply elasticity also depends on whether the firm is near its capacity. The closer it is to capacity, the less flexibility it has to increase its production capacity. Refer to the following graphs that show five different supply curves with varying price elasticities. We will discuss applications of demand elasticity and supply in the next chapter.

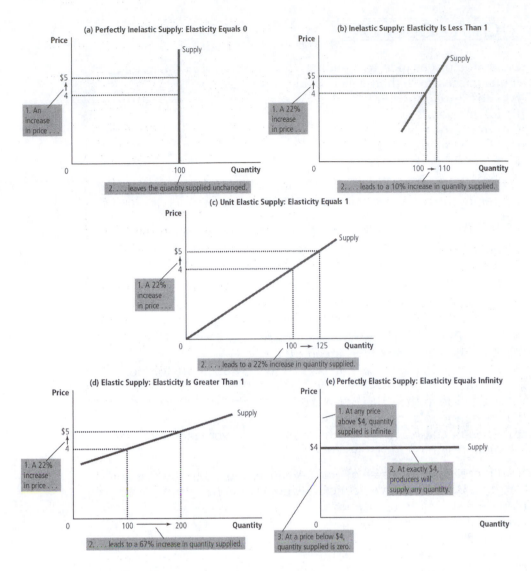

(a) Perfectly Inelastic Supply: Elasticity Equals 0

1. An increase in price . . .

2. . . . leaves the quantity supplied unchanged.

(b) Inelastic Supply: Elasticity Is Less Than 1

1. A 22% increase in price . . .

2. . . . leads to a 10% increase in quantity supplied.

(c) Unit Elastic Supply: Elasticity Equals 1

1. A 22% increase in price . . .

2. . . . leads to a 22% increase in quantity supplied.

(d) Elastic Supply: Elasticity Is Greater Than 1

1. A 22% increase in price . . .

2. . . . leads to a 67% increase in quantity supplied.

(e) Perfectly Elastic Supply: Elasticity Equals Infinity

1. At any price above $4, quantity supplied is infinite.

2. At exactly $4, producers will supply any quantity.

3. At a price below $4, quantity supplied is zero.

How Markets Work:
Student Objectives for the AP Exam

You should be able to:
- Define all key terms in bold
- Comfortably graph changes in supply and demand and identify resulting changes in market equilibrium price and quantity
- Clearly distinguish the difference between a change in the quantity demanded/supplies and a change in demand/supply
- Calculate both the price elasticity of demand and supply
- Know the difference between an elastic vs. an inelastic curve and its revenue implications

MULTIPLE-CHOICE QUESTIONS

1. If gasoline prices increase and there is an increase in the number of bus passes sold, then gasoline and bus rides are
    (A) substitute goods.
    (B) luxury goods.
    (C) inferior goods.
    (D) complementary goods.
    (E) normal goods.

2. If there is an increase in the supply of a good, what will most likely happen to the price and quantity of the good exchanged in the market?

	Price	Quantity
(A)	No change	No change
(B)	Increase	Increase
(C)	Increase	Decrease
(D)	Decrease	Increase
(E)	Decrease	Decrease

3. Which of the following will not change the demand for ice cream?
    (A) A change in consumers' incomes
    (B) A change in the price of frozen yogurt, a substitute for ice cream
    (C) A change in the price of ice cream
    (D) A change in consumers' taste for ice cream
    (E) An expectation that the consumption of ice cream may cause diabetes

4. If an increase in the price of good A causes a drop in the demand for good B, what can you conclude about good B?
    (A) Good B is an inferior good.
    (B) Good B is a luxury good.
    (C) Good B is a necessity.
    (D) Good B is a substitute for good A.
    (E) Good B is a complement to good A.

5. Of the following scenarios, which would necessarily shift the supply of cars to the right?
    (A) An increase in the efficiency of car production technology
    (B) An increase in the wages for workers in the car industry
    (C) A decrease in the number of people buying cars
    (D) A decrease in consumer income
    (E) A decrease in the number of car production companies in the industry

6. The demand curve for apples is downward sloping because an increase in the price of apples leads to
    (A) the increased consumption of alternative fruit, such as oranges.
    (B) a fall in the expected future price of apples.
    (C) a decrease in the number of apples available for purchase.
    (D) an increase in consumers' preferences for apples.
    (E) an increase in the wages for laborers in the apple market.

7. An increase in the demand for computers and an increase in the supply of computers will
   (A) decrease equilibrium price and increase equilibrium quantity sold in the computer market.
   (B) increase equilibrium price and decrease equilibrium quantity sold in the computer market.
   (C) increase equilibrium price and quantity sold in the computer market.
   (D) increase equilibrium quantity, but whether it increases equilibrium price is indeterminate.
   (E) increase equilibrium price, but whether it increases equilibrium quantity is indeterminate.

8. Which of the following would most likely cause a rightward shift in the demand curve for the *New York Times* newspaper?
   (A) A decrease in the costs of printing newspapers
   (B) An increase in the price of the *New York Daily News*—a rival newspaper
   (C) An improvement in cable television in the New York area
   (D) A decrease in income, assuming the newspaper is a normal good
   (E) A decrease in the population size in the New York area

9. The elasticity of demand for a product is likely to be greater
   (A) when the cross-price elasticity coefficient for a particular good is negative.
   (B) the greater the amount of time over which buyers adjust to a price change.
   (C) if the product is a *necessity,* rather than a *luxury* good.
   (D) the smaller the number of substitute products available.
   (E) the smaller the proportion of one's income spent on the product.

10. Which of the following must be true if the revenues of corn farmers increase when the price of corn increases?
    (A) The supply of corn is price elastic.
    (B) The supply of corn is income elastic.
    (C) The supply of corn is income inelastic.
    (D) The demand for corn is price elastic.
    (E) The demand for corn is price inelastic.

11. For which of the following pairs is the cross-price elasticity most likely negative?
    (A) Peanut butter and jelly
    (B) Air travel and train travel
    (C) Used cars and new cars
    (D) Live theater tickets and movie tickets
    (E) Blueberries and raspberries

12. Along a given demand curve for a product,
    (A) demand increases as price increases.
    (B) demand increases as incomes fall.
    (C) quantity demanded increases as incomes fall.
    (D) quantity demanded increases as price increases.
    (E) quantity demanded decreases as price increases.

13. A decrease in the input costs for the production of a certain good leads to
    (A) an increase in demand for the good.
    (B) an increase in the supply of the good.
    (C) an increase in the price of the good.
    (D) a shortage of the good.
    (E) a surplus of the good.

14. Which of the following changes will cause the demand for burgers to shift to the right?
    (A) An increase in the price of pizza, a substitute good
    (B) An increase in the price of French fries, a complementary good
    (C) An increase in the price of burgers
    (D) A decrease in the price of burgers
    (E) An increase in the cost of producing burgers

15. Which of the following situations would necessarily lead to an increase in the price of oranges?
    (A) There is ideal weather for growing oranges.
    (B) The price of apples, a substitute good, falls.
    (C) A technological breakthrough enables farmers to grow more oranges.
    (D) The wages of workers in the orange industry fall.
    (E) Medical researchers discover that eating oranges is good for one's health.

FREE-RESPONSE QUESTIONS

1. Assume that bagels and cream cheese are complementary goods.
   (a) Draw a correctly labeled graph for the bagel market and identify:
       (i) The equilibrium price of bagels, P_0
       (ii) The equilibrium quantity of bagels, Q_0
   (b) Draw a correctly labeled graph for the cream cheese market and identify:
       (i) The equilibrium price of cream cheese, P_0
       (ii) The equilibrium quantity of cream cheese, Q_0
   (c) Suppose that, holding all else constant, the price of milk, an input used in the production of cream cheese, has increased. How does this change affect the following in the cream cheese market? Explain.
       (i) The equilibrium price of cream cheese
       (ii) The equilibrium quantity of cream cheese
   (d) Explain how the cream cheese price increase in part (c) above will affect the bagel market? Specifically, graph and explain how this cream cheese price increase will affect:
       (i) The equilibrium price of bagels
       (ii) The equilibrium quantity of bagels

2. Suppose that cell phones have a relatively elastic demand and vitamins have a relatively inelastic demand.
    (a) Draw a correctly labeled graph for the cell phone market and identify:
        (i) The equilibrium price of cell phones
        (ii) The equilibrium quantity of cell phones
    (b) Draw a correctly labeled graph for the vitamin market and identify:
        (i) The equilibrium price of vitamins
        (ii) The equilibrium quantity of vitamins
    (c) If technological improvements enable both cell phone and vitamin producers to increase their supply of each good, what will happen to the market equilibrium price and quantity in each market? Explain your answer graphically and with words. (You may use your graphs in parts (a) and (b) above.)
    (d) Which product experiences a larger change in price? Explain.

Answers

MULTIPLE-CHOICE QUESTIONS

1. **A.** Since the demand for bus passes increase when the price of gasoline increases, we know that taking the bus is an alternative to driving a car which means that the two goods are substitutes for one another (*Principles of Economics* 5th ed. page 70/6th ed. page 70).

2. **D.** An increase in supply will shift the supply curve to the right while the demand curve remains constant. This will increase the quantity and decrease the price (*Principles of Economics* 5th ed. page 81/6th ed. page 81).

3. **C.** A change in the price of ice cream will affect the quantity of ice cream demanded, but will not shift the curve (*Principles of Economics* 5th ed. pages 69–72/6th ed. pages 69–72).

4. **E.** If the price of good A causes the demand for good B to drop, these two goods must be complements since the higher price of good A will lead to less consumption of good A. A decline in the quantity demanded of good A will result in a decrease in the demand for good B (*Principles of Economics* 5th ed. pages 69–72/6th ed. pages 69–72).

5. **A.** An improvement in technology enables a supplier to produce more of a good using fewer resources, so the supply increases (*Principles of Economics* 5th ed. pages 74–76/6th ed. pages 74–76).

6. **A.** An increase in the price of apples will result in a decrease in the quantity of apples demanded, which suggests that people are consuming alternative fruits due to the high price of apples (*Principles of Economics* 5th ed. pages 67–69/6th ed. pages 67–69).

7. **D.** There are two shifts in this scenario—the demand curve shifts to the right and the supply curve shifts to the right. This causes the quantity to increase, but, depending on the magnitude of each shift, the price may go up or down (*Principles of Economics* 5th ed. pages 81–82/6th ed. pages 81–82).

8. **B.** An increase in the price of a rival paper will bring more buyers into the market for the *New York Times*. More people will buy the *New York Times* because the price of its substitute has increased (*Principles of Economics* 5th ed. page 70/6th ed. page 70).

9. **B.** The longer the time horizon, the more elastic is the demand for a good because people have the time to find alternatives (*Principles of Economics* 5th ed. pages 90–91/6th ed. pages 90–91).

10. **E.** When the demand curve is inelastic, the extra revenue from the higher price is greater than the lost revenue from selling fewer units (*Principles of Economics* 5th ed. pages 94–97/6th ed. pages 94–97).

11. **A.** The cross-price elasticity is negative for complementary goods. Peanut butter and jelly are complementary goods. The other answers show pairs of substitute goods (*Principles of Economics* 5th ed. page 99/6th ed. pages 97–98).

12. **E.** Moving along a demand curve, the quantity demanded decreases as price increases (*Principles of Economics* 5th ed. pages 68–69/6th ed. pages 68–69).

13. **B.** A decline in input costs makes it cheaper for a producer to supply a good. This increases the supply, or shifts the supply curve to the right (*Principles of Economics* 5th ed. page 75/6th ed. 75).

14. **A.** An increase in the price of pizza, a substitute good, will increase the demand for hamburgers because pizza is more expensive relative to burgers. Since the two goods are substitutes, consumers will buy the good that is relatively cheaper. In this case, consumers will buy burgers (*Principles of Economics* 5th ed. page 70/6th ed. page 70).

15. **E.** With the medical discovery that eating oranges is good for one's health, more people will demand oranges because they *expect* that it will improve/maintain their health. This is an example of how consumer expectations can shift demand (*Principles of Economics* 5th ed. page 71/6th ed. page 71).

FREE-RESPONSE QUESTIONS

1. (a)

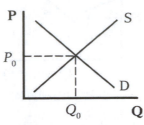

Bagel Market

(b)

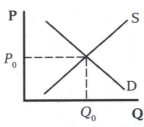

Cream Cheese
Market

(c) When the price of milk increases, it is more expensive for
cream cheese producers to make cream cheese and therefore,
the supply decreases or shifts to the left, as in the graph below.
The equilibrium quantity of cream cheese decreases and the
price increases.

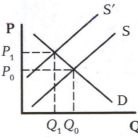

Cream Cheese
Market

(d) Since cream cheese and bagels are complementary goods,
when the price of cream cheese increases, the demand for
bagels fall. This decreases the price and the quantity of bagels
sold in the bagel market.

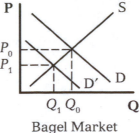

Bagel Market

(*Principles of Economics* 5th ed. pages 67–72/6th ed. pages 67–72)

2.

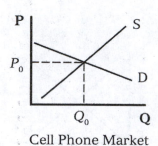

Cell Phone Market

(a)

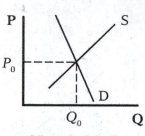

Vitamin Market

(b) Since the supply curve increases in both markets, the price in both markets will fall while the quantity in both will rise. Refer to the following graphs for support:

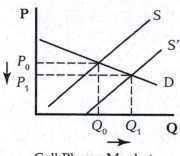
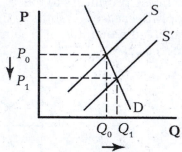

Cell Phone Market   Vitamin Market

(c) Since the supply increases by the same amount (both markets experience a doubling of supply), it is clear that the vitamin market, the good that has the more *inelastic* demand, will experience a larger price drop.
(*Principles of Economics* 5th ed. pages 103–107/6th ed. pages 101–104)

3

THE WELFARE OF MARKETS

In Chapter 2, we learned about supply and demand—how they work together to determine the price and quantity of goods and services sold in any given market and how the elasticity of demand and supply may affect market outcomes. In this chapter, we will focus on **welfare economics**, *the study of how the allocation of resources affects economic well-being,* and the impact of government policies on consumer and producer welfare.

In order to determine whether a market outcome is good, it helps to look at the outcome from the perspective of both the consumer and the producer. We will measure consumer welfare by looking at **consumer surplus**, *the amount that buyers are willing to pay for a good minus the amount they actually pay for it.* We will measure producer welfare by looking at **producer surplus**, *the amount a seller is paid for a good minus the seller's cost of providing it.* We will also look at the welfare impact of government policies, such as taxes and price ceilings and floors.

CONSUMER SURPLUS

(*Principles of Economics* 5th ed. pages 138–142/6th ed. pages 136–141)

The demand curve helps us to measure **consumer surplus**. We will use an example to illustrate how the demand curve is related to consumer surplus. Suppose that you are selling a rare album through an internet auction site. There are four people who are interested in your album—John, Paul, George, and Ringo. Each individual values your album differently and, therefore, has a different maximum amount that he is willing to pay for your album. If John is willing to pay $100 for your album, Paul is willing to pay $80, George is willing to pay $70, and Ringo is willing to pay $50, the demand curve for these four potential buyers is drawn in the figure below .

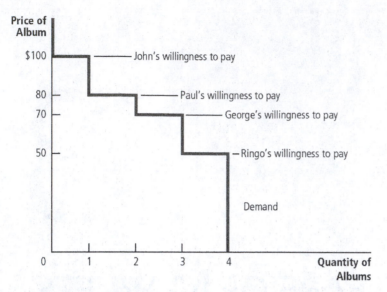

No one is willing to buy your album at a price higher than $100, but John is willing to buy your album at a price of $100, which is why the quantity of albums demanded is one. Paul is willing to buy your album for $80, and since John is willing to pay $100 for your album, we assume that he is also willing to buy your album for $80, which is why the quantity of albums demanded at $80 is two. Following this rationale for George and Ringo produces the demand curve in figure above.

At a price of $80 per album, John's consumer surplus is $20 because he is willing to pay $100, but only pays $80. Refer to the left figure below to see a graphical representation of this consumer surplus.

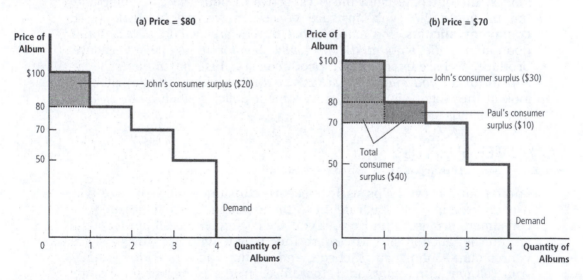

Continuing our analysis, if the price is $70, John's consumer surplus is $30 while Paul's consumer surplus is $10, since John is willing to pay $100 and Paul is willing to pay $80. The sum of John and Paul's consumer surplus is $40. Refer to the right figure above to see a graphical representation of total consumer surplus at a price of $70.

This example tells us that *the area below the demand curve and above the price measures the consumer surplus in a market.* The figure below shows the area of total consumer surplus at a price of P_1.

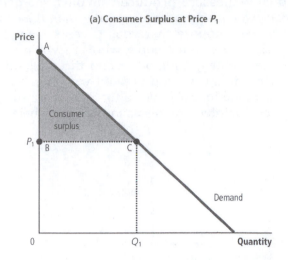

(a) Consumer Surplus at Price P_1

Note that, if the price dropped from P_1 to P_2, the consumer surplus would increase because existing consumers now pay an even lower price, represented by the area of the rectangle BCED in the figure below, and new consumers would enter the market at the lower price, represented by the triangle CEF. Study this figure below, which shows this increase in consumer surplus graphically.

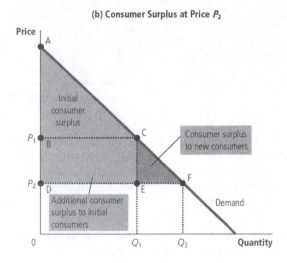

(b) Consumer Surplus at Price P_2

PRODUCER SURPLUS
(*Principles of Economics* 5th ed. pages 143–146/6th ed. pages 141–145)

The supply curve can help us to measure **producer surplus**, *the gain that producers receive because the market price is greater than the cost of producing a good or service.* Suppose that your parents want to have their house painted. There are four people who are willing to provide their painting services: your grandmother and three friends, Georgia, Frida, and Mary. Grandma is willing to paint your home for $500, Georgia will paint your home for $600, Frida for $800, and Mary for $900. If we plot out the four painters' prices as in the figure below, we would see the following:

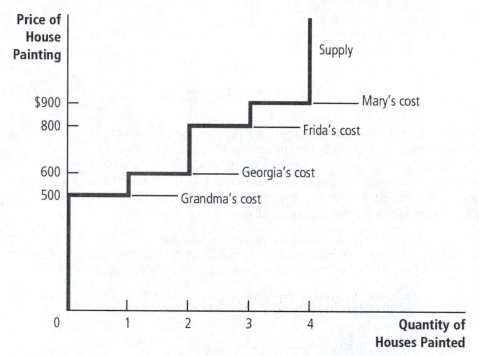

Each painter is willing to take the painting job as long as the price she would receive is greater than her opportunity cost of doing the work. If the price is below $500, no one is willing to do the job, which means that the quantity supplied is zero. At a price of $500 or greater, Grandma is willing to supply her painting services. At a price of $600 or greater, Georgia is also willing to supply her painting services. If we follow this rationale for Frida and Mary we will arrive at the supply curve depicted in the figure at the bottom of page 103.

If the price is $600, Grandma supplies her painting services and accrues a producer surplus of $100 since she was willing to paint for $500 but receives $600 instead. The left figure below depicts this surplus. If the price is $800, not only will Grandma supply her painting services, but Georgia is also willing to supply her painting services. Grandma's producer surplus is $300 while Georgia's surplus is $200. The total producer surplus is $500 and is depicted in the right figure below.

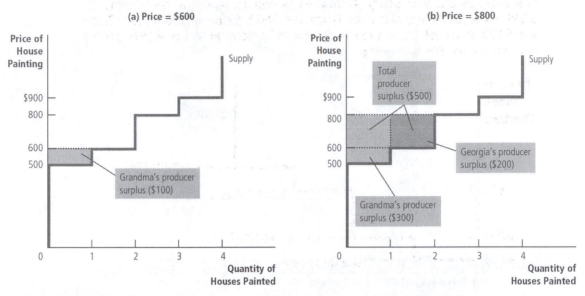

This example tells us that **the area above the supply curve and below the price measures the producer surplus in a market.** The following figure shows the area of total producer surplus at a price of P_1.

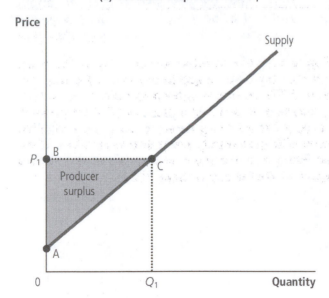

(a) **Producer Surplus at Price P_1**

Note that, if the price increased from P_1 to P_2, the producer surplus would also increase because existing producers are better off because they will get more for what they sell, represented by the area of the rectangle BCED in the preceding figure, and new producers enter the market at the higher price, represented by triangle CEF. The following graph shows this increase in producer surplus.

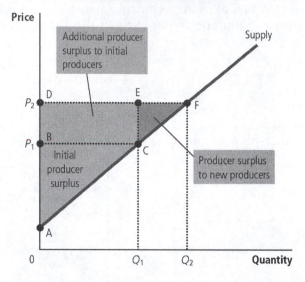

(b) Producer Surplus at Price P_2

CONSUMER AND PRODUCER SURPLUS AT EQUILIBRIUM
(Principles of Economics 5th ed. pages 147–150/6th ed. pages 145–148)

Economists use consumer and producer surplus to study the welfare of buyers and sellers in a market. If total consumer and producer surplus are maximized, then we can say that the market is **allocatively efficient**, *where the total surplus received by all members of society is maximized.* In addition to efficiency, we are also concerned about economic **equality**, *the uniform distribution of economic prosperity among members of society.* The graph below shows a market that demonstrates equality and efficiency.

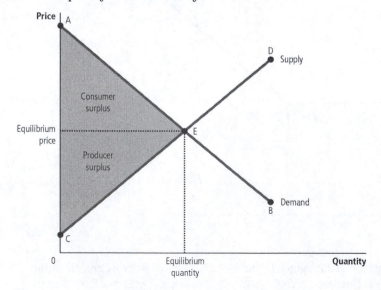

IMPACT OF TAXATION
(Principles of Economics 5th ed. pages 123–130, 159–169/6th ed. pages 121–128, 155–166)

Up until this point, we have considered economic welfare under a free market system. However, economic welfare may be hindered under certain circumstances, such as when the government imposes a tax on the market. When a tax is imposed, the market does not produce where supply and demand intersect. In fact, when there is a tax, both consumers and producers can be negatively affected. The impact of a tax on market welfare is the same regardless of whether the tax is placed on consumers or producers. For example, when a tax is imposed on consumers, the demand curve decreases or shifts downward. This decreases the quantity demanded for the good/service that is taxed, which means that sellers receive a lower price while buyers end up paying a higher price. On the other hand, when a tax is imposed on producers, the supply curve decreases or shifts upward by the size of the tax. This leads to the same result: the quantity demanded decreases and sellers receive a lower price for the good/service while buyers end up paying a higher price. The left graph below illustrates the impact of a tax on buyers whereas the right graph illustrates the impact of a tax on sellers. In both cases, the welfare impact is the same and is depicted in the third graph below

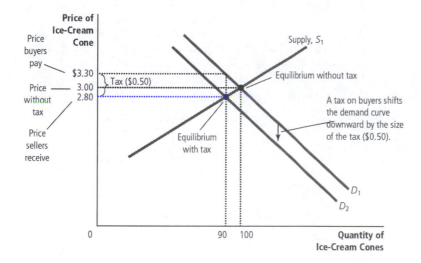

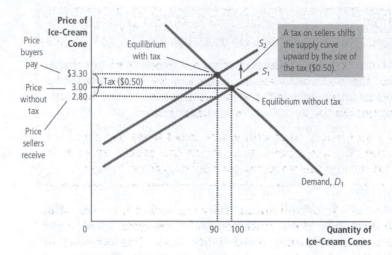

With a tax, both consumer and producer surplus are reduced and the market experiences a **deadweight loss**, *the fall in total surplus that results from a market distortion.* The following graph illustrates the impact of a tax on economic welfare.

	Without Tax	With Tax	Change
Consumer Surplus	A + B + C	A	−(B + C)
Producer Surplus	D + E + F	F	−(D + E)
Tax Revenue	None	B + D	+(B + D)
Total Surplus	A + B + C + D + E + F	A + B + D + F	−(C + E)

The area C + E shows the fall in total surplus and is the deadweight loss of the tax.

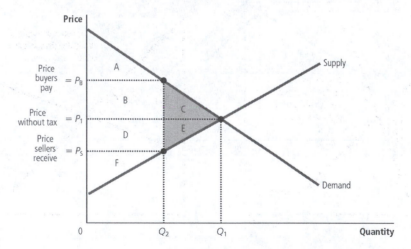

A tax on a good/service reduces consumer surplus by the area (B + C) and the producer surplus by the area (D + E). Since the quantity produced and purchased with the tax, Q_2, is less than the free market quantity, Q_1, there is a deadweight loss marked by the area (C + E). The area of rectangle (B + D) represents the **tax revenue**, *the money collected by the government and calculated by multiplying the size of the tax by the quantity sold.*

AP Tips

It is important that you can identify the consumer and producer surplus as well as the welfare losses in a market with and without a tax. You will need to know where the deadweight loss is and how the total surplus changes on the AP Microeconomics exam.

Students should also be able to calculate and read from a graph how much of the tax the consumer pays, how much the producer loses in revenue, and what money the government receives from the tax.

Based on our discussion on the impact of taxes so far, it is clear that a tax results in welfare loss. Both producer and consumer surplus are reduced and there is a resulting deadweight loss. The amount of deadweight loss is determined by the elasticity of either the supply and demand curves. Recall from Chapter 2 that **elasticity** is *a measure of the responsiveness of quantity demanded or quantity supplied to one of its determinants.* Let's assume that we impose the _same_ tax to a market with different supply and demand elasticities. What we see is that the _more elastic_ the supply or demand curve, the _larger the welfare loss_, represented by a larger area of deadweight loss. Conversely, the _less elastic_ the supply or demand curve, the _smaller the welfare loss_, represented by a smaller area of deadweight loss. The series of graphs below depict the welfare loss graphically.

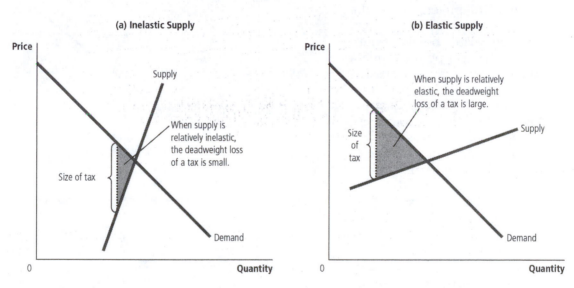

(a) Inelastic Supply

Price

Supply

When supply is relatively inelastic, the deadweight loss of a tax is small.

Size of tax

Demand

0   Quantity

(b) Elastic Supply

Price

When supply is relatively elastic, the deadweight loss of a tax is large.

Size of tax

Supply

Demand

0   Quantity

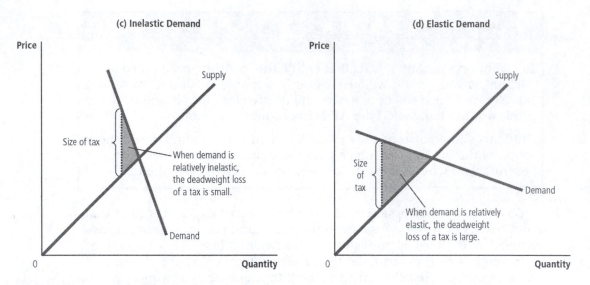

Not only does elasticity affect the amount of market deadweight loss when a tax is imposed, it also determines who, buyers or sellers, will pay the burden of the tax. If buyers have an inelastic demand relative to sellers, then the buyer bears a larger tax burden. If sellers have an inelastic demand relative to buyers, then the seller bears a larger tax burden. The below figure illustrates this point. When a good is a necessity, consumers will have a slight change in quantity demanded as the price rises, so producers are able to pass a greater percentage of the tax burden to the buyer.

The *size* of the tax imposed may also affect welfare loss. For example, a small tax has a small deadweight loss and raises a small amount of tax revenue while a larger tax has a larger deadweight loss and raises more tax revenue. This does not mean, however, that policymakers should impose extremely large taxes. There is a limit to the amount of revenue a very large tax can raise, but the welfare loss continues to increase as taxes are

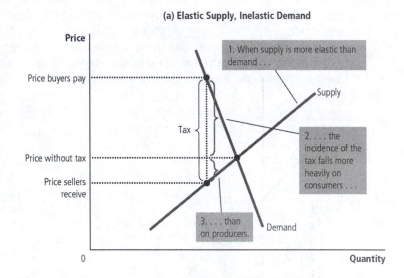

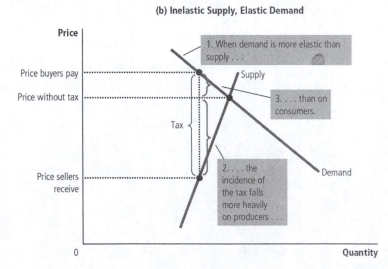

increased. The following set of graphs show the impact of different tax sizes on tax revenue and deadweight loss. As tax rates rise, tax revenue first rises, then falls, but deadweight loss continues to rise.

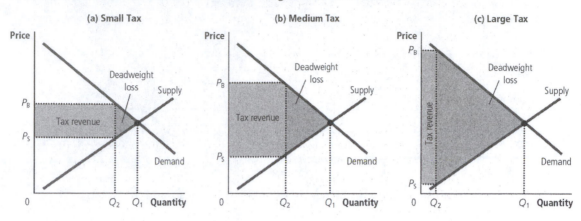

IMPACT OF PRICE CEILINGS AND PRICE FLOORS

(*Principles of Economics* 5th ed. pages 114–123/6th ed. pages 112–121)

So far we have looked at how to measure welfare loss and the impact of taxes on market welfare. In addition to tax policies, however, the government may affect market outcome through the establishment of price controls, such as **price ceilings**, *a legal maximum on the price at which a good can be sold,* and **price floors**, *a legal minimum on the price at which a good can be sold.* Government may impose a price ceiling when it feels the market price is too high. An example of a price ceiling is rent control. Local governments may choose to establish a rent control policy (a price ceiling) in order to help improve the affordability of housing. In order for a price ceiling to be effective, it must be set *below* the market equilibrium price. If a price ceiling is set above the market equilibrium price, for example if rent control prices were set above the market rental rates, then the price ceiling would be ineffective because the market rental rates would prevail. The below figure illustrates an effective price ceiling. An effective price ceiling creates a market shortage since the quantity demanded exceeds the quantity supplied at this lower-than-market price. A rent control law creates a shortage of apartments.

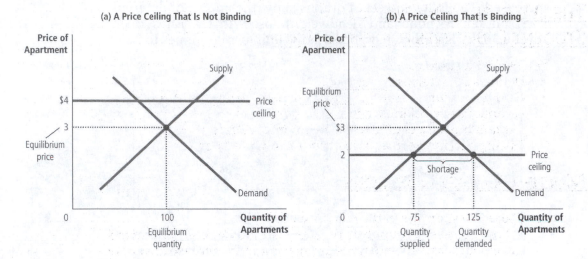

(a) A Price Ceiling That Is Not Binding

(b) A Price Ceiling That Is Binding

Suppose that the government imposes a price floor instead. An example of a price floor is minimum wage. Government may impose a minimum wage price floor in order to help increase wages for laborers. In order for a price floor to be effective, it must be set *above* the market equilibrium price. If a price floor is set below the market equilibrium price, for example a minimum wage is set below the market wage rates, then the price floor would be ineffective because the market wage rates would prevail. The graph below illustrates an effective price floor. An effective price floor creates a market surplus since the quantity supplied exceeds the quantity demanded at this higher-than-market price. An effective minimum wage results in a labor surplus, or unemployment.

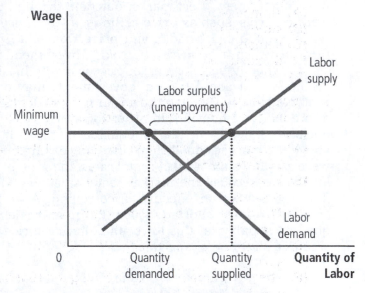

AP Tip

Students often get confused with price ceilings and price floors. Remember that a price floor is a minimum whereas a price ceiling is a maximum. Study the previous two figures to make sure that you understand the difference between the two.

THE WELFARE OF MARKETS: STUDENT OBJECTIVES FOR THE AP EXAM

You should be able to:
- Define all key terms in bold
- Graph: consumer and producer surplus, deadweight loss, tax revenue, price ceilings, and price floors
- Explain the impact of taxes on economic welfare
- Distinguish between a price ceiling and price floor

MULTIPLE-CHOICE QUESTIONS

1. There is a shortage in the market when
   (A) the increase in supply is greater than the increase in demand.
   (B) the increase in demand is greater than the increase in supply.
   (C) the quantity demanded is less than the quantity supplied.
   (D) the quantity demanded is greater than the quantity supplied.
   (E) the government has imposed an effective price floor.

2. Price is currently above equilibrium. There is a situation of excess _____. Assuming that there are no price controls in place, we would expect the price to _____.
   (A) supply; rise.
   (B) supply; fall.
   (C) demand; rise.
   (D) demand; fall.
   (E) demand; remain constant.

3. Suppose that the government would like to impose a 5% tax on either good X or Y. How should the government choose which good to tax?
   (A) The government should tax the good that has a perfectly inelastic demand.
   (B) The government should tax the good that has a perfectly elastic demand.
   (C) The government should tax the good that has a unit elastic demand.
   (D) The government should tax the good that has a perfectly elastic supply.
   (E) The government should tax the good that has a unit elastic supply.

4. An effective price floor in the corn market will result in
   (A) an increase in the price of corn and an excess supply of corn.
   (B) an increase in the price of corn and an excess demand for corn.
   (C) a decrease in the price of corn and an excess demand for corn.
   (D) a decrease in the price of corn and an increase in the quantity of corn sold.
   (E) a decrease in the price of corn and a decrease in the quantity of corn sold.

5. The welfare loss of a tax stems from the theory that
   (A) taxes decrease the incentive to work.
   (B) taxes increase the rate of inflation.
   (C) taxes lead to an output level that is less than market equilibrium.
   (D) government does not spend tax revenue efficiently.
   (E) producer surplus exceeds consumer surplus whenever a tax is imposed.

Use the following graphs to answer questions 6–9:

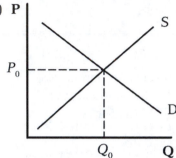

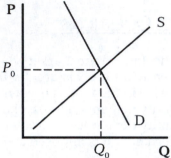

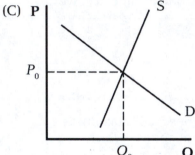

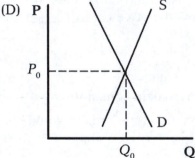

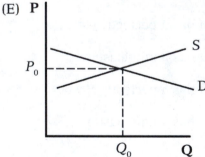

6. In which of the above market situations will the largest portion of a 3% tax per unit of output be borne by sellers (relative to buyers)?

7. In which of the above market situations will the largest portion of a 3% tax per unit of output be borne by buyers (relative to sellers)?

8. In which of the above market situations will the deadweight loss (or welfare loss) of a 3% per-unit tax be greatest?

9. In which of the above market situations will the tax revenue from a 3% per-unit tax be greatest?

10. If the supply of a product is perfectly inelastic, the incidence of a 5% per-unit tax will fall
    (A) entirely on the seller.
    (B) mostly on the seller.
    (C) neither party bears the burden.
    (D) mostly on the buyer.
    (E) entirely on the buyer.

Use the following graph to answer questions 11–15:

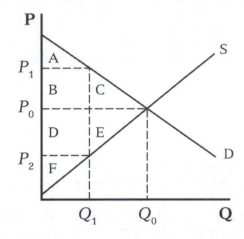

11. Using the labels in the graph above and assuming a free market system (no government intervention), identify the area of consumer surplus.
    (A) A
    (B) A + F
    (C) A + B + C
    (D) C + E
    (E) D + E + F

12. Using the labels in the graph above, what is the area of producer surplus when a tax of P_1 is imposed?
    (A) C + E
    (B) D + E + F
    (C) D + E
    (D) F
    (E) A

13. Using the labels in the graph above, identify the area that represents the loss in consumer surplus when a tax of P_1 is imposed.
    (A) A + B + C
    (B) D + E + F
    (C) B + C
    (D) D + E
    (E) C + E

14. Using the labels in the graph above, identify the price received by sellers and the price paid by buyers when a tax is imposed.
    (A) P_0 = price received by sellers; P_1 = price paid by buyers.
    (B) P_1 = price paid by buyers; P_2 = price received by sellers.
    (C) P_2 = price paid by buyers; P_1 = price received by sellers.
    (D) P_1 = price received by sellers; P_0 = price paid by buyers.
    (E) P_2 = price received by sellers; P_0 = price paid by buyers.

15. Using the labels in the graph on the previous page, identify the area that represents the welfare loss resulting from the imposition of a tax.
    (A) C + E
    (B) B + D
    (C) A + F
    (D) D + E
    (E) B + C

FREE-RESPONSE QUESTIONS

1. There is a highly inelastic supply of apartments in New York City. A new wave of unskilled laborers moves into New York City in search of work.
   (a) Using economic analysis and a supply-demand graph, show how the arrival of these unskilled laborers will affect each of the following.
       (i) The price of apartments in New York City
       (ii) The quantity of apartments available in New York City
   (b) The local New York City government passes a rent control law for apartments located within its city limits. On a new graph, show where the rent control should be set in order for it to be effective. Explain.
   (c) What is the impact of the rent control law on the market for apartments in New York City? In your answer, be sure to address the impact on the following.
       (i)   The quantity of apartments demanded
       (ii) The quantity of apartments supplied
       (iii) Is there a shortage or surplus in the market? Explain.

2. The government imposes a 5% per-unit tax on the purchase of computers.
   (a) Using a graph, identify the following areas before the imposition of the tax.
       (i)   Total consumer surplus
       (ii) Total producer surplus
       (iii) Deadweight loss
   (b) Using economic analysis and a supply-demand graph, show how the tax will affect each of the following in your graph in part (a) above.
       (i) The price of computers
       (ii) The quantity of computers sold

(c) On a new graph, identify the following after the imposition of the tax.
  (i)   Total consumer surplus.
  (ii) Total producer surplus.
  (iii) Government tax revenue.
  (iv) Deadweight loss.

Answers

MULTIPLE-CHOICE QUESTIONS

1. **D.** Refer to the figure depicting a price ceiling on page 112. When there is an effective price ceiling, the market experiences a shortage because the quantity demanded is greater than the quantity supplied at the lower-than-market price (*Principles of Economics* 5th ed. pages 114–117/6th ed. pages 112–115).

2. **B.** Without price controls, a price above equilibrium will have to adjust to balance supply and demand and return to market equilibrium by falling (*Principles of Economics* 5th ed. pages 118–119/6th ed. pages 116–117).

3. **A.** If the government taxes a good with a perfectly inelastic demand, the quantity demanded for the good does not change even when a tax is imposed. Therefore, the government is able to maximize tax revenues and minimize welfare loss since there is no deadweight loss (*Principles of Economics* 5th ed. pages 128–129, 164–168/6th ed. pages 125–126, 160–166).

4. **A.** An effective price floor is one that is imposed <u>above</u> market equilibrium. This creates a surplus of corn, where the quantity of corn supplied exceeds the quantity of corn demanded (*Principles of Economics* 5th ed. pages 118–123/6th ed. pages 116–121).

5. **C.** A tax increases the price which in turn decreases the quantity demanded and supplied in the market, resulting in deadweight loss (*Principles of Economics* 5th ed. pages 160–166/6th ed. pages 157–159).

6. **C.** Since the supply curve is more inelastic than the demand curve in this graph, the burden of a 3% per-unit tax will be borne by sellers. (*Principles of Economics* 5th ed. pages 128–130/6th ed. pages 125–128).

7. **B.** Since the demand curve is more inelastic than the supply curve in this graph, the burden of a 3% per-unit tax will be borne by buyers (*Principles of Economics* 5th ed. pages 128–130/6th ed. pages 125–128).

8. **E.** A 3% per-unit tax will result in the greatest welfare loss when both the demand and supply for the good/service are extremely elastic. Graph (E) depicts the greatest elasticity of both curves (*Principles of Economics* 5th ed. pages 164–167/6th ed. pages 160–163).

9. **D.** A 3% per-unit tax will result in the highest tax revenue collected when both the demand and supply for the good/service are extremely inelastic. Graph (D) depicts the greatest inelasticity of both curves (*Principles of Economics* 5th ed. pages 164–167/6th ed. pages 160–163).

10. **A.** If the government taxes a good with a perfectly inelastic supply, the quantity supplied of the good does not change even when a tax is imposed. Therefore, the government is able to maximize tax revenues and minimize welfare loss since there is no deadweight loss (*Principles of Economics* 5th ed. pages 128–129, 164–168/6th ed. pages 125–126, 160–166).

11. **C.** Consumer surplus is the area under the demand curve above the market equilibrium price. Since there is no government intervention, the area of consumer surplus is A + B + C (*Principles of Economics* 5th ed. page 162/6th ed. page 158).

12. **D.** The producer surplus decreases when a tax is imposed. The producer surplus with a tax is represented by the area F (*Principles of Economics* 5th ed. page 162/6th ed. page 158).

13. **C.** Consumer surplus, under a free market, is the area A + B + C. With a tax, the consumer surplus decreases to just the area A. The consumer surplus loss is B + C (*Principles of Economics* 5th ed. page 162/6th ed. page 158).

14. **B.** With a tax, the price increases, which decreases the quantity demanded of the good sold in the market. P_1 is the price paid by buyers at the lower quantity demanded, which means that the quantity supplied also decreases. Therefore the price received by sellers at this lower quantity is P_2 (*Principles of Economics* 5th ed. page 162/6th ed. page 158).

15. **C.** The welfare loss from the tax is represented by C + E. The market does not produce an efficient output level with a tax (*Principles of Economics* 5th ed. page 162/6th ed. page 158).

FREE-RESPONSE QUESTIONS

1. (a)

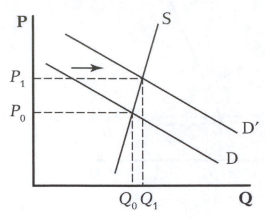

NYC Apartments

The price of apartments in NYC increase and the quantity of NYC apartments supplied increases, although the price increase is far greater than the quantity increase. Note that the supply curve is inelastic relative to the demand curve to reflect the high occupancy rates and limited quantities of apartments available in NYC.

(b)

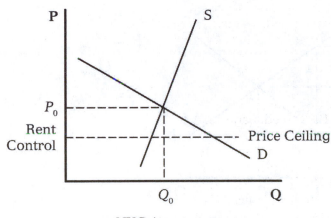

NYC Apartments

The rent control, a price ceiling, must be below the market equilibrium price in order for it to be effective because if it were established at any point above the market equilibrium price, the market equilibrium price would prevail and the rent control would be ineffective.

(c)

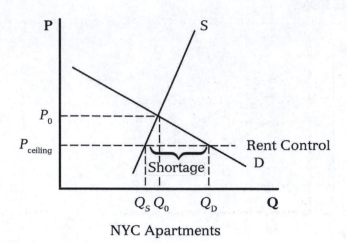

NYC Apartments

The quantity of apartments demanded exceeds the quantity of apartments supplied at this lower-than-market price ceiling. This creates a market shortage of apartments (*Principles of Economics* 5th ed. pages 114–123/6th ed. pages 112–121).

2. (a)

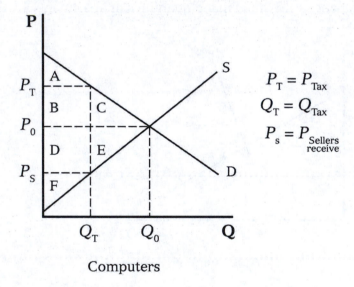

$$P_T = P_{Tax}$$
$$Q_T = Q_{Tax}$$
$$P_s = P_{Sellers \atop receive}$$

Computers

The pre-tax consumer surplus is A + B + C and the pre-tax producer surplus is D + E + F. There is no deadweight loss if the market is free to operate and the government doesn't intervene by imposing taxes.

(b)

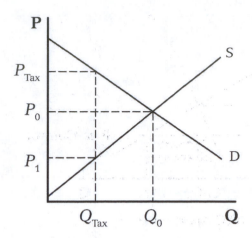

The price of computers increases while the quantity of computers sold decreases.

(c) Using the graph in part (a), the post-tax consumer surplus is area A and the post-tax producer surplus is area F. The government tax revenue is represented by area B + D and the deadweight loss is area C + E (*Principles of Economics* 5th ed. pages 160–169/6th ed. pages 156–166).

PRODUCTION COSTS AND COMPETITIVE MARKETS

In any given market, we assume that firms want to maximize their profit. In this chapter, we will cover the very technical topic of production costs. Specifically, we will look at how a firm's input hiring decisions affect the costs incurred by the firm in the short and long run. We will also apply our understanding of production costs to competitive markets. Be warned that this chapter is very technical, but understanding production costs and competitive markets are fundamental to our study of microeconomics and preparation for the AP Microeconomics exam.

THE PRODUCTION FUNCTION

(*Principles of Economics* 5th ed. pages 271–273/6th ed. pages 263–265)

In order to determine the costs of production, we need to first look at how productive our resources are. The **production function** shows *the relationship between the quantity of inputs used to make a good and the quantity of output of that good*. It is sometimes called the **total product curve (TP)**. For example, the TP tells us how much output increases when we hire more workers. While it is helpful for us to know how overall output changes when new inputs are hired, we are more interested in the marginal changes. Is it beneficial to hire an additional worker? In order to determine whether or not it makes sense to hire that worker, we need to know how output changes when one additional worker is hired. The **marginal product curve (MP)** shows us *the increase in output that arises from an additional unit of input hired*. The **average product curve (AP)** shows us *the average output produced by each worker*. The figure below illustrates these three production functions.

To develop a better understanding of how we measure production costs, we are going to continue our use of the cookie company example using the fictional company data presented in the following table.

Quantity of Cookie (dozen per hour)	Total Cost	Fixed Cost	Variable Cost	Average Fixed Cost	Average Variable Cost	Average Total Cost	Marginal Cost
0	$ 3.00	$3.00	$ 0.00	—	—	—	
							$0.30
1	3.30	3.00	0.30	$3.00	$0.30	$3.30	
							0.50
2	3.80	3.00	0.80	1.50	0.40	1.90	
							0.70
3	4.50	3.00	1.50	1.00	0.50	1.50	
							0.90
4	5.40	3.00	2.40	0.75	0.60	1.35	
							1.10
5	6.50	3.00	3.50	0.60	0.70	1.30	
							1.30
6	7.80	3.00	4.80	0.50	0.80	1.30	
							1.50
7	9.30	3.00	6.30	0.43	0.90	1.33	
							1.70
8	11.00	3.00	8.00	0.38	1.00	1.38	
							1.90
9	12.90	3.00	9.90	0.33	1.10	1.43	
							2.10
10	15.00	3.00	12.00	0.30	1.20	1.50	

The first and second columns show the number of cookies we can produce and the total cost associated with each production quantity. Total costs can be divided into two types, fixed and variable costs. **Fixed costs** are those *costs that do not vary with the quantity of output produced and must be paid even if nothing is produced,* such as the rent we might have to pay for use of the kitchen or the cost of taking out a loan for an oven to bake the cookies in. The cost of rent and the loans taken out to purchase the oven is fixed because, regardless of whether we are able to produce and sell the cookies, we <u>must</u> pay these costs. **Variable costs** are *costs that vary with the quantity of output,* such as the cost of labor and ingredients (flour, chocolate chips) necessary to make our cookies. Our **total costs** are the *sum of our fixed and variable costs.* The remaining columns include our per-unit costs: average fixed cost, average variable cost, average total cost, and marginal cost.

Average Fixed Cost (AFC)	*= total fixed cost (TFC)/Quantity (Q)*
Average Variable Cost (AVC)	*= total variable cost (TVC)/Quantity (Q)*
Average Total Cost (ATC)	*= total cost (TC)/Quantity (Q)*
Marginal Cost (MC)	*= change in TC/change in Q*

The following graph on the left plots out each of the per-unit cost curves according to the data from our cookie company taken from the table above. The marginal cost rises with increasing output and eventually reflects the law of diminishing marginal returns. Consider our cookie company example: if we produce a few cookies and hire a few workers, we have excess production capacity because a lot of our equipment is still unused. If we increase our cookie production, we have to hire more workers, causing our equipment to be more fully utilized and our workspace more crowded. If we want to increase our cookie production even further, we would hire more workers, but these new workers may have to wait to use the equipment, which is why the marginal cost of producing an extra cookie at higher production levels is high. The average total cost (ATC) curve is U-shaped and intersects the MC curve at its lowest point. The graph on the right illustrates the per-unit cost curves for a typical firm. This graph is the one you want to use in your AP preparation.

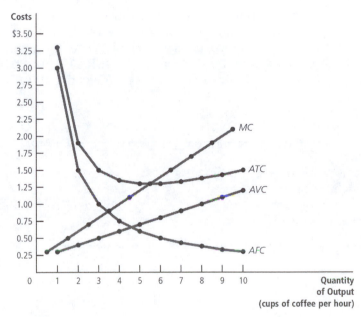

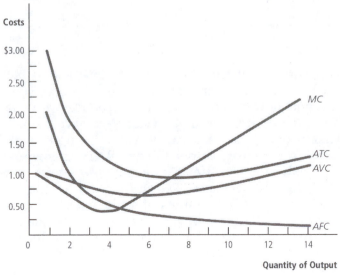

AP Tips

It is unlikely that you will have to create a production cost chart on a free-response question on the AP Microeconomics exam, but you must be prepared to answer multiple-choice questions on this topic. It is helpful to graph these per-unit curves in your test margins so that you have a visual aid as you answer the production cost multiple-choice questions.

You must be able to determine fixed and marginal costs.

SHORT-RUN VS. LONG-RUN COSTS

(*Principles of Economics* 5th ed. pages 123–130, 280–283/6th ed. pages 271–274)

In the short run, some costs are fixed. We make this assumption because it is difficult to negotiate the cost of rent or other input costs in the short run. In the long run, there is more time for us to find cheaper rental spaces, or build our own factories in order to keep production costs low, so all costs are variable. The long-run ATC (LRATC) is U-shaped just like the short-run ATC (SRATC), but because all costs are variable in the long run, the LRATC looks like this.

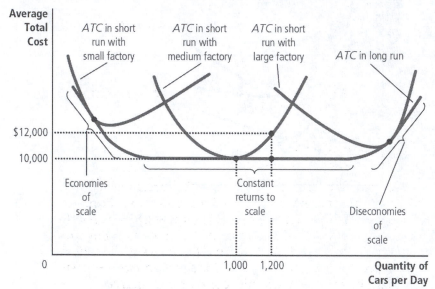

The LRATC consists of the SRATC over time and is helpful in deciding how big we want our factory to be. The SRATC curve is helpful in deciding how much we want to produce with that given plant size. Initially, the SRATC is high because we have a small factory with higher fixed costs, but over time, we can open up a large factory that will help us to cut costs, so our future SRATC is lower than the original. Eventually though, SRATC will increase again because of growing production inefficiencies. The first section of the LRATC is where the firm experiences **economies of scale**, *the property whereby LRATC falls as the quantity of output increases*. The middle section of the LRATC is where the firm has **constant returns to scale**, *the property whereby LRATC stays the same as the quantity of output changes*. The last section of the LRATC is where the firm experiences

diseconomies of scale, *the property whereby LRATC rises as the quantity of output increases.* Economies of scale may arise because workers may specialize in different aspects of production and therefore reduce overall production costs; whereas diseconomies of scale arise because the firm has become too large and cannot manage its production processes very efficiently. Before moving on to our next related topic, here is a table summarizing the many different types of cost curves.

Term	Definition	Mathematical Description
Explicit costs	Costs that require an outlay of money by the firm	
Implicit costs	Costs that do not require an outlay of money by the firm	
Fixed costs	Costs that do not vary with the quantity of output produced	FC
Variable costs	Costs that vary with the quantity of output produced	VC
Total cost	The market value of all the inputs that a firm uses in production	$TC = FC + VC$
Average fixed cost	Fixed cost divided by the quantity of output	$AFC = FC/Q$
Average variable cost	Variable cost divided by the quantity of output	$AVC = VC/Q$
Average total cost	Total cost divided by the quantity of output	$ATC = TC/Q$
Marginal cost	The increase in total cost that arises from an extra unit of production	$MC = \Delta TC/\Delta Q$

FIRMS IN COMPETITIVE MARKETS

(Principles of Economics 5th ed. pages 289–293/6th ed. pages 279–283)

Having a good understanding of production costs is important for our study of how firms within markets make decisions. In this section, we will examine the behavior of competitive firms. A **competitive market**, or a **perfectly competitive market**, is *a market that has the following characteristics: many buyers and sellers in the market, identical products, firms are price-takers, and it is easy for firms to enter or exit the market.* The goal of any firm in this competitive market is to maximize **profit**, *total revenue minus total cost.* To see how a firm can do this, we need to consider both the revenue and the costs for the firm in a competitive market. Let's continue to use our cookie company example. The table below shows the revenue data for our cookie company.

Quantity (Q)	Price (P)	Total Revenue (TR = P × Q)	Average Revenue (AR = TR/Q)	Marginal Revenue (MR = ΔTR/ΔQ)
1 dozen	$6	$ 6	$6	
				$6
2	6	12	6	
				6
3	6	18	6	
				6
4	6	24	6	
				6
5	6	30	6	
				6
6	6	36	6	
				6
7	6	42	6	
				6
8	6	48	6	

The first two columns show the amount of cookies we can produce and the price we could charge for the cookies that we produce. The third column is our total revenue, which is calculated by taking the price of a dozen cookies (which is $6) multiplied by the quantity sold. The fourth and last column show average and marginal revenue. **Average revenue** tells us how much revenue we receive for a typical sale of a dozen of our cookies and is calculated by taking the *total revenue divided by the quantity sold*. **Marginal revenue** tells us how much additional revenue we receive for each additional dozen of cookies produced and is calculated by taking *the change in total revenue from an additional unit sold*. The $6 price of the dozen of cookies is determined by the supply of and demand for cookies in the competitive market. Since there are so many buyers and sellers in the competitive market, firms <u>must</u> take the market price and sell their cookies for $6. Suppose that a firm decides to sell their cookies for $7. In a competitive market, cookie buyers would not buy a $7 dozen of cookies when they can buy an identical dozen of cookies for $6, so the firm will eventually have to lower its price and take the market price of $6. The following graph illustrates how a firm in a competitive market takes the market price. Note that the $6 price is also the firm's marginal revenue (MR) because each additional dozen of cookies sold brings in an additional $6 in revenue. It is also the average revenue price and the demand equilibrium price.

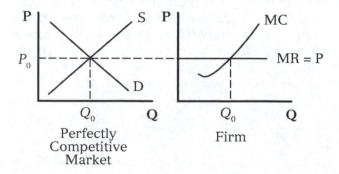

> ## AP Tips
>
> The AP Microeconomics exam will refer to perfectly competitive markets. If you are using the Mankiw *Principles of Economics* text, know that perfectly competitive markets are the same thing as competitive markets.
>
> It is very important to know the characteristics of perfectly competitive markets. Use the following pneumonic to help recall the characteristics: **P-I-L-E** (Price-takers, Identical products, Lots of buyers and sellers, and Easy entry/exit).
>
> One other thing to note is that, since the competitive firm is a price taker, it's **MR = D = AR = P**, or "MR. DARP." This is another pneumonic to remember what goes on the firm graph.

PROFIT MAXIMIZATION AND THE SHORT RUN

(*Principles of Economics* 5th ed. pages 292–302/6th ed. pages 282–293)

How do firms maximize profit? They do so by producing at an output level where its *marginal revenue (MR) is equal to its marginal costs (MC)*. Using the following data, we can see why MR = MC is the firm's profit maximizing output level.

Quantity (Q)	Total Revenue (TR)	Total Cost (TC)	Profit (TR − TC)	Marginal Revenue (MR = ΔTR/ΔQ)	Marginal Cost (MC = ΔTC/ΔQ)	Change in Profit (MR − MC)
0 dozens	$ 0	$ 3	−$3			
				$6	$2	$4
1	6	5	1			
				6	3	3
2	12	8	4			
				6	4	2
3	18	12	6			
				6	5	1
4	24	17	7			
				6	6	0
5	30	23	7			
				6	7	−1
6	36	30	6			
				6	8	−2
7	42	38	4			
				6	9	−3
8	48	47	1			

Profit is maximized when 4 or 5 dozen cookies are produced (total profit of $7). It makes sense that we should produce 5 dozen cookies since total profit is maximized, but it does not make sense that we produce 6 dozen since profits fall. When producing 5 dozen cookies, MR = MC = $6, and profit is maximized. The reason why we want to produce where MR = MC is because any other level of production gives us lower profits. Let's look at this graphically.

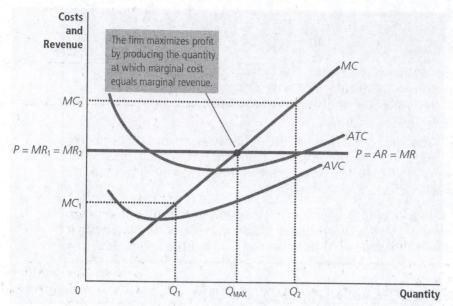

At quantity Q_1, MR exceeds MC, so increasing production will increase profit. At quantity Q_2, MC is above MR, so decreasing production will increase profit. The profit-maximizing level of output is where MR = MC, at quantity Q_{MAX}. **MR = MC is the profit-maximizing output level for _all_ types of firms, not just competitive firms.**

AP Tip

The profit-maximizing output level for any firm is <u>ALWAYS</u> where **MR = MC**. On both free-response and multiple-choice questions, you will be asked about the profit-maximizing price and quantity for firms in different markets. The way you find this is by locating the price and quantity that corresponds to where **MR = MC**.

In the short run, firms can earn profits or incur losses, but they cannot leave the market. The distinction between the long and short run is that in the long run, firms can easily leave or enter the competitive market, whereas in the short run, they remain in the market and will continue to produce as long as a firm's losses are less than its fixed costs. The following graphs show a firm in a competitive market that is earning a profit.

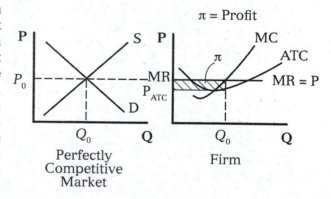

Note that the MR is greater than the firm's ATC at the profit maximizing output level. This is how we know that the firm is earning a profit, since its revenues exceed its costs. It is also possible for a firm to incur a loss in the short run. The following graphs show a firm in a competitive market that is incurring a loss.

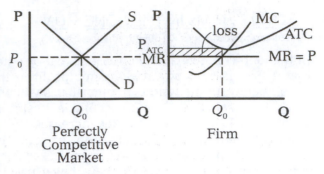

Note that the ATC is greater than the firm's MR, which is why the firm incurs a loss—costs exceed revenue. However, in the short run, the firm that incurs a loss has to make a decision regarding whether it will **shut down**, a *short-run decision to not produce anything*, or continue production even with a loss. If a firm decides to shut down in the short run, it will lose all revenue from the sale of its product and will still have to pay its fixed costs, so why would a firm consider shutting down in the short run? It considers shutting down in the short run because it can *save the variable costs of making the product*. This means that a firm will shut down if the <u>revenue it earns is less than the variable costs</u> of production. The following graphs illustrate the firm's shut down decision. In this first set of graphs, the firm's AVC exceeds its MR = P, so the firm shuts down.

Since AVC > MR = P, the firm shuts down in the short run.

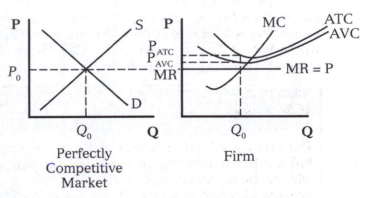

In this next set of graphs, the firm still incurs a loss, but chooses to stay open in the short run because MR = P > AVC. The firm will at least get a little money to use toward covering fixed costs and any excess might cover even some of its variable costs, making it worthwhile for it to remain in business. Firms are not concerned about covering its

Since MR = P > AVC, the firm incurs a loss but remains open in the short run.

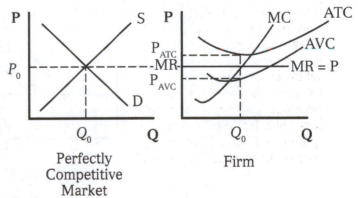

fixed costs in the short run because fixed costs are considered **sunk costs**, *a cost that has already been committed and cannot be recovered.*

COMPETITIVE FIRMS IN THE LONG RUN

(*Principles of Economics* 5th ed. pages 300–306/6th ed. pages 289–295)

In the long run, firms may choose to exit or enter the market. Suppose that a firm is earning an economic profit in the short run, as in the graph below. In the long run, other firms will want to enter the market since they see that it is a profitable business. An increase in the number of firms in the market increases the market supply (supply determinant: number of sellers, refer back to Chapter 2), which lowers the market price. Since the firm in a competitive market is a price-taker, the firm takes the new, lower price, up to the point where firms in this market no longer make an economic profit. The long-run condition for firms in competitive markets is that they do not earn an economic profit; instead, firms earn a **normal profit**, *minimum profit necessary to retain suppliers in the competitive market (in other words, a normal profit covers a supplier's opportunity costs),* in the long run. Study this graph series to make sure that you understand how the competitive market responds to short-run economic profit.

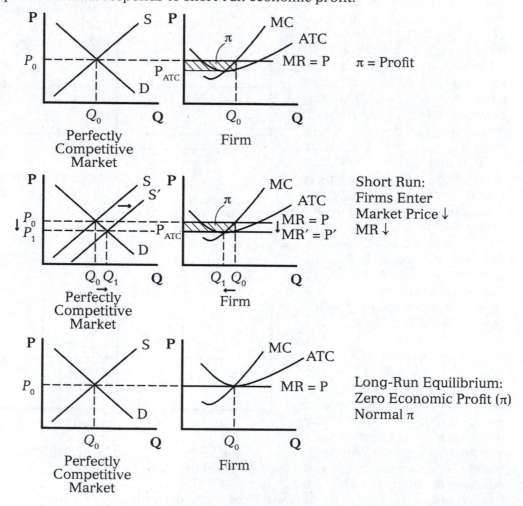

π = Profit

Short Run:
Firms Enter
Market Price ↓
MR ↓

Long-Run Equilibrium:
Zero Economic Profit (π)
Normal π

Suppose instead that a firm incurs a short-run loss, but stays open because its revenues exceed its variable costs. In the long run, firms will exit the market. This decreases the market supply, which increases the market price. Again, since firms are price-takers, they take this new, higher price up until the point where, again, each firm remaining in the market earns a normal profit.

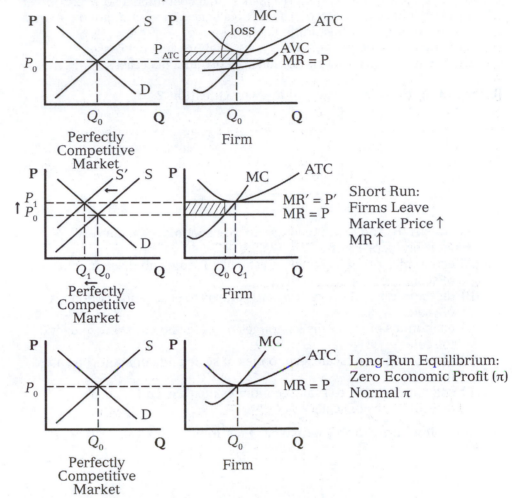

PRODUCTION COSTS AND COMPETITIVE MARKETS: STUDENT OBJECTIVES FOR THE AP EXAM

You should be able to:

- Define all key terms in bold
- Graph: production functions, per-unit cost curves, side-by-side perfectly competitive market and firm in various short-run situations (loss, profit), side-by-side perfectly competitive market and firm in the long run (zero economic profit)
- Determine if a firm should shut down or stay open in the short run
- Analyze long-run decisions to enter or exit the market

MULTIPLE-CHOICE QUESTIONS

1. Which of the following statements is correct?
   (A) Marginal cost measures the cost per unit of output associated with any level of production.
   (B) When marginal product rises, marginal cost must also rise.
   (C) Marginal cost is the cost of an extra variable input divided by the addition of one additional worker.
   (D) When average product rises, marginal product decreases.
   (E) When total product rises, marginal product decreases.

Refer to the following graph to answer Question 2:

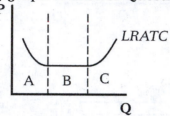

2 Sections A, B, and C of the long-run average total cost curve, respectively, represent
   (A) economies of scale, constant returns to scale and diseconomies of scale.
   (B) diseconomies of scale, constant returns to scale and economies of scale.
   (C) economies of scale, diseconomies of scale and constant returns to scale.
   (D) diseconomies of scale, economies of scale and constant returns to scale.
   (E) constant returns to scale, economies of scale, and diseconomies of scale.

Use the following graph to answer Questions 3–4:

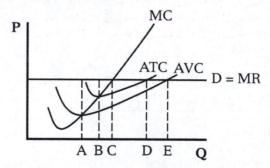

3. Using the graph above, the firm will produce at which level of output?
   (A) 0A.
   (B) 0B.
   (C) 0C.
   (D) 0D.
   (E) 0E.

4. Refer again to the above graph. Complete the following sentence to make it a correct statement: The firm is earning

    _____.

    (A) zero normal profit.
    (B) zero accounting profit.
    (C) zero economic profit.
    (D) positive economic profit.
    (E) a loss and should shut down in the long run.

Use the following table to answer Question 5:

Input	Total Product
0	0
1	5
2	11
3	18
4	26
5	30

5. Based on the data in the above table, after which unit does diminishing returns set in?
    (A) First unit of input.
    (B) Second unit of input.
    (C) Third unit of input.
    (D) Fourth unit of input.
    (E) Fifth unit of input.

6. What is the difference between the short run and the long run in regard to the theory of the firm?
    I.   All input costs are fixed in the short run.
    II. All input costs are variable in the long run.
    III. At least one input cost is fixed in the short run.
    (A) I only.
    (B) II only.
    (C) III only.
    (D) I and II only.
    (E) II and III only.

Use the following graph to answer Questions 7–9:

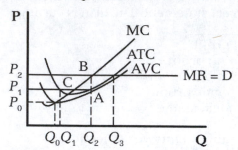

7. Using the above graph, at the price of P_2, the area of economic profit is
   (A) the area of the rectangle $0P_1AQ_2$.
   (B) the area of the rectangle P_1P_2AB.
   (C) the area of the rectangle $0P_1CQ_1$.
   (D) the area of the rectangle $0P_2BQ_2$.
   (E) the area of the rectangle Q_1Q_2AC.

8. Using the above graph, in the short run, the firm will stop production (shut down) when the price falls below
   (A) $0P_0$.
   (B) $0P_1$.
   (C) $0P_2$.
   (D) P_0P_1.
   (E) P_0P_2.

9. In the short run, an increase in the demand for a product produced by a competitive industry will cause
   (A) each firm to decrease its output.
   (B) each firm to increase its price.
   (C) an increase in the number of firms.
   (D) each firm to earn less profit.
   (E) an increase in the average size of firms.

10. Which of the following is *not* a feature of perfect competition?
    (A) Many firms.
    (B) Homogeneous products.
    (C) Ease of entry and exit.
    (D) Zero economic profit in the long run.
    (E) Advertisement.

11. Which of the following statements regarding normal profits are true?
    (A) They are zero under pure competition in the long run.
    (B) They are excluded from a firm's cost of production.
    (C) They are considered an explicit cost for the firm.
    (D) They are necessary to keep a firm in the industry in the long run.
    (E) They are necessary to keep a firm in the industry in the short run.

12. Which of the following represents the correct relationship between the demand curve for a perfectly competitive industry and the demand curve for a perfectly competitive firm?

        Competitive Market   Competitive Firm
- (A) downward sloping   downward sloping
- (B) downward sloping   perfectly elastic
- (C) perfectly elastic   downward sloping
- (D) perfectly elastic   perfectly elastic
- (E) perfectly inelastic   perfectly elastic

13. A perfectly competitive firm is operating where marginal revenue is greater than marginal costs. What should this firm do to increase profits?
- (A) Increase its price.
- (B) Decrease its price.
- (C) Do nothing.
- (D) Increase its production.
- (E) Decrease its production.

14. Which of the following statements is true of perfectly competitive firms in long-run equilibrium?
- (A) A firm's revenue will decrease if production is increased.
- (B) A firm's total revenues are at a maximum.
- (C) A firm does not earn an economic profit, but a normal profit.
- (D) A firm does not earn a normal profit, but an economic profit.
- (E) A firm does not earn a normal or an economic profit.

15. If a firm in a competitive market is experiencing losses, what will happen to industry supply and the equilibrium price in the long run?

        Market Supply   Equilibrium Price
- (A) Increase   Decrease
- (B) Increase   Increase
- (C) No change   Decrease
- (D) Decrease   Decrease
- (E) Decrease   Increase

FREE-RESPONSE QUESTIONS

1. A perfectly competitive manufacturing industry is in long-run equilibrium. Suppose that there is a technological advance that increases production in this manufacturing industry.
   (a) Explain how this technological improvement will affect the manufacturing industry's output and price in the short run.
   (b) Using side by side graphs of the industry and the firm, show the short-run effect of this technological advance on the price, output, and profit of a typical firm in this manufacturing industry.
   (c) Will firms be earning an economic profit or economic loss? Will firms enter or exit this manufacturing industry in the long run? Explain.

2. Assume that a perfectly competitive constant cost industry is in long-run equilibrium. Suppose that there is sharp population increase which causes an increase in the market demand for this good.
   (a) Draw a correctly labeled, side-by-side graph for the market and the firm and show each of the following.
      (i) Industry price and output.
      (ii) Firm price and output.
      (iii) Firm profit.
   (b) Following the increase in consumer demand, the industry adjusts to a new long-run equilibrium. Explain how the industry makes this long-run adjustment using your graphs in part (a) and be sure to identify the following.
      (i) Long-run industry price.
      (ii) Long-run firm output and price.
      (iii) Profits.

Answers

MULTIPLE-CHOICE QUESTIONS

1. **C.** This is the definition of marginal cost. Marginal cost = change in total cost/change in quantity (*Principles of Economics* 5th ed. page 276/6th ed. page 268).

2. **A.** LRATC has 3 components: economies of scale, constant returns to scale, and diseconomies of scale (*Principles of Economics* 5th ed. page 280/6th ed. page 272).

3. **C.** MR = MC is the profit-maximizing output level for ANY type of firm (*Principles of Economics* 5th ed. pages 292–294/6th ed. pages 282–284).

4. **D.** The firm's MR = P is greater than its ATC at the profit maximizing quantity, so the firm is earning an economic profit (*Principles of Economics* 5th ed. pages 300–301/6th ed. pages 290–291).

5. **E.** Returns continue to increase with each input hired until the 5th input is hired. The 5th input adds only 4 units to total output whereas inputs #1–4 add increasing quantities of output (*Principles of Economics* 5th ed. pages 271–273/6th ed. pages 263–265).

6. **E.** In the short run, at least one variable cost is fixed, whereas in the long run, all costs are variable. This is because there is more time to make adjustments to contracts so that costs can be changed (usually lowered) in the long run (*Principles of Economics* 5th ed. pages 280–283/6th ed. pages 271–274).

7. **B.** To find the area of economic profit, you need to identify the MR = P and the ATC at the profit-maximizing quantity. Recall that profit = TR – TC, so in our graph, profit = (PxQ) – (ATC xQ) (*Principles of Economics* 5th ed. page 300/6th ed. page 290).

8. **A.** When the price falls below AVC in the short run, the firm will stop production because it can no longer cover its variable costs (*Principles of Economics* 5th ed. pages 296–297/6th ed. pages 286–287).

9. **B.** Perfectly competitively firms are price-takers, so when the market demand increases, the market price increases as well, which means that the firm takes this new, higher price (*Principles of Economics* 5th ed. page 305/6th ed. page 294).

10. **D.** Competitive markets are characterized by: many buyers/sellers, identical products, firms are price takers, and it is easy to enter/exit the market in the long run (*Principles of Economics* 5th ed. pages 290–292/6th ed. pages 280–282).

11. **D.** A normal profit covers the opportunity cost for the supplier to remain in the competitive market. Without a normal profit, suppliers would not stay in the market in the long run (*Principles of Economics* 5th ed. pages 302–305/6th ed. pages 292 –293).

12. **B.** Make sure that you know how to graph the side-by-side graphs of a competitive market/firm. The market faces a downward sloping demand curve while the firm faces a perfectly elastic demand curve since it is a price-taker (*Principles of Economics* 5th ed. pages 294–305/6th ed. pages 284–293).

13. **D.** The firm should increase its production because it is not producing where MR = MC. It can maximize its profit by producing more (*Principles of Economics* 5th ed. pages 292–294/6th ed. pages 282–284).

14. **C.** In the long run, firms can enter or exit a competitive market. This adjusts the market equilibrium price which is taken by the firms in a way so that, in the long run, there are zero economic profits but the firm does still earn a normal profit (*Principles of Economics* 5th ed. page 305/6th ed. page 294).

15. **E.** If a firm in a competitive market is losing money, it (and others in the same situation) will leave the market, decreasing market supply and driving up the equilibrium price (*Principles of Economics* 5th ed. pages 292–305/6th ed. pages 280–294).

FREE-RESPONSE QUESTIONS

1. (a) The technological improvement increases production capability, which will increase the market supply. The market price will increase and the quantity produced in the market will also increase. Refer to the graph in part (b) to see the graphical answer.

(b) Since the firm in a competitive industry is a price taker, it takes this new, lower price which means that the firm's price and output decrease. Refer to the following graph for parts (a) and (b):

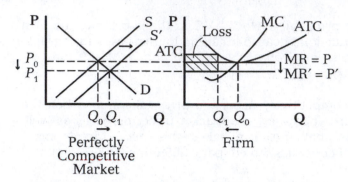

Perfectly
Competitive
Market

Firm

(c) Since the firm now incurs a loss, firms will exit the industry in the long run.

(*Principles of Economics* 5th ed. pages 297–305/6th ed. pages 288–295)

2. (a) The increase in demand shifts the market demand curve to the right. This increases the market price and output level. Since the firm is a price taker, it takes the new market price and produces at a higher output level because MR = MC at a higher quantity. The firm is making an economic profit in the short run, shown by the area (P – ATC) × Q.

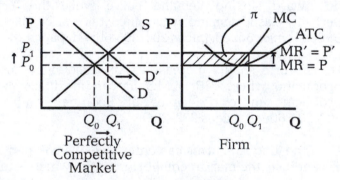

Perfectly
Competitive
Market

Firm

(b) Since firms have a profit in the short run, other firms will enter the market. This will increase the market supply and bring the market price back to its initial level, P_0. The firm takes this new lower market price, so $P_2 = P_0$ and its output level declines as well, returning to its original level Q_0 ($Q_0 = Q_2$) since MR = MC at a lower quantity. The firm loses its economic profit in the long run, but each firm has a normal profit.

The top set of graphs shows the LR adjustment process
while the bottom set of graphs shows the new LR equilibrium.

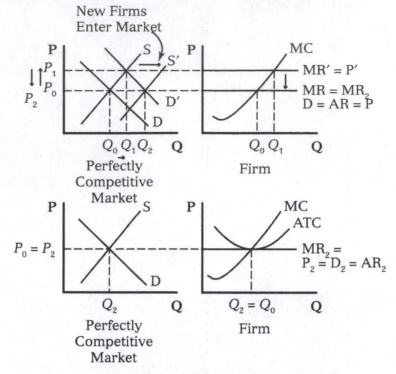

(*Principles of Economics* 5th ed. pages 297–305/6th ed. pages 288–295)

5

FIRMS IN IMPERFECTLY COMPETITIVE MARKETS

Most firms exist in markets that are not perfectly competitive. If you think about the characteristics of a perfectly competitive market (identical products, easy entrance/exit, numerous buyers/sellers), it should make sense that rarely would we have a market that sells identical products, for example. In this chapter, we will devote our time to the study of firms in imperfectly competitive markets: the monopoly, oligopoly, and monopolistically competitive firm. Before reading this chapter, please make sure that you have read Chapter 4 because the content here builds on our discussion from the last chapter.

THE CHARACTERISTICS OF A MONOPOLY
(*Principles of Economics* 5th ed. pages 312–314/6th ed. pages 300–301)

A **monopoly** is a *firm that is the sole seller of a product without close substitutes*. The monopolist becomes the only seller in its market because there are factors barring the entry of other firms into the market. These barriers to entry form due to three main reasons: (1) when a firm owns (and is the sole owner of) a key resource required for production, (2) when the government gives firm the exclusive right to produce a good or service (e.g., a patent), and (3) when a firm has economies of scale—where the firm can produce output at a lower cost than other firms, therefore prohibiting new firms from entering the market.

Since the monopolist is the sole seller in the market, it can set its own price (it is a price maker or price seeker), although they cannot charge a price higher than the demand curve (this is because people will not buy the good/service sold if the price exceeds the demand curve). In the next section, we will compare the characteristics and behavior of a monopoly to a perfectly competitive firm.

145

AP Tip

The characteristics of monopoly are: **S**ingle seller, **P**rice-maker, **U**nique product, and **D**ifficult entry into the market, or **S-P-U-D**. Again, feel free to use this or come up with your own pneumonic, but you must know the characteristics of the monopoly for the AP Microeconomics exam since it helps you to understand how the firm will behave.

THE MONOPOLIST'S PROFIT MAXIMIZATION DECISION

(*Principles of Economics* 5th ed. pages 315–322/6th ed. pages 303–310)

Similar to the perfectly competitive firm, the monopolist will choose a price and output quantity that will maximize its profit. If you recall our discussion from the previous chapter, the profit maximizing output is always determined by where marginal revenue (MR) = marginal cost (MC), even for a monopolist. The difference is that, since the monopolist is the sole seller in this market, the monopolist will charge a higher price than the competitive firm. Let's use an example to continue our discussion. Suppose that we live in a remote town where you are the only water supplier. The following table shows the price that buyers in the market are willing to pay for each gallon of water. Note that total revenue (TR) is maximized (MR is zero) at 6 gallons.

Quantity of Water (Q)	Price (P)	Total Revenue (TR = P × Q)	Average Revenue (AR = TR/Q)	Marginal Revenue (MR = ΔTR/ΔQ)
0 gallons	$11	$ 0	—	
				$10
1	10	10	$10	
				8
2	9	18	9	
				6
3	8	24	8	
				4
4	7	28	7	
				2
5	6	30	6	
				0
6	5	30	5	
				−2
7	4	28	4	
				−4
8	3	24	3	

If we plot the price and marginal revenue data from this table, it would look like this:

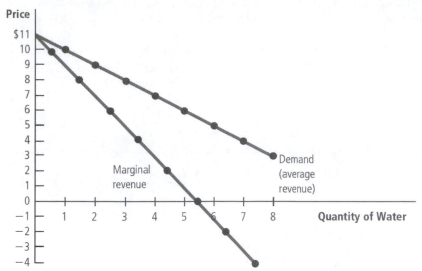

Note that the profit-maximizing monopolist will never choose a quantity corresponding to the inelastic portion of the D curve because MR < 0 and will not intersect MC in the inelastic portion. (This was a previous AP question, so something you should know.) Recall that the demand curve for a perfectly competitive firm is perfectly elastic because it is a price-taker. (The competitive firm's demand curve is equal to its marginal revenue curve, which is also perfectly elastic.) In contrast, the monopolist faces a downward sloping demand curve because it is the sole seller in the market and can charge any price along the market demand curve.

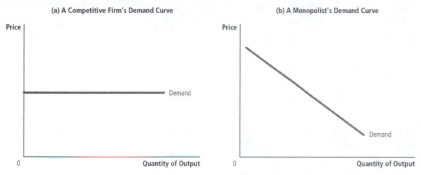

One thing to pay particular attention to is that the monopolist's MR curve is steeper than the market demand curve. Why is this? If you look at the data in the table again, you will see that marginal revenue falls at a faster rate than the demand curve. The reason for this is that, although the monopolist is the sole seller in the market, it cannot sell its good/service at different prices to different buyers. Looking back at the graph on page 2, you will see that, in order to sell one gallon of water, the monopolist can only charge $10 (corresponds with the market demand curve), but if the monopolist wants to sell 2 gallons of water, it must charge $9. Even though there is one buyer who is willing to pay $10 for water, the monopolist _must lower its price on **all units sold**_ and charge $9 to all buyers in order to sell more water. Because the price on _all_ units sold must fall if the monopolist wants to increase production, the monopolist's marginal revenue is always *less* than its price. Additionally, refer back to the graph and note that the MR curve becomes negative. At this point, as prices are lowered to sell more, it will decrease the TR. The demand curve becomes inelastic at this point.

How then, does a monopolist determine its profit maximizing output and price? A monopolist chooses its production level based on MR = MC and charges the highest market price. Refer to the following graph for a graphical explanation.

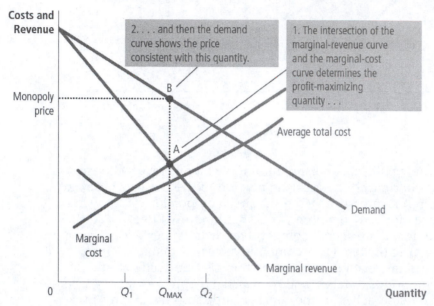

Note that the monopolist charges a price higher than a competitive firm. A competitive firm charges a price that is equal to marginal revenue and marginal cost whereas a monopolist charges a price that is *greater* than its marginal revenue and marginal costs. That is:

$$\text{Competitive firms } P = MR = MC$$

$$\text{Monopoly } P > MR = MC$$

Since the monopolist can charge a higher price, the monopolist's profit potential is larger than a competitive firm. Recall that profit is total revenue minus total costs (Profit = TR − TC), or Profit = (P − ATC) × Q. The following side by side graphs illustrate the profit for a competitive firm and a monopoly. Study the differences between the two.

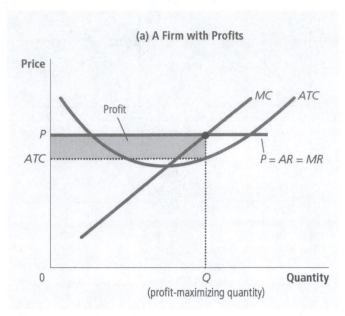

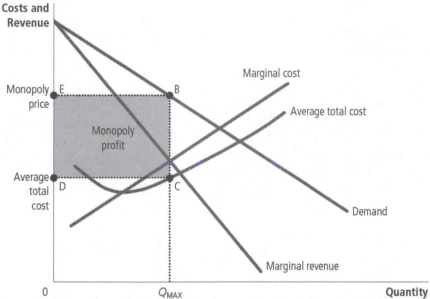

Despite a larger profit, a monopoly may not be the best way to organize a market because there are significant welfare losses to society. Recall our discussion of consumer and producer surplus from Chapter 3. In a competitive market, both consumer and producer surplus are maximized because the firm takes the market price. The competitive market is allocatively efficient. In a monopoly, there is market **deadweight loss**, *the fall in total surplus that results from a market distortion,* such as a higher monopoly price or lower quantity of output produced. The following side by side graphs compare the welfare differences between a competitive market and monopoly.

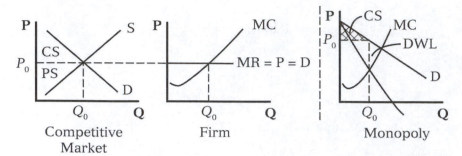

CS = Consumer Surplus
PS = ProducerSurplus
DWL = Deadweight Loss

Note that, in the monopolist graph, a portion of the consumer surplus has been taken by the monopolist as a part of its profit, and there is deadweight loss because the monopolist is not producing at the efficient, socially desirable output level. This next graph illustrates both the competitive market and the monopolist's price and output levels. It is important for you to understand that the competitive firm produces at a socially optimal, efficient level of output and price, whereas the monopolist produces too little and at too high of a price, resulting in a deadweight loss.

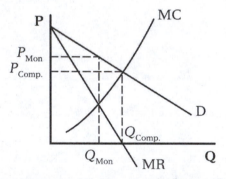

AP Tip

You must know the differences between a monopolist and the competitive firm and market for the AP Microeconomics exam. Study these graphs carefully so that you can clearly identify the differences between each market. For example, both competitive firms and a monopoly will choose an output where MR = MC, but the competitive firm faces a perfectly elastic MR curve whereas the competitive firm faces a downward sloping MR curve.

THE DIFFERENT TYPES OF MONOPOLIES

(*Principles of Economics* 5th ed. pages 321–322, 326–337/6th ed. pages 309–310, 314–323)

Up until this point, we have assumed that the monopoly exists only as a single-price monopolist. For the purposes of the AP Microeconomics exam, the single-price monopolist is the main monopolistic market form that you should know. However, there are price-discriminating monopolies, constant cost monopolies, and natural monopolies as well. Recall that a single-price monopolist faces a downward sloping demand curve and an even steeper marginal revenue curve because it must lower its price on all units sold in order to sell more output.

What happens if a monopolist could actually sell its output at different prices to different buyers? A monopolist who can charge different prices to different buyers engages in **price discrimination**, *the business practice of selling the same good at different prices to different customers.* Keep in mind that, in order to sell a good at different prices to different customers, the monopolist must be able to separate each market so that the customers are not upset at having to pay a different price for the same service. Some specific examples of price discrimination include: movie tickets that are priced differently at different times of day or for different customer groups (e.g., student verus senior citizens), airline tickets priced differently depending on the day of travel, and discount coupons (not all customers pay the discounted price). If a monopolist is a perfect price discriminator, meaning that the firm can successfully separate its customer base so that it can charge every single price along the market demand curve, the monopolist's profit will look like this:

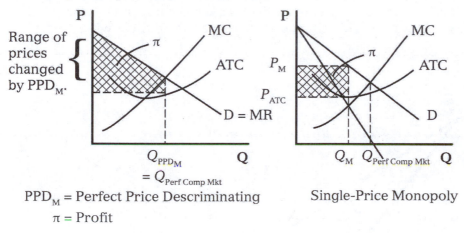

PPD$_M$ = Perfect Price Descriminating

π = Profit

Single-Price Monopoly

Note that, for the perfectly price discriminating monopolist, the *demand is equal to the marginal revenue*. This is because the monopolist charges different prices for different customers, so the marginal revenue from each additional unit sold is equal to price corresponding to the market demand curve. Compared with a single-price monopolist (the right graph above), it is clear that the perfectly price discriminating monopolist has greater profit and does not experience the welfare loss since the firm sells at an efficient quantity. (The perfect price discriminating monopoly produces at the efficient, competitive market level.)

A second variation to our monopoly firm is the **constant cost monopoly**, *a monopoly where the marginal cost is perfectly elastic because there are no diminishing marginal returns.* An example of a constant cost monopoly is a firm with a drug patent. The marginal cost for the production of each additional pill is roughly the same. During the life of the patent, the constant cost monopolist acts in the same way as a single-price monopolist, except that its graph looks like this:

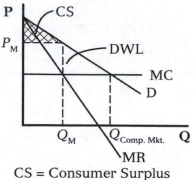

CS = Consumer Surplus

DWL = Deadweight Loss

The firm produces at the output where MR = MC and charges a price that corresponds to this point along the market demand curve. The constant cost monopolist, just like the single-price monopolist, experiences deadweight loss as well. Once the monopoly's patent expires, however, new firms can enter the market, so the price falls and the constant cost monopolist ends up producing at a price and quantity that is the same as a competitive market because they no longer have a monopoly. This change is illustrated in the following graph.

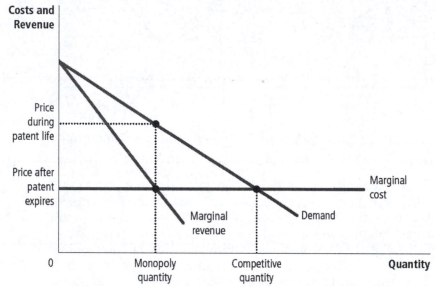

One final monopoly variation you should be familiar with is the **natural monopoly**, *a monopoly that arises because a single firm can supply a good or service to an entire market at smaller cost than could two or more firms*; in other words, the natural monopolist experiences an economies of scale advantage. Your local water company is a good example of a natural monopoly. Since a natural monopoly has this significant cost advantage, the firm's cost curves are more elastic. The following graph compares the natural monopoly to a single-price monopoly.

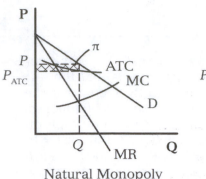

Natural Monopoly

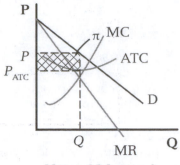

Natural Monopoly

Recall that a firm's LRATC curve is elastic in comparison to the SRATC, especially in the economies of scale region. The natural monopolist's ATC curve is more elastic for this reason. It will still eventually intersect the MC curve at its minimum point, but at a much higher output level. Both monopolies, the natural and single-price monopoly, earn a profit but create deadweight loss.

Government regulators may choose to correct the welfare losses created by monopolies. They may require a natural monopoly to charge a **fair return price**, *a price equal to its average total cost (and where the economic profit is zero)*, or a **socially optimal price**, *a price equal to its marginal cost*. The problem with regulating a monopolist in this way is that the monopolist loses money, which means that the government may need to subsidize the monopolist in order for the firm to continue producing the good/service. Refer to the following graph to see the impact of government regulation on a natural monopoly.

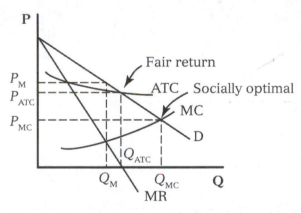

Q_{ATC} = Fair return quantity
Q_{MC} = Socially optimal quantity

AP Tip

When taking the AP exam, always assume that the monopoly in each question is a single-price monopolist *unless otherwise noted*. While the exam will test you on these other monopolistic forms (price discriminating and natural monopolies), assume that the exam is asking you about a single price monopolist unless the question explicitly states that it is an alternative type of monopoly.

Oligopoly

(*Principles of Economics*, 5th ed. pages 365–376/6th ed. pages 349–359)

An **oligopoly** is *a market structure in which only a few sellers offer similar or identical products*. The key to an oligopoly is that the few sellers may cooperate in order to produce the quantity and charge the price of a monopolist. The graph for successfully colluding oligopolists looks just like that of a single-price monopoly (refer to the graph on page 147). The challenge for firms in an oligopoly is that, in order to reach a monopoly outcome, firms *must work together and trust each other*. There is tension between cooperation and self-interest because on the one hand, if one firm lowers its prices a little, its revenues may increase a little, but if the oligopolist works with the other firms and charges the higher monopoly price, <u>all</u> of the firms within the oligopoly are better off. The Prisoners' Dilemma is a game that illustrates the difficulty of cooperation. Refer to the following table as we continue our discussion:

	Jack's Decision	
	High production: 40 Gallons	**Low production: 30 Gallons**
High production: 40 Gallons **Jill's Decision**	Jack gets $1,600 profit Jill gets $1,600 profit	Jack gets $1,500 profit Jill gets $2,000 profit
Low production: 30 Gallons	Jack gets $2,000 profit Jill gets $1,500 profit	Jack gets $1,800 profit Jill gets $1,800 profit

Suppose that Jack and Jill both own a well that produce safe drinking water. They each need to decide how many gallons of water to pump and sell. Jack and Jill have two production options—high production of 40 gallons, or low production of 30 gallons. If Jill produces 40 gallons and Jack also produces 40 gallons, they each make a profit of $1600. If Jill produces 40 gallons while Jack produces 30 gallons, Jill earns a $2000 profit while Jack earns a $1500 profit. However, if Jill produces 30 gallons and Jack produces 30 gallons, they each make a profit of $1800. If Jack and Jill would both agree to produce 30 gallons of water, they would be better off. Why, then, would Jack or Jill want to cheat and produce more? Suppose that Jack and Jill are producing 30 gallons each. Jill sees that, if she increases her production to 40 gallons while Jack continues to produce at the agreed-upon quantity of 30 gallons, her profit will increase to $2000 while Jack makes $1500. Jack may think along the same lines, so what ends up happening is that both Jack and Jill end up with high production levels (40 gallons each) and lower profit ($1600 versus $1800 if they had both cooperated).

The reason why it is difficult for firms in an oligopoly to cooperate is because there is a strong incentive for each firm to "play" its

dominant strategy, *a strategy that is best for a player in a game regardless of the strategies chosen by the other players.* In this example, the dominant strategy is to produce 40 gallons. Since both firms "play" their dominant strategy, each firm ends up making less money than if they had cooperated and produced at lower production levels. This resulting behavior is the **Nash equilibrium**, *a situation in which economic actors interacting with one another each choose* their best strategy given the strategies that all the other actors have chosen. In our example, when Jill chose to increase production to 40 gallons, Jack's best choice was to also increase his production to 40 gallons.

AP Tips

The characteristics of oligopolistic firms are: Co-operation, **A** few firms, **P**rice-makers, and (very) **S**imilar (if not identical) products, or **C-A-P-S**. Again, feel free to use this or come up with your own pneumonic. Remember, it is important for you to be able to distinguish between the different types of markets!

Recent AP Microeconomics free response questions have been on the Prisoners' Dilemma, so it is a good idea for you to know how to read the different strategies and identify both the Nash equilibrium (if applicable) and dominant strategy.

MONOPOLISTIC COMPETITION
(*Principles of Economics* 5th ed. pages 345–355/6th ed. pages 329–338)

A monopolistically competitive firm is a bit of a cross between a competitive firm and a monopoly. **Monopolistic competition** is *a market structure in which many firms sell products that are similar but not identical.* The monopolistically competitive firm is similar to a monopoly in that it creates barriers to entry through advertisement, but it is similar to a competitive market in that there are many buyers and sellers and it is relatively easy to enter/exit the market.

Because the monopolistically competitive firm has some monopoly power but at the same time has many buyers and sellers, the firm faces a relatively elastic demand curve. The following graph illustrates three side-by-side graphs of a competitive, monopolistically competitive and monopolistic firm in the short run.

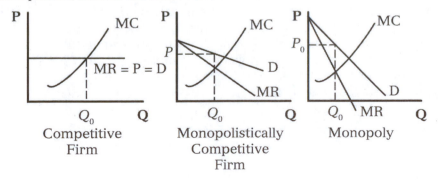

© 2012 Cengage Learning. All Rights Reserved. May not be scanned, copied or duplicated, or posted to a publicly accessible website, in whole or in part.

The competitive firm is a price taker and therefore faces a perfectly elastic demand. The monopoly is a price maker and therefore charges a price according to the downward sloping market demand curve. The monopolistically competitive firm faces a downward sloping demand curve that is less elastic than the monopoly but more inelastic than the competitive firm because it has some monopoly tendencies because of its reliance on advertisements as a means to carve out a consumer niche for its product. In the short run, the monopolistically competitive firm can earn a profit or incur a loss. The following graphs are for both situations. Note that, similar to a monopolist, the monopolistically competitive firm creates some welfare loss (there is deadweight loss and decreased consumer surplus).

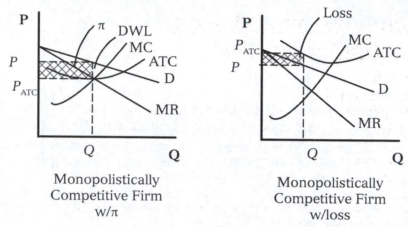

Monopolistically
Competitive Firm
w/π

Monopolistically
Competitive Firm
w/loss

In the long run, the monopolistically competitive firm earns zero economic profit, just as in the competitive firm's case, because new firms can enter and exit the market. The following graphs illustrate the long-run adjustment for a monopolistically competitive firm.

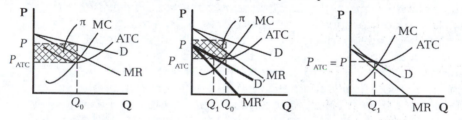

SR π → Firms Enter Market → Demand ↓ → LR:0 Economic Profit

Note that the monopolistically competitive firm begins with a profit in the short run. In the long run, new firms can enter the market. This decreases the demand for the existing firm's product. The demand continues to fall until the demand curve is tangent to the average total cost curve. In the long run, the monopolistically competitive firm's price is equal to its average total cost, and therefore, the firm earns a zero economic profit, but normal profit.

AP Tips

The characteristics of monopolistically competitive firms are: **S**imilar products, **E**asy entrance/exit to the market, **A**dvertisements to give it monopoly-like power, and **M**any buyers and sellers, or **S-E-A-M**. Again, feel free to use this or come up with your own pneumonic.

For all four firms (competitive, monopoly, oligopoly, and monopolistically competitive), be able to identify how a firm determines its price, output, and profit.

FIRMS IN IMPERFECTLY COMPETITIVE MARKETS: STUDENT OBJECTIVES FOR THE AP EXAM

You should be able to:
- Define all key terms in bold
- Graph: single-price monopoly, price discriminating monopoly, natural monopoly, constant cost monopoly, monopolistically competitive firm in the short and long run
- Explain how government may regulate a monopoly
- Analyze a prisoners' dilemma payoff matrix and dominant strategy
- Determine and graphically illustrate the long run outcome for a monopolistically competitive firm
- Clearly distinguish between the different market structures (competitive, monopoly, monopolistically competitive, and oligopoly) in the short and long run, under conditions of profit and loss

MULTIPLE-CHOICE QUESTIONS

1. Which of the following statements is true for a monopolist at the profit-maximizing level of output?
   (A) Price exceeds marginal revenue.
   (B) Marginal cost exceeds price.
   (C) Demand is price inelastic.
   (D) Price equals marginal cost, which equals average total cost.
   (E) The demand curve intersects the supply curve.

2. If a perfectly competitive market were monopolized without any changes to its cost conditions, the price and quantity produced would change in which of the following ways?

Price	Quantity
(A) Increase	Increase
(B) Increase	Decrease
(C) Increase	May increase or decrease
(D) Decrease	Increase
(E) Decrease	Decrease

Use the following graph to answer Questions 3–4:

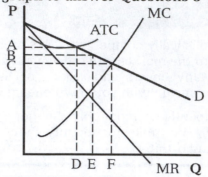

3. If the government were to regulate the monopolist (in the graph above) in order to achieve allocative efficiency, the socially optimal regulated price would be
   (A) A.
   (B) B.
   (C) C.
   (D) D.
   (E) E.

4. If the government were to regulate the monopolist in the diagram above at the fair return price, it would be at
   (A) A.
   (B) B.
   (C) C.
   (D) D.
   (E) F.

5. What happens to a monopolist's price, profits, and output if only its fixed costs decrease?

	Price	Profit	Output
(A)	No change	Increase	No change
(B)	No change	Increase	Increase
(C)	Decrease	Decrease	Decrease
(D)	Increase	Increase	Increase
(E)	Decrease	No change	No change

Use the following diagram to answer Question 6:

	Exxon's Decision	
	Drill Two Wells	**Drill One Well**
Drill Two Wells	Exxon gets $4 million profit Texaco gets $4 million profit	Exxon gets $3 million profit Texaco gets $6 million profit
Drill One Well	Exxon gets $6 million profit Texaco gets $3 million profit	Exxon gets $5 million profit Texaco gets $5 million profit

Texaco's Decision (row labels)

6. Based on the diagram with payoff information for two large oil companies, Exxon and Texaco, which of the following statements is true?
   (A) Exxon's best strategy would be to drill one well regardless of what Texaco does.
   (B) Exxon will definitely receive the highest profit if it drills two wells.
   (C) Exxon will receive the highest profit if it drills one well.
   (D) Exxon will receive the highest profit if it drills two wells, regardless of what Texaco does.
   (E) Exxon and Texaco will most likely both end up drilling two wells, according to Nash equilibrium.

7. Monopolistic competition is characterized by
   (A) one firm selling several products.
   (B) many firms selling the same product.
   (C) many firms selling slightly different products.
   (D) one firm selling one product.
   (E) a few large firms selling slightly different products.

8. In comparison to perfect competition, monopolistically competitive firms face
   (A) more elastic demand.
   (B) a vertical demand curve.
   (C) a horizontal demand curve.
   (D) perfectly inelastic demand.
   (E) less elastic demand.

9. Monopolistically competitive firms are inefficient because they
   (A) produce a lower level of output and sell at a higher price than do perfectly competitive firms.
   (B) use production processes that are more capital-intensive than do perfectly competitive firms.
   (C) face downward sloping demand curves, ensuring that marginal revenue is greater than marginal cost.
   (D) produce at that level of output where price equals marginal cost.
   (E) realize diseconomies of scale.

10. In the long run, a monopolistically competitive firm will make
    (A) more profit than a perfect competitor.
    (B) less profit than a perfect competitor.
    (C) more profit than a monopoly.
    (D) more profit than an oligopolist.
    (E) the same profit as a perfect competitor.

11. Which of the following barrier to entry would explain why a firm might have a natural monopoly?
    (A) Legal restrictions, such as patents or exclusive contracts
    (B) Control of a scarce resource, such as diamond mines
    (C) Predatory practices, such as lowering price below average total cost
    (D) Economies of scale due to large size
    (E) Large sunk costs necessary to compete with an existing firm

12. Which would definitely _not_ be an example of price discrimination?
    (A) A theater charges children less than adults for a movie.
    (B) Universities charge higher tuition for out-of-state residents than in-state residents.
    (C) School dances are more expensive for guests than for students who attend the school.
    (D) Tickets to a football game are more expensive than to a baseball game in the same stadium.
    (E) A cell phone company charges more for calls made on weekdays versus weekends.

13. To practice price discrimination, a monopolist must
    (A) be a natural monopoly
    (B) charge one price to all buyers.
    (C) permit the resale of the product by the original buyer.
    (D) be able to separate buyers into different markets with different price elasticities.
    (E) have a differentiated product.

14. Interdependence among firms is a characteristic primarily associated with
    (A) labor markets.
    (B) perfect competition.
    (C) monopolistic competition.
    (D) monopoly.
    (E) oligopoly.

15. Which of the following best explains why it is difficult to maintain lasting collusive agreements?
    (A) There is an unavoidable conflict in that a collusive agreement can increase the profits of some, but not all, firms in the industry.
    (B) There is little potential for gain from collusion unless there are a large number of consumers in the market.
    (C) Each firm in the industry views itself as facing a vertical demand curve, even though the market demand curve is downward sloping.
    (D) The firms in the industry have a common incentive to increase output to a more competitive level.
    (E) Each firm realizes that its profits would increase if it were the only firm to violate the collusive agreement by increasing its production slightly.

FREE-RESPONSE QUESTIONS

1. The Cleaning Company is a firm operating in the monopolistically competitive industry that produces a popular cleaning product. The company produces the profit-maximizing quantity of its cleaning product but is currently incurring a loss.
   (a) Draw a correctly labeled graph for The Cleaning Company and show
       (i) the profit-maximizing output and price
       (ii) the area of loss
   (b) Explain and show graphically what happens to The Cleaning Company's profit and output level in the long run.
   (c) If the company continues to produce its cleaning product in the long run, will it produce at an allocatively efficient level of output? Explain.

2. Suppose that the government grants you a patent which gives you, the owner of a profit-maximizing firm, the exclusive right to produce a new prescription drug.
   (a) Assume that your company is making an economic profit. Using a correctly labeled graph, identify the following:
       (i) Profit-maximizing price
       (ii) Profit-maximizing quantity
       (iii) Area of economic profit
   (b) Now assume that the government tries to regulate your firm by requiring you to produce at a fair return price. Using the same graph as in part (a) above, identify the following:
       (i) The area of welfare loss incurred before government regulation
       (ii) The fair return price
   (c) What will happen to your firm's profit if the government does regulate your firm as in part (b) above?
   (d) Now assume that your firm's patent expires. What will happen to your long-run profit? Explain in words and use a graph to support your answer.

Answers

MULTIPLE-CHOICE QUESTIONS

1. **A.** Recall that a monopoly's P > MR = MC (*Principles of Economics* 5th ed. page 320/6th ed. page 307).

2. **B.** Price increases while quantity would decrease because the monopolist faces an MR curve that is steeper than its demand curve. This means that the profit maximizing output is less than the perfectly competitive firm because MR = MC at a lower quantity. The price is higher because the monopolist can charge the highest price determined by the demand curve (*Principles of Economics* 5th ed. pages 319–322/6th ed. pages 306–309).

3. **C.** The socially optimal price is where P = MC (*Principles of Economics* 5th ed. pages 333–337/6th ed. pages 321–323).

4. **A.** The fair return price is where P = ATC (*Principles of Economics* 5th ed. pages 280–282/6th ed. pages 321–323).

5. **A.** When fixed costs fall, average total costs fall. That is the only change. The profit-maximizing output is still determined by MR = MC, which doesn't change when fixed costs fall (*Principles of Economics* 5th ed. pages 319–322/6th ed. pages 306–309).

6. **E.** Both Exxon and Texaco have the highest combined profit potential if they cooperate and agree to drill one well each. However, if Exxon drills two wells, its profit potential increases (the same is true for Texaco). It is therefore difficult for both firms to cooperate and drill one well since there is an incentive for both firms to drill two wells. The result is that both firms will drill two wells, ending at the Nash equilibrium point where both firms drill two wells (*Principles of Economics* 5th ed. pages 370–378/6th ed. pages 355–361).

7. **C.** A monopolistically competitive firm has many sellers who sell slightly differentiated products (*Principles of Economics* 5th ed. page 346/6th ed. page 330).

8. **E.** Review the graphs for a monopolistically competitive firm (*Principles of Economics* 5th ed. pages 349–350/6th ed. pages 335–336).

9. **A.** A monopolistically competitive firm experiences welfare losses similar to a monopoly because it produces at a quantity lower than and sell at a price higher than a competitive firm (*Principles of Economics* 5th ed. page 349/6th ed. page 335).

10. **E.** Long-run economic profit for both a competitive and a monopolistically competitive firm are zero because new firms can enter and exit the market in the long run (*Principles of Economics* 5th ed. pages 348–350/6th ed. pages 334–336).

11. **D.** This is the definition of a natural monopoly (*Principles of Economics* 5th ed. pages 335–336/6th ed. pages 319–322).

12. **D.** Price discrimination is when a firm charges a different price to different customers for *the same product or service*. A football game is not the same as a baseball game (*Principles of Economics* 5th ed. pages 326–332/6th ed. pages 314–318).

13. **D.** In order to charge different prices, the firm must be able to separate its customer base in a way that will still encourage buyers to buy the good/service. This is especially true since the good/service sold is identical (*Principles of Economics* 5th ed. pages 326–331/6th ed. pages 314–318).

14. **E.** Firms in an oligopoly can act as a monopoly <u>as long as</u> they work together to keep production low (*Principles of Economics* 5th ed. pages 366–372/6th ed. pages 350–356).

15. **E.** Refer to the Prisoners' Dilemma discussion in this chapter. Each firm can choose to cooperate and keep production low, which maximizes overall profit for <u>all</u> firms within the oligopoly or increase production slightly, which increases profit for itself in comparison to the other firms (*Principles of Economics* 5th ed. pages 370–376/6th ed. pages 355–361).

FREE-RESPONSE QUESTIONS

1. (a)

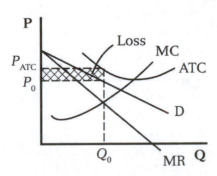

The Cleaning Co.
This graph shows the profit-maximizing output where MR = MC and the price corresponding to this point along the downward sloping demand curve. The area of economic loss is calculated by taking the P_{ATC} at the profit maximizing quantity and subtracting the $P_{profit\ max}$ (P_0) and multiplying it by the profit-maximizing quantity, Q_0.

(b)

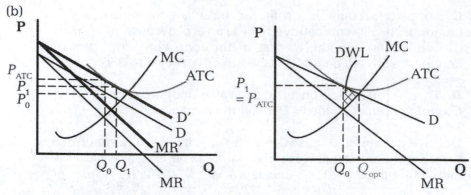

The Cleaning Co.

In the long run, firms will leave the industry since they are losing money. This means that there are fewer firms left in the market, so the demand for The Cleaning Company's product increases. When the demand increases, marginal revenue increases as well. This increases the profit-maximizing output to Q_1 and the price to P_1. In the long run, the firm does not earn an economic profit, but does earn a normal profit, $P_1 = P_{ATC}$. Refer to the second graph to see the long-run equilibrium.

(c) No, in the long run the monopolistically competitive firm does not produce at the socially optimal level of output. There is deadweight loss. The profit-maximizing quantity is less than the socially optimal quantity. Refer to the graph in part (b) to see the welfare loss.

(*Principles of Economics* 5th ed. pages 348–354/6th ed. pages 329–337)

2. (a)

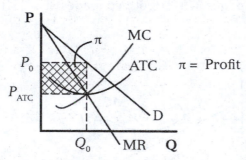

Your Monopoly

Profit-maximizing quantity is where MR = MC and the price is determined by the point on the demand curve corresponding to this profit-maximizing quantity. The profit is calculated by taking P_0 and subtracting P_{ATC} and multiplying it by the profit maximizing output, Q_0.

(b)

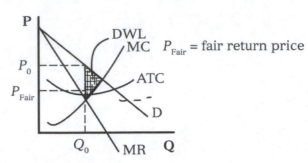

The fair return price is P = ATC. The welfare loss is shown in the graph as deadweight loss. The fair return price is identified on the graph where P_{F-R} = ATC.

(c) Your firm will no longer earn an economic profit if the government regulates as in part (b).

(d)

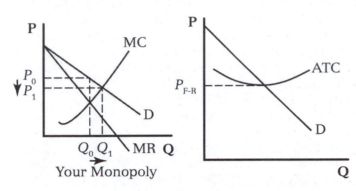

Your Monopoly

If your firm's patent expires, there will be more competitors in the market, which means that you will have to lower your price from P_0 to P_1 and increase your output from Q_0 to Q_1 in order to remain competitive. You will end up producing at the competitive market's price and quantity, which is also an efficient level of output.

(*Principles of Economics* 5th ed. pages 312–334/6th ed. pages 300–322)

6

THE MARKET FOR RESOURCES

Up until this point, we have primarily discussed product markets, the markets in which we sell goods/services. However, if you recall our circular flow model from Chapter 1, firms also need to buy resources in order to produce the goods/services purchased by households. In this chapter, we will focus on the resource market—the buying and selling of the factors of production.

THE RESOURCE MARKET
(Principles of Economics 5th ed. pages 391–407/6th ed. pages 375–389)

Recall that the factors of production are the inputs used by firms to produce goods and services that are sold in the market. Land, labor, and capital are the three most important factors of production, although entrepreneurial ability is an important one as well. In our discussion of resource markets, we will focus on the labor market because it is a bit different from the market for land and capital (although we will address both at the end of the chapter as well).

The demand for labor is different from demand in the product market. The demand for labor is a **derived demand**, meaning that *it is dependent upon the product market demand*. It is very important for you to remember that, in the circular flow of the economy, there are two markets: the **product market**, *where businesses supply* goods and services to households, who demand the goods and resources produced by businesses, and the resource market, where households supply their resources (mostly labor, but land and capital as well) in order to help businesses to produce the goods and services sold in the product market and businesses demand the resources provided by households. Suppose that a firm produces cookies in a competitive labor market. The cookie producing firm needs to decide how many workers to hire and what wage to pay. In order to determine how many workers to hire and what to pay, the firm looks to the cookie *product market*—if there is a steadily increasing demand for cookies by cookie consumers, it is more likely that the cookie firm will hire more laborers to work in its kitchen since there is demand for cookies. This illustrates the point that labor market demand is derived from demand in the product market. The resource market graph looks very similar to a product market graph, but remember, a key difference is that in the resource market, businesses demand the resources (such as labor) provided by households. Refer to the following graph to see the market graph for workers in the cookie industry. Note that, instead of price on the y-axis and quantity on the x-axis, wages are on the y-axis because wages are the price/cost of labor and quantity of laborers is on the x-axis. The equilibrium wage rate is determined by the demand for and supply of laborers in the market.

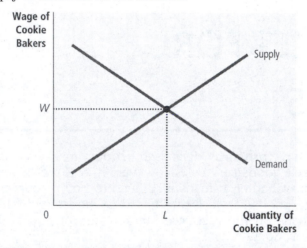

AP Tip

Students often mislabel their resource market graphs. Remember that the cost of the resource goes on the y-axis while the quantity of the resource goes on the x-axis. It is very important to label your graphs accurately for the AP Microeconomics exam. Always check your textbook for the correct labeling of graphs. No labels = No points.

We assume, for now, that this particular cookie producing firm exists in a competitive resource market—that is, there are many other cookie producing firms looking to hire cookie laborers in the industry. Similar to the competitive product market, this means that cookie-producing firms in this resource market must take the resource market wage rate. Firms' demand for labor depends on how productive its workers are in comparison to the revenue that the firm receives from the sale of cookies, so the firm will look at the marginal product of labor and the product price in order to determine its labor demand. Recall from our discussion in Chapter 4 that the marginal product is the additional product produced with the hiring of one more worker. The demand for labor is also known as its **marginal revenue product**

(MRP),[1] *the extra revenue that each additional laborer adds to total revenue.*

The MRP = Marginal product of labor × Price of the product
$$= MP_L \times P$$

Marginal revenue product is also known as the "value of the marginal product."

The MRP, or the demand for labor, is downward sloping and shifts when: (1) there is a change in the price of the product (the output price), (2) there is technological improvement, and (3) there is a change in the supply of other factors. Since the MRP is determined by the MP_L and product price, which is also the market value of the output produced by that labor, holding all else constant, when the output price changes, the MRP changes as well—that is, when P increases, MRP should also increase and vice versa. A technological improvement can either increase or decrease MRP. Technological improvement can improve the marginal productivity of labor, but if the technological improvement acts as a substitute for labor, then the marginal productivity of labor will decline. This means that, in the case of a technological improvement, you need to read the AP question carefully in order to determine whether the technology *helps* labor productivity or *hurts* labor productivity by taking over the work of laborers. The supply of other factors may also affect the demand for labor because it can limit how many workers you can hire. For example, if there is a decrease in the number of ovens available to bake chocolate chip cookies, you will not be able to hire as many bakers for your chocolate chip cookie business.

The supply of labor is an upward sloping curve and shifts when: (1) there is a change in work preferences, (2) there is an increase/decrease in the availability of alternative revenue-generating opportunities, and (3) there is a change in the number of people looking for work. More women may prefer to work in comparison to 50 years ago, which reflects a change in attitudes/preferences regarding work. When there are many other job alternatives, there will be a decrease in the supply of labor available for a specific resource market. Immigration usually leads to an increase in the labor supply because there are more people looking for work within specific markets. These are all examples of how the supply of labor can shift.

In order to determine the market equilibrium wage rate, let's take a quick look at how labor demand and labor supply work together using our cookie business example. Holding all else constant, suppose that there is a large immigration increase. This leads to an increase in the supply of workers looking for work as cookie bakers, but the demand for workers remains constant. The market wage rate falls and the number of cookie bakers employed increases. Refer to the graph below to see the result on the equilibrium wage rate.

---

[1]Note that in the *Principles* text, Mankiw refers to the MRP as the *value of marginal product*. This is the same as the MRP. The AP exam uses *marginal revenue product*.

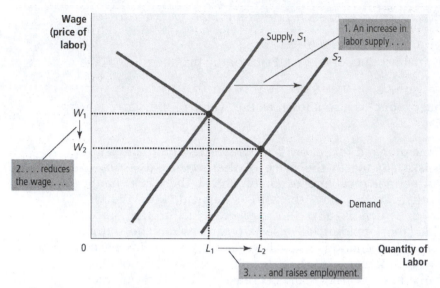

Suppose, instead that the price of cookies has increased, holding all else constant. Since the demand for labor is a derived demand (dependent on the product market), the demand for labor (or the MRP) increases. The supply of labor remains unchanged, the wage rate increases, and the quantity of cookie bakers hired in the market increases. Refer to the following graph to see the result on the market.

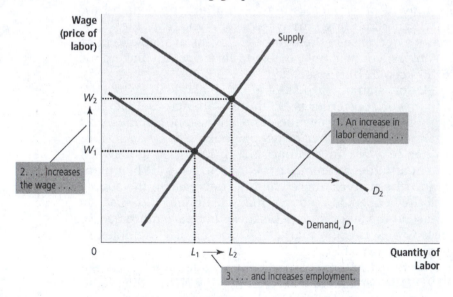

FIRMS IN THE RESOURCE MARKET

(*Principles of Economics* 5th ed. pages 395–398/6th ed. pages 377–389)

Similar to the competitive product market, the competitive resource market also consists of many buyers and sellers. The key difference is that the firms are buying resources, such as labor, instead of output. Firms within a competitive resource market are wage-takers, meaning that since there are so many firms in the market, no single firm can influence the wages paid to workers and, therefore, each firm in the competitive resource market must *take* the market equilibrium wage rate. The wage rate (WR) is also the firm's **marginal resource (or**

factor) cost (MRC or MFC), *the extra cost associated with the hiring of an additional worker.* The firm in the resource market, your apple farm for example, will choose to hire the number of workers where the demand for labor is equal to the marginal resource cost of labor. In other words, you will hire where the **marginal revenue product (MRP) = marginal resource cost (MRC)**. All profit-maximizing resource firms want to hire where MRP = MRC because this maximizes their profit.

Note that this is very similar to the MR = MC rule in the competitive product market, but this is also very different, because we are talking about *resource* revenue and costs. Refer to the following graph to see side-by-side graphs of the resource market and the firm in equilibrium. You do not need to include all three labels on the y-axis. We have included these options to show what you may include, but any one of these options will do. Note that, where MRP = MRC, the resource firm maximizes its revenue per worker hired.

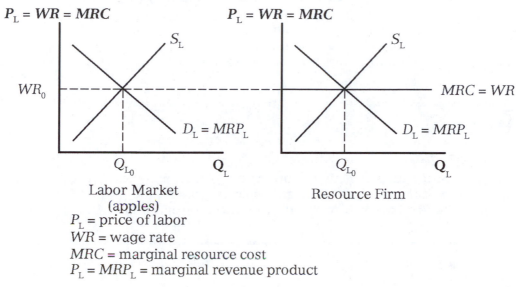

Labor Market
(apples)
P_L = price of labor
WR = wage rate
MRC = marginal resource cost
$P_L = MRP_L$ = marginal revenue product

Remember that a perfectly competitive resource market is similar to the perfectly competitive product market in that there are many buyers and sellers, it is easy to enter and exit, and it produces an identical product. The key difference is that, in the resource market, businesses are buying the resources sold by households and the labor skills offered are identical. The behavior of any firm that exists in this type of perfectly competitive resource market is therefore highly dependent upon the activities in the resource market. Suppose that we have a perfectly competitive resource market for unskilled labor. When the demand for unskilled labor increases in the resource market, the equilibrium wage rate paid for unskilled labor increases. Any firm hiring unskilled workers must take (or pay) the higher wage to its workers, thus decreasing the number of unskilled workers it hires. Refer to the following graph to see the changes in the wage rate and quantity of unskilled laborers hired.

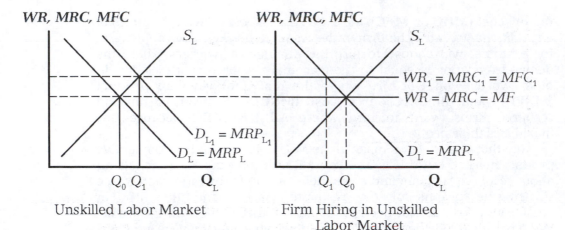

Unskilled Labor Market   Firm Hiring in Unskilled
                                        Labor Market

Please note that, when the market equilibrium wage rate increases, the firm's MRC will also increase. This is because the firm must take and pay the industry wage rate, which means that its marginal resource cost increases. Refer to the above side-by-side graphs to see the firm's response to a market wage rate change. The firm faces a higher MRC and therefore, hires fewer workers at this higher wage rate.

AP Tip

The AP Microeconomics exam emphasizes both the product market and the resource market. It is important for you to know how to graph side-by-side resource firm and market graphs and how a change in the product price may affect both the resource firm and the market.

MONOPSONY

(*Principles of Economics* 5th ed. page 406/6th ed. page 389)

Up until this point, we have built our analysis of labor markets on the assumption that they are competitive (that there are many buyers and sellers in the market so that each buyer or seller cannot effectively influence the wage rate). It is possible, especially in remote areas, that a single firm is the only source of employment. *A resource market in which there is a single buyer of labor* is called a **monopsony**. Similar to the monopoly in the product market, the monopsonist hires fewer workers than the competitive firm and pays a lower wage. The following graph illustrates the monopsony's resource maximizing decision:

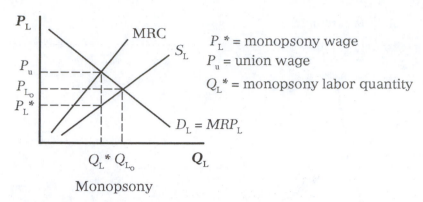

Monopsony

The marginal resource cost (MRC) is steeper than the labor supply curve because, in order to hire more workers, the monopsonist must increase wages for *all* workers. This rationale is very similar to why the marginal revenue (MR) curve is steeper than the demand curve for a monopoly. Since the monopsonist faces an upward sloping labor supply curve, the firm must offer a higher wage to hire an additional worker. The monopsonist cannot wage discriminate (offer different employees different wages for the same work), so in order to hire enough workers, the monopsonist must increase wages for all workers so that every worker is paid the same for the same work. This increases the marginal resource cost (MRC) and explains why it is steeper than the labor supply curve. The monopsonist, similar to the competitive resource firm, still hires where MRP = MRC. The difference is that, since the monopsonist is the sole *demander* of labor, it can pay a lower wage, P_L^*, and hire fewer workers, Q_L^*, than the competitive resource firm (who hires at P_{L0} and Q_{L0}). Unless there is a union to negotiate on behalf of the workers, the monopsonist will pay the lower wage. We have included a potential union wage, P_U, to illustrate the maximum wage a union might help to negotiate for workers in a monopsonist market.

AP Tip

While not generally on the AP Microeconomics exam, the monopsony did show up as a free-response question on the most recent exam, so it would be helpful for you to study the monopsony graph on page 173.

OTHER RESOURCES: LAND AND CAPITAL

(*Principles of Economics* 5th ed. pages 405–410/6th ed. pages 389–393)

Now that we understand how firms determine how much labor to hire and how much to pay its workers, we will move our discussion to other factors of production, land and capital. The markets for land and capital are very similar to the market for labor. The following is a graph of the market for land.

(a) The Market for Land

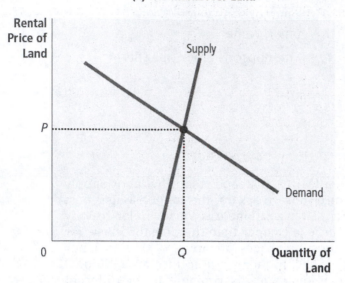

Note that the supply curve is very inelastic. This is because the quantity of land is limited. In some cases, the supply of land may even be perfectly inelastic. The price paid for the use of land is called **its rental price**. Recall our circular flow model in Chapter 1. Firms buy factors of production (land, labor, capital, and entrepreneurial ability) from households while households receive wages, interest, rent, and profit in return. Wages are paid in exchange for labor. Rent is paid in exchange for land. Interest is paid in exchange for capital. Profit is paid in exchange for entrepreneurial talent. The rest of the land market graph is familiar—a downward sloping demand curve and quantity of land on the x-axis.

The market for capital (recall that capital is the equipment or structures used to produce goods and services) is also very similar to the labor market. The following is a graph of the market for capital.

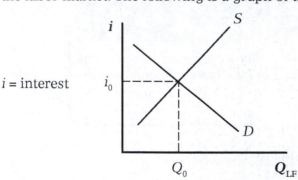

Market for loanable funds

The market for capital is determined by the interest rate in the loanable funds market, which is a macroeconomic concept that we discuss in the Macroeconomics section of this book. Since capital is usually very expensive, firms often need to borrow money in order to purchase the capital necessary for production. Note in the graph that interest, i, is on the y-axis, while the quantity of loanable funds, Q_{LF}, is on the x-axis. In both markets, the market for land and capital, the laws of supply and demand apply—any change to one of the supply or demand determinants will shift the curve and affect the equilibrium price and quantity.

What happens when a firm wants to use more than one resource? What if a firm wants to hire labor and use capital equipment in its production process? How does a firm decide what combination of resources will maximize profit? We know that, if a firm uses one resource, the profit maximizing rule is to hire where MRP = MRC. When a firm uses more than one input in its production process, it wants to hire a combination of inputs where costs are minimized. The **least cost rule** states that *a firm should hire a combination of resources so that the last dollar spent on each resource results in the same marginal product.* Stated another way:

$$\frac{\text{Marginal Product of Labor } (MP_L)}{\text{Price of Labor } (P_L)} = \frac{\text{Marginal Product of Capital } (MP_C)}{\text{Price of Capital } (P_C)}$$

A profit maximizing firm should hire multiple resources so that the marginal product of each resource per dollar spent on each resource are equal.

PUBLIC POLICY AND THE RESOURCE MARKET

(*Principles of Economics* 5th ed. pages 414–429/6th ed. pages 397–411)

The U.S. government does sometimes intervene in the resource market. For example, the government has implemented a policy that all employers must pay their employees a living, or minimum wage. A minimum wage works to increase wages in markets that have a low market equilibrium wage rate. A minimum wage is a price floor—it increases wages, but results in a surplus of laborers (unemployment). Refer to the following graph to see the result of a minimum wage policy on the market.

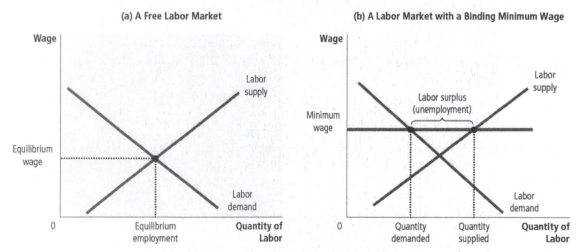

The graph on the left shows a labor market without government intervention. Suppose the government intervenes and sets a price floor, a minimum wage law, that increases the wage paid to all workers hired in the market. Note that the quantity of workers demanded at this higher, minimum wage rate decreases while the quantity of workers supplied is higher. The implementation of a minimum wage results in unemployment, which is marked by the difference between the quantity of labor supplied and the quantity of labor demanded.

AP Tip

Remember that, in the resource market, MRP = MRC. MRP stands for *marginal **revenue** product,* while MRC stands for *marginal **resource** cost.* Students often confuse these two. Make sure that you know the difference. Another way to remember the resource maximizing rule is this:

MRP = MRC = MFC (marginal *factor* cost)

THE MARKET FOR RESOURCES: STUDENT OBJECTIVES FOR THE AP EXAM

You should be able to:
- Define all key terms in bold
- Graph: side-by-side competitive resource market and firm, monopsony, and land and capital markets
- Analyze resource firms' hiring options

MULTIPLE-CHOICE QUESTIONS

1. The marginal resource cost (MRC) curve of a firm hiring resources in a competitive resource market
   (A) is always more elastic than the resource market supply curve.
   (B) is equal to the resource market supply curve.
   (C) lies below the resource market supply curve because the higher wage paid to an additional worker must also be paid to all other employees.
   (D) is unit elastic.
   (E) lies above the resource market supply curve because the higher wage paid to an additional worker must also be paid to all other employees.

2. The critical feature of a monopsonistic labor market is that the employer
   (A) faces an upward sloping labor supply curve.
   (B) faces a perfectly inelastic labor supply curve.
   (C) has a perfectly elastic demand curve for labor.
   (D) can hire any number of workers it chooses at the "going" wage rate.
   (E) must also be a monopolist in the product market.

3. Which of the following statements is not correct?
   (A) A firm hiring in a competitive resource market will hire where MRP = MRC.
   (B) A monoposony will hire where MR = MC.
   (C) A purely competitive seller will pay workers a wage rate equal to their MRP.
   (D) An imperfectly competitive seller will pay workers a wage rate equal to their MRP.
   (E) A union will bargain for wages above the equilibrium wage rate.

4. Resource market demand is a derived demand because
   (A) the firms hiring in the resource market take the market wage rate.
   (B) it is dependent upon the demand for output produced by the labor.
   (C) the equilibrium wage in the labor market is determined by the number of firms hiring in the resource market.
   (D) the labor supply curve for the firm is perfectly elastic.
   (E) the market labor supply curve is upward sloping.

5. Labor, capital, and natural resources are all examples of which of the following?
   (A) Public goods.
   (B) Inferior goods.
   (C) Factors of production.
   (D) Output.
   (E) Substitutes in production.

6. The market demand curve for labor (MRP_L) will shift to the right when
   (A) the number of firms increases.
   (B) the price of output decreases.
   (C) the labor supply curve shifts to the right.
   (D) the labor supply curve shifts to the left.
   (E) the marginal product of labor increases.

7. The relationship between the marginal revenue curve and the demand curve for a monopoly is most similar to the relationship between the marginal resource cost (MRC) curve and what curve for a monopsony?
   (A) Labor demand.
   (B) Labor supply.
   (C) Marginal external cost.
   (D) Total cost.
   (E) Marginal cost.

8. The value of the marginal revenue product (MRP) of labor always equals the marginal resource cost (MRC) of labor for which type of firm?
   (A) Perfectly competitive resource firm.
   (B) Monopolistically competitive firm.
   (C) Monopoly.
   (D) Perfectly competitive product firm.
   (E) Oligopoly.

(a) Given the production information above, respond to each of the following:
  (i) Draw a side-by-side market and firm graph showing your firm's demand and supply curve for workers.
  (ii) Explain how you will determine the number of workers to hire.
  (iii) Indicate how many workers you will hire on your graph drawn for part (i) above.
  (iv) In what type of resource market does your apple picking business operate? Explain.
(b) Assume that the government imposes a minimum daily wage in the apple market. The new minimum wage rate at which you can hire all the workers you want is now $120/day and the selling price of apples is now $6.
(c) Explain how your demand for workers will change graphically and with words. Please be sure to indicate how many workers you will hire and how many dozens of apples you will sell on your graph.

2. Assume that a small town firm is a monopsony.
  (a) Draw the monopsonist's labor market graph and show the following:
    (i) The number of workers hired by the monopsony
    (ii) The wage rate paid to workers hired by the monopsony
  (b) Using the same graph as in part (a), compare the monopsonist's wage and the number of workers hired to the wage and number of workers hired by the competitive resource market. Explain why there is a difference between the two markets.

Answers

MULTIPLE-CHOICE QUESTIONS

1. **A.** A firm hiring resources in a competitive resource market must take the market wage and therefore, its marginal resource cost (MRC) is going to be the same for every resource unit hired. The firm's MRC curve is perfectly elastic (*Principles of Economics* 5th ed. page 405/6th ed. page 389).

2. **A.** Without an upward sloping labor supply curve, the monopsonist would be able to hire a given number of workers at any wage rate (assuming that the only alternative to an upward sloping supply curve is that there is a perfectly inelastic supply curve). The upward sloping supply curve is the feature that makes the MRC curve steeper than the labor supply curve and determines the number of workers hired and the wages that they are paid in a monopsonistic market (*Principles of Economics* 5th ed. page 405/6th ed. page 389).

3. **B.** All firms hiring in resource markets maximize the use of their resources where MRP = MRC. This means that a

monopsony also hires where MRP = MRC. MR = MC is the profit maximizing production output in the product market, not the resource market (*Principles of Economics* 5th ed. page 405/6th ed. page 389).

4. **B.** The demand for resources depends on the output price, which is determined by product demand and supply (*Principles of Economics* 5th ed. pages 391–399/6th ed. pages 376–383).

5. **C.** Factors of production include: land, labor, capital, and entrepreneurial ability. These are also refered to as inputs or resources (*Principles of Economics* 5th ed. pages 391–392/6th ed. pages 375–376).

6. **E.** MRP = MP × P. When MP increases, MRP increases (*Principles of Economics* 5th ed. pages 395–398/6th ed. pages 380–382).

7. **B.** For the monopoly, the MR is steeper than the D-curve. For the monopsonist, the MRC is steeper than the labor supply curve (*Principles of Economics* 5th ed. page 405/6th ed. page 389).

8. **A.** Of the five options, "wage taking" is the only resource firm. The profit maximization rule in the resource market is where MRP = MRC. All of the other options are product firms, where MR = MC is the profit maximization rule (*Principles of Economics* 5th ed. pages 392–405/6th ed. pages 379–389).

9. **E.** All three statements are true. Firms in a competitive labor market hire where MRP = MRC, but they still face a downward sloping labor demand curve (MRP_L) and have a perfectly elastic MRC = MFC = WR curve since they are wage takers. The resource market demand is derived from the marginal product of the resource and the product price (*Principles of Economics* 5th ed. page 396/6th ed. page 380).

10. **B.** By hiring one waiter, the number of dinners served increases from 0 to 50. When the second waiter is hired, the number of dinners served increases from 50 to 75. Although still increasing, the second waiter's marginal product is 25 in comparison to the first waiter's marginal product of 50 (*Principles of Economics* 5th ed. pages 561–562/6th ed. pages 541–542).

11. **D.** The MP_L of the 5th waiter is 5 dinners. Multiply this by the product price of $5, the MRP_L of the 5th waiter is $25 (*Principles of Economics* 5th ed. pages 395–396/6th ed. pages 380–381).

12. **B.** The MP_L of the 4th waiter is 7 dinners. Multiply this by the dinner price of $5, the MRP = $35, which is also equal to the

MRC = $35 (*Principles of Economics* 5th ed. pages 395–396/6th ed. pages 380–381).

13. **B.** The firm should hire 3 waiters. The MP_L of the 3rd waiter is 22 dinners. The MRP of the 3rd waiter is $110 ($22 × $5). Although this is considerably higher than the MRC of $50, it is better than hiring 4 waiters, where the MRP_{4th} = $35. When MRP does not equal to MRC, you want to err on the side of a higher MRP than MRC, so that you don't lose money. Note that, with a minimum wage law, the restaurant hires fewer waiters, resulting in at least one waiter who is now unemployed (*Principles of Economics* 5th ed. pages 395–396/6th ed. pages 380–381).

14. **E.** This is the least cost rule. A profit maximizing firm should hire multiple resources so that the marginal product of each resource per dollar spent on each resource are equal (*Principles of Economics* 5th ed. pages 391–409/6th ed. pages 375–393).

15. **B.** An increase in the number of unskilled laborers will increase the supply of unskilled laborers in the unskilled labor market. This increase in supply will increase the number of unskilled laborers hired in the market and will lower the equilibrium wage rate paid to the workers who are hired (*Principles of Economics* 5th ed. pages 396–405/6th ed. pages 380–389).

FREE-RESPONSE QUESTIONS

1. The MRC = $75 and the output price = $5.
   Here is the MP_L for each worker hired:

Number of Workers	Dozens of Apples Picked	MP_L
3	60	
4	80	20
5	105	25
6	125	20
7	140	15
8	150	10

(a) Refer to the following graph.

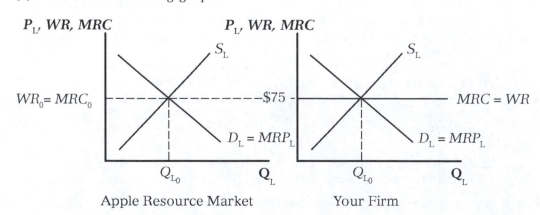

Apple Resource Market   Your Firm

You will determine the number of workers to hire where MRP = MRC. Since the 7th worker's marginal product is 15, you would hire 7 workers because the MRP = 15 × $5 = $75, which is equal to the MRC of $75. Your apple picking business is a firm in a competitive resource market. You should know this because your firm is always taking the market wage.

(b) The MRC is now $120 and the output price is $6. Since the output price has increased, the demand for labor also increases. You should now hire 12 workers, because the MRP$_{12th worker}$ = $120, which is equal to MRC of $120.

Notice again, that with a minimum wage, you hire fewer workers.

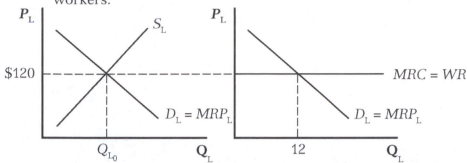

Apple Resource Market   Your Firm

(*Principles of Economics* 5th ed. pages 396–405/6th ed. pages 375–389)

2. (a) Refer to the following monopsony graph. The number of workers hired is determined by MRP = MRC and the wage paid is determined by the number hired and the labor supply curve. (The 2011 AP Microeconomics Form B exam asks a similar monopsony question that you can also refer to.)

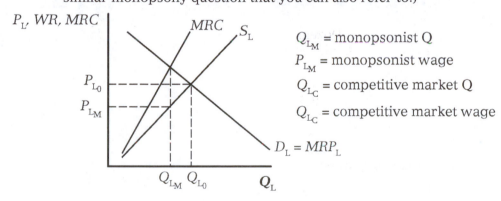

Q_{L_M} = monopsonist Q
P_{L_M} = monopsonist wage
Q_{L_C} = competitive market Q
Q_{L_C} = competitive market wage

Monopsony

(b) The monopsonist's wage is lower than a competitive firm's wage. The monopsonist hires fewer workers than a competitive firm. The monopsonist is the sole supplier of jobs and therefore, can pay a lower wage and hire fewer workers. (*Principles of Economics* 5th ed. page 405/6th ed. page 389)

7

MARKET FAILURES

Markets are a good way to organize economic activity; in fact, in most cases, they are the best way to allocate resources. They allow buyers and sellers to come together to exchange goods and services so that everyone can be better off. We have shown the conditions under which competitive markets are efficient, but the reality is that markets do not always produce an efficient outcome. In this chapter, we will discuss the instances where the market fails to produce an optimal outcome. Specifically, we will look at the market failure generated by negative and positive externalities, public goods, and common resources and at its potential solutions.

EXTERNALITIES

(*Principles of Economics* 5th ed. pages 203–209/6th ed. pages 195–202)

The market equilibrium price and quantity in competitive markets usually represents the most efficient allocation of the resource. In other words, market equilibrium is the point of allocative efficiency. There are times, however, when the market activity of a group of buyers and sellers inadvertently affects the well-being of a bystander and results in a less than optimal market outcome. An **externality**, *the uncompensated impact of one person's actions on the well-being of a bystander*, causes the market to produce a suboptimal outcome. *If the impact on the bystander is beneficial*, the market failure is called a **positive externality**. *If the impact on the bystander is harmful*, the market failure is called a **negative externality**.

Recall from our welfare discussion in Chapter 3 that, in competitive markets, the quantity produced and consumed at equilibrium is efficient in the sense that it maximizes consumer and producer surplus and enables all mutually beneficial trades. In other words, the market allocates its resources in a way that maximizes the total value to the consumers who buy the good or service minus the total costs to the producers who make and sell the good or service. Refer to the following graph to refresh your memory.

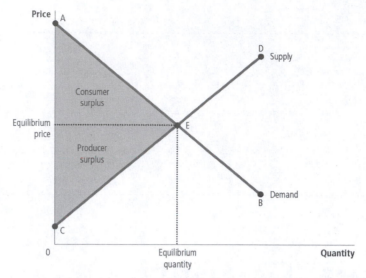

Let's use the aluminum market as an example to illustrate the effect of an externality on the market outcome. It is often the case that aluminum factories emit pollution as a part of their production process. A certain amount of smoke enters the atmosphere every time the factory produces an aluminum product. The smoke creates a health risk for those who breathe the air. This health risk is an example of a negative externality because the individuals who breathe the air incur a health "cost" that the aluminum producing factory does not factor into its production and supply decision. There is a social cost to the production of aluminum that is not included in a typical aluminum market analysis. The following graph shows the impact of the negative externality on the aluminum market.

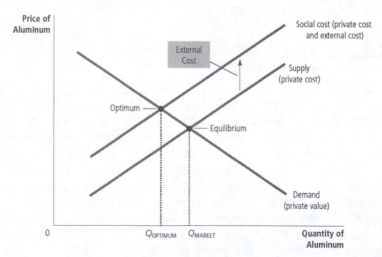

The supply curve represents the private cost of production for aluminum producers, while the social cost curve represents the private cost of production of aluminum plus the external cost to bystanders who breathe in the polluted air emitted by the aluminum producers. The AP Microeconomics exam may sometimes refer to this social cost curve as the marginal social cost (MSC) and the demand curve as the marginal social benefit (MSB). In the presence of a negative externality such as pollution, the social cost of a good is greater than the private cost, as shown in the graph. Note that the equilibrium quantity of aluminum, Q_{market}, is greater than the socially optimal quantity, $Q_{optimal}$. This is a market failure, or market inefficiency, because the market equilibrium reflects just the private cost, not the social cost, of aluminum production. The aluminum market is producing more aluminum than is optimal and should reduce its aluminum production in order to raise overall societal well-being.

While some market activity may result in negative externalities, there are also other market actions that actually yield benefits to bystanders who do not pay for the product or service. Education is a good example of a market with a positive externality. The benefits of education extend beyond the individual. Better education does not only result in higher productivity and wages for the individual, but an educated population leads to more informed voters, potentially less crime, and greater technological advances that may lead to even greater productivity and higher wages. In other words, it would be beneficial to society if we "consumed" more education. The education market currently does not "produce" an optimal quantity of education, as depicted in the following graph.

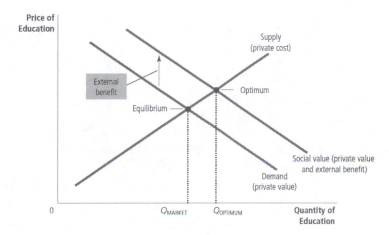

The education demand curve does not reflect the societal value of education. The social value of education is greater than the private value, as shown by the curve to the right of the education demand curve. The optimal quantity is where the social value and the private cost (supply curve) intersect. In the case of a positive externality, the market does not produce enough of a good or service.

AP Tip

Students should know how to graph a market with a negative and positive externality. Remember that a negative externality means that the market produces too much of a good or service at too low of a price, while a positive externality means that the market produces too little of a good or service than is socially desirable.

PUBLIC SOLUTIONS TO EXTERNALITIES
(*Principles of Economics* 5th ed. pages 209–215/6th ed. pages 202–209)

In the case of market failures, how can we encourage markets to produce the optimal quantity of a good or service? The government may choose to intervene in order to help the markets to **internalize the externality**, *altering market incentives so that people take account of the external effects of their actions.* In simple terms, the government may use public policy to encourage the market to produce the optimal quantity of a good or service. In the case of a negative externality, where aluminum producers produce more than the optimal quantity of aluminum, the government may impose a **corrective tax**, *a per-unit tax designed to induce private decision makers* (such as aluminum producers) *to take account of the social costs that arise from a negative externality,* on the market. A corrective tax will shift the supply curve to the left since the tax is imposed on and paid by the producer. (These taxes are also referred to as a *Pigovian tax*, named after the economist Arthur Pigou.) An ideal corrective tax is one that is equal to the external cost paid by market bystanders. Refer to the following graph to see how a corrective tax can work.

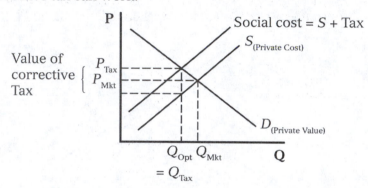

Note that, in an ideal market, the corrective tax is equal to the external cost to society, thus, internalizing the negative externality because the tax decreases the supply provided by aluminum producers (since costs are now higher with a tax) and the new equilibrium quantity with the corrective tax is now equal to the optimal quantity. In reality, a corrective tax is set just high enough to encourage the market to produce at the socially optimal quantity. Gasoline is an example of a good that is heavily taxed in the United States. A gas tax may be used to reduce gas consumption and other negative externalities that result from gasoline production such as increased road congestion, pollution, and car accidents. Refer back to Chapter 2 to review the impact of taxes on the market.

Instead of imposing a corrective tax, the government may choose to issue tradable pollution permits in order to internalize a negative externality. Tradable pollution permits allow the government to cap the amount of production at the optimal quantity while allowing pollution emitting firms to trade pollution permits privately in a pollution permit market. The benefit of using tradable pollution permits is that the market will produce the optimal quantity of a good or service because the quantity is fixed based on the number of pollution permits available. In both cases of a corrective tax and a pollution permit, the firm pays the pollution cost, shifting the supply curve to the left. With a corrective tax, the firm pays the pollution cost to the government. With pollution permits, the polluting firm must buy the permit to pollute. Both of these policy options help to internalize the negative externality by raising the marginal cost of polluting.

How might the government internalize a positive externality? Recall that, in the case of a positive externality, the market produces too little of a good or service. In order to encourage a greater quantity of education, the government intervenes in the market for education by creating incentives for individuals to go to school. For example, the government may provide an education subsidy in order to make education more affordable. Education in the United States is heavily subsidized by the government. For example, the U.S. government gives college grants to lower-income individuals in order to encourage the pursuit of higher education. It is socially beneficial for more people to own fuel efficient cars and energy efficient appliances, but the quantity purchased in the market for both goods is less than the socially optimal level. In other words, there is a positive externality in both markets. Our government has decided to internalize this positive externality by providing tax benefits to those who buy fuel efficient cars or energy efficient appliances. Refer to the following graph to see how a subsidy can internalize a positive externality.

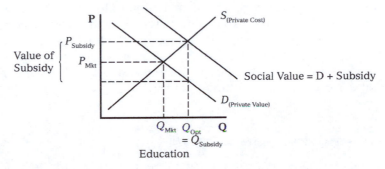

AP Tip

Negative externalities lead to a $Q_{mkt} > Q_{optimal}$. To internalize this externality, government may impose a *tax, or other restrictions* to encourage optimal production.

Positive externalities lead to a $Q_{mkt} < Q_{optimal}$. To internalize this externality, government may provide a *subsidy* to encourage optimal production.

PRIVATE SOLUTIONS TO EXTERNALITIES
(*Principles of Economics* 5th ed. pages 215–220/6th ed. pages 209–213)

Government action is not always needed to address market failures. In fact, when certain conditions are met, some economists argue that little to no government intervention is needed. For example, economist Ronald Coase made the argument that: (1) when property rights are clear and enforceable, (2) when all parties involved in the market have complete information, and (3) when transaction costs are low, there is no need for government intervention to correct externalities because the individual parties can negotiate or bargain in order to achieve an efficient allocation of resources. Specifically, the **Coase theorem** (named after economist Ronald Coase) *proposes that if private parties can bargain without cost over the allocation of resources, they can solve the problem of externalities on their own.* Let's use an example to illustrate how the Coase theorem might work. Suppose that a chemical company pollutes into a river where many individuals like to swim. These individuals are citizens of the town in which the river runs, so these individuals have the property right to swim in clean water. There is a negative externality because the chemical firm produces more than the socially optimal quantity. In our previous discussion where the government intervenes to correct the externality, the government may impose a corrective tax on the firm to decrease production. According to the Coase theorem, this externality may be more effectively addressed privately between the chemical firm and the town citizens because the property rights are clearly defined and enforceable (the town citizens have the right to clean water; this is enforceable by the town leaders) and the transaction costs are low. Since the town citizens have the property right to clean water, the chemical firm may negotiate with the citizens and agree to pay a certain amount of money to the town and its citizens in order to be able to pollute. If the town citizens agree to the terms of the firm's negotiated proposals, they have corrected this negative externality privately without government intervention. Note that the result is the same as when there is public (government) intervention—the firm's marginal costs increase as a result of negotiating with the town citizens and therefore the firm produces at a lower, socially optimal quantity.

PUBLIC GOODS

(Principles of Economics 5th ed. pages 225–232/6th ed. pages 217–224)

Markets allocate goods according to what people are willing to pay for and what sellers are willing to receive for the good. Goods without prices result in another sort of market failure because the market cannot use prices to send the necessary signals to allocate resources efficiently. There are many types of goods in our economy, which all fall into one of four categories—private goods, common resources, club goods, and public goods. In order to distinguish between the different types, we consider two questions. (1) Is the good **excludable**? That is, *can people who don't want to pay be prevented from using the good?* (2) Is the good **rival in consumption**? That is, *does one person's use of the good reduce another person's ability to use it?* A **public good** is *a good that is neither excludable nor rival in consumption.* Examples of public goods include our system of national defense and basic research.

Why do public goods present a problem for society? Let's consider the example of a fireworks display to answer this question. A fireworks display is not excludable because you cannot prevent someone from seeing the fireworks since it is displayed in the sky and it is non-rival in consumption because one person's enjoyment of the fireworks display does not take away from another person's enjoyment of the same display. A fireworks display is a good example of a public good because it meets both criteria. Suppose that it costs a town $1,000 to put on a fireworks display. The city is willing to put on the fireworks show because its citizens receive a benefit from watching the display that is greater than its $1,000 cost. Very rarely would we see a fireworks show put on by a private profit-maximizing firm or individual. Why wouldn't the private market want to produce the fireworks show when the benefit exceeds the cost? The private market recognizes that, since the fireworks show is not excludable or rival, it cannot make money from a fireworks show because people know that they can watch the fireworks show regardless of whether or not they've paid. A **free rider** is *a person who receives the benefit of a good but avoids paying for it*. The reason why the private market does not produce a public good is because people have an incentive to be free riders. The private market would then fail to provide the efficient outcome. This is why public goods, such as national defense and police security, must be provided by the government.

COMMON RESOURCES
(*Principles of Economics* 5th ed. pages 232–237/6th ed. pages 224–229)

Common resources, *goods that are rival in consumption but are not excludable*, also lead to an inefficient market outcome. Examples of common resources include clean air and water. Common resources, like public goods, are available free of charge. The difference is that an individual's use of a common resource can reduce another individual's use of the same resource. Consider public restrooms—they are free to use, but if someone does not clean up after using the restroom, it reduces your ability to "enjoy" your public restroom experience. **The Tragedy of the Commons** is *an economic concept that illustrates why common resources are used more than is desirable from the standpoint of society as a whole*. Suppose that we are in a small town where fishing is an important economic activity. The lake where people fish isn't owned by anyone (it is not excludable) and everyone is allowed to fish in it. As the population grows and more people go fishing at the lake, the lake becomes overfished. Overfishing can lead to a depletion of fish populations and other environmental issues such as a loss of biodiversity. The overfishing of the lake will make it impossible for the townspeople to catch fish to sell, which causes the town to lose one of its main sources of income. The Tragedy of the Commons arises because of an externality. When increasing numbers of people fish in the common lake, the quality and quantity of fish available is reduced. Individuals who fish do not consider this negative externality when deciding whether or not to fish in the lake, and so the common town lake becomes overfished as more and more people fish in it. The main lesson from the Tragedy of the Commons is that, when property rights are poorly defined, individuals will act in ways that result in negative externalities. If the lake were owned by specific individuals, the individuals would have a vested interest in caring for the biodiversity of the lake.

The government can internalize this externality by regulating the amount of time each individual can fish in the lake or by charging a fee to fish in the lake. It can also turn the lake, which is a common resource, into a private good by selling it to any individual willing to pay for the exclusive rights to the lake in order to encourage an optimal usage of the common resource. In some U.S. cities, the local governments have started to charge a small fee for use of public bathrooms to encourage more responsible usage of this common resource.

MARKET FAILURES:
STUDENT OBJECTIVES FOR THE AP EXAM

You should be able to:
- ▨ Define all key terms in bold
- ▨ Graph: negative and positive externality, the impact of government policy on negative and positive externalities
- ▨ Explain why public goods and common resources result in market failures
- ▨ Present potential solutions to market externalities

MULTIPLE-CHOICE QUESTIONS

1. In a market economy, public goods, such as community police protection, are unlikely to be provided in sufficient quantity by the private sector because
   (A) private firms are less efficient at producing public goods than is the government.
   (B) the use of public goods cannot be withheld from those who do not pay for them.
   (C) consumers have no demand for public goods.
   (D) consumers can produce public goods more efficiently than private firms.
   (E) public goods are inherently too important to be left to private firms to produce.

2. Which of the following is true when the production of a good results in a negative externality?
   (A) The government must produce the good.
   (B) The private market will produce too little of the good.
   (C) The private market will produce too much of the good.
   (D) The private market price will be too high.
   (E) The government must prevent the production of the good.

3. Imposing taxes that increase as a firm's pollution increases is often recommended by economists as a means to reduce pollution. The reason for this recommendation is that such taxes would likely
   (A) eliminate pollution completely.
   (B) increase the government's revenues.
   (C) encourage firms to increase production.
   (D) encourage firms to use the most efficient method to reduce pollution.
   (E) be paid out of firms' profits and not paid for by higher consumer prices.

4. Which of the following types of goods are non-rival in consumption?
   (A) Public goods.
   (B) Private goods.
   (C) Common resources.
   (D) Inferior goods.
   (E) All goods provided by the government.

5. Market failures can be reduced by which of the following?
(A) A corrective, Pigovian tax
(B) Government regulation
(C) Tradable permits
(D) The assignment of private property rights
(E) All of the above

6. The socially optimal level of pollution is
(A) less than that created by the market, but not zero.
(B) more than that created by the market.
(C) the market quantity.
(D) determined by private firms.
(E) zero.

7. Which of the following is a potential source of a negative externality?
(A) A loud conversation in a library
(B) Smokestack scrubbers which clean air released by factories
(C) National defense
(D) A graduate degree
(E) A subsidy

8. The Coase theorem asserts that, under the right circumstances, inefficiencies created by externalities can be dealt with through
(A) meditation.
(B) a lawsuit.
(C) vigilante action.
(D) government policy.
(E) private bargaining.

9. An effective Pigovian tax for a good that results in a negative externality is one that
(A) raises the marginal private cost of production so that the market produces at the socially optimal quantity.
(B) raises the external cost of production so that the market produces at the socially optimal quantity.
(C) decreases the marginal social benefit to society.
(D) decreases the marginal private cost of production so that the market produces at the socially optimal quantity.
(E) decreases the external cost of production so that the market produces at the socially optimal quantity.

Use the following graph to answer Question 10:

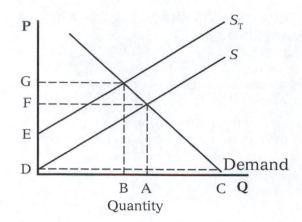

10. In the graph, point A is the current equilibrium level of output of a good and point B is the optimal level of output from society's perspective. S_T is the supply curve with a tax.
    One possible solution to this negative externality is to
    (A) give the consumers a subsidy in the amount of EF.
    (B) give producers a subsidy in the amount of AB.
    (C) tax producers by the amount of FG.
    (D) tax consumers by the amount of EF.
    (E) regulate the market so that the price remains at point F.

11. Of the following, one example of a positive externality is
    (A) a technology spillover.
    (B) traffic congestion.
    (C) pollution.
    (D) a subsidy for polluters.
    (E) a pollution tax.

12. If the production of a good results in a positive externality, the government might be able to improve economic efficiency in this market by
    (A) eliminating private production of the good.
    (B) promoting the export of the surplus output.
    (C) initiating antitrust (antimonopoly forming) action.
    (D) granting a subsidy to private producers.
    (E) imposing a tax on private producers.

13. Which of the following is true of the marginal cost of providing a pure public good to one more consumer?
    (A) It is equal to zero.
    (B) It is positive.
    (C) It is equal to the original cost of the good.
    (D) It decreases as the number of consumers increases.
    (E) It increases as the number of consumers increases.

14. Which of the following is true regarding consumer welfare when the government imposes a corrective tax in a market?
    (A) Consumer surplus increases.
    (B) Consumer surplus decreases.
    (C) Producer surplus increases.
    (D) There is a decrease in government tax revenue.
    (E) There is an external value that is not recognized by the market.

15. When the government imposes a corrective tax, the market produces a socially optimal quantity, but there is a welfare loss because
    I.   there is a decrease in consumer surplus
    II. there is a decrease in producer surplus
    III. the tax decreases employees' incentives to work
    (A) I only.
    (B) II only.
    (C) III only.
    (D) I and II only.
    (E) I, II, and III only.

FREE-RESPONSE QUESTIONS

1. One approach to the problem of pollution control in a market economy is to impose a corrective tax on producers emitting the pollution. Suppose that the government imposes such a tax on the aluminum-producing firms.
   (a) Draw and label the supply and demand curves for the aluminum market before the tax is imposed.
   (b) Using your graph in part (a) above, show the impact of a corrective tax on the following and label:
       (i)   the equilibrium quantity
       (ii) the equilibrium price
       (iii) the total tax revenue

2. Education provides benefits to those who receive the education as well as others in their community. Assume a competitive market for education.
   (a) Draw a correctly labeled supply and demand graph for education and identify:
       (i)   the market price
       (ii) the market output
       (iii) the socially efficient or socially optimal level of output
   (b) Identify a solution to the education market externality. Explain how your solution helps to internalize the externality.

Answers

MULTIPLE-CHOICE QUESTIONS

1. **B.** Public goods result in a free rider problem. This decreases the incentive for private firms to produce public goods, since they cannot keep free riders from consuming the public good (*Principles of Economics* 5th ed. page 228/6th ed. page 220).

2. **C.** $Q_{mkt} > Q_{opt}$ when there is a market negative externality (*Principles of Economics* 5th ed. pages 205–207/6th ed. pages 198–199).

3. **D.** A corrective or Pigovian tax encourages firms to reduce production in order to account for the external cost of their production (*Principles of Economics* 5th ed. pages 210–211/6th ed. pages 203–205).

4. **A.** Public goods are always non-rival in consumption—one person's enjoyment and use of the good does not take away from another person's enjoyment and use. Private goods are excludable and rival in consumption, while common resources are not excludable but rival in consumption. Inferior goods are goods where, as income falls, more people consume the good, so this is irrelevant to the question (*Principles of Economics* 5th ed. page 226/6th ed. page 218).

5. **E.** All policy options can address the market inefficiencies resulting from the overuse of common resources (*Principles of Economics* 5th ed. pages 232–237/6th ed. pages 224–229).

6. **A.** While we do not want pollution, given that we want to have the goods and services provided by markets, the socially optimal level of pollution corresponds to a specific production quantity that is less than the market and greater than zero (*Principles of Economics* 5th ed. pages 206–207/6th ed. pages 198–199).

7. **A.** A loud conversation in the library can take away from your ability to concentrate and study in the library (*Principles of Economics* 5th ed. page 206/6th ed. page 198).

8. **E.** There are some circumstances when private bargaining works as a better (and less costly) solution to externalities than government policy intervention (*Principles of Economics* 5th ed. pages 217–218/6th ed. pages 210–211).

9. **A.** An effective corrective tax is one that increases the cost of the pollution caused by production back onto the producers. The producers' marginal private cost (MPC) should ideally increase by the amount of the external cost of production/pollution to society. This shifts the supply curve to the left (*Principles of Economics* 5th ed. page 210/6th ed. page 203).

10. **C.** The tax is equal to the vertical distance between the two supply curves, which is the amount FG (*Principles of Economics* 5th ed. page 210/6th ed. page 203).

11. **A.** Technological advances can provide unintended benefits to society that may lead to higher production and wages (*Principles of Economics* 5th ed. page 208/6th ed. page 201).

12. **D.** A subsidy encourages private producers to produce more of a good where there is a positive externality (*Principles of Economics* 5th ed. pages 207–208/6th ed. pages 199–200).

13. **A.** A public good is non-rival and non-excludable, therefore, it does not cost anything extra to provide more of the public good to an additional person (*Principles of Economics* 5th ed. pages 227–230/6th ed. pages 220–222).

14. **B.** Consumer surplus decreases because the tax increases the market price paid by consumers. However, society as a whole benefits because the market will produce a more optimal quantity of the good or service that is resulting in a negative externality (*Principles of Economics* 5th ed. page 210/6th ed. page 203).

15. **D.** In an efficient market where there are no externalities, a tax results in deadweight loss because the market produces less, which results in a smaller consumer and producer surplus. We do not know whether a tax would affect workers' incentives to work, although we would expect that a corrective tax would have no effect on worker incentives since the tax is placed on producers, not its employees. We do not have enough information to know that option III is true. Note that a corrective tax encourages a socially optimal production level and allocates resources more efficiently, so while consumer and producer surplus are smaller after the imposition of a corrective tax, there is no deadweight loss because production levels are more efficient (*Principles of Economics* 5th ed. pages 210–211/6th ed. pages 203–205).

FREE-RESPONSE QUESTIONS

1. (a)

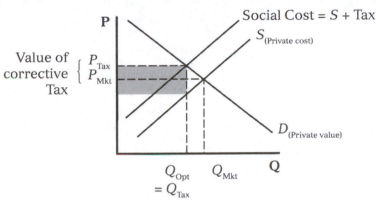

Aluminum Market

Without a corrective tax, the market produces at Q_{mkt} and P_{mkt}. Note that the market produces too much aluminum at too low of a price. $Q_{mkt} > Q_{optimal}$

(b) With a corrective tax, aluminum producing firms internalize the external cost of pollution because the tax increases its marginal costs of production and shifts the supply curve to the left. The new equilibrium quantity is $Q_{opt} = Q_{tax}$ and the new equilibrium price is P_{tax}. The tax revenue collected by the government is shown by the shaded area of the rectangle above.

(*Principles of Economics* 5th ed. pages 212–214/6th ed. pages 206–207)

2. (a)

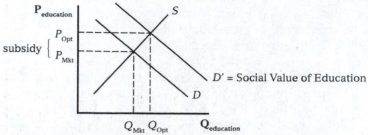

(b) In order to encourage a greater consumption of education, the government may provide a subsidy. The subsidy makes it more affordable for people to go to school and therefore increases market consumption of education and reduces the gap between Q_{mkt} and Q_{opt}, internalizing the externality.

(*Principles of Economics* 5th ed. pages 207–209/6th ed. pages 199–202)

8

NATIONAL INCOME AND PRICE DETERMINATION

Macroeconomic analysis often revolves around the topic of national income—total income earned by residents of an economy through the production of goods and services. Whether it involves discussion of output fluctuations over time (known as the business cycle) or simply the composition of gross domestic product, national income is a constant theme in macroeconomic theory. Analysis of national income frequently comes in the form of the aggregate demand-aggregate supply model.

MEASUREMENT OF NATIONAL INCOME: GROSS DOMESTIC PRODUCT

(*Principles of Economics* 5th ed. pages 510–515 /6th ed. pages 496–499)

The most commonly used measure of national income is gross domestic product (GDP). GDP measures the market value of all final goods and services produced within a country in a given period of time. It is the sum of four components: consumption, investment, government purchases and net exports.

CONSUMER SPENDING

The largest component of GDP is consumer spending, purchases of goods and services by private domestic households. Goods are further broken down into the categories of durable and non-durable goods; durable goods are those expected to last a minimum of 3-7 years (cars, washing machines, dishwashers) while non-durable goods are meant for more immediate consumption (food and clothing). Services are intangible items such as haircuts, education and legal, medical or financial services.

INVESTMENT SPENDING

The most volatile component of GDP is investment spending. Investment spending may be divided into three primary parts: business spending on capital, new real estate construction within the given year, and additions to inventory in a given year.

GOVERNMENT PURCHASES

Purchases by local, state and federal governments is also included in the calculation of GDP. It is important to note that transfer payments are not included in GDP. Transfer payments (such as social security benefits) are not transactions for any productive good or service; including them in GDP would overestimate the value of a nation's GDP.

NET EXPORTS

Purchases of American made goods by foreigners are also included in GDP as net exports. Net exports equate to a nation's exported goods and services minus the goods and services it imports. For America, a net importer, this component of GDP is actually negative and represents a decrease in GDP.

While GDP is intended to be an indicator of a nation's productive activity, there will always be productive activity which does not count towards its calculation. These activities are called non-market activities; many argue that the fact that they are not calculated means that GDP is actually undervalued.

MACROECONOMIC ISSUES: BUSINESS CYCLE, INFLATION AND UNEMPLOYMENT
(*Principles of Economics* 5th ed. pages 739–742 /6th ed. pages 720–722)

In a market economy, it is understood that GDP will fluctuate in the short run. Despite the unpredictable nature of the duration of these swings, the fluctuations in GDP are collectively known as the business cycle. The normal state of the economy is one of positive growth in GDP known as expansion. Generally speaking, unemployment decreases and inflationary pressures are greater during expansion. Eventually, expansions come to an end; the final period of expansion is known as the peak, which is then followed by a contraction. Contractions are periods characterized by a relative downturn in economic activity, namely declining GDP and increasing unemployment. With some exceptions, inflation is usually not a major concern during a contraction. If a contraction lasts long enough (most economists agree upon a two quarter, or six month, minimum), it may be referred to as a recession. While damaging to the economy in the short run, recessions also come to an end. The final quarter of negative growth is known as a trough.

THE AGGREGATE DEMAND AND AGGREGATE SUPPLY MODEL

(*Principles of Economics* 5th ed. pages 745–760/6th ed. pages 724–730)

One of the most commonly used and referred to models in macroeconomics is the aggregate demand-aggregate supply model (AD-AS). As the name implies, the model aggregates (or combines) demand and supply for all goods and services produced in an economy so as to provide a comprehensive depiction of an economy. Aggregate demand represents the total amount of goods and services households, firms, government, and foreigners are willing to purchase at a set of price levels. Likewise, aggregate supply illustrates the total amount of goods and services firms are willing and able to produce at a set of price levels. It is important to point out that AD is seen from the perspective of buyers; AS, on the other hand, comes from the perspective of producing firms.

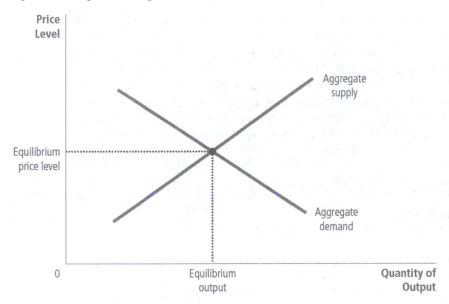

REASONS WHY THE AGGREGATE DEMAND CURVE IS DOWNWARD SLOPING

(*Principles of Economics* 5th ed. pages 746–748 /6th ed. pages 726–729)

In introductory chapters of most economics courses, it is taught that demand curves slope downward due to the income and substitution effects. These effects relate the change in price of a good with the effects on real income and relative price of related goods. While the effects are true when discussing demand for a particular good, they do not apply when analyzing the demand for an economy as a whole. To explain the downward slope of the aggregate demand curve, it is necessary to understand three separate, yet not entirely unrelated, reasons: the wealth effect, the interest rate effect, and the exchange rate effect.

THE WEALTH EFFECT

Changes in price level affect household wealth, the purchasing power of households based on total assets owned. As the general price level rises, the amount of goods each dollar can purchase decreases. In reaction to this decrease in wealth, consumers cut back on spending and output demanded decreases. Of course, the opposite is also true. As price level falls, each dollar is capable of purchasing more and total output demanded increases. The negative sloping AD curve illustrates this relationship.

THE INTEREST RATE EFFECT

A lower price level causes consumers to have excess money balances. As a result, they increase their lending, reducing the interest rate and stimulating investment spending.

THE EXCHANGE RATE EFFECT

When constructing aggregate demand, it's not just domestic consumers that demand output from domestic producers; purchases by foreign consumers must be considered as well. Therefore, changes in price level do have an effect on net exports as relative price level changes result in changes in the relative values of currencies among nations. With these exchange rate changes come changes in output demanded by foreign buyers. More specifically, when price level falls, interest rates fall with it. A decrease in domestic price level and interest rates leads to a decrease in the value of the domestic currency and an increase in exported goods. Hence, the aggregate demand curve displays a negative slope.

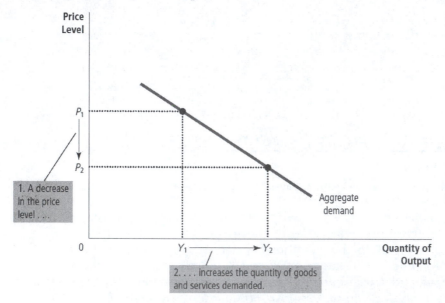

SHIFTING THE AGGREGATE DEMAND CURVE
(Principles of Economics 5th ed. pages 749–751/6th ed. pages 729–731)

The factors which cause the aggregate demand curve to shift are the four components which, when summed, equal aggregate demand: consumption, investment, government spending and net exports, as seen in the following equation:

$$AD = Y = C + I + G + NX$$

While this direct relationship is easily explained and learned, it requires slightly more explanation to comprehend what makes each of these four components change. In each case, it is important to recall that an increase (decrease) in aggregate demand simply means that consumers are willing and able to purchase more (less) goods at all price levels than they were before.

CONSUMER SPENDING

Consumer spending makes up roughly 70% of the United States' GDP in any given year. For that reason, changes in consumption have a direct and significant effect on aggregate demand. One can associate these changes with changes in disposable income and consumer confidence. As consumers witness an increase in either, they tend to spend more money at all price levels, creating an increase in aggregate demand. Likewise, as incomes and confidence fall, consumer spending falls and AD shifts to the left.

INVESTMENT SPENDING

In the context of AD and GDP, investment is broadly defined as spending on capital by firms, new home purchases and additions to inventories. Fluctuations in investment, often driven by changes in interest rates or expected rates of return, have a direct effect on aggregate demand. As firms see prevailing interest rates below their expected rates of return for particular investment projects, they are more likely to spend (or borrow) money. Aggregate demand, therefore, increases with the rise in investment as firms are demanding more capital goods at all price levels. When interest rates rise, investment will fall due to firms desire to earn higher rates on interest-bearing assets; AD will then decrease as well.

GOVERNMENT SPENDING

Governments may have a direct effect on aggregate demand by increasing purchases of domestically produced goods and services. These products may include the purchase of defense materials or the contracting of private businesses to carry out infrastructure projects on behalf of the government. Regardless, the effect on aggregate demand is the same; increased government spending shifts AD to the right while cuts in government spending shift AD to the left.

NET EXPORT SPENDING

Foreign purchases of domestic goods also have an effect on the aggregate demand curve. As net exports equal exports minus imports, any action which alters the purchase of goods shipped to other countries (exports) or those purchased from other countries (imports) will shift AD. For example, when foreign economies prosper—as indicated by a rising national income—it is likely that citizens there will buy more goods, including imported goods. Consistent with this theory, an increase in the national income of Japan can be expected to increase the United States' net exports. Likewise, fluctuations in exchange rates have similar effects. When the U.S. dollar weakens, it becomes cheaper for foreign consumers to purchase U.S. goods, increasing demand for output by U.S. firms at all price levels and shifting AD to the right.

REASONS WHY THE SHORT RUN AGGREGATE SUPPLY CURVE IS UPWARD SLOPING
(*Principles of Economics* 5th ed. pages 755–759 /6th ed. pages 734–738)

THE STICKY WAGE THEORY

Nominal wages, those wages seen on an employee's paycheck, tend to be slow to adjust to inflation in the short run. There are two reasons for this: one is due to workers' inability to recognize relative price changes in the short run; the second is the fact that many wages are locked into a contract which cannot be renegotiated whenever prices change. When prices rise and the wage stays the same, firms are more profitable and they produce more.

THE STICKY PRICE THEORY

Just as wages can be slow to adjust over time, prices also tend to change slowly over time (albeit for different reasons). Reasons for this include a hesitancy of retailers to change prices due to costs associated with doing so; these costs are known as menu costs. Actions of competitors will also be considered. A firm may hesitate in adjusting retail prices until they are certain about a competitor's pricing plans. When the price level rises, those firms that have not raised their prices look inexpensive, and the sell more.

THE MISPERCEPTIONS THEORY

Sometimes market activities can be misread by market participants. It is possible for suppliers to misread the messages sent by unexpectedly high or low price levels. When the price level rises, firms may only notice that the price of their product went up. This causes them to temporarily produce more.

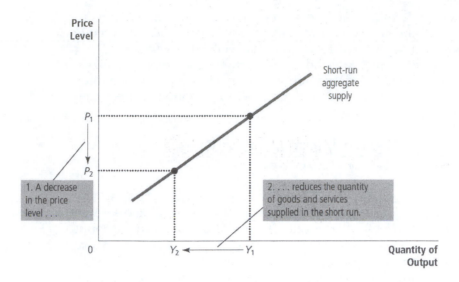

SHIFTING THE SHORT RUN AGGREGATE SUPPLY CURVE

(*Principles of Economics* 5th ed. pages 760–761/6th ed. pages 738–740)

It is important to remember that the SRAS curve illustrates the quantity of goods and services produced by an economy in the short run for a given set of prices. One way to approach this definition is to say that SRAS gives an indication of what an economy is currently producing, as opposed to LRAS which indicates what an economy is capable of producing. Changes in the current output of an economy come about at all price levels when the SRAS curve shifts; shifts in SRAS occur due to changes in the levels of the factors of production, changes in the productivity of resources and expectations of changes in the price level.

CHANGES IN THE AVAILABILITY OF RESOURCES

Changes in the availability of land, labor, and capital (physical or human) will demonstrate a positive relationship with the SRAS curve. As quantities of these resources increase, SRAS will shift to the right. This is primarily due to decreasing factor prices associated with the increased availability of resources, resulting in lower production costs.

CHANGES IN TECHNOLOGY

Gains in technology increase the productivity of resources used by firms. As a result, firms are more efficient and become capable of producing more output from the same level of inputs. Therefore, increases in the level of technology shift the SRAS curve to the right; decreases have the opposite effect and shift the SRAS curve to the left.

CHANGES IN EXPECTED PRICE LEVEL

Expectations in price level have the potential to cause firms to adjust their levels of production. If firms expect price levels to rise, it is reasonable to believe they will increase output levels. These expectations may be the result of everyday business activity, or they may be in reaction to regulatory or legislative actions by a government agency. When government actions affect the day-to-day operations of firms, such as changes in corporate tax levels or subsidies, it is likely that overall output will have to change as well. SRAS will shift left when firms are adversely affected by government actions (tax hikes, cuts in subsidies, increased regulations), and shift right when they gain from the same actions (tax decreases or loopholes, increased subsidies, decreased regulations).

VERTICAL AGGREGATE SUPPLY IN THE LONG RUN

(Principles of Economics 5th ed. pages 752–753 /6th ed. pages 731–734)

The Long Run Aggregate Supply (LRAS) curve is a vertical line intersecting the x-axis at full employment level of output, also known as the natural rate of output. The natural rate of output is the amount of goods and services an economy will produce when all resources are being utilized at their full productive capacity given the current level of technology and capital stock. LRAS is dependent upon the economy's quantities of labor, capital and natural resources given the prevailing level of technology. As a result, fluctuations in price level have no effect on potential GDP and the LRAS curve is a vertical line at the natural rate of output.

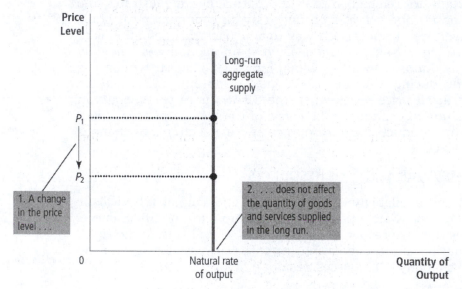

In practical terms, LRAS represents an economy's potential GDP. From this perspective, one should see a parallel between LRAS and the PPC. Both curves give a visual interpretation of how much a country's economy is capable of producing, holding resources and technology constant. Changes in the levels of capital and technology have the power to alter a nation's productivity, therefore adjusting the potential output of an economy changes as well. As a result, we witness shifts in the LRAS and PPC (in the same direction).

AP Tip

Know your shifters! Working with the AD-AS model is like playing a game. In any game, one must know the rules—the shifters of AD and AS are the rules to the game. A working knowledge of what causes aggregate demand, short-run aggregate supply and long-run aggregate supply to increase or decrease will allow you to manipulate the graph with ease and make determinations about changing levels of prices, output and unemployment.

MACROECONOMIC EQUILIBRIUM

(*Principles of Economics* 5th ed. pages 761–765/6th ed. pages 740–750)

Equilibrium in the AD-AS model may be classified as either short-run or long-run. The intersection of AD and SRAS represents an economy's current output and price level; this is referred to as the short-run equilibrium. When all three curves intersect, the economy has reached its long-run equilibrium; this indicates that both output and price level have reached their full employment levels. Changes in macroeconomic equilibrium occur whenever exogenous variables shift AD, SRAS or LRAS. These fluctuations, and the subsequent changes in economic activity, illustrate the ebb and flow that occurs as the economy moves through the business cycle.

In the long run, it is understood that output and price levels will return to their full employment levels. In the short run, the exogenous aggregate supply and aggregate demand shocks move equilibrium away from LRAS. When short-run equilibrium occurs at output levels below full employment output, we say a contractionary (or recessionary) gap exists. Occasionally, and for relatively short periods of time, expansionary gaps arise as short-run equilibrium moves beyond potential GDP.

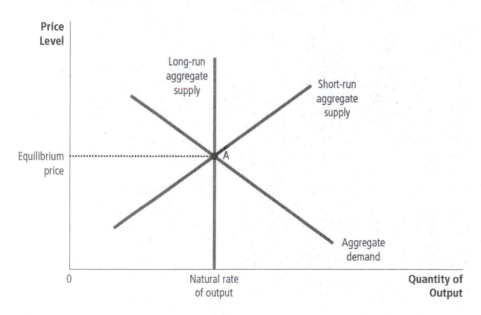

Recall that aggregate demand shifts due to changes in consumption, investment, government purchases and net exports at each price level. An increase in any of these components will shift AD to the right, resulting in an increase in output and price level (known as demand-pull inflation). Decreases in the four AD shifters are followed by a shift of AD to the left; price level and output subsequently decrease with this change.

Likewise, shifts in short run aggregate supply also alter short-run equilibrium. An adverse shift in SRAS causes cost-push inflation as prices and unemployment rise with a decrease in output (this is a way of correctly illustrating stagflation). Rightward shifts in SRAS actually decrease price level and unemployment as output increases.

NATIONAL INCOME AND PRICE DETERMINATION: STUDENT OBJECTIVES FOR THE AP EXAM

You should be able to:
- Define all key terms in bold
- Graph the Aggregate Demand-Aggregate Supply (AD-AS) model
- Explain the reasons for the shapes of the AD curve, the SRAS curve and the LRAS curve as well as the causes of changes in each
- Use quarterly growth rates to identify the phases of the business cycle and illustrate these changes on the AD-AS model

MULTIPLE-CHOICE QUESTIONS

1. Which of the following is not considered by one of the four components of the expenditures approach to calculating GDP?
   (A) Purchases of physical capital by American businesses.
   (B) Consumer spending on American made goods.
   (C) Purchase of shares of stock in American owned businesses.
   (D) Foreign purchases of American made goods.
   (E) American purchases of foreign made goods.

2. GDP increases occurring as a result of firms' purchases of new equipment from other domestic firms are counted as this.
   (A) Consumption.
   (B) Investment.
   (C) Government Purchases.
   (D) Net Exports.
   (E) Financial assets.

3. The normal state of the economy, in which GDP is experiencing positive growth while firms find plentiful customers and growing profits, is commonly referred to as a
   (A) contraction.
   (B) expansion.
   (C) recession.
   (D) integration.
   (E) depression.

4. Recessions are most frequently correlated with
   (A) increasing unemployment and decreasing levels of economic activity.
   (B) increasing unemployment and increasing levels of economic activity.
   (C) decreasing unemployment and decreasing levels of economic activity.
   (D) decreasing unemployment and increasing levels of economic activity.
   (E) improvements in physical capital which force workers out of their jobs.

5. The wealth effect, interest rate effect and net export effect help explain this important concept.
   (A) The negative relationship between price level and output demanded.
   (B) The negative relationship between price level and output supplied.
   (C) The positive relationship between price level and output demanded.
   (D) The positive relationship between price level and output supplied.
   (E) The negative relationship between output demanded and output supplied.

6. Which of the following would result in a shift of the aggregate demand curve to the right?
   (A) An increase in the expected price level.
   (B) A decrease in the availability of labor.
   (C) A reduction in the level of physical capital.
   (D) A decrease in government spending intended to balance the budget.
   (E) A decrease in marginal income tax rates.

7. A drop in the value of major stock indices often leads to a decrease in the amount of output demanded and movement down the aggregate demand curve. Which of the following explains this?
   (A) Interest rate effect.
   (B) Net export effect.
   (C) Sticky wage theory.
   (D) Wealth effect.
   (E) Misperceptions theory.

8. The belief that prices are slow to adjust to changes in the real economy helps to explain
   (A) the negative slope of aggregate demand.
   (B) the positive slope of short run aggregate supply.
   (C) the vertical shape of long-run aggregate supply.
   (D) the various adverse shifts of short run aggregate supply.
   (E) the reasons for shifts in aggregate demand.

9. Assume massive new sources of natural gas are discovered in the continental United States. What will be the expected change in short-run aggregate supply?
(A) Increase in SRAS.
(B) Decrease in SRAS.
(C) Movement up along the SRAS curve.
(D) Movement down along the SRAS curve.
(E) SRAS will not be affected by this discovery.

10. As the level of capital stock and technology increases, we can expect
I.   short-run aggregate supply to increase.
II. long-run aggregate supply to increase.
III. aggregate demand to increase.
(A) I only.
(B) II only.
(C) III only.
(D) I and II only.
(E) I, II and III.

11. Assume business and consumer confidence is down. What will be the expected effect on aggregate demand, output and price level in the short run?

AD	Output	Price Level
(A) Increase	Increase	Increase
(B) Decrease	Decrease	Decrease
(C) No Change	Increase	Decrease
(D) Increase	Decrease	Increase
(E) Decrease	Increase	Decrease

12. Long term growth, as determined by capital formation and gains in technology, is best illustrated by a
(A) rightward shift of aggregate demand.
(B) leftward shift of short-run aggregate supply.
(C) rightward shift of long-run aggregate supply.
(D) leftward shift of aggregate demand.
(E) leftward shift of long-run aggregate supply.

13. Stagflation, a prolonged period of relatively high inflation and falling output, is unique and associated with
(A) decreasing rates of unemployment.
(B) a leftward shift of short-run aggregate supply.
(C) long-run corrections of aggregate demand.
(D) a rightward shift of aggregate demand.
(E) increases in productivity due to technological gain.

14. Assume the economy is operating at its natural rate of output. A contractionary gap would emerge as a result of
(A) a decrease in aggregate demand.
(B) a decrease in short-run aggregate supply.
(C) a decrease in long-run aggregate supply.
(D) A and B only.
(E) A, B, and C.

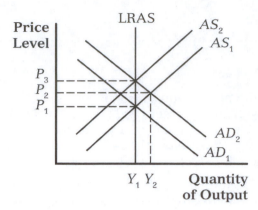

15. Which of the following explanations best describes the above scenario?
    (A) A decrease in corporate taxes and an increase in levels of technology.
    (B) An increase in consumer confidence followed by an increase in wage rates.
    (C) A decrease in government spending and massive new discoveries of crude oil.
    (D) An increase in population and a decrease in the price of steel.
    (E) A decrease in the purchase of new homes and an increase in rental rates.

FREE-RESPONSE QUESTIONS

1. Gross domestic product (GDP) measures the amount of goods and services produced by an economy.
    a. List and define the four components of GDP.
    b. Identify whether each of the following situations increase, decrease, or have no effect on the GDP of the United States.
        i. Purchase of a new car produced in the United States
        ii. U.S. Government contract with a private firm for the manufacturing of weapons
        iii. The purchase of stock on the New York Stock Exchange
        iv. A world-class chef cooks dinner at home for his wife and children
        v. Imported apparel sold at low prices at a major retail outlet

2. Assume the U.S. economy has been operating beyond full employment levels of output and price level.
    a. On a correctly labeled graph of AD-AS, identify the following:
        i. Current equilibrium output, Y, and price level, P_1
        ii. Long-run aggregate supply
        iii. Full employment output, labeled FE
    b. Due to a prolonged period of relatively high inflation expectations, labor demands higher wages and firms respond accordingly. On your graph from part (a), show the following:
        i. The change in aggregate supply
        ii. The new short run equilibrium output, Y_1, and price level, P_1
    c. Based on the change that occurred in part (b), what phase of the business cycle is the economy now in? Explain.

Answers

MULTIPLE-CHOICE QUESTIONS

1. **C.** GDP measures the production of goods and services in an economy; stocks are financial assets and the purchase of them does not represent the production of a good, but rather of a transfer of ownership. (*Principles of Economics* 5th ed. pages 512–514/6th ed. pages 497–499).

2. **B.** Investment consists of business fixed investment, residential fixed investment and additions to inventory for a given year. (*Principles of Economics* 5th ed. pages 513–514/6th ed. pages 497–499).

3. **B.** The economy is normally growing, or expanding. Contractions are due to fluctuations in the normal state of affairs. (*Principles of Economics* 5th ed. pages 739–742/6th ed. page 720).

4. **A.** Due to the decrease in output during recessions, one may expect employment figures to fall as job opportunities decrease and economic activity falters. (*Principles of Economics* 5th ed. pages 739–742/6th ed. page 722).

5. **A.** The negative relationship between price level and output demanded is explained by the wealth effect, interest rate effect and net export effect, resulting in a downward sloping aggregate demand curve. (*Principles of Economics* 5th ed. pages 746–748/6th ed. page 727).

6. **E.** AD shifts to the right due to increases in consumption, investment, government spending and net exports. A decrease in marginal tax rates causes disposable income to increase, leading to an increase in consumption and aggregate demand. (*Principles of Economics* 5th ed. pages 749–751/6th ed. pages 729–730).

7. **D.** Levels of household wealth decrease when stock indices fall. As a result, individuals reduce their amount of spending and we witness a correlation between increases in price level and decreases in output demanded. (*Principles of Economics* 5th ed. page 747/6th ed. pages 727–728).

8. **B.** Sticky price theory helps explain the upward sloping SRAS curve as prices do not change instantaneously to reflect market conditions. (*Principles of Economics* 5th ed. page 758/6th ed. pages 736–737).

9. **A.** A decrease in production costs allows firms to produce more with the same amount of resources; as a result, SRAS shifts to the right. (*Principles of Economics* 5th ed. pages 760–761/6th ed. pages 738–739).

10. **D.** Increases in the levels of capital stock and technology increase the amount of output produced per unit of input; this is an increase in productivity. Both short-run and long-run

aggregate supply increase as firms increase current and potential output. However, productivity changes have no effect on aggregate demand. (*Principles of Economics* 5th ed. pages 753–755, 760–761/6th ed. pages 733–34, 738–739).

11. **B.** With a decrease in business confidence, expected rates of return will fall, leading to a decrease in investment spending. This will shift AD to the left, therefore causing decreases in output and price level. (*Principles of Economics* 5th ed. pages 749–751/6th ed. pages 740–742).

12. **C.** Long term economic growth is represented by a rightward shift in the LRAS curve because the curve is an illustration of an economy's potential GDP. (*Principles of Economics* 5th ed. pages 753–755/6th ed. pages 733–734).

13. **B.** Shifting the SRAS curve to the left will cause output to fall, unemployment to rise and price level to rise. Stagflation is defined as a prolonged period of high unemployment and inflation rates; a leftward shift of SRAS is the only way to show this on the AD-AS model. (*Principles of Economics* 5th ed. pages 761–765/6th ed. page 749).

14. **D.** A contractionary gap emerges whenever output falls below full employment levels. A decrease in either AD or SRAS would cause short run equilibrium output to fall below the natural level of output. (*Principles of Economics* 5th ed. pages 761–765/6th ed. pages 749–750).

15. **B.** Increases in consumer confidence cause buyers to spend more money, shifting AD to the right. In the long run, wages will increase to reflect the demand pull inflation, therefore shifting SRAS back to the left. (*Principles of Economics* 5th ed. pages 761–765/6th ed. pages 749–750).

FREE-RESPONSE QUESTIONS

1. a. Consumption: spending by households on goods and services
        Investment: spending on capital, equipment, inventories, and structures, including household purchases of new housing
        Government purchases: spending on goods and services by local, state and federal governments
        Net export spending: spending on domestically produced goods by foreigners (exports) minus spending on foreign made goods by domestic residents (imports)
    b. i.   Increase
        ii. Increase
        iii. No change
        iv. No change
        v.   Decrease
    (*Principles of Economics* 5th ed. pages 512–514/6th ed. pages 497–499)

2. a. Correctly labeled graph of AD-AS

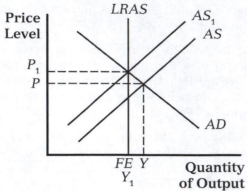

   i.   See graph; Y and P
   ii. See graph; LRAS
   iii. See graph; FE
   b. Labor demands higher wages and firms respond
   i.   See graph; short-run aggregate supply decreases
   ii. See graph; output decreases and price level increases
   c. Contraction; due to the increase in wages and decrease in short-run aggregate supply, output has decreased
   (Principles of Economics 5th ed. pages 761–765/6th ed. pages 749–750)

9

FINANCIAL SECTOR AND THE FEDERAL RESERVE

Much of the economic activity which takes place in any economy is facilitated by that economy's financial sector. The financial sector is the mechanism by which individuals looking to lend money find those looking to borrow. Through this market interaction, much consumer and business spending is financed, leading to increases in national income and subsequent decreases in unemployment. The central bank, through its monetary policy decisions, has considerable influence on the pace of lending and therefore, indirectly, influence on any changes in national income, unemployment and inflation.

MONEY AND FINANCIAL MARKETS

(*Principles of Economics* 5th ed. pages 642–646 and 576–578/6th ed. pages 620–625 and 556–558)

One of the roles of a market economy is to facilitate trade and the transfer of private property among parties. While this process is quite obvious when the purchasing party has available finances on hand to make the transaction happen, what happens when they do not? Financial markets play a key role in allowing transactions to occur by matching potential borrowers who are in need of liquid assets with those willing and able to lend.

Financial assets make borrowing and lending possible. Financial assets can come in the form of money, stocks and bonds. Any thorough understanding of the financial system begins with an understanding of money. Therefore, one must ask: what is money?

MONEY

Money is *the set of assets in an economy that people regularly use to buy goods and services from other people.* Literally speaking, money allows for the transfer of ownership and eliminates the need for a

215

double coincidence of wants that is required in a barter transaction. Money serves three purposes in any economy, known as the three main functions of money.

It is also important to understand from where money establishes its value. Historically, items used as money were utilized because of their intrinsic value—the item had value even when not used as money. The most common form of this type of money was gold and is called commodity money. Currencies were originally able to be converted to commodities with intrinsic value. Over time, this faded away and commodity money was replaced by fiat money, money without intrinsic value that derives its worth due to government decree. In other words, fiat money has value because government says it does.

The most common function of money is to serve as a **medium of exchange**. In this role, *money represents the item buyers give sellers in exchange for a good or service*. It is important that a form of money is stable in value and widely acceptable in order to fulfill this function.

A second function of money is to serve as a **unit of account** (sometimes called a standard of value). As a unit of account, money is used as *a form of measurement from which prices, debts and values of goods can be compared*. Because we all have a concept of what a dollar is worth, we can formulate from that unit (the dollar) comparable values of goods based on their dollar price.

The third function of money is to *transfer purchasing power from the present to the future*; in this role, money is called a **store of value**. Many commodities serve as a store of value (gold comes to mind). To serve as a store of value, a commodity must maintain a degree of worth over time. With regard to money, it is important to recognize the impact of inflation on its ability to serve in this capacity; currencies with high levels of inflation do not maintain their value as well as those with low, predictable inflation rates.

M1 AND M2

In order to properly and accurately account for the nation's money supply, it is necessary for the central bank to categorize money in different ways. In the United States, the Fed uses the M1 and M2 definitions of money.

The **M1** definition of money *includes all currency (cash and coin), traveler's checks and checkable deposits*. Forms of money included as M1 are the most liquid forms of money, meaning they are easily transferred from one individual to another.

M2 is a larger definition of money; in calculating **M2**, the Fed *includes all forms of M1, and then adds a variety of money held in less liquid forms. This includes, but is not limited to, savings, small time deposits, and money market mutual funds.*

AP Tip

Associate the M1 and M2 definitions of money with the functions of money. M1 includes only the most liquid forms of money; associate M1 with forms of money which serve as a medium of exchange. M2 money (beyond counting M1) is considerably less liquid; associate exclusively M2 money with serving as a store of value.

STOCKS AND BONDS

In discussing financial markets, one must expand their perspective beyond money alone. Stock and bond markets are essential in understanding alternate systems by which resources are moved between borrowers and lenders. Although not counted towards a nation's GDP, these transfers of ownership facilitate economic activity that does contribute to GDP through both investment and consumption.

Stocks are *financial assets that represent a claim to partial ownership in a firm*. Stockholders, as owners of firms, also may claim portions of profits coming from the firms they own. Literally speaking, each individual stock is worth a fraction of a company divided among the various shareholders.

Bonds are *certificates of indebtedness, or IOUs*. They represent an obligation from the issuer of the bond to the owner of the bond. Generally speaking, firms (and governments) issue bonds in order to borrow money from potential lenders. When lenders purchase a bond, they are purchasing a promise from the issuer to pay back the full amount of the bond plus a predetermined amount of interest over a set period of time. When this period of time has ended, we say the bond has reached its date of maturity.

FINANCIAL INTERMEDIARIES AND THE BANKING SYSTEM

(*Principles of Economics* 5th ed. pages 578–580/6th ed. pages 558–560)

Financial intermediaries are *institutions which bring together borrowers and savers in an economy*. Examples of financial intermediaries include institutions such as banks, mutual funds, credit unions, and savings and loan associations.

Banks are the most obvious and familiar of financial intermediaries in most economies. Most are familiar with banks' role as the keepers of demand deposits, also known as checking accounts or checkable deposits. Demand deposits are given the name because they are funds which may be redeemed or transferred at the owner's request. A checking account is an example of a demand deposit.

It is also the job of a bank to take in and ensure deposits of people looking to save their money while also making loans to people wanting to borrow money. Interest is used as payment for these funds; banks pay interest to savers for the use of their funds while charging interest to borrowers for the lending services provided. This process, while profitable for the bank, also facilitates the consumption and investment that drives economic activity. A secure and fluid banking industry is essential in a thriving economy.

Banks are not the only option for savers and borrowers. Mutual funds offer to the public a portfolio (variation) of stocks and bonds. By varying investment options, mutual funds allow savers to reduce their risk of loss by diversifying their holdings. Credit unions, in many ways, operate just as banks do, their only difference being that depositors are also members of the credit union itself. These often are associated with particular industries or occupations (teachers unions, military, etc.). Finally, savings and loan associations are financial institutions which specialize in just what the name implies, savings and loans.

THE LOANABLE FUNDS MARKET

(*Principles of Economics* 5th ed. pages 583–589/6th ed. pages 564–570)

The market representing savers and borrowers in the economy is called the **loanable funds market**. The model for the market illustrates the supply of loanable funds (savers) versus the demand for loanable funds (borrowers). Because we are talking about lending, the price for funds is the real interest rate, the return lenders expect to receive after inflation has been accounted for.

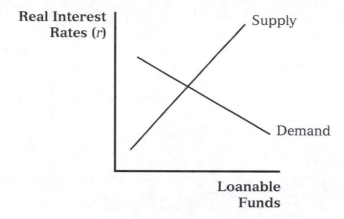

Incentives to save more money will increase the supply of loanable funds and cause a decrease in real interest rates. The supply of loanable funds decreases when money is taken out of savings; this causes an increase in real interest rates. An example of an incentive to save (or not save) may be related to tax policy regarding interest earned on savings. When money is put into a savings account, it earns interest for the saver. The incentive to save decreases as tax rates on those earnings increase. A reduction in taxes on interest earned may have the effect of increasing savings and increasing the supply of loanable funds.

The demand for loanable funds may be correlated with demand for investment. As investment demand increases, so does the demand for loanable funds; the opposite is also true. Optimistic expectations for business conditions may be one cause for an increase in the demand for loanable funds. Another may be the intervention of government. Through investment tax credits, firms may receive tax credits when they purchase new capital, meaning they will owe less in taxes for the given year.

Finally, government may have an indirect effect on the loanable funds market through its own budgetary actions. When the federal government spends more money on outlays than it brings in through tax receipts, the status of the budget is that of a deficit. When a federal budget deficit occurs, government must borrow money in order to finance the promised spending. This money comes from the loanable funds market. In response to a federal budget deficit, national savings decreases and the supply of loanable funds decreases as well.

A budget surplus will have the opposite effect. When government revenue exceeds outlays, the additional funds received are added to national savings as government pays off a portion of its accumulated national debt. This increase in savings leads to an increase in the supply of loanable funds and real interest rates fall.

CENTRAL BANK AND THE CONTROL OF MONEY SUPPLY

(*Principles of Economics* 5th ed. pages 648–649/6th ed. pages 625–627)

Central banks oversee the financial system of a nation. In general, they do so by manipulating the amount of money in circulation. Changes in money supply influence interest rates, which in turn cause the levels of borrowing and saving to fluctuate. In the United States, this role is filled by the Federal Reserve System.

THE FEDERAL RESERVE SYSTEM

As already stated, *the central bank of the United States* is known as the **Federal Reserve System**, or simply, the Fed. The Fed, begun in 1913 with the Congressional passage of the Federal Reserve Act, has a variety of responsibilities. As the primary regulator of the U.S. banking industry, it oversees all financial institutions throughout the nation. Further, the Fed serves a stabilizing role in the economy as the determinant of monetary policy, a topic that will be addressed in the next chapter. For now, the focus of this section is to recognize how the Fed is organized in order to sufficiently fulfill its many roles.

We call the Fed a system primarily because it has been designed to spread across the nation through a system of district banks. There are 12 Federal Reserve district banks located in various cities throughout the U.S. Spreading the system throughout the nation serves a number of purposes.

On a practical level, the system allows for the logistical role of issuing currency throughout the nation via the district banks, as well as allowing the Fed to keep an accurate count of money supply. In addition, the district banks serve as regional information hubs for the Fed; district bank presidents communicate with banking and business leaders in their area and report back to the Board of Governors in Washington on the progress of the economy. This brings us to the next component of the Fed.

The Federal Reserve Board of Governors is a seven-member board charged with providing leadership and direction for the Fed. The members are nominated by the President and confirmed by the Senate to serve one 14-year term. Fed governors, who are usually bankers or academic economists by trade, often serve as leaders in formulating economic opinions throughout the nation. They give speeches and make numerous public appearances communicating the Fed's stance on economic issues while working to maintain the Fed's credibility among citizens.

When policy decisions must be made, it is the Federal Open Market Committee (FOMC) that meets to determine the best course of action. The FOMC consists of all seven governors and five of the twelve district bank presidents (four seats rotate on an annual basis while the New York bank president is always on the committee). The decisions of the FOMC, based on what is known as the dual mandate (discussed in detail next chapter), essentially come down to one thing: should money supply be increased or decreased? Therefore, it is essential that the Fed has an accurate count of how much money is in circulation at any given time.

THE MONEY MARKET

When the Fed causes fluctuations in money supply, the effect on nominal interest rates will have an inverse effect on economic activity in the nation. This is due to changes in the levels of investment and interest-sensitive consumption that occur in reaction to interest rate changes. The relationship between changes in money supply and nominal interest rates (those rates charged by financial institutions) is best illustrated by the money market graph.

The money market graph (see below) illustrates the intersection of money supply and money demand. In this model, money supply is a general representation of total money currently in circulation; it is shifted by monetary policy (right for an increase in MS, left for a decrease in MS). The money supply curve is vertical (perfectly inelastic) because changes in nominal interest rates have no effect on the quantity of money in circulation. Money demand is the demand for liquid forms of money and has a negative slope to represent the inverse relationship between interest rates and quantity of money demanded.

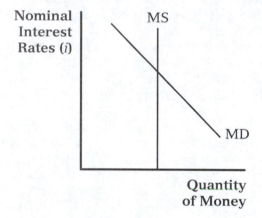

Fed decisions to increase money supply will cause money supply to shift to the right and nominal interest rates to fall. With a decrease in interest rates, investment and consumption will increase. This is an example of how expansionary monetary policy is intended to encourage growth in an economy. The opposite, known as contractionary monetary policy, occurs when the Fed decreases money supply, driving nominal interest rates up and sending levels of investment and consumption down; this will shift aggregate demand to the left.

THE FISHER EFFECT

(*Principles of Economics* 5th ed. pages 674–676/6th ed. pages 655–656)

Economist Irving Fisher was an early-20th century American economist known for his many contributions to monetarist theory. Among them, he his most regarded for explaining the relationship between real and nominal interest rates, based on the actual and anticipated rate of inflation.

As mentioned earlier in the chapter, nominal interest rates are the rates charged by a lender to a borrower for the use of funds for a specific amount of time. By lending money to another individual, lenders are forgoing a certain amount of consumption at the present time in order to gain an additional amount of purchasing power in the future. That additional purchasing power lenders hope to gain is called the real interest rate.

The Fisher effect explains that prior to lending money banks determine what to charge borrowers (the nominal interest rate) by adding their desired return (the real interest rate) and the anticipated inflation rate. After the loan has been repaid, the real return may be determined by subtracting the actual inflation rate from the interest rate charged. This relationship is illustrated by the Fisher equation: nominal interest rate (i) = real interest rate (r) + expected inflation (Π_e).

THE EQUATION OF EXCHANGE

(*Principles of Economics* 5th ed. pages 670–672/6th ed. pages 650–652)

Monetarist theory is based upon a simple equation known as the equation of exchange. It is always true and it serves as the basis of the **quantity theory of money**, that belief that *changes in price level are directly proportional to changes in money supply in the long run*. The monetary equation of exchange is: MV = PQ.

To fully understand the equation, one must first recognize and understand the variables. M represents money supply; in the monetarist interpretation, the M2 definition of money supply is most relevant. V is the velocity of money, a measurement of how many times each dollar changes hands in a given year. P represents price level, or more specifically, the implicit price deflator used in making the inflationary adjustment between real and nominal GDP. Q is real GDP, national income after adjusting for inflation.

As it is used in monetarist theory, the equation of is exchange is interpreted as implying that changes in money supply lead to similar changes in price level. This is because monetarists assume that velocity (specifically M2 velocity) is relatively stable and that real GDP is slow to change. Therefore, monetarists conclude, by controlling the growth of money supply, the central bank can control inflation.

MONEY CREATION AND THE MONEY MULTIPLIER

(*Principles of Economics* 5th ed. pages 650–653/6th ed. pages 627–630)

Inherent in the discussion of the Federal Reserve is the ability of the Fed to create money. The Fed "creates" money by influencing the amount of money banks can lend, a money creation process that occurs as a result of what is called the fractional reserve system.

In the case of 100-percent-reserve banking, all deposits are held as reserves; no loans are made by banks in this type of system. This is not how the U.S. system of reserves operates.

Fractional-reserve systems, such as that in place among U.S. banks, are different. Under this system, only a fraction of deposits are kept as reserves; the remainder is loaned out to borrowers. As a result, more than one person may have a claim on each dollar of reserves and the act of bank lending actually "creates" new money.

As part of its monetary policy and federal regulator roles, the Fed actually dictates how much money banks must keep on reserve. The reserve requirement is determined by the board of governors and requires banks to keep a certain amount of deposits on reserve; anything above that legal minimum is considered excess reserves and may be loaned out.

By using excess reserves and the reserve ratio, one may predict how much money can be created by a given deposit. Assume a reserve ratio of 10 percent. This means that for every $1 deposited in the bank, $0.10 must be kept on reserve. If a deposit of $100 is made, the bank must keep $10, but is capable of loaning out $90. By loaning out excess reserves, the bank is creating a situation where two people have claims on the same reserves, hence, a fractional-reserve system.

To determine how much money can be created by each deposit, one must use the money multiplier. The money multiplier illustrates how much money can be generated with each dollar of reserves; it is equal to the reciprocal of the reserve ratio. For our example above, the money multiplier is 1/0.1, or 10. We calculate the amount of potential money created by multiplying the amount of money able to be loaned (excess reserves) by the money multiplier. In our example, excess reserves equaled $90, therefore this deposit may create up to $900.

We would state in this situation that $900 may be created through new loans. This is only possible if two conditions are met: 1. Banks lend out their entire excess reserves (which they often do not) and 2. Borrowers re-deposit all funds into the banking system. Without both of these conditions, the full multiplier effect will not take place and less than $900 will be created. In the end, the $100 of reserves can support $1,000 of deposits – the original $100 plus $900 generated through additional bank lending. Thus, the multiplier tells us the total deposits that may result from the original $100 increase in bank reserves.

FINANCIAL SECTOR AND THE FEDERAL RESERVE: STUDENT OBJECTIVES FOR THE AP EXAM

You should be able to:
- Define all key terms in bold
- Graph: be able to accurately draw and manipulate the loanable funds market and money market graphs
- Explain how the equation of exchange supports the quantity theory of money
- Demonstrate the relationship between real and nominal interest rates based on the Fisher effect

MULTIPLE-CHOICE QUESTIONS

1. Determine the amounts of M1 and M2 based on the data on the following table:

Type of Money	Amount
Cash & Coin	$5,000
Small time deposits	$2,000
Traveler's Checks	$1,000
Savings	$3,000
Checking Accounts	$2,500

	M1	M2
(A)	$5,000	$5,000
(B)	$7,000	$12,000
(C)	$7,000	$13,500
(D)	$8,500	$13,500
(E)	$8,500	$5,000

2. When money is being held in savings, it is fulfilling this function:
   (A) Medium of exchange.
   (B) Standard of value.
   (C) Store of value.
   (D) Unit of account.
   (E) Measure of wealth.

3. The distribution of currency and clearing of checks are among the roles of this component of the Federal Reserve System.
   (A) Board of Governors.
   (B) The Twelve District Banks.
   (C) The Federal Open Market Committee.
   (D) Discount Window.
   (E) Chairman of the Board of Governors.

4. The paper money issued by the U.S. government is
   (A) The equivalent of a U.S. Treasury security
   (B) Backed by silver.
   (C) Backed by gold.
   (D) A fiat currency.
   (E) A commodity currency.

5. Which group is responsible for determining and implementing the Federal Reserve's monetary policy?
   (A) Federal Reserve Thrift Advisory Councils.
   (B) Secretary of the Treasury.
   (C) Federal Open Market Committee.
   (D) Office of Management and Budget.
   (E) Council of Economic Advisors.

6. For a given economy, money supply is valued at $4,000 while the implicit price deflator is 1.5 and real GDP is $8,000. According to the equation of exchange, what is the velocity of money?
    (A) 3.
    (B) 2.
    (C) 1.5.
    (D) 1.
    (E) 0.75.

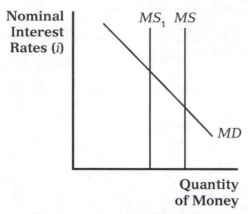

7. Assume that Fed policy causes the change in money supply from MS to MS$_1$ illustrated in the graph above. What is the intended goal of this policy?
    (A) Encourage growth by increasing interest rates as motivation for increased investment.
    (B) Slow down rates of inflation by contracting money supply and driving up interest rates, therefore lowering investment.
    (C) Decrease unemployment by increasing the amount of money demanded.
    (D) Increase investment opportunities by creating more optimistic business expectations.
    (E) Reach full employment by increasing consumption.

8. In the money market graph, the vertical shape of the money supply curve illustrates:
    (A) Potential changes in money supply due to changing central bank policy.
    (B) That interest rates have no effect on the quantity of money supplied.
    (C) Whether money demand will increase or decrease when interest rates fluctuate.
    (D) The inverse relationship between interest rates and money supply.
    (E) A positive relationship between changes in money supply and changes in interest rates.

9. Assuming a reserve requirement of 20%, what is the money multiplier?
    (A) 20.
    (B) 10.
    (C) 5.
    (D) 2.
    (E) 0.5.

10. According to the quantity theory of money, price level and money supply
(A) are directly proportional in the long run.
(B) are always equal amounts because velocity is constant.
(C) are inversely related in the long run.
(D) are stable in the short run.
(E) exhibit no relationship in the long run.

11. An increase in households' desire to save money for a later date will cause the following change in the loanable funds market:
(A) An increase in the demand for loanable funds and an increase in real interest rates.
(B) A decrease in the demand for loanable funds and a decrease in real interest rates.
(C) A decrease in the supply of loanable funds and an increase in real interest rates.
(D) An increase in the supply of loanable funds and a decrease in real interest rates.
(E) No change will occur in the loanable funds market.

12. The Fed decreases money supply. Based on the resulting change in nominal interest rates in the money market, what will be the expected change in investment and aggregate demand?

	Investment	Aggregate Demand
(A)	Decrease	Increase
(B)	Decrease	Decrease
(C)	No change	Increase
(D)	Increase	No Change
(E)	Increase	Increase

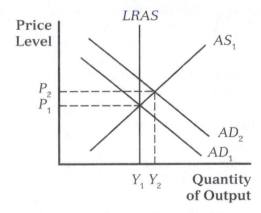

13. The change in aggregate demand illustrated in the graph above may have come as a result of which of the following?
(A) An increase in the demand for loanable funds.
(B) A decrease in money supply.
(C) An increase in the supply of loanable funds.
(D) An increase in money demand.
(E) A decrease in the velocity of money.

14. What name is given the rate that represents the amount of consumption banks hope to gain in the future by forgoing consumption today?
    (A) Nominal interest rate.
    (B) Discount rate.
    (C) Prime rate.
    (D) Real interest rate.
    (E) Inflation rate.

15. Assume banks desire a 2 percent return on all loans. If the anticipated level of inflation is 3 percent, how much should banks charge on new loans?
    (A) 6%.
    (B) 5%.
    (C) 3%.
    (D) 1%.
    (E) – 1%.

FREE-RESPONSE QUESTIONS

1. The central bank is charged with maintaining price stability and encouraging economic growth by controlling changes in the money supply.
   a. Assume that, in the interest of lowering unemployment, the central bank increases money supply.
      i. Illustrate the effects of this policy on a correctly labeled graph of the money market.
      ii. What will be the expected effect on nominal interest rates as a result of this policy?
      iii. What will happen to aggregate demand as a result of this policy? Explain.
   b. At the same time, the federal government decides on a massive tax cut which will lead to a federal budget deficit. Show on a correctly labeled graph of the loanable funds market the effect of the deficit on real interest rates.
   c. In response to the policies listed above in parts (a) and (b), what will happen to investment? Explain.

2. Assume the reserve requirement is 10 percent.
   a. A bank has $150,000 in deposits. What amount of new loans can be created by this money?
   b. Calculate the money multiplier.
   c. A new customer deposits $1,000. What is the maximum increase in money supply that may occur as a result of this deposit?
   d. The Fed purchases $1,000 in securities from this bank. What is the maximum increase in money supply that may occur as a result of this purchase?

Answers

MULTIPLE-CHOICE QUESTIONS

1. **D.** M1 is the sum of currency ($5,000), traveler's checks ($1,000) and demand deposits ($2,500); M2 is the sum of M1 plus small time-deposits ($2,000) and savings ($3,000). (*Principles of Economics* 5th ed. pages 645–646/6th ed. pages 624–625).

2. **C.** Money held in savings represents the forgoing of consumption now for consumption in the future; as a function of money, it is a store of value. (*Principles of Economics* 5th ed. page 643/6th ed. page 621).

3. **B.** Among the roles of the 12 district banks are to distribute currency and clear checks in order to facilitate economic activity. (*Principles of Economics* 5th ed. page 648/6th ed. page 626).

4. **D.** The paper money distributed by the Treasure has no backing and is labeled fiat money. (*Principles of Economics* 5th ed. page 644/6th ed. page 622).

5. **C.** The FOMC consists of the Fed Board of Governors and five district bank presidents; they are responsible for determining monetary policy (*Principles of Economics* 5th ed. page 648/6th ed. page 626–627).

6. **A.** The equation of exchange is MV = PQ. Because PQ = 8,000 * 1.5, or 12,000, V must equal 3 so that MV also equals 12,000. (*Principles of Economics* 5th ed. pages 670–672/6th ed. pages 650–652).

7. **B.** A decrease in money supply will drive interest rates up, which decreases AD by decreasing levels of investment and consumption. The Fed does this to slow down potential rates of inflation. (*Principles of Economics* 5th ed. page 668/6th ed. page 648).

8. **B.** The inelastic money supply curve is unaffected by changes in interest rates; movement along the curve does not change the quantity of money supplied. (*Principles of Economics* 5th ed. page 780/6th ed. page 760).

9. **C.** The money multiplier is the reciprocal of the reserve requirement; with a reserve ratio of 20%, the money multiplier equals 1/0.2, or 5. (*Principles of Economics* 5th ed. pages 650–653/6th ed. pages 628–630).

10. **A.** Monetarists conclude from the equation of exchange that there exists a directly proportional relationship between the growth of money supply and increases in price level. (*Principles of Economics* 5th ed. pages 670–672/6th ed. pages 650–652).

11. **D.** When households put more money into savings, national savings increases, causing the supply of loanable funds to increase. The increase in supply of loanable funds will drive down real interest rates as banks attempt to attract borrowers. (*Principles of Economics* 5th ed. pages 583–589/6th ed. pages 564–570).

12. **B.** A decrease in money supply will cause nominal interest rates to rise. When interest rates rise, investment decreases, leading to a decrease in aggregate demand. (*Principles of Economics* 5th ed. pages 783–784/6th ed. pages 764–765).

13. **C.** As the supply of loanable funds increases, interest rates fall, causing investment and consumption to increase. This leads to an increase in aggregate demand. (*Principles of Economics* 5th ed. pages 583–589/6th ed. pages 564–570).

14. **D.** A real interest rate is defined as the amount of consumption lenders hope to gain by forgoing present consumption; it measures this by taking inflation into account. (*Principles of Economics* 5th ed. page 540/6th ed. page 524).

15. **B.** The Fisher equation states nominal interest rates equal real interest rates plus anticipated inflation: 2% + 3% + 5%. (*Principles of Economics* 5th ed. pages 674–676/6th ed. pages 655–656).

FREE-RESPONSE QUESTIONS

1. a.

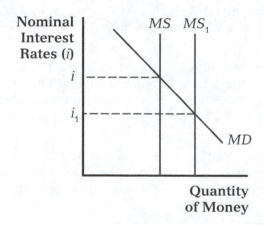

   i.   Correctly labeled graph of the money market; money supply shifts to the right, causing interest rates to fall.
   ii. Nominal interest rates will decrease.
   iii. Aggregate demand will increase; investment and consumer spending will increase when interest rates fall.

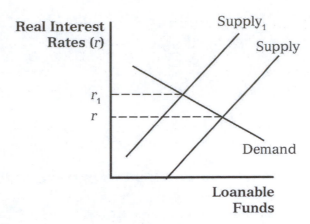

b. Correctly labeled graph of the loanable funds; decrease in the supply of loanable funds causing interest rates to rise (an increase in the demand for loanable funds is also acceptable).

c. The change in investment is indeterminate; the increase in money supply will increase investment, but the decrease in the supply of loanable funds (or increase in demand for loanable funds) will decrease private investment. The cumulative change is unknown.

(*Principles of Economics* 5th ed. pages 779–781 and 583–589/6th ed. pages 758–761 and 564–570)

2. a. $135,000.
   b. 10.
   c. $9,000.
   d. $10,000.

(*Principles of Economics* 5th ed. pages 650–653/6th ed. pages 627–631)

10

INFLATION, UNEMPLOYMENT, AND STABILIZATION POLICY

The dual economic concerns of inflation and unemployment have historically shared headlines. Rising prices and job loss are two of the more commonly recognized sources of economic stress faced by individuals and economies. Comprehension of rising prices and job losses may help in alleviating some of the stress associated with these two situations; for this reason, numerous theories have emerged regarding the causes of and potential solutions to inflation and unemployment.

INFLATION

(*Principles of Economics* 5th ed. pages 529–537/6th ed. pages 513–520)

Over time and with economic growth, *the average price of goods and services tend to rise*; this situation is known as **inflation**. Inflation creates numerous problems for an economy ranging from uncertainty regarding future price levels to a depreciation of the value of a nation's currency in international markets. To fully understand the effects of inflation, one must first have an idea of what it is and how it is measured.

MEASURING INFLATION

There are many methods used for measuring fluctuating price levels in an economy. The most commonly used indicator of consumer inflation in the U.S. is the consumer price index (CPI), measured monthly by the Bureau of Labor Statistics (BLS). The CPI is one example of a **price**

index, *the measurement of the price of a market basket of goods from one period to another.* In this case, a basket of consumer goods is measured each month and used as an indicator of any changes in average prices paid by consumers. To do so requires a great amount of data collection and analysis by economists at the BLS. Other examples of a price index include the producer price index (PPI) and GDP price deflator, discussed in Chapter 11.

A general price index is determined by comparing the value of a basket of goods in the current year to the value of the same basket in a fixed base year. The process begins with the collection of prices for a specific set of goods and services and computation of the basket's total cost. To compute the index, simply take the cumulative price of the basket in the current year and divide by the price of the same basket of goods in the chosen base year. Multiplying the answer by 100 gives the price index for the current year.

Price index = (Price of a basket of goods and services in current year/Price of basket in base year) × 100

By calculating a price index this way, it should be clear that the index for the base year will always equal 100.

From this price index, we can determine the inflation rate by calculating the percent change in prices from one period to the next. For example, if in year 1, the price index is 100 and in year 2 it is 110, we can say that prices increased 10% from year 1 to year 2.

AP Tip

Be able to calculate the percent change in any given indicator. An easy way to remember how is by memorizing the phrase: New minus Old over Old. For example, in the case of a price index, percent change in found by subtracting the old PI from the new PI, then dividing by the old PI (and multiplying by 100). This method works for any data, whether CPI, unemployment or Real GDP.

UNEMPLOYMENT

(*Principles of Economics* 5th ed. pages 613–622/6th ed. pages 593–597)

While inflation is often a bewildering subject to those without a background in economics, unemployment is generally more easily understood. Fluctuations in price level can be deceiving and the causes not very obvious; job loss—and the causes—are easily observed.

MEASURING UNEMPLOYMENT

Unemployment as it is measured in the United States *is an indication of how many people in the labor force are not working.* The labor force is loosely defined as the number of people aged 16 and above who are both willing and able to work. This generally consists of just over half the population. Unemployment measures the percentage of this subset that is actually out of work at any given time; it does not illustrate the number of people without a job as a percentage of the total population.

The calculation of unemployment is a simple one. Monthly surveys completed by the Bureau of Labor Statistics determine how many citizens make up the labor force at any given time as well as how many are employed or unemployed. The unemployment rate is found by dividing the number of unemployed by the total labor force.

Unemployment Rate = (# unemployed/Labor force) × 100

While it sounds ideal to shoot for an unemployment rate of zero, it is much more realistic to say most economists would prefer an unemployment rate within the range of 4–6 percent. It is impractical to expect zero percent unemployment—that condition where everyone who wants a job has one. Likewise, history has shown that there are certain types of unemployment always present in an economy, even the healthiest ones.

TYPES OF UNEMPLOYMENT

People find themselves unemployed for many different reasons. To better understand the employment situation, analysts have defined unemployment in three different ways.

Frictional unemployment *occurs due to the extended time a person takes to find a job best suited for their skills*. Recent high school or college graduates searching for their first job are considered frictionally unemployed, as are individuals who leave a job in search of a better one. Implied in the definition of frictional unemployment is that job seekers feel an extended job search is worth the cost of being unemployed.

Structural unemployment *occurs when the job skills of potential workers are no longer needed or the skills of job seekers are worth less than prevailing wage rates*. This often occurs as a result of technological advances which make certain jobs obsolete. For example, in the mid-twentieth century the introduction of refrigeration made the jobs of milk and ice delivery men obsolete or wages being held above the equilibrium wage. In order to find gainful employment, structurally unemployed people must improve or add to their current job skills.

A third type of unemployment is **cyclical unemployment**. Cyclical unemployment occurs when *workers lose their jobs due to downturns in the business cycle*. In other words, jobs are lost because people aren't buying as much as they used to.

Understanding the three types of unemployment allows one to comprehend what is meant by **the natural rate of unemployment**. The natural rate of unemployment is *that rate of unemployment that occurs in the long run when cyclical unemployment is zero and the economy is producing at what is called full employment levels of output*. While the natural rate of unemployment can vary over time, in the U.S. it usually hovers within the 4–6 percent range.

STABILIZATION POLICY

(*Principles of Economics* 5th ed. pages 777–798/6th ed. pages 757–778)

Stabilization policy is the act of government entities intervening in the economy in order to encourage economic growth, maintain stable prices and/or achieve full employment. Although classical economic theory states that economies will self-correct, governments often decide that waiting for self-correction takes too long (and is politically unwise). Stabilization policies have emerged as short-run fixes for economic downturns.

Stabilization policies may be directed in one of two ways: expansionary or contractionary. **Expansionary policies** are intended to encourage short-run increases in output and subsequently provide a boost to employment. **Contractionary policies** slow down economic growth as a deterrent to high inflation rates.

FISCAL POLICY AND ITS IMPACT ON AD-AS

Theories regarding the appropriate use of fiscal policy are derived from the twentieth century economist John Maynard Keynes. Keynes proposed that downturns in the business cycle were the result of inadequate aggregate demand. While classical and neoclassical economic theories preached that self-correction would occur in the long run, Keynes believed a short-run solution was needed because, as he famously put it, "in the long run, we'll all be dead." Therefore, in order to stimulate aggregate demand and encourage short run increases in national income, Keynesian economic theory supports the manipulation of aggregate demand through the two tools of fiscal policy: government spending and taxation.

Fiscal policy is *the attempt of a government to stabilize the economy through government spending and taxation.* It has a direct effect on aggregate demand and economic activity. In the case of government spending, policy makers can have a direct influence on aggregate demand by increasing or decreasing the amount of government purchases made. Expansionary action would increase aggregate demand and output, leading to lower unemployment. A decrease in taxes would have the same effect; by lowering tax rates, consumption will increase due to higher levels of disposable income and aggregate demand will increase. An increase in output and decrease in unemployment should soon follow this policy.

It should be noted that expansionary fiscal policies will likely have an adverse effect on the federal budget. Due to the combination of increased spending and/or decreased taxes, federal outlays will increase while revenue decreases. This combination will lead to a federal budget deficit, causing the government to issue securities in order to cover the full cost of the government spending. While this may be encouraged in the short-run, there are long-run implications that must be realized (and addressed later in the chapter).

Contractionary fiscal policies operate just as expansionary actions did, yet in the opposite direction. To slow down economic growth and any problematic inflationary issues, government spending would have to decrease and/or increase taxes. Either of these actions would cause aggregate demand to decrease, bringing down price levels and output.

THE MULTIPLIER EFFECT

Keynes' theories regarding the effects of fiscal policy are dependent on his understanding of the **multiplier effect**. The multiplier effect states that as expansionary fiscal policies are implemented, subsequent increases in income will lead to further increases in consumer spending and the final increase in GDP will be greater than the initial increase in government spending. In other words, for every $1 increase in government spending, GDP will increase by more than $1.

Determining the multiplier effect of fiscal policy relies upon knowledge of the marginal propensity to consume (MPC) and marginal propensity to save (MPS). The **MPC** indicates *how much household spending increases whenever income increases;* **MPS** is *the measure of increases in saving that results from increased income.* For example, assume a household's income increases by $10,000 and, in response, the household's consumption goes up $8,000. In this case, MPC equals the percentage of the change in income that was spent, or 80% (8,000/10,000). MPS—the amount saved—makes up the remaining 20% (2,000/10,000). As a rule, MPC plus MPS must equal 100% as spending and saving are the only two ways additional after tax income may be used.

With this knowledge, we can determine the amount of the spending multiplier. Again refer to the example above. If—as we assume—all households treat their additional income the same way, the spending multiplier will be the reciprocal of MPS, or 1/MPS. In this case, the multiplier is 5 (1/0.2).

Just as there is a spending multiplier used to estimate the effects of a change in government spending, there is also a tax multiplier which predicts the effects of a change in taxes. To find the tax multiplier, simply divide negative MPC by MPS. The tax multiplier is always negative; this is so because an increase in taxes will decrease GDP while a decrease in taxes will increase GDP. In the example above where MPC equaled 0.8, the tax multiplier will be – 0.8/0.2, or – 4.

To use either multiplier, simply multiply the proposed change in government spending or taxes by the multiplier to determine the potential change in GDP that will result due to the policy change. If the multiplier is 5 and policy makers intend to increase government spending by $1,000, one can expect GDP to increase by $5,000 ($1,000 × 5). If, in the same situation, taxes were increased by $1,000, GDP would decrease by $4,000 ($1,000 × -4).

AUTOMATIC STABILIZERS

To this point, we have only considered the case of **discretionary stabilization policy**—*those policy changes requiring new legislation to be passed.* In many other cases, prior legislation has paved the way for **automatic stabilization policy**, *policy actions that do not require new legislation.* Examples of automatic stabilization include the progressive income tax and unemployment benefits.

MONETARY POLICY AND ITS IMPACT ON AD-AS

Central bank intervention in the economy also has an effect on aggregate demand known as **monetary policy**, *the determination of money supply as a way of stabilizing the economy.* In the United States, this means the Federal Reserve is designed to fulfill a stabilizing role; this role is defined as the dual mandate. The dual mandate, as the name implies, indicates that the Fed has two goals when determining monetary policy; those two goals are to maintain price stability and to promote economic growth. One could paraphrase these goals has fighting inflation and fighting unemployment. Similar to fiscal policy, monetary policy accomplishes this goal by manipulating aggregate demand, albeit more indirectly. The Fed has three main tools to utilize when applying its stabilization policy: open market operations, discount window lending and the reserve requirement.

AP Tip

Be certain you can relate monetary policy actions with the graphs of the money market and loanable funds market. Any expansionary monetary policy will increase money supply, shifting MS (in the money market) and the supply of loanable funds (in the loanable funds market) to the right. As a result, in both graphs interest rates will decrease, causing an increase in consumption and investment, therefore an increase in aggregate demand. Contractionary monetary policies will have the opposite effect.

Open market operations, simply defined, *is the buying and selling of government securities on the open market.* Government securities, or bonds, are issued by the Treasury department as a form of borrowing whenever the federal government has a budget deficit (see Chapter 9 for further explanation). Individuals and banks can purchase these bonds from the Treasury in an auction and, if they choose, re-sell them on the open market. This is where the Fed enters the picture.

In order to manipulate money supply, the Fed can buy or sell bonds. To increase money supply, the Fed buys bonds, which increases bank reserves, drives down interest rates and encourages economic activity through investment and consumption. The FOMC would decide on this course of action when the economy needs a boost and unemployment is high; we call this an expansionary monetary policy. When inflation is high, the opposite set of events occurs: the Fed sells securities, decreasing bank reserves, causing interest rates to rise and economic activity to fall. This is the proper use of open market operations under a contractionary monetary policy.

Open market operations is the most commonly used tool of monetary policy. Every day at the New York Federal Reserve Bank, securities are bought and sold on the open market in order to manipulate money supply and to reach a pre-determined target for the federal funds rate. The federal funds rate is an interest rate private banks charge each other for overnight loans; by increasing or decreasing money supply, the Fed is able to effectively alter the federal funds rate which has a great deal of influence on rates charged to borrowers, therefore altering the amount of investment and consumption occurring throughout the economy.

The second tool of the Fed is **discount window lending**. At the discount window, the Fed is acting as the "lender of last resort" by *lending money directly to private banks.* Private banks, facing liquidity problems, may borrow money from the central bank. When they do, they borrow at the discount window (think of it as a drive-thru teller for bankers). Of course, the Fed doesn't lend money for free; banks are charged the discount rate—an interest rate banks must pay the Fed for borrowing money. When the Fed wants to encourage more lending in order to stimulate economic activity (expansionary policy), they lower the discount rate. To fight inflation by slowing down lending activity, the Fed raises the discount rate.

The third, and least used, tool of monetary policy is the **reserve requirement**. As stated in Chapter 9, the reserve requirement dictates to banks *how much of each deposit must be held in reserves*. These reserves may be held as cash in the bank's vault or deposited at the appropriate Federal Reserve district bank. When the Fed wants to encourage more lending, they decrease the reserve ratio, essentially increasing the amount of funds available for loans; this is expansionary policy aimed at lowering unemployment. By raising the reserve ratio, the central bank decreases the amount of funds available for loans and slows economic activity; this is contractionary policy and is meant to lower inflation.

LAGS IN POLICY MAKING

Policy does not have an instantaneous effect on the economy. In fact, it takes time for the effects of policy to be felt; these gaps in time are known as lags in policy making and can differ from policy to policy.

Inside lags are those *lags that occur between the time an economic problem arises and potential solutions are actually decided upon*. This includes recognition lags (the time it takes policy makers to identify a problem) and response lags (the time spent determining a proper policy solution). Due to the timely legislative process, fiscal policy traditionally exhibits much larger inside lags than monetary policy.

Outside lags *take place after a stabilization policy has been implemented*. They refer to the amount of time it takes for the effects of policy to be felt by the economy. Because of the nature of monetary policy and its necessity to work though the banking system, monetary outside lags are considerably longer than those of fiscal policy.

SHORT-RUN TRADE OFF BETWEEN INFLATION AND UNEMPLOYMENT: THE PHILLIPS CURVE

(*Principles of Economics* 5th ed. pages 801–815/6th ed. pages 785–798)

Research from the mid-twentieth century revealed to economists a short-run relationship between the two indicators, inflation and unemployment. A.W. Phillips, the British economist credited with this discovery, claimed that there exists an inverse relationship between inflation and unemployment; when unemployment is low, people spend more money and cause prices to rise; when unemployment is high, people cut back their spending and inflation rates fall. Data from the 1960s appeared to confirm Phillips' theory and the **Phillips Curve**, *illustrating the short-run trade-off between inflation and unemployment,* was born (see below).

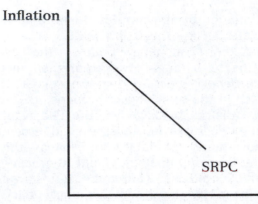

The 1970s, however, told a different story. Due to drastic increases in production costs, aggregate supply fell throughout much of the decade. As AS shifted left, output decreased, unemployment rose and cost-push inflation occurred at relatively high rates. This prolonged period of high unemployment and high inflation—named stagflation to represent a stagnant economy with inflation—defied the lessons of the Philips Curve. Upon further analysis, though, economists discovered two things: (1) The changes of the 1970s were the result of a shift of the short-run Phillips Curve and (2) There is no relationship between inflation and unemployment in the long-run.

The first of these conclusions reveals much about the nature of the short-run Phillips curve (SRPC), its relationship to AD-AS, and what makes it shift. In general, we can say that changes in the SRPC are inversely related to shocks of short-run aggregate supply; rightward shifts in SRAS correlate with leftward shifts of SRPC while decreases in SRAS occur when SRPC increases. Likewise, movements of aggregate demand indicate movement along the SRPC; an increase in AD will increase price level while decreasing unemployment—synonymous with movement up the SRPC—while a decrease in AD has the opposite effect and causes movement down the SRPC.

The second conclusion, that there is no long-run relationship between inflation and unemployment, led economists to derive the vertical long-run Phillips curve (LRPC). This curve (see below), intersects the x-axis at the natural rate of unemployment and indicates that in the long-run, unemployment will return to its full employment rate (that rate of unemployment where cyclical unemployment is zero), regardless of any changes in inflation. The LRPC may shift left or right, but only as a result of a change in the natural rate of unemployment. The natural rate of unemployment changes when there is an extension of the duration of unemployment due to extensions of unemployment benefits and/or general economic conditions which restrict hiring by firms for a long period of time.

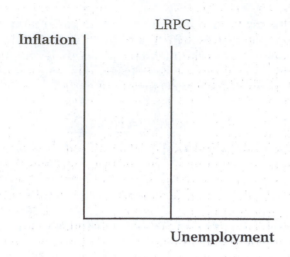

LONG-RUN TRADE OFF BETWEEN GROWTH AND STIMULUS: THE CROWDING OUT EFFECT

(*Principles of Economics* 5th ed. pages 791–792/6th ed. pages 771–772)

The intention of expansionary fiscal policy is obvious: encourage short-run gains in output in order to decrease high levels of unemployment. What isn't as obvious is the long-run effect of such policies. Because of the budget deficit created by expansionary policies, it is very likely that, absent any accommodative monetary policy, interest rates will rise in the short-run. This happens as a result of increased money demand (due to inflationary expectations) and a decrease in supply of (or an increase in demand for) loanable funds by government. In either case, increases in interest rates cause levels of investment and interest-sensitive consumption to decrease. With these decreases, any increase in AD created by the fiscal policy is partially offset and the predicted multiplier effect does not occur. This scenario is known as **crowding out**, *the decrease in investment brought on by high federal deficits*. Essentially, government borrowing has the potential to "crowd out" private investors.

Explained above is merely the short-run effect of crowding out. The long-run consequences are more severe. It should be understood that investment spending, while shifting AD in the long-run, may lead to economic growth in the long-run. This will be discussed in more detail in the next chapter, but in essence, investment spending leads to capital formation and advancements in technology, the two key drivers of productivity growth. With increases in productivity comes long-term economic growth. When crowding out occurs, a trade-off is occurring; long-term growth is being sacrificed in order to achieve short-run gains in output and employment.

ACCOMMODATIVE MONETARY POLICY

Even with expansionary fiscal policies and federal budget deficits in place, it is possible to avoid crowding out if the central bank determines short-run growth is needed. The Fed may choose to accommodate, or aide, the expansionary fiscal policy with an expansionary policy of its own. In doing so, the Fed can maintain interest rates at their previous levels, effectively negating crowding out as investment and consumption also maintain previous levels due to consistent interest rates. In doing so, the FOMC has determined unemployment is a bigger problem than inflation.

INFLATION, UNEMPLOYMENT, AND STABILIZATION POLICY: STUDENT OBJECTIVES FOR THE AP EXAM

You should be able to:
- Define all key terms in bold
- Graph the Phillips curve
- Explain the logic behind and reasons for fiscal and monetary stabilization policies
- Present the reasons why crowding out may occur and how accommodative policies may limit its effects

MULTIPLE-CHOICE QUESTIONS

1. Given below are prices and quantities for a basket of goods in two given years. Calculate a price index for year 2 using the following data and year 1 as the base year.

	Quantity	Price (year 1)	Price (year 2)
Item 1	5	$10	$12
Item 2	10	$7.50	$20

   (A) 55.
   (B) 80.
   (C) 208.
   (D) 250.
   (E) 480.

2. If the consumer price index for an economy increases from 125 to 150 in one calendar year, what is the percent increase in consumer prices for that year?
   (A) 50%.
   (B) 20%.
   (C) 25%.
   (D) 5%.
   (E) 10%.

3. Given the following data, calculate the unemployment rate for this economy:

Adult Population	Employed	Unemployed
200	95	5

   (A) 2.5%.
   (B) 5%.
   (C) 10%.
   (D) 27.5%.
   (E) 50%.

4. As the economy enters a recession, a major manufacturer lays off hundreds of factory workers. What type of unemployment is this?
   (A) Structural.
   (B) Seasonal.
   (C) Cyclical.
   (D) Frictional.
   (E) Recessional.

5. Facing the prospects of a recession and potential economic decline, the federal government chooses to lower marginal income tax rates and increase government spending. What type of policy is this and what effect will it have on the federal budget?

Policy Type	Effect on budget
(A) Expansionary monetary	Towards surplus
(B) Expansionary fiscal	Towards deficit
(C) Contractionary fiscal	Towards surplus
(D) Contractionary monetary	Towards deficit
(E) Expansionary fiscal	Towards surplus

6. Calculate the spending multiplier when MPC is 0.9.
   (A) 10.
   (B) −10.
   (C) 9.
   (D) −9.
   (E) 1.

7. Assume an individual's income increases $20,000 in a given year. If this person saves $5,000 of the change in income and spends the rest, what is the MPC?
   (A) 0.9.
   (B) 0.8.
   (C) 0.75.
   (D) 0.25.
   (E) 0.2.

8. Given an MPC of 0.75, by how much would a government have to change spending in order to cause a $4 trillion increase in real GDP, holding taxes constant and assuming the full multiplier effect?
   (A) $5.33 trillion.
   (B) $4 trillion.
   (C) $2 trillion.
   (D) $1 trillion.
   (E) −$1.33 trillion.

9. Which of the following is an example of an automatic stabilizer?
   (A) Congress votes for an increase in marginal income tax rates and the President signs the new bill into law.
   (B) The Fed lowers the target for the federal funds rate.
   (C) Banks facing a shortage of liquid funds borrow from the Fed at the discount window.
   (D) Unemployed workers receive unemployment benefits to help pay their bills.
   (E) The federal government constructs a stimulus package of new spending to encourage growth in a stagnant economy.

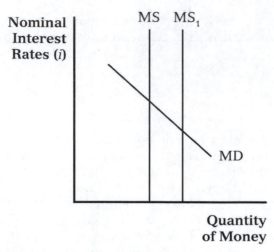

10. Which of the following Fed policies would cause the above change in money supply from MS to MS₁?
    (A) Selling Treasury securities on the open market.
    (B) Raising the discount rate.
    (C) Increase in government spending.
    (D) Buying Treasury securities on the open market.
    (E) Decrease in marginal tax rates.

11. Which of the following combinations of fiscal and monetary policies would have the most expansionary effect?

	Discount Rate	Taxes	Government Spending
(A)	Lower	Lower	Increase
(B)	Raise	Raise	Decrease
(C)	Lower	Raise	Increase
(D)	Raise	Lower	Increase
(E)	Lower	Lower	Decrease

12. Assume the CPI indicates that inflation is a growing problem in the economy. What would be an appropriate monetary policy response by the Federal Reserve aimed at slowing inflation?
    (A) Raise the discount rate in order to slow lending activity.
    (B) Raise corporate income taxes.
    (C) Buy additional treasury securities on the open market.
    (D) Lower the reserve ratio.
    (E) Instruct the Treasury to print less money.

13. Which of the following is an example of an inside lag of fiscal policy making?
    (A) Savvy investors shift funds in order to avoid a new capital gains tax.
    (B) Politicians of opposing parties disagree on amounts of new stimulus spending.
    (C) Lending opportunities increase due to the Fed's decision to lower the federal funds rate.
    (D) Two members of the Federal Reserve board of governors disagree on inflationary expectations.
    (E) Unemployment benefits are extended in response to an extended recession.

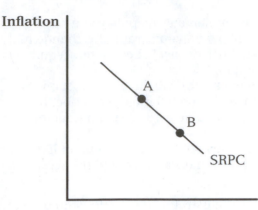

14. Which of the following best explains the movement along the short-run Phillips curve from point A to point B seen on the graph above?
    (A) An increase in aggregate demand due to increased consumer spending.
    (B) A decrease in short-run aggregate supply due to increased production costs.
    (C) An increase in long-run aggregate supply due to gains in productivity.
    (D) An increase in short-run aggregate supply due to decreased government regulations on firms.
    (E) A decrease in aggregate demand due to decreased investment spending.

15. Assume that high federal government deficits over a number of years decrease the supply of loanable funds and cause interest rates to rise. If the Fed wants to prevent crowding out from occurring, which of the following would be the most effective open market operation?
    (A) Lower the discount rate.
    (B) Cut marginal income tax rates.
    (C) Lower the reserve ratio.
    (D) Buy treasury securities.
    (E) Increase discretionary government spending.

FREE RESPONSE QUESTIONS

1. Assume the economy is operating at output levels $5 trillion below full employment.
    a. Illustrate the current state of the economy on a correctly labeled graph of AD-AS.
        i. Label equilibrium price level, P_e and output, Y_e.
        ii. Draw the long run aggregate supply curve and label full employment output Y_f.
    b. MPC equals 0.8. How much would fiscal policy makers have to increase spending, holding taxes constant, in order to close the contractionary gap?

   c. Assume policy makers implement the policy you have described in part (b). Show on your graph the change in aggregate demand that will occur. Label the new equilibrium price level, P_2, and output, Y_2.

   d. The policy described in part (b) will have an effect on the federal budget which keeps the full multiplier effect from being realized. What is this situation called? Explain how this happens.

   e. Describe a policy the central bank may implement if it wants to accommodate fiscal policy makers and avoid the scenario described in part (d).

2. The short-run Phillips curve illustrates the relationship between inflation and unemployment in the short-run.
   a. Draw a correctly labeled short-run Phillips curve.
   b. With a natural rate of unemployment of 5%, show—on the same graph as part (a)—the long-run Phillips curve.
   c. Assume that currently unemployment is 8%. Label point A on the short-run Phillips curve.
   d. In order to ease the hardships of unemployment, policy makers decide to extend unemployment benefits from 27 to 54 weeks. Show the change that will likely occur on your graph above. Explain.

Answers

MULTIPLE-CHOICE QUESTIONS

1. **C.** The price of the basket of goods increases from $125 in year 1 to $260 in year 2. This is calculated by multiplying the quantity of each item purchased by the price each year. The index number is determined by dividing the year 2 total by the base year total (year 1) and multiplying by 100. 260/125 equals 2.08, times 100 equals 208. (*Principles of Economics* 5th ed. pages 529–537/6th ed. pages 513–520) .

2. **B.** The CPI changed from 125 to 150. This is a 20 percent change, calculated as 150 minus 125 divided by 125 (times 100). 25/125 equals 0.2, times 100 equals 20 percent. (*Principles of Economics* 5th ed. pages 529–537/6th ed. pages 513–520)

3. **B.** Unemployment represents the percentage of the labor force not working. The labor force in this problem is 100 (employed plus unemployed). Of the 100 members of the labor force, 5 are unemployed, meaning a 5 percent unemployment rate. (*Principles of Economics* 5th ed. pages 613–622/6th ed. pages 593–597).

4. **C.** Cyclical unemployment occurs when jobs are lost due to downturns in the business cycle. (*Principles of Economics* 5th ed. pages 613–622/6th ed. pages 593–597) .

5. **B.** Changes in government spending and taxes are the domain of fiscal policy. When spending increases and taxes decrease, the effect on the economy is expansionary; the effect on the budget is to cause a deficit due to increased spending versus decreased revenues. (*Principles of Economics* 5th ed. pages 787–793/6th ed. pages 767–773)

6. **A.** The spending multiplier is calculated by dividing 1 by MPS. In this case, 1 divided by 0.1 equals 10. (*Principles of Economics* 5th ed. pages 789–790/6th ed. pages 769–770).

7. **C.** MPC is the change in consumption divided by the change in income. With income increasing $20,000 and $5,000 devoted to savings, the change in spending is $15,000. 15,000 divided by 20,000 equals 0.75. (*Principles of Economics* 5th ed. page 789/6th ed. page 769).

8. **D.** With an MPC of 0.75, the spending multiplier is 4. Therefore, any increase in spending will cause an increase in output four times that amount. To close a $4 trillion gap, spending must increase by ¼ the amount of the gap, or $1 trillion. (*Principles of Economics* 5th ed. pages 789–790/6th ed. pages 769–770).

9. **D.** Automatic stabilizers take effect without any new legislation; unemployment benefits automatically apply whenever people lose their jobs. (*Principles of Economics* 5th ed. page 797/6th ed. pages 777–778).

10. **D.** An increase in money supply occurs due to expansionary monetary policy; only D, buying Treasury securities, is an example of this type of policy. (*Principles of Economics* 5th ed. pages 778–784/6th ed. pages 758–764).

11. **A.** Only answer A appropriately indicates three consistent expansionary policies: lowering the discount rate, lowering tax rates and increasing spending. (*Principles of Economics* 5th ed. pages 777–798/6th ed. pages 757–778).

12. **A.** To slow inflation, the Fed must implement a contractionary monetary policy; of the options given, only raising the discount rate fits the necessary description. (*Principles of Economics* 5th ed. pages 777–798/6th ed. pages 757–778).

13. **B.** Inside lags take place before legislation is passed. As policy makers discuss alternate options for policy, the amount of time passed is referred to as an inside lag. (*Principles of Economics* 5th ed. pages 830–831/6th ed. pages 812–813).

14. **E.** Movement along the short-run Phillips curve occurs as a result of shifts of aggregate demand. When AD decreases, unemployment rises and price level falls, shown as movement down the SRPC. (*Principles of Economics* 5th ed. pages 801–815/6th ed. pages 785–798).

15. **D.** In order to avoid crowding out, the Fed must maintain interest rates at their previous levels. To do so, expansionary monetary policies are needed, such as buying treasury securities. (*Principles of Economics* 5th ed. pages 791–792/6th ed. pages 771–772).

FREE-RESPONSE QUESTIONS

1.

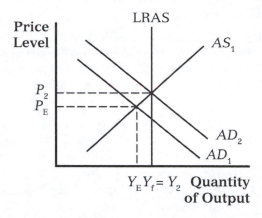

a. Correctly labeled graph of AD-AS
   i. LRAS indicating full employment.
   ii. Equilibrium price and quantity at output below full employment.
b. $1 trillion.
c. See graph above, AD increases; new equilibrium price and quantity.
d. Crowding out; the expansionary fiscal policy creates a federal budget deficit. As government borrows money, it increases interest rates due to a decrease in the supply of loanable funds; the increase in interest rates decreases investment and consumption, slowing any increases in AD brought on by the policy.
e. Any expansionary monetary policy is acceptable: buy securities on the open market, lower the discount rate, or lower the reserve ratio.

(*Principles of Economics* 5th ed. pages 777–798/6th ed. pages 757–778)

2.

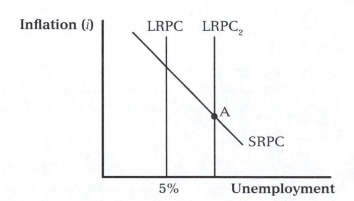

a. Correctly labeled short-run Phillips curve.
b. See graph above, correctly labeled long-run Phillips curve at 5 percent unemployment.
c. See graph above, point A to the right of LRPC.
d. See graph above, $LRPC_2$ The extension of unemployment benefits will increase the duration of unemployment, causing an increase in the natural rate of unemployment and shifting the LRPC to the right.

(*Principles of Economics* 5th ed. pages 801–815/6th ed. pages 785–798)

11

ECONOMIC GROWTH AND PRODUCTIVITY

Discussions of economic growth can be misleading. The concept, in the context of the long-run stability of an economy, refers to long-term economic growth, as opposed to short-run fluctuations. This means that short-term increases in consumption, investment, government spending, and net exports do not necessarily count as examples of economic growth. Rather, the term is meant to be connected with the concept of productivity, that term referring to the amount of output created from a given input.

DEFINING ECONOMIC GROWTH
(*Principles of Economics* 5th ed. pages 550–572/6th ed. pages 531–552)

In a word, it is gains in productivity that causes long-term economic growth. **Productivity** is defined as *the amount of output produced by an individual unit of an input.* Simply put, think of productivity as output per worker. When each worker is capable of producing more output from the same amount of time, productivity has increased and economic growth has occurred.

THE FACTORS THAT CAUSE ECONOMIC GROWTH

There are a number of events that potentially create economic growth. To uncover the events which increase productivity, one must ask: Why would a worker be capable of producing more? The answer is simple: increased physical capital, development of human capital, acquisition of more natural resources or improvements in the level of technology. Any of these will allow for each individual worker to produce more in the same amount of time.

> ## AP Tip
>
> Don't confuse the terms production and productivity. Production refers to an amount of output being produced by an economy. Productivity, however, refers to the amount of output produced per unit of input. While the two terms are very closely related, their use can have extremely different meanings. For example, increases in production may occur due to increased levels of consumer spending; this does not mean productivity has gone up.

PHYSICAL CAPITAL PER WORKER

When the term capital is used as a description of one of the four factors of production, it is likely that it is referring to physical capital. **Physical capital** consists of *the machines and equipment utilized by firms to produce the goods and services they provide*. In other words, physical capital is the "stuff that makes the stuff." The amount of physical capital in an economy (or capital stock) is a major determinant of that economy's productivity and rate of economic growth. As the amount of physical capital per worker increases, it can be assumed that labor is more capable of producing goods and economic growth occurs, increasing potential GDP. Therefore, increases in the capital stock cause long-term economic growth.

HUMAN CAPITAL PER WORKER

While the increased use of tangible equipment is an obvious determinant of economic growth, a less apparent one may be human capital per worker. **Human capital** is defined as *the knowledge and skills workers acquire through education, training, and experience*. As levels of human capital increase, labor becomes more skilled at their jobs and therefore more capable of producing goods. Economic growth occurs as productivity gains increase the natural rate of output due to individual workers' increased abilities. This may occur through formal education, worker training programs or—although immeasurable—experience, often referred to as learning by doing.

NATURAL RESOURCES PER WORKER

The discovery or acquisition of more natural resources may also lead to economic growth. In many cases, the amount of a natural resource available to an economy is either fixed or very difficult to change. For example, oil producing nations have a fixed amount of a non-renewable resource from which they derive their product. They may develop new ways to find and extract the oil, but the amount they have is a given. Acquisition or discovery of a natural resource, however, may have a significant impact on an economy's rate of economic growth.

TECHNOLOGICAL KNOWLEDGE

Gains in technological knowledge are the fourth and final determinant of economic growth. With greater technological knowledge, firms and workers become capable of producing more products faster and more efficiently. For example, with the technological gains of the late-1990s, access to relatively new technologies such as the internet, fiber-optic cable, fax machines, and cellular phones allowed firms to communicate more efficiently, to transport inputs more quickly, and, eventually, to produce more goods per unit of input than ever before. This era created unusually high productivity gains in the United States as workers and machines were capable of producing more than ever from a given amount of resources.

MEASURING GROWTH: REAL VS. NOMINAL GDP

(*Principles of Economics* 5th ed. pages 516–518/6th ed. pages 500–502)

Economic growth implies that a nation is capable of producing more finished goods and services with the same amount of resources than it did in a previous year. In order to accurately measure that this has occurred, one must understand the difference between real and nominal GDP and be able to convert between the two.

MEASURING GROWTH

The fundamental difference between any real and nominal variable is inflation. Simply comparing nominal output levels from year to year is an invalid way of measuring economic growth. Because of inflation, the value of a currency fluctuates from year to year. **Nominal GDP** is the *measurement of the production of goods and services valued at current prices*; it is not adjusted for inflationary (or deflationary) changes. As a result, the output level for consecutive years may be measured in units (dollars) that are not equal. To equalize units, we convert nominal to **real GDP**, *the measurement of the production of goods and services valued at constant prices*.

Think of it this way: imagine you are tracking your height from the ages of ten to fourteen years. This is perfectly acceptable so long as you use a consistent unit of measurement from year to year, such as inches. But what if the length of an inch varied from year to year? Your annual height comparisons would no longer be a valid history of your growth because the unit of measurement itself changed. This is what would happen if economic growth was measured using nominal (non-adjusted) GDP. Inflation causes the value of the dollar (our unit of measurement) to decrease. Nominal GDP does not account for this; for accurate depictions of economic growth, we must use real GDP.

When making the adjustment from nominal to real GDP, an index number (such as the CPI discussed in Chapter 10) must be used. Sometimes in place of CPI, a **GDP deflator** is used. This figure is *a measure of the price level calculated as the ratio of nominal GDP to real GDP times 100*. To convert from nominal GDP to real GDP, it is helpful to recall the following equation:

$$(\text{Nominal/price deflator}) \times 100 = \text{Real}$$

What this means is that to adjust for inflation (or deflate) nominal GDP, we simply divide GDP in current dollars by the price deflator. The following example shows how this is done.

Assume nominal GDP in year 1 is $10 trillion. If the GDP deflator is 200, a few mathematical calculations will give you real GDP.

(Nominal GDP/price deflator) × 100 = Real GDP

($10 trillion/200) × 100 = Real GDP

$50 billion × 100 = Real GDP

$5 trillion = Real GDP

The adjustment for inflation actually deflates (or lowers) GDP from its nominal figure ($10 trillion) down to its real figure ($5 trillion). Now the data is in constant prices and may serve as a valid measure of positive or negative economic growth.

AP Tip

One easy way to remember how to convert from nominal to real GDP is to use the equation of exchange that was discussed in Chapter 9. Recall the equation MV = PQ. Now, take the right side, PQ, where P equals the price deflator and Q is real GDP. Recall that P × Q equals nominal GDP. Therefore, if PQ = nominal GDP, real GDP must equal nominal GDP divided by the price deflator (times 100).

ILLUSTRATING GROWTH: THE PRODUCTION POSSIBILITIES CURVE

(*Principles of Economics* 5th ed. pages 25–28/6th ed. pages 26–28)

Any fundamental economics class addresses the production possibilities curve (PPC) very early in the course, as in Chapter 1 of this book. The PPC illustrates the maximum combination of two goods and/or services that a nation's economy can produce given a fixed amount of fully employed resources. As a result, it indicates the amount of product produced when that nation is operating at full employment levels of output.

ECONOMIC GROWTH ON THE PPC

Because it shows potential GDP, the PPC is capable of illustrating growth. When the curve shifts outward, it implies that more of both goods graphed may be produced by the economy in question. This indicates economic growth as the total amount of goods and services the economy is capable of producing has increased. The following figure shows how economic growth is illustrated on a standard PPC.

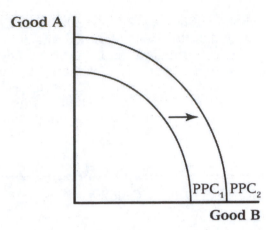

The shift from PPC₁ to PPC₂ shown above may be the result of any of the previously listed determinants of economic growth. Development of new physical capital (better machinery and equipment), advancement of human capital (through education and/or training), acquisition or discovery of natural resources, and/or increases in the level technology all cause potential GDP to rise and the PPC to shift outward.

ILLUSTRATING GROWTH: THE LONG-RUN AGGREGATE SUPPLY CURVE

(Principles of Economics 5th ed. pages 753–756/6th ed. pages 731–734)

The long-run aggregate supply curve (LRAS) represents an economy's natural rate of output, the amount of goods and services produced when the nation is operating at full employment. The output level, also known as the economy's potential GDP, is reached when an economy is utilizing its factors of production at their optimal level, given the levels of technology and capital stock available at the time. A shift of LRAS curve, therefore, indicates a change in the natural rate of output and will occur as a result of the previously mentioned determinants of economic growth.

ECONOMIC GROWTH ON THE LRAS

Long-run economic growth is illustrated by a rightward shift of the LRAS curve, as seen in the following figure.

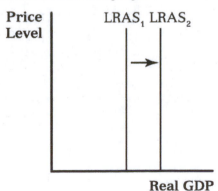

What this means is that when an economy is utilizing its land, labor, capital, and entrepreneurial ability to their highest capacity, the natural rate of output is being produced and the economy is functioning on the LRAS curve. A rightward shift of the LRAS curve indicates that even with no change in the amount of resources, the economy is capable of producing more due to productivity gains. Like with the PPC, this occurs due to gains in physical capital, human capital, natural resources, or technology.

LONG-RUN GROWTH VERSUS SHORT-RUN FLUCTUATIONS AND LONG-TERM CORRECTIONS OF AN ECONOMY

(*Principles of Economics* 5th ed. pages 762–765/6th ed. pages 734, 738–740)

Classical economic theory teaches that an economy will correct itself in the long run. It is important to understand the mechanisms that drive this process and how they differ when the economy is operating beyond or below full employment output levels.

Take first the situation when output levels are beyond full employment as a result of increased aggregate demand (shown below as the movement from AD_1 to AD_2). Implied by this scenario is that the economy is strong, as is the labor market. Without economic growth, LRAS will remain at its original position and current output levels will move to points beyond the natural rate. While this can occur for short periods of time, the economy cannot sustain this level of output in the long run and something must adjust to bring output back to full employment levels. That adjustment occurs due to input prices, especially wage rates.

In the short run, **nominal wages**—*wages at current dollar values*—do not change (or change very slowly). **Real wages**—*the purchasing power of wages*—do adjust with price level, even in the short run. Therefore, when AD shifts to the right and demand-pull inflation occurs, real wages fall and labor sees their purchasing power decline. In the long run, as workers realize they can't buy as much, they demand (or negotiate) for higher nominal wages. Because the economy is operating beyond full employment and labor markets are strong, workers' demands are met and nominal wages rise. The increase in nominal wages (an input price) cause the SRAS curve to decrease, as shown by the shift from $SRAS_1$ to $SRAS_2$ on the following graph. This is the theoretical illustration of a self-correcting economy when output reaches levels beyond full employment.

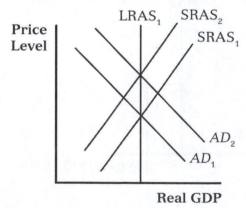

A similar story is told when output is below full employment. Once again, in theory, it is nominal wages that cause the long-run adjustment.

Assume the opposite of the above scenario occurs: aggregate demand shifts left as the economy weakens and resulting output levels occur below the natural rate. In this case, price levels have fallen and the labor market is relatively weak. Due to low output and high unemployment, workers are willing to take pay cuts in order to stay employed or, if out of work, to get a job and begin earning an income again. As a result, in the long run nominal wages fall and the SRAS curve shifts back to the right ($SRAS_1$ to $SRAS_2$), bringing output back to full employment levels.

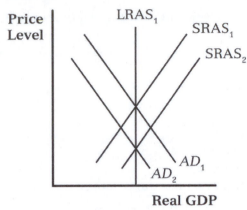

ECONOMIC GROWTH AND PRODUCTIVITY: STUDENT OBJECTIVES FOR THE AP EXAM

You should be able to:
- Define all key terms in bold
- Graph: economic growth on the PPC and LRAS curve; long-run self-correction on the AD–AS model
- Explain: the difference between long-term growth and short-term fluctuations of output
- Demonstrate an understanding of the classical explanation for long-term self-correction

MULTIPLE-CHOICE QUESTIONS

1. An increase in productivity may be defined as
   (A) an increase in output.
   (B) an increase in the number of inputs needed to produce a given output.
   (C) an increase in output per unit of input.
   (D) a short-run increase in output resulting from an increase in consumer spending.
   (E) a long-run decrease in the units of labor within an industry.

2. Which of the following is considered a cause of positive economic growth?
   (A) Government spending decreases.
   (B) Personal consumption expenditure increases.
   (C) A decrease in natural resources.
   (D) An increase in the stock of capital goods.
   (E) The purchase of exports by foreign consumers.

3. Negative economic growth may be shown as a
   (A) leftward shift of the PPC.
   (B) rightward shift of the PPC.
   (C) movement of output from within the PPC to a point outside the PPC.
   (D) movement of output from beyond the PPC to a point within the PPC.
   (E) movement of output from a point within the PPC to a point on the PPC.

4. Which of the following is NOT a factor directly related to the development of long-term economic growth?
   (A) Development of human capital.
   (B) Consumption spending.
   (C) Level of technology.
   (D) Creation of new physical capital.
   (E) Discovery of new sources of a natural resource.

5. The GDP deflator for year 1 is 125. If year 1 nominal GDP is $1,250, what is real GDP in year 1?
   (A) $100.
   (B) $1,000.
   (C) $1562.50.
   (D) $156,250.
   (E) Cannot be determined by the data given.

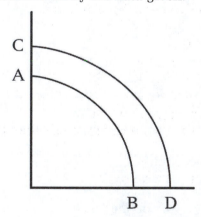

6. If the economy of a nation represented by the PPC above shifts from AB to CD, which of the following is most likely to have caused the shift to occur?
   (A) Full employment of all resources.
   (B) Advances in human capital.
   (C) More efficient use of resources.
   (D) Increases in government spending.
   (E) Decreases in imported goods.

7. Assume that federal grants result in increased access to higher education for millions of citizens. The resulting gains in human capital will create
   (A) long-term economic growth due to increases in productivity.
   (B) decreases in real GDP as a result of decreased investment spending.
   (C) decreases in SRAS due to elevated wage rates.
   (D) a decrease in LRAS as natural rates of unemployment fall.
   (E) inflated price levels and decreased levels of aggregate demand.

8. A PPC of an economy and the LRAS curve are similar in that they both
   (A) consist of combinations of two manufactured goods.
   (B) are measured in nominal terms.
   (C) are capable of illustrating opportunity cost.
   (D) represent the natural rate of output and illustrate economic growth when expanding outward.
   (E) only apply to the short-run time horizon.

9. Real GDP provides a more accurate depiction of economic growth than nominal GDP because
   (A) it is adjusted for the effects of inflation.
   (B) nominal GDP includes intermediate goods but real GDP does not.
   (C) real variables are more likely to fluctuate than nominal.
   (D) real GDP is calculated by private sector economists while nominal GDP is altered by government agents for political gain.
   (E) they are inversely related.

10. Research indicates that investments in research and development by firms have produced massive new amounts of sophisticated physical capital within a given economy. What would be the expected effect on the LRAS curve for this economy?
    (A) It will shift to the left.
    (B) It will become more elastic.
    (C) It will become perfectly elastic.
    (D) It will shift to the right.
    (E) It will be unaffected.

11. Nominal wages will fall in the long run when
    (A) the economy self-corrects from a position of less than full employment output.
    (B) the unemployment rate is very low.
    (C) output levels are above the natural rate.
    (D) real wages also fall.
    (E) demand-pull inflation occurs.

12. While only shifting AD in the short run, which of the following increases in government spending is most likely designed to encourage economic growth in the long run?
    (A) Expansion of the national park system.
    (B) Increased spending on new educational facilities and equipment.
    (C) Defense spending on new weapons, tanks, and helicopters to bolster national security.

(D) Raises for police officers and firefighters.

(E) Increased healthcare benefits for government employees.

13. Which of the following may lead to an increase in nominal wages?
    (A) Prolonged periods of high inflation and high unemployment.
    (B) Decreases in aggregate demand leading to widespread unemployment and output levels below full employment.
    (C) Short-run increases in investment spending.
    (D) A rightward shift of the LRAS curve.
    (E) Demand-pull inflation occurring while output levels are beyond full employment levels.

14. The purchasing power of the money workers are paid is called
    (A) salary.
    (B) nominal wages.
    (C) income.
    (D) real wages.
    (E) inflationary income.

15. An economy operating beyond the natural rate of output will self-correct
    (A) over the course of ten or more years.
    (B) only if the government balances the federal budget.
    (C) when the PPC shifts inward.
    (D) as inflation rates subside.
    (E) through the upward adjustment of nominal wages in the long run.

FREE-RESPONSE PROBLEMS

1. Assume the U.S. economy is operating at full employment output levels.
   (a) Illustrate the following on a correctly labeled graph of AD–AS.
       (i)   Long-run aggregate supply.
       (ii) The full employment output level, labeled Y_f.
       (iii) The current output level, labeled Y_1.
       (iv) The current price level, labeled P_1.
   (b) An increase in consumption spending occurs.
       (i)   Show on your graph from part (a) the change in aggregate demand.
       (ii) Label the new equilibrium output, Y_2, and the equilibrium price level, P_2.
       (iii) Is this considered economic growth?
   (c) Assume further that gradual technological developments occur in this economy and become accessible to firms at the same time.
       (i)   Using your graph from part (a), illustrate the effect of this development on the LRAS and SRAS curves.
       (ii) Label the new equilibrium output, Y_3, and the price level, P_3.
       (iii) Is this considered economic growth?

2. The following data is for a nation's economy over three years.
   (a) Given the data in the table, determine real GDP for years 1–3:

Year	Nominal GDP	Real GDP	GDP Deflator
1	$1,000		100
2	$1,500		125
3	$2,000		200

   (b) After adjusting for the effects of inflation, in what year(s) did real output increase? Decrease?
   (c) Based on the GDP deflator, in what year was inflation greatest?

Answers

MULTIPLE-CHOICE QUESTIONS

1. **C.** Productivity is an increase in the total output produced by each unit of input (*Principles of Economics* 5th ed. page 555/6th ed. page 537).

2. **D.** Of the options given, only an increase in the amount of physical capital will increase productivity (*Principles of Economics* 5th ed. pages 555–557/6th ed. pages 537–539).

3. **A.** A leftward shift of the PPC implies that the given economy now produces less with the same amount of resources; this is negative economic growth (*Principles of Economics* 5th ed. pages 25–28/6th ed. pages 26–28).

4. **B.** Spending by consumers will increase AD and output in the short run; this is not the same as economic growth which occurs in the long run (*Principles of Economics* 5th ed. pages 555–557/6th ed. pages 537–539).

5. **B.** To convert from nominal to real GDP, one must divide nominal GDP by the price deflator and multiply by 100. 1250/125 = 10, 10 × 100 = 1000 (*Principles of Economics* 5th ed. pages 516–518/6th ed. pages 500–502).

6. **B.** The outward shift of the PPC represents an increase in productivity and economic growth; advances in human capital may cause this (*Principles of Economics* 5th ed. pages 25–28/6th ed. pages 26–28).

7. **A.** Increases in human capital increase the productivity of labor and fuel long-term economic growth (*Principles of Economics* 5th ed. pages 555–557/6th ed. pages 537–539).

8. **D.** The PPC and LRAS curve are similar in that they both represent the natural rate of output (*Principles of Economics* 5th ed. pages 25–28, 753/6th ed. pages 26–28, 734).

9. **A.** Adjusting for inflation keeps prices at a constant value and allows for more accurate output comparisons over time (*Principles of Economics* 5th ed. pages 516–518/6th ed. pages 500–501).

10. **D.** New sources of a valuable natural resource will create economic growth and shift the LRAS curve to the right (*Principles of Economics* 5th ed. pages 555–557/6th ed. pages 537–539).

11. **A.** Nominal wages fall in the long run when unemployment is high due to output levels being below full employment levels. Workers are willing to accept lower wages in order to gain or maintain employment (*Principles of Economics* 5th ed. pages 760–761/6th ed. pages 738–740).

12. **B.** Increased spending on education is intended to increase human capital, a determinant of economic growth in the long run (*Principles of Economics* 5th ed. pages 555–557/6th ed. pages 537–539).

13. **E.** Nominal wages will rise in response to high inflation when output is beyond full employment and firms feel the need to pay workers more in order to maintain such high levels of production (*Principles of Economics* 5th ed. pages 760–761/6th ed. pages 738–740).

14. **D.** Real wages account for the effects of inflation and therefore represent the purchasing power of money (*Principles of Economics* 5th ed. page 669/6th ed. page 649).

15. **E.** The increase of nominal wages in the long run will cause input prices to rise as well, shifting the SRAS curve back to the left and bringing output back to full employment levels (*Principles of Economics* 5th ed. pages 760–761/6th ed. pages 738–740).

FREE-RESPONSE QUESTIONS

1.

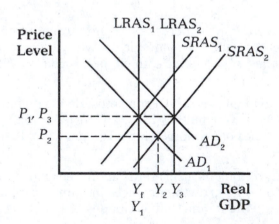

(i)   See graph (LRAS$_1$)
(ii)   See graph (Y$_f$)
(iii)   See graph (Y$_1$)
(iv)   See graph (P$_1$)
(v)   See graph (Y$_2$)
(vi)   See graph (P$_2$)

  (vii) No, an increase in AD is not economic growth.
  (viii) See graph (Y_3)
  (ix) See graph (P_3)
  (x) Yes, an increase in LRAS is economic growth.

(*Principles of Economics* 5th ed. pages 555–557, 746–761/6th ed. pages 537–539, 726–739)

  (b) Real GDP (year 1) = $1,000
    Real GDP (year 2) = $1,200
    Real GDP (year 3) = $1,000
  (c) Real output increased from year 1 to year 2.
    Real output decreased from year 2 to year 3.
  (d) Year 3 had the highest rate of inflation.

(*Principles of Economics* 5th ed. pages 516–518/6th ed. pages 500–502)

12

THE OPEN ECONOMY

Most of our economic analysis up until this point has been based on the assumption that we have a **closed economy**, *an economy that does not interact or engage in trade with other economies in the world.* As you know, our economy is closely intertwined with that of other nations. In this chapter, we will discuss the economic issues relating to an **open economy**, *an economy that interacts freely with other economies around the world.* An open economy interacts with other economies in two ways—(1) it buys and sells goods and services in world product markets, and (2) it buys and sells financial capital assets, such as stocks and bonds in world financial markets. We will dedicate the first half of this chapter to global economic interaction in product markets and the second half to financial markets.

INTERNATIONAL TRADE
(*Principles of Economics* 5th ed. pages 691–696/6th ed. pages 671–676)

Recall from our discussion in Chapter 1 that trade may help to increase the consumption possibilities of and bring economic gain to a nation (since trade allows a nation to consume outside of its PPF). Review the material on comparative and absolute advantage and trade gains in our discussion of the production possibilities model in Chapter 1 before continuing on. International trade allows nations to specialize in the production of goods and services in which it has a comparative advantage and improves resource productivity.

Exports (X) are *the goods and services that are produced domestically and sold abroad.* **Imports (M)** are *the goods and services that are produced abroad and sold domestically.* A **trade surplus** is when a country has *an excess of exports over imports* and a **trade deficit** is *an excess of imports over exports.* The United States has increased its level of international trade dramatically over the last few decades and, as the next graph shows, has had a trade deficit since the late 1970s. The increase in trade is partly due to improvements in transportation, telecommunications, and technological progress. This trade increase closely correlates with U.S. economic growth and higher living standards.

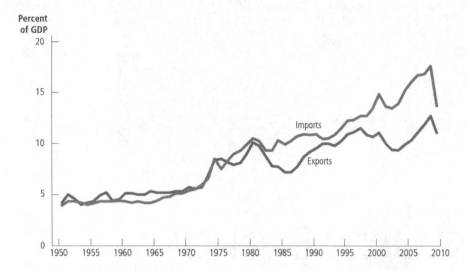

Similar to our analysis of microeconomic markets, we can use supply and demand analysis to find the equilibrium price and quantity of exports and imports. Whether a nation imports or exports a good or service depends on the world equilibrium price. If our economy was a closed economy, the domestic market equilibrium price would prevail; by opening the economy to international trade, we must now also consider the world price. Let's use the wheat market to illustrate how the world price is determined and how a nation determines whether they will export or import a particular good. In order to determine whether the United States should import or export wheat, we need to first look at the domestic wheat market. Refer to the following graph of the U.S. domestic wheat market as we continue our discussion.

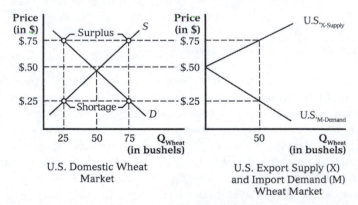

U.S. Domestic Wheat Market

U.S. Export Supply (X) and Import Demand (M) Wheat Market

The domestic market equilibrium price of wheat in the U.S. is $0.50 per bushel. At this price, 50 bushels are purchased. If the United States decided to remain a closed market, then this is all of the information that we would need to know about the wheat market. Once we decide to open our markets to trade however, we need to dig a little deeper. Notice that, at a price of $0.75/bushel, there is a 50 bushel wheat surplus in the U.S. (75 bushels – 25 bushels = 50 bushels of surplus). At a price of $0.25/bushel, there is a 50 bushel wheat shortage in the U.S.

This means that, at any price above the market equilibrium price of $0.50/bushel, U.S. suppliers will want to export its wheat surplus to receive a higher price, and at any price below the market equilibrium price of $0.50/bushel, the U.S. will want to import wheat since there is a wheat shortage at any price below $0.50/bushel and the U.S. will want to purchase the cheaper foreign wheat. The graph on the right shows the U.S. wheat export supply curve and the U.S. wheat import demand curve. The U.S. export supply curve is upward sloping because if the world price is greater than the domestic price of wheat ($0.50/bushel), the quantity of U.S. wheat exported increases. The U.S. import demand curve is downward sloping because if the world price is below the domestic price of wheat, the quantity of wheat imported by the U.S. will increase.

In order to determine the world price of wheat, we must look at other nations' wheat export supply and import demand curves. To simplify our analysis, we will compare the U.S. wheat market to that of just one other country. Suppose that Mexico is also a wheat producing country. Assuming that it is a little bit cheaper to produce wheat in Mexico, the Mexican wheat market graphs might look like the following:

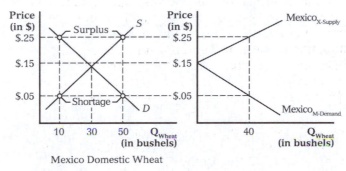

Mexico Domestic Wheat

Notice that the graphs are very similar to the U.S. wheat market graphs, except that the equilibrium price and quantity of wheat sold in Mexico is less than in the U.S. At a price of $0.25/bushel, Mexico has a 40 bushel wheat surplus and at a price of $0.05/bushel, Mexico has a 40 bushel wheat shortage. This means that Mexico is willing to export wheat if the price is above $0.15/bushel and will need to import wheat if the price is below $0.15/bushel. To determine the world price of wheat, we combine the export supply and import demand curves of all wheat producing nations and find the equilibrium. Remember that we are simplifying our analysis by assuming that Mexico and the United States are the only two nations that produce wheat. If we combine both nations' wheat export supply and import demand curves, the graph would look like this:

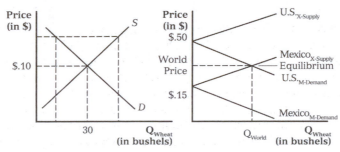

This world wheat market graph includes the export supply and import demand curves of both countries. Since the United States will import at a price below $0.50/bushel and Mexico will export at any price above $0.15/bushel, the equilibrium world price will be somewhere between $0.15/bushel and $0.50/bushel. This means that the United States will import wheat and Mexico will export wheat in the world market. Why would the United States and Mexico want to engage in this kind of trade? The United States would gain because it pays less for wheat since Mexico has the comparative advantage in wheat production. Mexico also gains because it receives U.S. dollars in exchange for the wheat that it exports. Mexico can use the U.S. dollars to acquire other imported goods, thus gaining through trade.

AP Tip

It is unlikely that you will have to graph the export supply and import demand curves on the AP Microeconomics exam, but you need to understand why nations engage in trade and how each nation decides whether they will export or import a particular good or service.

TRADE BARRIERS
(*Principles of Economics* 5th ed. pages 728–730/6th ed. pages 706–707)

While in theory, nations can freely trade with one another, the reality is that nations do put up barriers to free trade. A country often chooses to protect its own industries by imposing trade barriers, such as a **tariff**, *a tax on goods produced abroad and sold domestically*, or an **import quota**, *a legal limit on the quantity of imported goods allowed in the domestic market*. Regardless of whether a nation's government imposes a tariff or an import quota on foreign goods imported into the domestic market, the economic impact of the tariff and quota are much the same—they lead to an increase in domestic production of the good and a decline in the consumption of the good. Let's look first at the economic impact of a tariff on the U.S. wheat market.

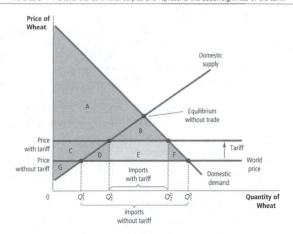

	Before Tariff	After Tariff	Change
Consumer Surplus	A + B + C + D + E + F	A + B	–(C + D + E + F)
Producer Surplus	G	C + G	+C
Government Revenue	None	E	+E
Total Surplus	A + B + C + D + E + F + G	A + B + C + E + G	–(D + F)

The area D + F shows the fall in total surplus and represents the deadweight loss of the tariff.

If this were a closed economy, the market equilibrium price and quantity would correspond to the intersection of the domestic supply and domestic demand curves. In an open economy like that of the United States, however, the world price, $P_{withouttariff}$, is the equilibrium price. At this price, the United States has a wheat shortage and therefore will import $(Q_{D1}-Q_{S1})$ units of the good. Suppose that the United States places a protective tariff on wheat. This tariff leads to an increase in the market price of wheat, from $P_{withouttariff}$ to $P_{withtariff}$. The quantity of wheat consumed decreases from $Q_{D1}-Q_{D2}$ and the suppliers of wheat in the United States increase the quantity of wheat supplied, from $Q_{S1}-Q_{S2}$.

Mexican wheat exporters are hurt by this tariff, because they still only receive the price, $P_{withouttariff}$ for wheat sold to the United States after paying the U.S. government the tariff, $P_{withtariff}$. In fact, rather than exporting quantity $(Q_{D1}-Q_{S1})$ units, Mexico exports quantity $(Q_{D2}-Q_{S2})$ units of wheat, so the quantity of wheat exported from Mexico to the United States falls. The U.S. government collects tariff revenue equal to the shaded area E. U.S. (domestic) consumers also lose with a tariff, as shown by the decline in consumer surplus, from the area A + B + C + D + E + F to A + B only, but U.S. producers are better off when there is a protective tariff, as shown by the slight increase in producer surplus, from the area G to G + C. The deadweight loss resulting from a tariff is shown by areas D + F.

The impact of an import quota is very similar to that of a protective tariff. One difference is that the tariff is a source of income to the importing country's government. If quotas are imposed, what might have been tariff income to the government becomes profit to the foreign seller, be it the producer or the middle man. Suppose that the United States places an import quota in its wheat market instead of a tariff. The supply of wheat in the United States increases by the amount of the quota and shifts to the right, as shown in the following graph. Note that Mexican wheat producers would not supply any wheat to the U.S. market at a price below P_w.

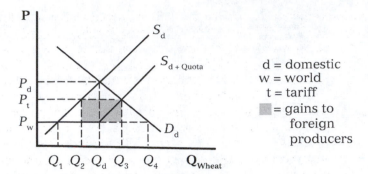

In the case of an import quota, the amount of wheat imported by the United States decreases from (Q_4-Q_1) units to (Q_3-Q_2) units and the domestic supply of wheat increases from Q_1 to Q_2, just as in the case of a tariff. The difference is that the shaded area is now economic gain earned by foreign wheat producers. If you look at both the tariff and import quota graphs, you will see that, in both cases, domestic consumers are hurt by these protective policies because they end up paying a higher price and lose consumer surplus, and domestic producers are helped by these protective policies because they receive a higher price for their goods/services and gain producer surplus. As in the case of a tariff, there is deadweight loss with an import quota, represented by the two triangles in the above import quota graph that correspond to areas D + F in the tariff graph. This is why many economists argue that trade barriers lead to excessive economic inefficiencies and should not be used.

A government may choose to protect its industries because they are **infant industries**, *newly formed industries* (in which case, the tariff protection should be for a limited time period, until the industry can be competitive in the global market) or because they want to help expand domestic industries that do not yet have a comparative advantage.

AP Tip

You need to know who benefits and who loses as a result of trade barriers. Be sure that you can draw correctly labeled graphs of the impact of trade barriers on supply and demand of goods.

BALANCE OF PAYMENTS

International trade allows nations to buy and sell foreign and domestic goods, services, and financial assets. In order to engage in international trade, nations must pay in the foreign currency of the nation from whom they are buying goods. For example, if the United States wants to buy wheat from Mexico, it would have to pay for the wheat in Mexican pesos. The United States (the importer) must exchange dollars for pesos in the foreign exchange market in order to buy wheat from Mexico (the exporter). We will discuss the logistics of the foreign exchange market in the next section. For now, note that when people in other countries want to buy U.S. goods (U.S. exports), they demand U.S. dollars. This increases our supply of foreign currency, since foreigners have to exchange their currency for U.S.

dollars. On the other hand, when U.S. citizens want to buy goods from another country (U.S. imports), they demand foreign currency. This decreases our supply of foreign currency, since U.S. citizens have to exchange their U.S. dollars for foreign currency. A nation's **balance of payments** is *the sum of all of the transactions that take place between itself and other nations.* It includes the trade of goods and services between nations, but it also includes the trade of assets between nations. The balance of payments has three separate accounts: the **current account**, *the account in the balance of payments that records a nation's trade in currently produced goods and services,* the **capital account**, *the account in the balance of payments that records the purchase or sale of financial assets,* and the **official reserves account**, *the account of the balance of payments that holds foreign currencies.* International trade similar to our discussion of U.S. import of Mexican wheat would be included in the current account while other foreign financial transactions, such as a U.S. bank buying stock in a Mexican company, would be included in the capital account.

AP Tips

Do not confuse capital stock with foreign capital in the capital account. Capital stock is a factor of production that includes machinery and equipment needed for the production of goods whereas foreign capital in the capital account refers to foreign investment in the United States What we are talking about here in this chapter is foreign investment.

Also, know that transactions that are imported or exported are recorded in the current account. If you are buying foreign assets or investing in financial markets in another country, it is recorded in the capital account.

The United States can draw on its official reserves to make up a deficit in either its current or capital accounts in order to ensure that the balance of payments is equal to zero. Why does the balance of payments equal to zero? In order to buy Mexican wheat, the United States must pay for it. This payment is a **debit**, *an item that decreases the value of an asset,* on the U.S. balance sheet. However, the payment by the United States for the Mexican wheat shows up as a **credit**, *an item that increases the value of an asset,* on the Mexican balance sheet. Since every transaction has both a debit and a credit, the balance of payments must be equal to zero. Another way to look at this is that we must pay for what we buy. We may pay with our current income (current account) or with savings from past income or promises to pay from future income (capital account).

AP Tips

One way to remember that the balance of payment must equal to zero is to think about the balance of payments as BoP. The "o" in "BoP" is = 0.

For the AP Microeconomics exam, you will need to remember that a nation will draw down its official reserves when it has either a current or capital account deficit so that its BoP = 0.

THE INTERNATIONAL MARKET FOR CURRENCIES

(*Principles of Economics* 5th ed. pages 704–732/6th ed. pages 682–690, 696–713)

The size and frequency of a nation's balance of payment adjustments to ensure a zero balance depends on the foreign exchange market. The **nominal exchange rate** is *the rate at which a person can trade the currency of one country for the currency of another* and the **real exchange rate** is *the rate at which a person can trade the goods and services of one country for the goods and services of another*. There are two ways to determine exchange rates: through a flexible exchange rate system or a fixed exchange rate system. Similar to our discussion about market versus command economies in Chapter 1, a flexible exchange rate is comparable to a market system (free market) whereas a fixed exchange rate is comparable to a government system within the market. A **flexible exchange rate system** is *one where market supply and demand determine exchange rates without government intervention*. A **fixed exchange rate system** is *one where the government determines what the exchange rate should be and attempts to manipulate markets to reach the target exchange rate*.

Let's first look at flexible exchange rates. In the following market graph for pesos, the supply is upward sloping because Mexicans will be able to buy more U.S. goods when the dollar price of the peso increases because it means that the peso is stronger (has appreciated in value relative to the dollar). The demand for pesos curve is downward sloping because all Mexican goods will be cheaper to Americans if pesos are less expensive (since the dollar has appreciated relative to the peso). As in most other market graphs, the exchange rate is determined by the intersection of the supply and demand curves and is equal to $1 = 12 pesos.

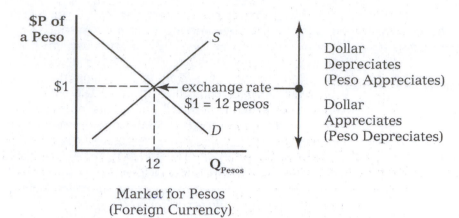

Market for Pesos
(Foreign Currency)

Note that, in the upper half of the graph, the dollar loses value relative to the peso because more dollars are needed to buy pesos. This means that the dollar has depreciated relative to the peso. **Depreciation** is *a decrease in the value of a currency as measured by the amount of foreign currency it can buy*. In the bottom half of the graph, the dollar appreciates relative to the peso because it costs fewer dollars to buy pesos. **Appreciation** is *an increase in the value of a currency as measured by the amount of foreign currency it can buy*. Flexible exchange rates mean that the exchange rate will continuously change as market demand and supply in the foreign currency market change. Any change in the demand for foreign currency or the supply of foreign currency will result in a new exchange rate under a flexible exchange rate system.

AP Tips

Familiarize yourself with the flexible exchange rate graph at the top of this page. You may be asked to find the foreign exchange rates as a part of the free-response questions on the AP Microeconomics exam, so it is helpful to know how exchange rates are determined.

Students often struggle with the foreign exchange market graph. To help you learn the graph, try this: remember that "whatever *goes on the bottom stays on the bottom.*" So if the market Q is for pesos, as in our example, you should label your y-axis with pesos in the denominator (the *"bottom"* of the fraction).

There are five main determinants that lead to changes in either the demand for or supply of foreign currency: (1) changes in consumer tastes for foreign or domestic goods, (2) relative income changes, (3) relative price-level changes, (4) relative interest rate changes, and (5) speculation. The following table provides an example of each determinant and explains its impact on the exchange rate and the value of the U.S. dollar. It is important for you to know that *an increase in the S of one currency necessitates an increase in the D for another and vice versa.*

(1) Changes in consumer tastes	If German cars become more popular in the U.S., for example, there will be an increase in the demand for euros, since more Americans will need to exchange their dollars for euros in order to buy a German car. The supply of U.S. dollars increases and the demand for euros decreases, causing the dollar to depreciate and the euro to appreciate.
(2) Relative income changes	The U.S. is in a recession and will therefore demand less of everything, including imports. Mexico's economy is growing relative to the U.S. and increases its demand for U.S. exports. The demand for dollars increases and the supply of pesos increases, causing the dollar to appreciate and the peso to depreciate.
(3) Relative price-level changes	China has a 2% inflation rate while the U.S. has a 7% inflation rate. Chinese goods are therefore relatively less expensive to those in the U.S. The supply of dollars decreases and the demand for the Chinese yuan increases, causing the Chinese yuan to appreciate and the dollar to depreciate.
(4) Relative interest rate changes	The U.S. Fed increases interest rates while the Mexican central bank does nothing. People in Mexico find that it is more profitable to put their money in U.S. banks, so the demand for dollars increases and the supply of pesos increases, causing the dollar to appreciate and the peso to depreciate.
(5) Speculation	Currency traders think that the U.S. interest rates will decrease relative to Germany, so they sell dollars, increasing the supply of dollars, and buy euros, which increases the demand for euros. The dollar depreciates and the euro appreciates.

AP Tip

If the demand for one currency increases; the supply of the other will also increase. If the supply of one currency decreases; the demand for the other will decrease.

The theory of **purchasing-power-parity (PPP)**, *a theory of exchange rates whereby a unit of any given currency should be able to buy the same quantity of goods in all countries*, tells us that exchange rates will adjust so that a given basket of goods will cost the same in all countries. If a basket of goods costs $100 in the U.S. and 1,000 pesos in Mexico, the exchange rate would be $1 = 10 pesos. If, for some reason, the actual exchange rate is $1 = 12 pesos, as in our previous example, according to PPP, the dollar will depreciate and the peso will appreciate so that we reach the PPP exchange rate of $1 = 10 pesos. In reality, exchange rates do not always make this adjustment.

The main disadvantage in using a flexible exchange rate system is that it leads to economic uncertainty. Without knowing what a nation's currency is worth in the foreign exchange market, people may be more reluctant to engage in trade because there is greater risk of potential economic losses especially if the nation's currency depreciates significantly.

To avoid economic uncertainty, some nations choose to have a fixed exchange rate system. Suppose, for example, that the governments of the United States and Mexico decide to fix their exchange rates so that $1 = 10 pesos. Even with a fixed exchange rate, they cannot do anything to prohibit the increase in the demand for or the supply of dollars or pesos. If there is an increase in the demand for Mexican pesos because Americans want to buy Mexican goods, there will be a shortage of pesos at the fixed exchange rate, as shown in the graph below.

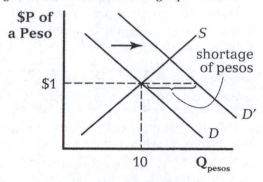

Market for Pesos
(Foreign Currency)

Under a flexible rate system, the exchange rate would just follow the intersection of the new demand and existing supply curve. Under a fixed exchange rate system, however, although there is upward pressure on the exchange rate due to the increased demand for pesos, the U.S. government tries to prevent the shortage of pesos by adjusting market supply or demand for pesos so that the exchange rate of $1 = 10 pesos can be maintained. One way the government can keep the exchange rate at $1 = 10 pesos when there is an increased demand for pesos is to use its official reserves. For example, the U.S. government can draw upon its official reserves to increase the supply of pesos in the market. The supply curve will shift to the right, and the exchange rate returns to $1 = 10 pesos. Another way to try to keep exchange rates fixed is for the government to implement trade policies to control the flow of trade, such as a tariff or import quota, which discourages imports and helps to control the demand for foreign currency.

NET EXPORTS AND CAPITAL FLOWS
(*Principles of Economics* 5th ed. pages 696–700, 716–733/6th ed. pages 676–680, 696–711)

Up until this point, we have focused our discussion on the global market for goods and services, but residents of an open economy also participate in global financial markets. You can use your money to buy an imported car from Japan or purchase stock in a Japanese corporation. **Net capital outflow (NCO)** is *the purchase of foreign assets by domestic residents minus the purchase of domestic assets by foreigners.* When a U.S. resident buys stock in a Japanese corporation, it is an example of a purchase of foreign assets by domestic residents and increases U.S. net capital outflow. When a Japanese resident buys bonds issued by the United States, it is an example of a purchase of domestic assets by foreigners and decreases U.S. net capital outflow. Net capital outflow can be positive or negative—when NCO > 0, the country has a net purchase of capital overseas and when NCO < 0, the country has more capital resources coming in from abroad. In an open economy, national saving is equal to domestic investment plus net capital outflow. In addition, net capital outflow equals net exports (NX), or exports minus imports.

AP Tips

Students must be able to distinguish between the current account and capital account and know what happens in one when the other changes.

International economics makes up 10–15% of the AP Macroeconomics exam. The following net capital outflow (NCO) model presented in Mankiw's *Principles of Economics* book is not necessary for your AP preparation, although full credit will be given for correct use of his economic models on the free-response portions of the AP exam. Studying Mankiw's NCO model, which is presented in the following section, is *optional*.

In an open economy, the loanable funds market and the foreign exchange market work together to determine important macroeconomic variables, such as the exchange rate and interest rate. The following graphs illustrate how these two markets work together.

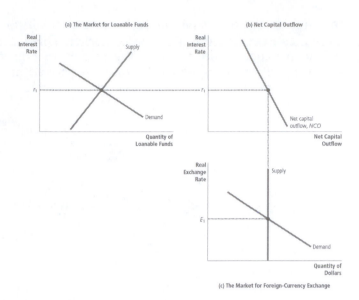

(a) The Market for Loanable Funds

(b) Net Capital Outflow

(c) The Market for Foreign-Currency Exchange

As discussed in Chapter 9, national savings is made up of private savings + public savings and provides the money for the loanable funds market. Note, though, that the supply of loanable funds also includes foreign savings in addition to private and public savings. Domestic investment and net capital outflow make up the demand for loanable funds. The equilibrium interest rate in the loanable funds market determines net capital outflow. A high domestic interest rate makes domestic assets cheaper and reduces net capital outflow. This is why the net capital outflow is downward sloping. The net capital outflow provides the supply of dollars in the foreign exchange market and is vertical because the exchange rate does not affect net capital outflow. The demand for dollars is downward sloping because a higher exchange rate means that the dollar has depreciated relative to another nation's currency. The series of graphs above show an open economy at equilibrium.

To develop a better understanding of how this NCO model works, let's look at the effects of an import quota. Recall that we have already discussed the economic impact of an import quota earlier in this chapter. You can compare the results of that analysis with this one. Please use the graphs below to help you visualize this discussion. An import quota means that the quantity of imports decreases, which in turn affects the demand for dollars in the foreign exchange market. There is an increase in the demand for dollars because there are fewer imports and therefore, a greater demand for U.S. goods. The increase in the demand for dollars increases the real exchange rate, causing the dollar to *appreciate*. Nothing in the loanable funds market is affected by an import quota—the interest rate does not change, which means that the net capital outflow also does not change. Since there is no change to the net capital outflow, net exports have not changed either. How can net exports remain unchanged when the amount of imports has decreased? Remember that the dollar has appreciated, which makes American goods more expensive relative to foreign goods and reduces net exports. According to this model, we see that trade policies do not affect a country's overall trade balance, although it does affect specific sectors of the domestic economy. For example, a U.S. import quota on Japanese cars may help American car producers, but the appreciation of the dollar will make it more difficult for other American companies to compete in the world market. This leads to a decline in American exports and a rise in the import of non-import quota goods. The result is the same as the one we arrived at in our earlier section on trade barriers: trade restrictions reduce overall economic well-being.

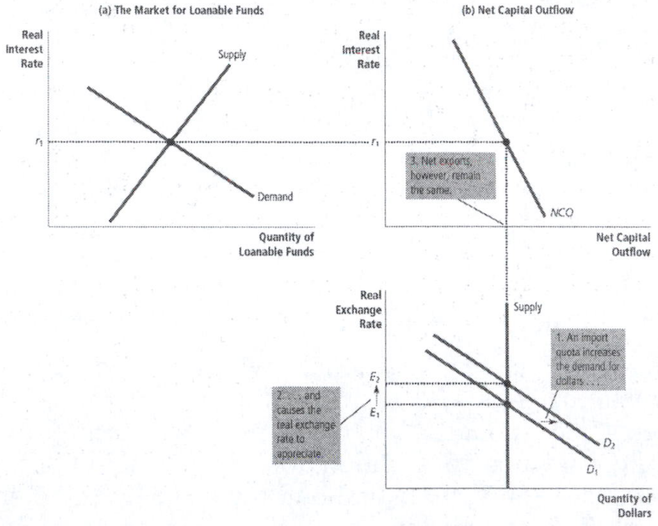

(c) The Market for Foreign-Currency Exchange

> **AP Tip**
>
> Loanable funds and the foreign exchange market are VERY important and will almost always be on the AP exams.

THE OPEN ECONOMY: STUDENT OBJECTIVES FOR THE AP EXAM

You should be able to:

- Define all key terms in bold
- Graph: economic impact of an import quota and tariff
- Demonstrate a solid understanding of: the export supply and import demand graphs, flexible and fixed exchange rate graphs, balance of payment accounts
- Analyze currency valuation changes

MULTIPLE-CHOICE QUESTIONS

1. In a system of flexible exchange rates, what happens to the money supply, the interest rate, and the international value of the dollar when the Federal Reserve sells bonds in the open market?

	Money Supply	Interest Rate	Value of the Dollar
(A)	Increase	Decrease	Decrease

(B) Increase	Decrease	Increase
(C) Decrease	Decrease	Decrease
(D) Decrease	Increase	Increase
(E) Decrease	Increase	Decrease

2. Suppose that you are a lawyer who can earn $150/hour, but you are also an excellent landscape gardener and can help others build beautiful gardens twice as quickly as the best landscape gardener in town, who earns $20/hour. Based on this information, which of the following statements is correct?
    (A) You have a comparative advantage in law, so you should practice law and hire your own landscape gardener to build your garden.
    (B) You have an absolute and a comparative advantage in both law and landscape gardening, so you should do both, build your garden and practice law, on your own.
    (C) You are twice as fast as the next best landscape gardener, so you should give up your law practice to become a landscape gardener.
    (D) Landscape gardeners should charge a higher rate so that there is less inequality between lawyers and landscape gardeners.
    (E) The best landscaper in town has the absolute advantage in gardening while you have the absolute advantage in practicing law.

3. Which of the following would be most likely to occur if the United States placed a high tariff on imported goods?
    (A) Workers in the United States would have more jobs in the long run.
    (B) There would be a redistribution of income in the United States from the rich to the poor.
    (C) The standard of living in the United States would increase.
    (D) The U.S. economy would become less efficient.
    (E) The quantity of U.S. exports would increase.

4. Which of the following are potential domestic benefits of production specialization and engagement in international trade?
    I.   A more efficient allocation of domestic resources
    II. An improved standard of living
    III. Increased national self-sufficiency
    (A) I only
    (B) II only
    (C) III only
    (D) I and II only
    (E) I, II, and III

5. An increase in China's demand for U.S. goods would cause the value of the dollar to
    (A) depreciate because of inflation.
    (B) depreciate because the U.S. is selling more dollars to China.
    (C) depreciate because the U.S. money supply increases as exports rise.
    (D) appreciate because China is selling more U.S. dollars.
    (E) appreciate because China is buying more U.S. dollars.

6. Which of the following best explains why many United States economists support free trade?
   (A) Workers who lose their jobs can collect unemployment compensation.
   (B) It is more important to reduce world inflation than to reduce United States unemployment.
   (C) Workers are not affected; only businesses suffer.
   (D) The long-run gains to consumers and some producers exceed the losses to other producers.
   (E) Government can protect United States industries while encouraging free trade.

7. If Mexicans increase their purchase of financial assets in the United States, the supply of Mexican pesos to the foreign exchange market and the dollar price of the peso will most likely change in which of the following ways?

	Supply of Pesos	Dollar Price of the Peso
(A)	Increase	Increase
(B)	Increase	Decrease
(C)	Decrease	Increase
(D)	Decrease	Decrease
(E)	Decrease	No change

8. If the real interest rate in the United States increases relative to the real interest rate in England and there are no trade barriers between the two countries, then which of the following will be true for the United States?

	Capital Flow	U.S. Currency	U.S. Exports
(A)	Inflow	Appreciation	Increase
(B)	Inflow	Appreciation	Decrease
(C)	Inflow	Depreciation	Increase
(D)	Outflow	Depreciation	Increase
(E)	Outflow	Appreciation	Decrease

9. Country X can produce either 2 cars or 4 computers with 10 units of labor. Country Y can produce 5 cars or 5 computers with 10 units of labor. Based on this information, which of the following is true?
   (A) Country X has an absolute advantage in the production of cars, while Country Y has a comparative advantage in the production of cars.
   (B) Country X has a comparative advantage in the production of computers, while Country Y has a comparative advantage in the production of cars.
   (C) Country X has an absolute advantage in the production of cars, while Country Y has a comparative advantage in the production of computers.
   (D) Neither country has a comparative advantage in the production of either good.
   (E) Country X has the comparative disadvantage in the production of both goods.

10. If a country has a current account deficit and does not want to draw down its official reserves, which of the following must be true?
    (A) It must also show a deficit in its capital account.

(B) It must show a surplus in its capital account.

(C) It must increase the purchases of foreign goods and services.

(D) It must increase the domestic interest rates on its bonds.

(E) It must limit the flow of foreign capital investment.

11. With an increase in investment demand in the United States, the real interest rate rises. In this situation, the most likely change in the capital stock in the United States and in the international value of the dollar would be which of the following?

U.S. Capital Stock	International Value of the Dollar
(A) Increase	Decrease
(B) Increase	No change
(C) Increase	Increase
(D) Decrease	Increase
(E) No change	Decrease

12. Of the following, which would cause the U.S. dollar to appreciate relative to the British pound?

(A) An increase in the money supply in the United States

(B) An increase in interest rates in the United States

(C) An increase in the United States trade deficit with Great Britain

(D) The United States purchase of gold on the open market

(E) The sale of $1 billion dollars worth of English tea to the United States

13. Assume that the supply of loanable funds increases in Econland. The international value of Econland's currency and exports will most likely change in which of the following ways?

Econland's Currency	Econland's Exports
(A) Decrease	Decrease
(B) Decrease	Increase
(C) Increase	Decrease
(D) Increase	Increase
(E) No change	No change

14. Which of the following statements regarding tariffs is true?

(A) A tariff decreases imports and increases the quantity supplied by domestic producers.

(B) A tariff decreases imports and decreases the quantity supplied by domestic producers.

(C) A tariff increases imports and raises revenue for the government that imposed the tariff.

(D) A tariff protects infant industries and raises revenue to foreign importers.

(E) A tariff results in an efficient market outcome.

15. A tariff may be preferable over an import quota because

(A) the level of domestic imports decreases.

(B) the government collects the tariff revenue.

(C) an import quota results in economic inefficiency.

(D) domestic consumers pay higher prices.

(E) domestic producers have greater gains with a tariff.

FREE-RESPONSE QUESTIONS

1. Assume that the United States and France are the only two countries in the world and that the exchange rate between the two countries is flexible.
   (a) Suppose that there is an increase in the United States demand for French goods. Draw a correctly labeled graph showing how this increase in demand will affect each of the following.
      (i) The supply of dollars
      (ii) The international value of the dollar
   (b) Assume that there is an increase in real interest rates in the United States, but not in France. Graph how this increase in interest rates will affect each of the following. Explain.
      (i) The international value of the dollar in the foreign exchange market
      (ii) The quantity of dollars supplied in the foreign exchange market

2. Over the past decade, China has used its savings to finance American investment. In other words, the Chinese have been buying American capital assets.
   (a) If the Chinese decided that they no longer wanted to buy U.S. assets, what would happen in the U.S. market for loanable funds? Specifically, address the impact on:
      (i) U.S. interest rates
      (ii) U.S. savings
      (iii) U.S. investment
   (b) Will the dollar appreciate or depreciate? Explain.

Answers

MULTIPLE-CHOICE QUESTIONS

1. **D.** When the Federal Reserve sells bonds in the open market, the money supply decreases, which increases the interest rates. Higher interest rates help to increase foreign investment in U.S. financial assets, which increases the demand for dollars and causes the dollar to appreciate (*Principles of Economics* 5th ed. page 668/6th ed. page 648).

2. **A.** You have the absolute advantage as a lawyer and as a landscape gardener, but you have the comparative advantage in practicing law <u>only</u>. The opportunity cost for you to switch professions, from law to landscape gardening, is much higher than the opportunity cost of the best landscaper in town, so it does not make sense for you to quit your job as a lawyer. This question revisits the idea that it makes sense to specialize and trade in the good/service where you have the comparative advantage (*Principles of Economics* 5th ed. pages 54–56/6th ed. pages 52–55).

3. **D.** The economy is less efficient with a tariff because it imports less then under free trade conditions. Although there is an increase in the domestic supply of the good/service, domestic consumers also

lose because they have to pay the higher tariff price (*Principles of Economics* 5th ed. pages 728–730/6th ed. pages 706–709).

4. **D.** Specialization and trade help to improve overall economic efficiency because resources are better used since each country produces goods/services it has the comparative advantage in. This leads to an improved standard of living because higher production leads to higher wages. There is increased dependency on other nations, not increased self-sufficiency (*Principles of Economics* 5th ed. pages 54–56/6th ed. pages 52–55).

5. **E.** In order to pay for the U.S. goods that it wants to buy, China must exchange yuan for dollars. This increases the demand for dollars in the foreign exchange market and causes the dollar to appreciate relative to the yuan (*Principles of Economics* 5th ed. pages 728–730/6th ed. pages 706–709).

6. **D.** Economists argue that trade barriers hurt domestic consumers and protect few domestic producers. Economists argue that free trade is beneficial because it will reap benefits to consumers that exceed the costs (*Principles of Economics* 5th ed. pages 729–730/6th ed. pages 708–709).

7. **B.** In order to increase investment in the U.S., Mexican residents must exchange their pesos for dollars. This increases the supply of pesos available on the foreign exchange market and decreases the dollar price of the peso, appreciating the dollar and depreciating the peso (*Principles of Economics* 5th ed. pages 728–730/6th ed. pages 706–709).

8. **B.** Since the U.S. interest rate is higher relative to Great Britain, more Britons will want to invest their pounds in U.S. financial assets. This results in an influx of capital into the United States and appreciates the dollar. The dollar appreciation means that U.S. goods are now more expensive relative to Great Britain and so exports fall (*Principles of Economics* 5th ed. pages 728–730/6th ed. pages 706–709).

9. **B.** Country X has the comparative advantage in the production of computers because it has a lower opportunity cost relative to Country Y. Country Y has the absolute advantage in the production of both goods, but the comparative advantage in the production of cars only (*Principles of Economics* 5th ed. pages 54–56/6th ed. pages 52–55).

10. **B.** Remember that the balance of payments must equal zero. In order for this to be true, if there is a current account deficit, there must be a capital account surplus, otherwise the government will have to draw on its official reserves to make up the imbalance (*Principles of Economics* 5th ed. page 700/6th ed. page 677).

11. **C.** An increase in the investment in the United States increases the amount of capital it has, so its capital stock increases. The dollar appreciates because there is greater demand for U.S. dollars needed to pay for the increased U.S. investment (*Principles of Economics* 5th ed. pages 711–721/6th ed. pages 697–707).

12. **B.** Higher U.S. interest rates increase foreign investment demand. This increases foreign demand for U.S. dollars (*Principles of Economics* 5th ed. pages 711–721/6th ed. pages 697–707).

13. **B.** An increase in the supply of loanable funds decreases the real interest rate. A lower interest rate deters foreign investment, which decreases the demand for dollars. The dollar depreciates, which makes Econland's goods cheaper relative to the rest of the world. This increases our exports (*Principles of Economics* 5th ed. pages 728–730/6th ed. pages 706–709).

14. **A.** Study the graph on page 267 of this chapter. A tariff reduces imports and increases the quantity of the good supplied by domestic producers (*Principles of Economics* 5th ed. pages 187–189/6th ed. pages 177–179).

15. **B.** The economic impact of a tariff and an import quota are the same. The key difference is that, with a tariff, the government can collect the tariff revenue whereas with an import quota, the gains go to foreign producers (*Principles of Economics* 5th ed. pages 187–189/6th ed. pages 177–179).

FREE-RESPONSE QUESTIONS

1. (a)

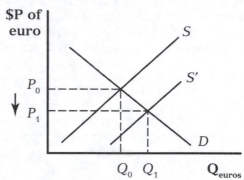

If there is an increase in U.S. demand for French goods, there will be an increase in the demand for euros (to pay for the French goods) and an increase in the supply of dollars, since Americans will have to exchange their dollars for euros. This results in the depreciation of the dollar and an appreciation of the euro.

(b)

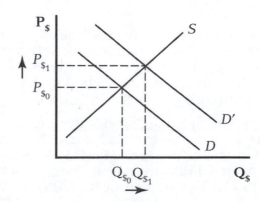

An increase in U.S. interest rates will result in increased foreign investment in U.S. assets. This leads to an increase in the demand for dollars, which appreciates the dollar, and the quantity of dollars supplied in the exchange market increases. (*Principles of Economics,* 5th ed. pages 728–730/6th ed. pages 706–709)

2. (a) If the Chinese decided that they no longer want to purchase U.S. financial assets, there will be an increase in the net capital outflow, which decreases the supply of loanable funds and raises real interest rates. U.S. savings increases with higher interest rates because people will want to keep their money in U.S. financial assets and U.S. investment falls because it now is more expensive to buy capital equipment for production.

   (b) The increase in the real interest rates (rir) entices foreigners to invest in U.S. foreign assets. This increases the demand for dollars and causes the dollar to appreciate. This would, in turn, increase U.S. imports and decrease U.S. exports, leaving a negative impact on net exports and a decrease in Investment due to the higher rir.

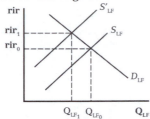 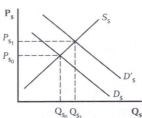

For those who want to use the Mankiw model, here is how you would answer this question with the graphs in Mankiw's *Principles* text. The increase in NCO increases the supply of the dollar in the foreign exchange market and causes the dollar to depreciate.

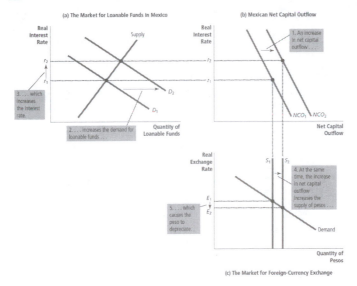

(*Principles of Economics,* 5th ed. pages 730–734/6th ed. pages 709–712)

Part III

Practice Tests:
Microeconomics and
Macroeconomics

PRACTICE TEST 1: MICROECONOMICS

This test will give you some indication of how you might score on the AP Microeconomics Exam. Of course, the exam changes every year, so it is never possible to predict a student's score with certainty. This test will also pinpoint strengths and weaknesses on the key content areas covered by the exam.

AP MICROECONOMICS EXAMINATION
Section I: Multiple-Choice Questions
Time: 70 minutes
60 Questions

Directions: Each of the following questions or incomplete statements is accompanied by five suggested answers or completions. Select the one that best answers the question or completes the statement.

1. A local government increases its gasoline tax. If this tax increase results in an increase in tax revenue, the price elasticity of demand for gasoline is
   (A) elastic.
   (B) unit elastic.
   (C) inelastic.
   (D) equal to one.
   (E) equal to the price elasticity of supply.

2. The law of increasing opportunity costs states that
   (A) as the production of a product increases, output costs increase.
   (B) as the production of a product decreases, input costs increase.
   (C) as the production of a product increases, input costs decrease.
   (D) as the production of a product decreases, inputs are not easily adaptable for the production of other goods.
   (E) as the production of a product increases, input costs increase because inputs are not easily adaptable for the production of other goods.

3. Mr. Economics, a high school economics teacher, hires two teaching assistants to help him grade student papers and create lecture slides for his students. Per hour, Teaching Assistant A can grade 3 papers or create 60 lecture slides, while Teaching Assistant B can grade 1 paper or create 50 lecture slides.

Based on the information presented above, which of the following statements is true?
(A) Teaching Assistant A has a comparative advantage in grading student papers and Teaching Assistant B has a comparative advantage in creating lecture slides.
(B) Teaching Assistant A has an absolute advantage in grading student papers, and Teaching Assistant B has an absolute advantage in creating lecture slides.
(C) Teaching Assistant B has a comparative advantage in grading student papers, and Teaching Assistant A has a comparative advantage in creating lecture slides.
(D) Teaching Assistant B has a comparative advantage in both grading student papers and creating lecture slides.
(E) Teaching Assistant B has an absolute advantage in both grading student papers and creating lecture slides.

4. Which of the following will occur if the government imposes a price floor above the equilibrium price of a good?
(A) The quantity supplied will exceed the equilibrium quantity and the quantity demanded.
(B) Firms' total revenues will increase if demand is price elastic.
(C) There will be a shortage in the market.

(D) No one will buy the good, since the price is above the equilibrium price.
(E) Price will exceed the average total cost of producing the good.

5. Which of the following will decrease the demand for hamburgers?
(A) An increase in the price of hot dogs, if hot dogs and hamburgers are substitute goods
(B) An increase in the price of french fries, if french fries and hamburgers are complementary goods
(C) A decrease in the cost of producing hamburgers
(D) An increase in the income levels of most consumers, if hamburgers are a normal good
(E) Research showing hamburgers are better for your health than chicken patties

6. The hourly wage of the labor used by a firm operating in a competitive cookie baking market increases. Assuming that labor is the only variable hired by this competitive cookie business, which of the following will occur as a result of this wage increase?
(A) The firm will decrease its level of production.
(B) The price of the good will decrease in the short run.
(C) The firm's marginal costs will decrease at every level of output.
(D) The firm's average fixed cost will decrease.
(E) More firms will enter the industry in the long run.

GO ON TO NEXT PAGE

7. Your friend, who enjoys sweets, is eating marshmallows. As she continues to eat more marshmallows, she tells you that the enjoyment she receives from eating each additional marshmallow declines. This gradual decline in enjoyment is an example of
   (A) diminishing marginal utility.
   (B) diminishing marginal product.
   (C) diminishing marginal returns.
   (D) increasing costs.
   (E) scarce resources.

8. Which of the following is true of a monopolistically competitive firm in the long run?
   (A) Price is equal to average total cost and marginal revenue is greater than marginal cost.
   (B) Price is equal to average total cost and marginal revenue is equal to marginal cost.
   (C) Price is greater than marginal revenue and marginal cost is greater than average total cost.
   (D) Price is greater than marginal revenue and marginal cost is equal to average total cost.
   (E) Price is greater than marginal cost and marginal revenue is equal to average total cost.

9. Which of the following is true of a firm in a perfectly competitive industry?
   (A) Firms engage in product differentiation.
   (B) Firms advertise to increase their market share.
   (C) Firms earn positive economic profits in the long run.
   (D) Firms are free to enter or exit an industry in the long run.
   (E) Firms face a downward-sloping demand curve.

10. A firm is currently producing at a loss because marginal cost exceeds its price. What does the firm need to do in order to increase its production efficiency?
    (A) The firm should ask the government to place an effective price ceiling on the good sold by the firm.
    (B) The firm should ask the government to tax the good sold by the firm.
    (C) The firm should decrease production.
    (D) The firm should increase production.
    (E) The firm should maintain its current level of production.

11. Which of the following statements about the relationship between the marginal cost curve and the average variable cost curve is true?
    (A) When the average variable cost curve is rising, the marginal cost curve is above the average variable cost curve.
    (B) When the average variable cost curve is falling, the marginal cost curve is above the average variable cost curve.
    (C) When the average variable cost curve is rising, the marginal cost curve is below the average variable cost curve.
    (D) When the average variable cost curve and marginal cost curve intersect, marginal cost is at a minimum.
    (E) When the average variable cost curve is falling, the marginal cost curve is also falling.

12. An effective tax results in market inefficiency because
    (A) it decreases the price below equilibrium and increases output above equilibrium.
    (B) it decreases the price below equilibrium and decreases output below equilibrium.
    (C) it increases the price above equilibrium and decreases output below equilibrium.
    (D) producer surplus increases and consumer surplus decreases.
    (E) producer surplus decreases and consumer surplus increases.

13. Betsy is the most recently hired employee at Bestseller Books. Her contribution to Bestseller Books' total revenue is greater than the additional cost of hiring her. Assuming that Bestseller Books' hires in a competitive market, what should Bestseller Books do to maximize its profit and use of resources?
    (A) Bestseller Books should consider laying off workers.
    (B) Bestseller Books should consider hiring more workers.
    (C) Bestseller Books should increase employee wages.
    (D) Bestseller Books should expand its business by leasing new retail space.
    (E) Bestseller Books does not need to do anything to maximize profit.

14. Suppose that a large number of unskilled workers enter a nation's labor market. If the labor market is competitive, the number of unskilled workers hired and the wage rate will most likely change in which of the following ways?

	Number of Unskilled Workers Hired	Wage Rate
(A)	Increase	Increase
(B)	Increase	Decrease
(C)	Increase	No change
(D)	Decrease	Increase
(E)	Decrease	Decrease

15. Monopolies are not allocatively efficient because they
    (A) produce at a point where marginal cost is less than marginal revenue.
    (B) produce at a point where marginal cost exceeds price.
    (C) produce more output than does a competitive industry with similar cost conditions.
    (D) produce less output than does a competitive industry with similar cost conditions.
    (E) engage in non-price competition.

16. Economics is the study of
    (A) the scientific method of research.
    (B) the allocation of scarce resources, given unlimited wants.
    (C) the fair and equal treatment of all households.
    (D) the behavior of groups.
    (E) profit-maximizing strategy.

17. A nation only produces two goods—cars and computers. An increase in the demand for cars will result in
    (A) an increase in the demand for computers.
    (B) a decline in total national revenue.
    (C) a decrease in the price of inputs used to produce cars.
    (D) a decrease in the price of cars.
    (E) an increase in the opportunity cost of producing computers.

18. Assume that bologna is an inferior good and that turkey is a normal good. An increase in consumers' incomes will most likely affect the equilibrium price and quantity of bologna and turkey in which of the following ways?

	Bologna Price	Bologna Quantity	Turkey Price	Turkey Quantity
(A)	Decrease	Decrease	Increase	Increase
(B)	Decrease	Increase	Increase	Decrease
(C)	Decrease	Decrease	Decrease	Decrease
(D)	Increase	Increase	Decrease	Decrease
(E)	Increase	Decrease	Increase	Decrease

GO ON TO NEXT PAGE

19. Assume that there is a technological breakthrough that improves the efficiency of the production of trains. What is the impact of this technological breakthrough on the market for trains?
    (A) The price of trains will increase and the quantity of trains will decrease.
    (B) The price of trains will decrease and the quantity of trains will decrease.
    (C) The price of trains will increase and the quantity of trains will increase.
    (D) The price of trains will decrease and the quantity of trains will increase.
    (E) The price of trains will decrease but the quantity of trains is indeterminate.

20. How would the imposition of an effective price floor on a particular good affect its market?
    (A) The demand would increase and the supply would decrease.
    (B) The supply would increase and the demand would decrease.
    (C) The quantity supplied would exceed the quantity demanded.
    (D) The quantity demanded would exceed the quantity supplied.
    (E) It would result in a market shortage.

21. Economies of scale exist when
    (A) the doubling of all inputs doubles the output produced.
    (B) short-run average total cost decreases as output increases.
    (C) short-run average total cost remains constant as output increases.
    (D) long-run average total cost increases as output increases.
    (E) long-run average total cost decreases as output increases.

22. In what ways is a monopoly different from a perfectly competitive firm?
    (A) A monopoly does not have a U-shaped average total cost curve.
    (B) A perfectly competitive firm has an average fixed cost curve that is perfectly horizontal.
    (C) A monopoly has a marginal revenue curve that lies below its demand curve.
    (D) A perfectly competitive firm always earns economic profits.
    (E) A perfectly competitive firm operates in the inelastic segment of its demand curve.

23. If a few firms in an oligopolistic market can successfully collude to maximize their collective profit, they will set their price so that it is
    (A) above the monopoly price.
    (B) above the marginal cost of production.
    (C) equal to the perfectly competitive firm's price.
    (D) equal to the marginal cost of production.
    (E) below the average total cost of production.

24. Which of the following is true regarding the demand curve for firms in a perfectly competitive industry? In the short run, perfectly competitive firms' demand curves are
    (A) upward sloping and equal to marginal revenue.
    (B) downward sloping and equal to marginal cost.
    (C) downward sloping and equal to marginal revenue.
    (D) horizontal and equal to average total cost.
    (E) horizontal and equal to marginal revenue.

Use the following information to answer Question 25:

# of Workers	Total Product
1	5
2	11
3	18
4	27

25. What is the marginal product of the 3rd worker?
    (A) 5.
    (B) 7.
    (C) 9.
    (D) 11.
    (E) 18.

26. If a 3 percent wage increase in a particular labor market results in a 6 percent decrease in employment, the demand for labor is
    (A) perfectly inelastic.
    (B) relatively inelastic.
    (C) unit elastic.
    (D) relatively elastic.
    (E) perfectly elastic.

27. Which of the following would definitely not be an example of price discrimination?
    (A) A gym charges senior citizens less than adults for membership.
    (B) A city charges more for admission to basketball games than baseball games held in the same stadium.
    (C) A cell phone company charges more for an individual phone service plan than a family service plan.
    (D) A local university charges higher tuition for non-state residents than for in-state residents.
    (E) A grocery store sells the same box of cereal for $0.50 less to customers who have a cereal savings coupon.

Use the following information to answer Question 28:

# of Workers	Marginal Resource Cost	Marginal Revenue Product
1	$5.00	$9.50
2	$5.75	$8.75
3	$6.50	$8.00
4	$7.25	$7.25
5	$8.00	$6.50
6	$8.75	$5.75

28. According to the information in the above table, how many workers should the firm hire to maximize the use of its labor?
    (A) 2 workers.
    (B) 3 workers.
    (C) 4 workers.
    (D) 5 workers.
    (E) 6 workers.

29. Which of the following statements regarding a pure public good is true?
    I. Consumption of the good by another person may reduce the availability of the good to others.
    II. The good is non-excludable.
    III. The private market produces too little of the good.
    (A) I only.
    (B) II only.
    (C) III only.
    (D) I and II only.
    (E) II and III only.

30. A monopsonistic employer's marginal resource cost curve
    (A) is always more elastic than the labor supply curve.
    (B) coincides with the labor supply curve.
    (C) lies below the labor supply curve because the higher wage paid to an additional worker must also be paid to all other employees.
    (D) lies above the labor supply curve because the higher wage paid to an additional worker must also be paid to all other employees.
    (E) is perfectly elastic.

GO ON TO NEXT PAGE

31. Which of the following is true for an economy with a straight-line production possibilities frontier?
    I. Resources are used efficiently.
    II. Resources are perfectly adaptable to alternative uses.
    III. The opportunity cost of switching production between two goods is constant.
    (A) I only
    (B) II only
    (C) III only
    (D) I and II only
    (E) II and III only

32. Producer surplus is defined as
    (A) the opportunity cost of producing a good minus the total revenue received from the sale of the good.
    (B) the difference between the price a consumer is willing to pay and the price they actually pay for a good.
    (C) the difference between the resource cost and the price that a consumer pays for a good.
    (D) the difference between the amount that a producer receives and the minimum amount a producer is willing to accept for a good.
    (E) the difference between the resource cost and the price for which a producer is willing to produce the good.

33. Assume that ice cream is a normal good. Which of the following would cause the equilibrium price of ice cream to increase?
    (A) Ice cream producers find a new technology that reduces the cost of producing ice cream.
    (B) The price of milk, an important input used in the production of ice cream, increases.
    (C) Ice cream and chocolate syrup are complements, and the price of chocolate syrup increases.
    (D) The government imposes a 5% income tax.
    (E) New health research shows that eating ice cream may increase one's risk of heart disease.

34. Holding all else constant, there is a new national health report announcing that drinking a glass of orange juice a day will improve one's resistance to the common cold and the cold winter weather has damaged sizable orange crops in Florida. As a result of these two changes, which of the following will definitely occur?
    (A) Orange farmers' profits will fall.
    (B) There will be a surplus of oranges in the market.
    (C) The demand for oranges will decrease.
    (D) The supply of oranges will increase.
    (E) The price of oranges will increase.

35. Assume that a firm uses only two inputs, labor (L) and capital (K) to produce its output. The marginal product of labor is MP_L and the price of labor is P_L while the marginal product of capital is MP_K and the price of capital is P_K. The least cost combination of capital and labor needed to produce any given level of output is where
    (A) $MP_L = MP_K$.
    (B) $MP_L/P_K = MP_K/P_L$.
    (C) $MP_L \times P_K = MP_K \times P_L$.
    (D) $MP_L/P_L < MP_K/P_K$.
    (E) $MP_L/P_L = MP_K/P_K$.

36. In general, technological improvements will lead to
    (A) a decrease in the average total cost of production.
    (B) a decrease in demand for the good produced by the technology.
    (C) an increase in the demand for the good produced by the technology.
    (D) an increase in marginal cost or production.
    (E) an increase in average fixed cost of production.

37. Marginal cost is defined as the
    (A) change in total cost divided by the change in output produced.
    (B) change in total cost resulting from using an additional unit of input.
    (C) difference between total variable cost and total fixed cost.
    (D) difference between total cost and total fixed cost.
    (E) difference between average total cost and average variable cost divided by output produced.

Use the following to answer Questions 38–39:

		Firm X's Pricing Strategy	
		High	Low
Firm Y's Pricing Strategy	Low	$40, $40	$25, $75
	High	$75, $25	$50, $50

The payoff matrix gives the profits associated with the strategic choices of two firms in an oligopolistic market. The first entry in each cell is Firm Y's profit and the second is Firm X's profit.

38. If the two firms collude, what would each firm's profit be?

	Firm X	Firm Y
(A)	$75	$25
(B)	$50	$50
(C)	$25	$75
(D)	$50	$75
(E)	$40	$40

39. Using the matrix above, what is the Nash equilibrium for these two firms?
    (A) Firm X prices high, Firm Y prices high
    (B) Firm X prices high, Firm Y prices low
    (C) Firm X prices low, Firm Y prices high
    (D) Firm X prices low, Firm Y prices low
    (E) The Nash equilibrium cannot be determined from the given information.

40. Which of the following must be true when average product is rising?
    (A) Marginal product is below average product.
    (B) Marginal product is decreasing.
    (C) Marginal product is increasing.
    (D) Marginal product is above average product.
    (E) Total product is at its maximum.

41. Assume that a perfectly competitive industry is in long-run equilibrium and the demand for the good increases. Which of the following will occur in the short run?
    (A) The price will remain unchanged.
    (B) The price will increase.
    (C) The price will decrease.
    (D) Economic profits will be equal to zero.
    (E) Economic profits will decrease.

42. The more substitutes a good has, all else constant,
    (A) the lower its price elasticity of demand.
    (B) the less elastic the demand for the good.
    (C) the more inelastic the demand for the good.
    (D) the greater the product's income elasticity.
    (E) the greater its price elasticity of demand.

43. A firm's demand curve for labor is equal to a portion of its
    (A) average variable cost curve.
    (B) total revenue curve.
    (C) marginal cost curve.
    (D) marginal revenue product curve.
    (E) marginal resource cost curve.

GO ON TO NEXT PAGE

44. In a competitive labor industry, the marginal revenue product of the last cake baker hired is $35 and the marginal revenue product of the last cookie baker hired is $15. The bakery must pay cake bakers $40/day and cookie bakers $10/day. How should the bakery adjust its labor force in order to maximize profits? The bakery
    (A) should hire more cake bakers and fewer cookie bakers.
    (B) should hire fewer cake bakers and more cookie bakers.
    (C) should hire fewer cake bakers and fewer cookie bakers.
    (D) should hire more of both cake bakers and cookie bakers.
    (E) is currently hiring the correct number of cake and cookie bakers to maximize profit.

45. The production of aluminum emits toxins in the air that are likely to cause cancer in those who breathe the polluted air. Which of the following will be true if the price of aluminum is determined in a free market?
    (A) The price of aluminum will be too low and the quantity sold will be too high.
    (B) The price of aluminum will be efficient, but the quantity sold will be too high.
    (C) The aluminum market will produce the socially optimal quantity.
    (D) The price of aluminum and the quantity sold will be too high.
    (E) The price of aluminum will overstate the true social cost imposed on those who breathe in the polluted air.

46. A perfectly competitive firm should shut down in the short run when
    (A) it is operating at an economic loss.
    (B) minimum average total cost exceeds price.
    (C) minimum average variable cost exceeds price.
    (D) marginal cost exceeds marginal revenue.
    (E) marginal revenue exceeds marginal cost.

47. If the demand for chocolate syrup increases as the price of ice cream decreases, it can be concluded that
    (A) chocolate syrup is an inferior good, and ice cream is a superior good.
    (B) chocolate syrup is a superior good, and ice cream is an inferior good.
    (C) both chocolate syrup and ice cream are inferior goods.
    (D) chocolate syrup and ice cream are substitute goods.
    (E) chocolate syrup and ice cream are complementary goods.

48. If the market demand for cigarettes is inelastic while the supply is elastic, which of the following is true when there is an increase in a cigarette tax?
    (A) Cigarette consumers will bear more of the burden of the tax.
    (B) Cigarette producers will bear the entire burden of the tax.
    (C) Cigarette producers will bear most of the burden of the tax or risk losing sales.
    (D) Both cigarette consumers and producers will share the burden of the tax equally.
    (E) The price of the cigarettes will not change with the tax.

49. Which of the following is true if a firm in a perfectly competitive market increases its price above the market equilibrium price?
    (A) The firm's total revenue will increase.
    (B) The quantity of the good sold by the firm will fall, but profit will increase.
    (C) The firm will face a downward sloping demand curve.
    (D) The firm will not be able to sell any output.
    (E) The firm's marginal costs will increase.

50. Bagels and cream cheese are complementary goods. If the cost of producing cream cheese increases, which of the following is true?
    (A) There will be a decrease in the price of bagels.
    (B) There will be a decrease in the price of cream cheese.
    (C) There will be an increase in the equilibrium quantity of cream cheese sold.
    (D) There will be an increase in the demand for bagels.
    (E) There will be an increase in the supply of bagels.

51. In which of the following scenarios is an opportunity cost incurred?
    I.   A student decides to buy a laptop computer for $500.
    II. A student decides to attend college full time starting in the fall.
    III. A student decides to get a summer job.
    (A) I only
    (B) II only
    (C) III only
    (D) I and III only
    (E) I, II, and III

52. Which of the following statements regarding an effective minimum wage is true?
    (A) The wage must be set below the market equilibrium.
    (B) There will be a shortage of workers in the labor market.
    (C) There will be unemployment.
    (D) The quantity of workers hired in the labor market will increase.
    (E) The quantity of jobs available in the labor market will increase.

53. A single-price monopolist's marginal revenue is
    (A) equal to its price.
    (B) greater than its price.
    (C) negative when it maximizes total revenue.
    (D) zero when it maximizes total revenue.
    (E) zero when it maximizes profit.

54. Holding all else constant, if the price of a firm's variable inputs were to fall
    (A) one could not predict how unit costs of production would be affected.
    (B) marginal cost, average variable cost, and average total cost would all fall.
    (C) marginal cost, average variable cost, and average fixed cost would all fall.
    (D) average variable cost would fall, but marginal cost would remain unchanged.
    (E) average variable cost and average fixed cost would fall.

55. Which of the following is true if a monopolist's marginal revenue curve is negative?
    (A) Demand for its product is unit elastic.
    (B) Demand for its product is price elastic.
    (C) Demand for its product is price inelastic.
    (D) Marginal cost is equal to its marginal revenue.
    (E) Average total cost is at its minimum point.

GO ON TO NEXT PAGE

56. Which of the following correctly describes what will happen to the market price and quantity if a few firms collude and act as a profit-maximizing monopoly?

Price	Quantity
(A) Decrease	Decrease
(B) Decrease	Increase
(C) Increase	Increase
(D) Increase	Decrease
(E) Increase	No change

57. Assume that a firm in a perfectly competitive market is earning short run profits. Which of the following accurately describes what will happen to the market equilibrium price and quantity in the long run?
    (A) Firms will enter the market, increasing the market price and quantity sold.
    (B) Firms will enter the market, decreasing the market price and quantity sold.
    (C) Firms will enter the market, decreasing the market price and increasing the quantity sold.
    (D) Firms will exit the market, increasing the market price and decreasing the quantity sold.
    (E) The number of firms remaining in the market will not change in the long run.

58. Marginal revenue product is defined as the
    (A) total revenue divided by the quantity of labor employed.
    (B) change in total cost that occurs when one additional unit of an input is employed.
    (C) change in income that occurs when an individual works additional hours.
    (D) change in total revenue that occurs when one additional unit of the good is produced.
    (E) change in total revenue that occurs when one additional unit of an input is employed.

59. A market will produce more than is socially optimal when
    (A) the market produces a public good.
    (B) the market privatizes a common resource.
    (C) the production of a good results in a positive externality.
    (D) the production of a good results in a negative externality.
    (E) the production of a good results in higher input costs.

60. Pure economic rent is the price of a resource with a perfectly
    (A) inelastic supply curve.
    (B) inelastic demand curve.
    (C) elastic demand curve.
    (D) elastic supply curve.
    (E) elastic supply curve and an inelastic demand curve.

STOP

END OF SECTION I
IF YOU FINISH BEFORE TIME IS CALLED, YOU MAY CHECK YOUR WORK ON THIS SECTION. DO NOT GO ON TO SECTION II UNTIL YOU ARE TOLD TO DO SO.

Section II: Free-Response Questions
Planning Time—10 minutes
Writing Time—50 minutes

Directions: You have 50 minutes to answer all three of the following questions. <u>It is suggested that you spend approximately half your time on the first question and divide the remaining time equally between the next two questions.</u> In answering the questions, you should emphasize the line of reasoning that generated your results; it is not enough to list the results of your analysis. Include correctly labeled diagrams, if useful or required, in explaining your answer. A correctly labeled diagram must have all axes and curves clearly labeled and must show directional changes. <u>Use a pen with black or dark blue ink.</u>

FREE-RESPONSE QUESTIONS

1. WonderWheat sells wheat in a perfectly competitive market and is currently in long-run equilibrium.
   (a) Draw correctly labeled side-by-side graphs for WonderWheat and the wheat market. On your graphs, identify the following.
       (i) Market equilibrium price and output
       (ii) WonderWheat's price and output
   (b) There is a stock market boom that increases the wealth of wheat consumers. Assuming that wheat is a normal good, how does this increase in wealth affect the wheat market and WonderWheat? Use your graph in part (a) above to show the impact on the following.
       (i) Market equilibrium price and output
       (ii) WonderWheat's price and output
   (c) Using your results from part (b) above, is WonderWheat earning a profit or incurring a loss? Show your answer graphically using the graph in part (b) above.
   (d) Given the short-run circumstances presented in part (b) and (c) above, how does the price and output of wheat adjust in the long run? Using your graphs, specifically address the following.
       (i) Market equilibrium price and output
       (ii) The number of firms in the market
       (iii) WonderWheat's price and output level, assuming that it remains in the market

2. Technological advances helped to increase the production capacity of U.S. farmers in the 20th century.
   (a) Using a correctly labeled graph, explain how technological advances affected the market price and quantity corn sold in the U.S.
   (b) The U.S. government passed the Agricultural Marketing Act in 1929 as a measure to help farmers during the Great Depression. The program provides an agricultural subsidy to farmers and guarantees a price floor in specific agricultural markets. Using a new, correctly labeled graph, explain the effect of the price floor on the following in the U.S. corn market.
       (i) The quantity of corn supplied
       (ii) The quantity of corn demanded
       (iii) The consumer surplus
       (iv) The producer surplus

(c) The government's implementation of a price floor results in an inefficient allocation of resources. Aside from looking at consumer or producer surplus, graph the area of deadweight loss to show why the price floor leads to an inefficient allocation of resources.

3. The table below provides the production information for Stacey's Soda Shack. Stacey hires workers in a competitive labor market and can hire workers to help make and bottle her soda for $20 a day. She sells her soda for $1 each.

Workers	Total Output
0	0
1	50
2	90
3	120
4	140
5	150
6	159

(a) Given the above production information, address each of the following.
  (i) Draw a graph showing Stacey's Soda Shack's demand and supply for workers.
  (ii) Use your graph in part (i) above to explain how Stacey will determine how many workers she will hire in order to maximize her profit and use her labor force. State how many workers Stacey will hire.
(b) Assume that Stacey's sodas are a normal good. If consumer income increases, how will Stacey's hiring decision change? Specifically, use appropriate graphs to explain how:
  (i) the income increase will affect the quantity of sodas sold in the market.
  (ii) Stacey's demand for workers will change as a result of this consumer income increase.
  (iii) the wage rate paid to Stacey's employees will change.
  (iv) the number of workers Stacey actually hires will change.

ANSWERS TO MICROECONOMICS PRACTICE TEST 1

SECTION I: MULTIPLE-CHOICE ANSWERS

Using the table below, score your test.

Determine how many questions you answered correctly and how many you answered incorrectly. You will find explanations to the answers on the following pages.

1. C	7. A	13. B	19. D	25. B	31. E	37. A	43. D	49. D	55. C
2. E	8. B	14. B	20. C	26. D	32. D	38. B	44. B	50. A	56. D
3. A	9. D	15. D	21. E	27. B	33. B	39. A	45. A	51. E	57. C
4. A	10. C	16. B	22. C	28. C	34. E	40. D	46. C	52. C	58. E
5. B	11. A	17. E	23. B	29. E	35. E	41. B	47. E	53. D	59. D
6. A	12. C	18. A	24. E	30. D	36. A	42. E	48. A	54. B	60. A

1. **C.** A tax increase increases the price of gasoline. If tax revenue increases with a tax (or price increase), the demand is inelastic. If tax revenue decreases with a tax, the demand is elastic. In this case, the tax revenue increases, so the demand is price inelastic (*Principles of Economics* 5th ed. pages 123–128/6th ed. pages 121–127).

2. **E.** Resources used in the production of one good are not necessarily adaptable for the use of another good. In order to switch from the production of one good to another, a firm incurs higher opportunity costs because resources that are good for the production of one good are not perfectly adaptable to the production of another good, since the firm will have to give up more of the resources used to produce one good in order to acquire the necessary resources to switch production to another good (*Principles of Economics* 5th ed. page 25/6th ed. page 26).

3. **A.** Teaching Assistant A has the comparative advantage in grading papers because he has a lower opportunity cost (20 lecture slides) than Teaching Assistant B, whose opportunity cost is 50 lecture slides. Teaching Assistant B has the comparative advantage in creating lecture slides because he has a lower opportunity cost (1/50 student paper) than Teaching Assistant A, whose opportunity cost is 1/20 student paper (*Principles of Economics* 5th ed. pages 49–58/6th ed. pages 49–57).

4. **A.** An effective price floor is one that is set <u>above</u> the market equilibrium price and will result in a surplus of the good sold, since the quantity supplied will be greater than the quantity demanded (*Principles of Economics* 5th ed. pages 114–121/6th ed. pages 112–117).

5. **B.** If hamburgers and fries are complementary goods, then an increase in the price of fries would decrease the demand for hamburgers because people consume the two goods together. If the price of one complementary good increases, the demand for the other good decreases (*Principles of Economics* 5th ed. pages 66–85/6th ed. pages 67–77).

6. **A.** Labor is a variable input. Since wages increase, the variable costs for the firm increase, which increases the firm's marginal costs. The firm's marginal cost curve increases and the marginal cost curve now intersects the marginal revenue curve at a lower output quantity, so the firm produces fewer cookies as the hourly wage rate for labor increases (*Principles of Economics* 5th ed. pages 290–303/6th ed. pages 280–289).

7. **A.** Utility is an economic measure of satisfaction. Diminishing marginal utility is the concept that the satisfaction, or utility, that we receive from the consumption of a good is highest with the first unit than subsequent units (*Principles of Economics* 5th ed. pages 66–85/6th ed. pages 67–77).

8. **B.** A monopolistically competitive firm does not earn economic profit in the long run, but does earn a normal profit. Firms will enter or exit the industry in the long run, which adjusts demand for the goods/services produced by monopolistically competitive firms who remain in the industry. This long-run adjustment continues to the point where the firm's price is equal to its average total costs (*Principles of Economics* 5th ed. pages 346–361/6th ed. pages 330–338).

9. **D.** The characteristics of firms in perfectly competitive industries: P-I-L-E. That is, they are **p**rice-takers, sell **i**dentical products, exist in a market with a **l**ot of buyers and sellers, and can **e**asily enter/exit the market (*Principles of Economics* 5th ed. pages 290–303/6th ed. pages 280–289).

10. **C.** The profit-maximizing quantity is where marginal revenue (MR) = marginal cost (MC). If the marginal cost exceeds price, marginal cost exceed marginal revenue, which means that the firm must decrease its production so that MR = MC (*Principles of Economics* 5th ed. pages 290–303/6th ed. pages 280–289).

11. **A.** The average variable cost (AVC) curve intersects the marginal cost (MC) curve at its minimum point. This is true for the average total cost curve as well. Since the AVC is at a minimum when it intersects the MC, when AVC is rising, the MC is above the AVC and when AVC is falling, the MC is below the AVC. Option E is not correct because, as AVC falls, the MC curve is *below* the AVC, but can either be rising or falling (*Principles of Economics* 5th ed. pages 268–281/6th ed. pages 260–272).

12. **C.** An effective tax is one that increases the price to a level above the market equilibrium. At this higher tax price, P_T, the quantity

demanded decreases, resulting in deadweight loss. Both consumer surplus and producer surplus decrease (*Principles of Economics* 5th ed. pages 138–148/6th ed. pages 136–146).

13. **B.** The marginal revenue product (MRP) is currently greater than the marginal resource/factor cost (MRC or MFC). In order to maximize resource use, Bestseller Books should hire workers where MRP = MRC, so the firm should consider hiring more workers. Note though, that if hiring an additional worker leads to MRP < MRC, then Bestseller Books should not hire an additional worker (*Principles of Economics* 5th ed. pages 392–409/6th ed. pages 376–392).

14. **B.** An increase in the number of unskilled workers shifts the supply of unskilled labor in the competitive labor market. This increases the quantity of unskilled laborers hired and lowers the equilibrium wage paid to unskilled laborers (*Principles of Economics* 5th ed. pages 392–409/6th ed. pages 376–392).

15. **D.** A monopoly still produces where MR = MC, but charges a higher price and sells fewer units of output. The monopolist's profit-maximizing output results in deadweight loss because the monopolist produces less output than the perfectly competitive industry and decreases consumer surplus (*Principles of Economics* 5th ed. pages 312–336/6th ed. pages 300–323).

16. **B.** Economics is the study of how society allocates its scarce resources given unlimited wants (*Principles of Economics* 5th ed. pages 15–24/6th ed. pages 15–24).

17. **E.** Since there is greater demand for cars, the nation will devote more of its resources to the production of cars. This increases the opportunity cost of producing computers (*Principles of Economics* 5th ed. page 25/6th ed. page 26).

18. **A.** If incomes fall, the quantity of inferior goods consumed increases. In this case, incomes increase, so the demand for bologna will decrease and the demand for turkey, a normal good, will increase. The decrease in the demand for bologna will result in a lower price and quantity consumed/sold. The increase in turkey will result in a higher price and quantity consumed/sold (*Principles of Economics* 5th ed. pages 66–85/6th ed. pages 67–77).

19. **D.** The supply curve for trains will increase (shift to the right) with a technological breakthrough. This will decrease the price of trains and increase the quantity of trains (*Principles of Economics* 5th ed. pages 66–85/6th ed. pages 67–77).

20. **C.** An effective price floor is one that is set above the market equilibrium price. At this price, the quantity supplied is greater than the quantity demanded and there is a surplus in the market (*Principles of Economics* 5th ed. pages 114–121/6th ed. pages 112–117).

21. **E.** Economies of scale occur in the downward sloping portion of the long-run average total cost curve. It is a cost advantage for firms when they expand (*Principles of Economics* 5th ed. pages 268–281/6th ed. pages 260–272).

22. **C.** A monopoly's marginal revenue (MR) curve is steeper than its demand curve, whereas for a perfectly competitive firm, the MR curve is equal to its demand (*Principles of Economics* 5th ed. pages 312–336/6th ed. pages 300–323).

23. **B.** An oligopoly with firms that successfully collude will want to charge the same price as a single-price monopolist, so the price will be greater than the marginal cost and the firms will produce at a level where MR = MC (*Principles of Economics* 5th ed. pages 366–384/6th ed. pages 350–362).

24. **E.** Since firms are price takers, the marginal revenue = price = demand = average revenue for a perfectly competitive firm (*Principles of Economics* 5th ed. pages 290–303/6th ed. pages 280–289).

25. **B.** The marginal product is the additional output produced by an additional worker. Total product increases from 11 to 18 with the addition of the 3rd worker, so his/her marginal product is 7 (*Principles of Economics* 5th ed. pages 268–281/6th ed. pages 260–272).

26. **D.** When a price increase results in a greater percentage decrease in quantity demanded, the demand is relatively price elastic (Ed > 1), but when a price increase results in a smaller percentage increase in quantity demanded, the demand is relative price inelastic (Ed < 1) (*Principles of Economics* 5th ed. pages 90–108/6th ed. pages 89–101).

27. **B.** Price discrimination occurs when a firm (or institution) is able to charge different prices to different customers for the same product. Firms must be able to separate the market according to differing price elasticity. In all of the options except for B, different prices were charged for the same good/service (*Principles of Economics* 5th ed. pages 333–336/6th ed. pages 320–323).

28. **C.** The resource maximizing rule is where marginal revenue product (MRP) = marginal resource/factor cost (MRC or MFC). The MRC ($7.25) = MRP ($7.25) for the 4th worker (*Principles of Economics* 5th ed. pages 392–409/6th ed. pages 376–392).

29. **E.** A public good is a good that is non-rival and non-excludable. Private firms have little incentive to produce an optimal quantity of public goods because the goods are non-excludable and non-rival. This is why the government often steps in to provide public goods, such as police security (*Principles of Economics* 5th ed. pages 204–237/6th ed. pages 195–235).

30. **D.** A monopsony is where one buyer faces many sellers and usually relates to the resource market. If a firm is the only employer ("buyer" of labor) that hires laborers ("seller" of labor) in a town, the monopsonistic firm will have to pay every laborer the same wage since all laborers are doing the same work. This results in a marginal resource cost curve that is above the labor supply curve (*Principles of Economics* 5th ed. pages 392–409/6th ed. pages 376–392).

31. **E.** A production possibilities curve that is bowed out from the origin reflects increasing opportunity costs whereas a production possibilities curve that is a straight line reflects constant opportunity costs. The resources used for the production of the two goods must be perfectly adaptable for switching from the production of one good to the other (*Principles of Economics* 5th ed. page 25/6th ed. page 26).

32. **D.** Producer surplus is the benefit to producers when they sell a good at a market price that is higher than what the producer is willing to supply the good for. It is the area located below the market equilibrium price and above the supply curve up to the market equilibrium quantity (*Principles of Economics* 5th ed. pages 138–148/6th ed. pages 136–146).

33. **B.** An increase in input costs will decrease the supply curve. This increases the price of ice cream and decreases the quantity of ice cream (*Principles of Economics* 5th ed. pages 66–85/6th ed. pages 67–77).

34. **E.** The demand for oranges will increase with the expectation that drinking orange juice will improve one's health and the supply of oranges will decrease as a result of the severe winter weather. The price of oranges definitely increases but the quantity of oranges is indeterminate and depends on the magnitude of the shifts of each curve (*Principles of Economics* 5th ed. pages 66–85/6th ed. pages 67–77).

35. **E.** The least cost rule helps firms to produce at least cost when using more than one input in production. The rule states that firms should hire where $MP_L/P_L = MP_K/P_K$ (*Principles of Economics* 5th ed. pages 392–409/6th ed. pages 376–392).

36. **A.** Input costs generally fall when there are technological improvements. This lowers the average total cost of production and an increase in supply as well (*Principles of Economics* 5th ed. pages 66–85/6th ed. pages 67–77).

37. **A.** MC = Δ in TC/Δ in Q; in other words, the marginal cost is the additional cost that is incurred with the production of an additional unit of output produced (*Principles of Economics* 5th ed. pages 268–281/6th ed. pages 260–272).

38. **B.** If the two firms collude, they will want to follow a low pricing strategy since each firm will earn $50 in profit (*Principles of Economics* 5th ed. pages 366–384/6th ed. pages 350–362).

39. **A.** Although it would make most sense for the firms to collude, there is an incentive for each firm to increase its price, since if one firm prices high the profit is $75 vs. $50 with collusion. Nash equilibrium is where both firms pick a strategy based on what the other firm will do, so the Nash equilibrium is where both firms pick the high pricing strategy (*Principles of Economics* 5th ed. pages 366–384/6th ed. pages 350–362).

40. **D.** The average product (AP) curve intersects the marginal product (MP) curve at its highest point. When the AP is rising, the MP is above the AP and when the AP is falling, the MP is below the AP. Refer to the graphs in the production costs chapter (*Principles of Economics* 5th ed. pages 268–281/6th ed. pages 260–272).

41. **B.** An increase in demand will increase the price of the good and the quantity of the good consumed/sold in the market (*Principles of Economics* 5th ed. pages 290–303/6th ed. pages 280–289).

42. **E.** The price elasticity of demand measures how much the quantity demanded of a good responds to a change in the price of that good. The more close substitutes there are, the higher the price elasticity of demand for the good. Other factors that affect price elasticity include time horizon and whether the goods are luxuries or necessities (*Principles of Economics* 5th ed. pages 114–121/6th ed. pages 112–117).

43. **D.** A firm's labor demand curve is a derived demand curve that corresponds to the downward sloping portion of the marginal revenue product curve (*Principles of Economics* 5th ed. pages 392–409/6th ed. pages 376–392).

44. **B.** The MRP/P for cake bakers is $35/$40 and the MRP/P for cookie bakers is $15/$10. In order to maximize the use of both resources, the firm hiring labor in this market should hire more cookie bakers since the MRP ($15) is currently greater than its MRC ($10) and fewer cake bakers since the MRP ($35) is less than its MRC ($40) (*Principles of Economics* 5th ed. pages 392–409/6th ed. pages 376–392).

45. **A.** This is an example of a negative externality, where aluminum producers in the aluminum market produce too much aluminum at too low of a price. In a free, unregulated market, the price is too low and the quantity sold too high (*Principles of Economics* 5th ed. pages 204–237/6th ed. pages 195–225).

46. **C.** A perfectly competitive firm should shut down when P < AVC in the short run because it can no longer cover its variable costs and is losing money. The firm does not consider its fixed costs because

they are sunk (*Principles of Economics* 5th ed. pages 290–303/6th ed. pages 280–289).

47. **E.** Complementary goods are goods that are consumed together. Therefore, when the demand for one good (chocolate syrup) increases when the price of another (ice cream) decreases, the two goods are complementary since the quantity consumed of both increase (*Principles of Economics* 5th ed. pages 66–85/6th ed. pages 67–77).

48. **A.** Since the demand for cigarettes is relatively more inelastic than the supply of cigarettes, the consumers of cigarettes will bear a larger burden of the tax. Refer to the graphs and discussion in Chapter 2 for more detail (*Principles of Economics* 5th ed. pages 123–128/6th ed. pages 121–127).

49. **D.** A firm in a perfectly competitive industry must take the market price. If the firm tries to increase its price, customers will not buy from that firm because there are many other sellers in that market from whom they can purchase the identical good from (*Principles of Economics* 5th ed. pages 290–303/6th ed. pages 280–289).

50. **A.** An increase in the cost of producing cream cheese will shift the cream cheese supply curve to the left and result in an increase in the price of cream cheese. A higher cream cheese price will lead to a decrease in the demand for bagels, since they are complementary goods. This decrease in bagel demand will decrease the equilibrium price of bagels (*Principles of Economics* 5th ed. pages 66–85/6th ed. pages 67–77).

51. **E.** An opportunity cost is what you give up in order to obtain something else. There are opportunity costs with every decision that we make. The opportunity cost of the $500 laptop purchase includes all of the other things the student may have spent his/her money on; new clothes, for example. The opportunity cost of going to college are all of the other things the student might have chosen to do; the wages he/she might have earned if he/she got a job instead, for example (*Principles of Economics* 5th ed. pages 49–58/6th ed. pages 49–57).

52. **C.** An effective minimum wage is set above the market equilibrium, price. This results in a surplus of workers, or unemployment because the quantity of workers supplied at the effective minimum wage is greater than the quantity of workers demanded at this wage (*Principles of Economics* 5th ed. pages 114–121/6th ed. pages 112–117).

53. **D.** When MR = 0, TR is at its maximum. Refer to the graphs in Chapter 4 for review (*Principles of Economics* 5th ed. pages 312–336/6th ed. pages 300–323).

54. **B.** A change in variable input prices will only be reflected in calculations for variable cost curves: marginal cost, average total

cost, and average variable cost (*Principles of Economics* 5th ed. pages 268–281/6th ed. pages 260–272).

55. **C.** When MR = 0, the firm's price elasticity of demand is equal to 1, which means that it is at its point of unit elasticity. When MR < 0, the price elasticity of demand is inelastic. Refer to the total revenue and elasticity graph in Chapter 2 (*Principles of Economics* 5th ed. pages 90–108/6th ed. pages 89–101).

56. **D.** A successfully colluding oligolopolistic market produces a higher quantity at a lower price than a monopolist. If firms collude to act as a monopoly, they will increase their price and lower their quantity produced/sold (*Principles of Economics* 5th ed. pages 366–384/6th ed. pages 350–362).

57. **C.** Short-run economic profit entices new firms to enter the market. This increases the market supply (since the number of sellers has increased) and lowers the market price and increases the quantity sold (*Principles of Economics* 5th ed. pages 290–303/6th ed. pages 280–289).

58. **E.** Marginal revenue product (MRP) = MP × $P_{product}$. MRP measures the change in total revenue when an additional resource unit is employed for production (*Principles of Economics* 5th ed. pages 392–409/6th ed. pages 376–392).

59. **D.** A market will produce too much at too low of a price when there is a negative externality (*Principles of Economics* 5th ed. pages 204–237/6th ed. pages 195–225).

60. **A.** Pure economic rent is collected when there is a perfectly inelastic supply curve. Economic rent is collected most commonly for the use of land, which is fixed in its supply and is perfectly inelastic (*Principles of Economics* 5th ed. pages 90–108/6th ed. pages 89–101).

SECTION II: FREE-RESPONSE ANSWERS

1. (12 points total)
   (a)

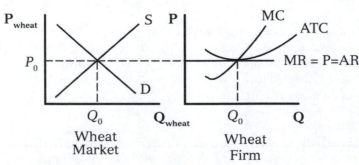

   4 points, 1 each for:
   - correctly labeled wheat market graph: Q_{wheat}, P_{wheat}, upward sloping S-curve and downward sloping D-curve
   - correctly labeled market equilibrium P_0 and Q_0, where S and D intersect

- correctly labeled WonderWheat firm graph, linked to the wheat market by price: P_{wheat}, Q_{wheat}, upward sloping MC curve and perfectly elastic MR curve
- MC = MR is the profit maximizing quantity produced by WonderWheat and ATC intersects MC = MR at its minimum point, showing LR equilibrium where the firm earns a normal profit but no economic profit.

(b) 3 points:

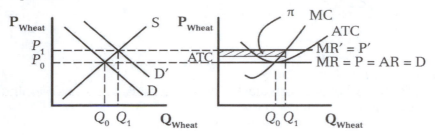

WonderWheat

- 1 for correctly labeled market and firm graph and an increase in market D (because increase in income is a demand determinant and wheat is a normal good)
- 1 for correctly labeled increase in market price and output
- 1 for correctly labeled increase in firm price and output

(c) see graph in part (b)

1 point: WonderWheat experiences an economic profit because MR > ATC at the profit maximizing quantity. (Be very careful with your graph here—make sure that the economic profit is graphed correctly. Start at the profit maximizing quantity and identify the ATC. From that point, draw your area of economic profit.).

(d 4 points, 1 each for:

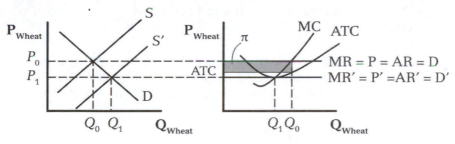

WonderWheat

- New firms enter the market because they are enticed by the economic profit earned by firms currently in the market.
- This increases the market supply.
- Market equilibrium price decreases and output increases.
- WonderWheat's output level and price decreases and returns to the same quantity as in the long-run equilibrium.

(*Principles of Economics* 5th ed. pages 290–303/6th ed. pages 280–289).

2. (9 points total)
   (a)

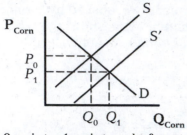

3 points, 1 point each, for:
   - Correctly labeled corn market graph: Q_{corn}, P_{corn}, upward sloping S, downward sloping D
   - Rightward shift in S due to technological advancement
   - Correctly labeled market equilibrium before and after the technological improvements

   (b)

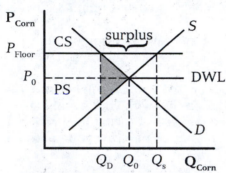

5 points, 1 point each, for:
   - Price floor above market equilibrium price
   - Q_s increases
   - Q_d decreases
   - CS decreases in comparison to market without price floor
   - PS increases in comparison to market without price floor
   (c) 1 point for correctly identifying the area of DWL (see graph in part (b) above)

3. (8 points total)
   MRC = MFC = WR = $20/day
   $P_{product}$ = $1

Workers	Total Output	Marginal Product
0	0	
1	50	50
2	90	40
3	120	30
4	140	20
5	150	10
6	159	9

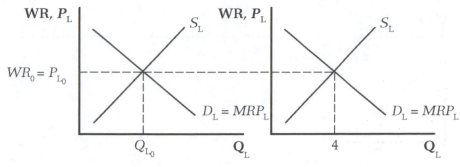

Stacy's Soda

(a) 4 points, 1 point each for:
- Correctly labeled labor market graph: Q_L, P_L, upward sloping S_L curve and downward sloping D_L curve
- Correctly labeled firm graph with perfectly elastic MRC or MFC or WR curve
- Stacey hires where MRP = MRC.
- She hires 4 workers since MRC ($20) = MRP ($20) when 4 workers are hired.

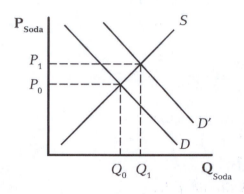

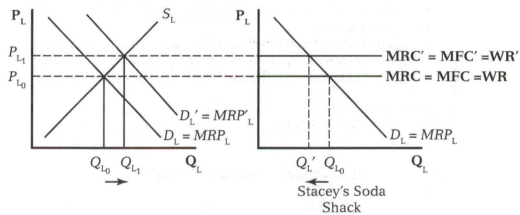

Stacey's Soda
Shack

(b) 4 points, 1 point each for:
- Consumer income increases will increase the demand for soda since it is a normal good; the quantity and price of soda sold will increase.
- The market price increases, so the demand for workers increases as well since it is a derived demand that is dependent on MP_L and product price.
- The increase in demand for labor increases the market wage rate. Stacey takes this new, higher wage rate.
- Since the MRC has increased, Stacey will hire fewer workers because MRC = MRP at a lower quantity of laborers.

CALCULATING YOUR SCORE

SECTION I: MULTIPLE-CHOICE QUESTIONS

[_____] × 1.25 = _____
Number Correct   Weighted Section I Score
(out of 60)   (Do not round)

SECTION II: FREE-RESPONSE QUESTIONS

Question 1 _____ × (1.2500) = _____
(out of 12)   (Do not round)

Question 2 _____ × (0.8333) = _____
(out of 9)   (Do not round)

Question 3 _____ × (0.9375) = _____
(out of 8)   (Do not round)

Sum = _____
Weighted Section II Score
(Do not round)

COMPOSITE SCORE

_____ + _____ = _____
Weighted   Weighted   Composite Score
Section I Score   Section II Score   (Round to nearest
                                          whole number)

Composite Score Range	Approximate AP Grade
73–90	5
58–72	4
45–57	3
33–44	2
0–32	1

Practice Test 2: Microeconomics

This test will give you some indication of how you might score on the AP Microeconomics Exam. Of course, the exam changes every year, so it is never possible to predict a student's score with certainty. This test will also pinpoint strengths and weaknesses on the key content areas covered by the exam.

AP MICROECONOMICS EXAMINATION
Section I: Multiple-Choice Questions
Time: 70 minutes
60 Questions

Directions: Each of the following questions or incomplete statements is accompanied by five suggested answers or completions. Select the one that best answers the question or completes the statement.

Use the following to answer Question 1:

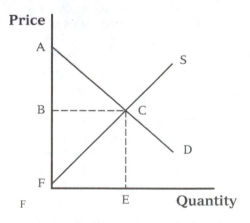

1. Using the above graph, which area represents consumer surplus?
   (A) 0ACE
   (B) BCF
   (C) 0BCE
   (D) ABC
   (E) 0BCE

2. A new government welfare program that collects tax revenue from those with higher income and redistributes the wealth to those with lower income will
   (A) decrease income inequality and decrease economic efficiency.
   (B) increase income inequality and increase economic efficiency.
   (C) increase income inequality and decrease economic efficiency.
   (D) decrease income inequality and increase economic efficiency.
   (E) decrease income inequality and have no effect on economic efficiency.

GO ON TO NEXT PAGE

Use the following graph to answer Questions 3–4:

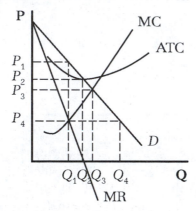

3. If the government wants to regulate the monopoly in the graph above so that it produces at a socially optimal level of output, the government should set the price equal to
   (A) P1
   (B) P2
   (C) P3
   (D) P4
   (E) 0

4. Which of the following is true regarding the above monopolist's profit at the socially optimal output level?
   (A) It is earning zero economic profit.
   (B) It is earning a positive economic profit.
   (C) It is earning a normal profit.
   (D) It is earning an accounting profit.
   (E) It is incurring an economic loss.

5. A firm has monopoly power because
   (A) of its constant use of advertisement.
   (B) of existing market entry barriers.
   (C) it sells identical products to other firms.
   (D) it uses scarce resources in production.
   (E) there is elastic demand for its product or service.

6. Assume that a firm in a perfectly competitive market is producing at the profit-maximizing level of output. If the cost of labor, a variable input, increases, which of the following is true?
   (A) The firm's marginal cost and average total cost will increase.
   (B) The firm will hire more workers.
   (C) The firm's marginal cost and average fixed cost will increase.
   (D) The firm's average fixed cost will increase and the firm will hire fewer workers.
   (E) The firm will earn an economic profit.

7. Which of the following is true for a monopoly but not for a firm in a perfectly competitive industry?
   (A) The firm produces where marginal cost is equal to marginal revenue.
   (B) The firm's marginal revenue curve is equal to its demand curve.
   (C) The firm earns zero economic profit in the long run.
   (D) The firm faces a downward sloping demand curve.
   (E) The firm produces at an efficient output level.

8. Which of the following is true of a perfectly competitive firm in the long run?
   (A) Price is equal to average total cost and marginal revenue is greater than marginal cost.
   (B) Price is equal to average total cost and marginal revenue is equal to marginal cost.
   (C) Price is greater than marginal revenue and marginal cost is greater than average total cost.
   (D) Price is greater than marginal revenue and marginal cost is equal to average total cost.
   (E) Price is greater than marginal cost and marginal revenue is equal to average total cost.

9. Which of the following is true of a firm in a monopolistically competitive industry?
   (A) Firms do not engage in product differentiation.
   (B) Firms advertise to increase their market share.
   (C) Firms earn positive economic profits in the long run.
   (D) Firms must collude in order to earn a monopoly profit.
   (E) Firms face a perfectly elastic demand curve.

10. A firm's demand for labor is often referred to as a derived demand because
    (A) the amount of labor hired by the firm depends on the number of laborers hired by the firm's competitors
    (B) the wages paid to the firm's employees depend on the firm's marginal utility from hiring an additional worker
    (C) the amount of labor hired by the firm depends on the firm's average fixed costs
    (D) the amount of labor hired by the firm depends on the firm's average total costs
    (E) the amount of labor hired by the firm depends on the demand for the firm's product or service

11. If the price of pizza decreases from $4/slice to $3/slice and the quantity of pizza demanded increases from 20 to 30, which of the following is true regarding this price range of the pizza demand curve?
    (A) The demand is perfectly elastic.
    (B) The demand is elastic.
    (C) The demand is unit elastic.
    (D) The demand is inelastic.
    (E) The demand is perfectly inelastic.

12. Assuming that the price of a good produced by a competitive industry increases, which of the following is true?
    (A) The marginal product of capital will increase.
    (B) The demand for labor will decrease in the short run.
    (C) The marginal revenue product of capital will increase.
    (D) The supply of labor will increase in the short run.
    (E) The supply of labor will decrease in the short run.

13. Reilly earns $10 per hour working at a local coffee shop. His parents purchased a pair of concert tickets to his favorite band for $50 each. In order to go to the concert, Reilly must take 6 hours off from work. What is Reilly's opportunity cost for attending the concert?
    (A) $10
    (B) $60
    (C) $100
    (D) $110
    (E) $160

14. Suppose that stricter immigration laws have decreased the number of unskilled workers that enter a nation's labor market. If the labor market is competitive, the number of unskilled workers hired and the wage rate will most likely change in which of the following ways?

Number of Unskilled Workers Hired	Wage Rate
(A) Increase	Increase
(B) Increase	Decrease
(C) Increase	No change
(D) Decrease	Increase
(E) Decrease	Decrease

15. Which of the following is true if a firm's long-run average total costs increase as output increases?
    (A) The firm is experiencing diseconomies of scale.
    (B) The firm is experiencing economies of scale.
    (C) The firm is experiencing constant returns to scale.
    (D) The firm is maximizing long-run economic profit.
    (E) The firm is engaging in efficient production expansion.

Use the following to answer Question 16:

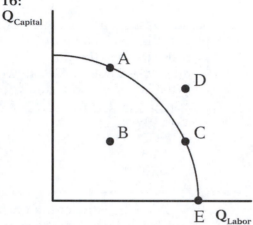

16. According to the above diagram of a production possibilities frontier for a firm in a competitive market, which of the following is true?
    (A) The firm is using its labor and capital efficiently at point C.
    (B) The firm is using its labor and capital efficiently at point B.
    (C) The firm should produce at point A rather than point C because it is socially optimal.
    (D) The firm is producing below its potential at point D.
    (E) The firm is maximizing profit at point B.

17. A nation produces two goods—machines and butter. A decrease in the demand for butter will result in
    (A) a decrease in the price of machines.
    (B) an increase in total national revenue.
    (C) a decrease in the price of inputs used to produce machines.
    (D) an increase in the price of butter.
    (E) a decrease in the opportunity cost of producing machines.

18. Assume that macaroni pasta and cheddar cheese are complementary goods. A decrease in the price of cheddar cheese will most likely affect the equilibrium price and quantity of macaroni in which of the following ways?

    MACARONI

	Price	Quantity
(A)	Decrease	Decrease
(B)	Decrease	Indeterminate
(C)	Decrease	Increase
(D)	Increase	Indeterminate
(E)	Increase	Increase

19. Suppose that the National Institute of Health releases research findings stating that the daily consumption of bananas will improve one's overall digestive health. How might this news affect the following in the banana market?
    (A) The price of bananas will increase, and the quantity of bananas sold will decrease.
    (B) The price of bananas will decrease, and the quantity of bananas sold will decrease.
    (C) The price of bananas will increase, and the quantity of bananas sold will increase.
    (D) The price of bananas will decrease, and the quantity of bananas sold will increase.
    (E) The price of bananas will decrease, but the quantity of bananas sold is indeterminate.

20. How would the imposition of an effective price ceiling on a particular good affect its market?
    (A) The demand would increase and the supply would decrease.
    (B) The supply would increase and the demand would decrease.
    (C) The quantity supplied would exceed the quantity demanded.
    (D) The quantity demanded would decrease.
    (E) It would result in a market shortage.

21. Which of the following regarding a firm's short-run average total cost is true?
    (A) It is equal to average fixed cost plus average variable cost.
    (B) It is equal to average fixed cost plus marginal cost.
    (C) It is equal to marginal cost plus average variable cost.
    (D) It is the total cost divided by the marginal cost.
    (E) It is fixed in the long run.

22. In what ways is a monopoly different from a monopolistically competitive firm?
    (A) A monopoly does not have a U-shaped average total cost curve.
    (B) A monopolistically competitive firm has zero economic profit in the long run.
    (C) A monopoly has a marginal revenue curve that lies below its demand curve.
    (D) A monopolistically competitive firm always earns an economic profit.
    (E) A monopoly faces a more elastic demand curve relative to a monopolistically competitive firm.

23. The reason why it is difficult for firms to collude successfully in an oligopolistic market is because
    (A) the dominant strategy for each firm is not the same.
    (B) each firm faces a different demand curve.
    (C) each firm is tempted to act in its own self-interest.
    (D) each firm can increase its own revenue by increasing its product price.
    (E) there are too many firms in the market to successfully coordinate action.

24. Which of the following is true regarding the marginal revenue curve for firms in a perfectly competitive industry? Perfectly competitive firms' marginal revenue curves are
    (A) upward sloping and equal to average revenue.
    (B) downward sloping and equal to marginal cost.
    (C) downward sloping and equal to average revenue.
    (D) horizontal and equal to average revenue.
    (E) horizontal and equal to average fixed cost.

Use the following information to answer Question 25:

# of Workers	Total Product
0	0
1	3
2	7
3	12
4	18
5	22

25. Which of the following regarding the 4th worker hired is true?
    (A) The firm's total product is maximized with the employment of the 4th worker.
    (B) The firm's marginal product is zero with the employment of the 4th worker.
    (C) The 4th worker's marginal product is less than the marginal product of the 5th worker due to increasing marginal returns.
    (D) The 4th worker's marginal product is greater than the marginal product of the 5th worker due to decreasing marginal returns.
    (E) The 4th worker's marginal product is higher than all of the other workers hired due to decreasing marginal returns.

26. Assume that Good X has a constant price elasticity demand equal to −1.0, Good Y has a constant price elasticity demand equal to −4.0, and that the supply curve for both goods are identical. Which of the following is true if the government imposes a $0.10 per unit production tax on both goods?
    (A) The tax burden paid by producers of both goods will be the same.
    (B) The tax burden paid by consumers of Good Y will be greater than the burden paid by consumers of Good X.
    (C) The tax burden paid by consumers of Good X will be greater than the burden paid by consumers of Good Y.
    (D) The tax burden paid by consumers of both goods will be the same.
    (E) The tax burden paid by producers of Good Y will be greater than the burden paid by consumers of Good X.

Use the following graph to answer Question 27:

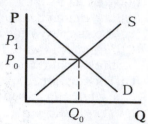

27. Using the above market graph and assuming no government intervention, if the current market price is at P_1, there will be a
    (A) shortage and an increase in the quantity supplied.
    (B) shortage and an increase in the quantity demanded.
    (C) shortage and a decrease in the quantity supplied.
    (D) surplus and a decrease in the quantity demanded.
    (E) surplus and the market price will fall.

28. Suppose that the labor market is perfectly competitive and in equilibrium. What will happen in the market if the government establishes an effective minimum wage law?
    (A) There will be higher unemployment in the short run.
    (B) There will be an increase in the supply of workers seeking jobs in the market.
    (C) Income inequality will increase in the short run.
    (D) There will not be enough workers to fill the newly available jobs.
    (E) Firms hiring in from this labor market will earn economic profit.

29. A pure public good is
    (A) provided in socially optimal quantities by the private market.
    (B) always provided by the government.
    (C) rival and excludable in consumption.
    (D) rival and non-excludable in consumption.
    (E) non-rival and non-excludable in consumption.

30. Which of the following is most likely to reduce national income inequality?
    (A) A national flat tax
    (B) A sales tax
    (C) Education subsidies to low income individuals
    (D) The removal of minimum wage laws
    (E) An increase in the national debt

31. Which of the following is true for an economy with a production possibilities frontier that is bowed out from the origin?
    I.   At any point along the frontier, resources are used efficiently.
    II. Resources are not perfectly adaptable to alternative uses.
    III. The opportunity cost of switching production between two goods is constant.
    (A) I only
    (B) II only
    (C) III only
    (D) I and II only
    (E) II and III only

32. Labor, capital, entrepreneurship, and land are all examples of
    (A) public goods.
    (B) inferior goods.
    (C) factors of production.
    (D) complementary goods.
    (E) substitute goods.

33. The study of economics attempts to answer which of the following questions?
    I.   What goods and services should be produced?
    II. Where will these goods and services be produced?
    III. For whom will these goods and services be produced?
    (A) I only
    (B) II only
    (C) III only
    (D) I, II, and III
    (E) I and III only

34. A firm in a perfectly competitive industry is currently earning zero economic profit. Based on this information, which of the following is true?
    (A) The firm should exit the market because it cannot cover its fixed costs.
    (B) The firm should remain open because the owner of the firm is earning exactly what he/she would make in his/her next best alternative job.
    (C) The firm should exit the market because its marginal revenue will be less than its average variable costs in the long run.
    (D) The firm is earning zero normal profit as well.
    (E) The firm will likely earn economic profit if it decides to stay in the market in the long run.

35. Assume that a chocolate factory uses only two inputs, labor (L) and capital (K) to produce its chocolate. Wages paid to labor are $10 per hour per worker and the marginal product of labor is 40 units of chocolate. The cost of capital is $20 per hour per unit and the marginal production of capital is 60 units of chocolate. In order for the chocolate factory to use its resources at least cost, it should
    (A) increase capital.
    (B) increase capital and decrease labor.
    (C) decrease labor.
    (D) increase labor.
    (E) increase labor and decrease capital.

36. When a market ignores the external costs of its production,
    (A) the market equilibrium price will be greater than the marginal social cost.
    (B) the market equilibrium price will be equal to the marginal social cost.
    (C) the market equilibrium price will be less than the marginal social cost.
    (D) the marginal social cost will be equal to the marginal private cost.
    (E) the marginal social cost will be less than the marginal private cost.

37. Pete's Pizza sells a slice of New York pizza for $2.50. Pete spends $0.50 worth of cheese for each slice of pizza that he makes and sells. The cost of the cheese Pete buys is calculated as one component of his
    (A) total variable costs.
    (B) total fixed costs.
    (C) marginal costs and total fixed costs.
    (D) average fixed costs.
    (E) decreasing opportunity costs.

Use the following to answer Question 38:

	Firm X's Pricing Strategy	
	Collude	Cheat
Firm Y's Pricing Strategy — Collude	$25, $5	$5, $20
Firm Y's Pricing Strategy — Cheat	$20, $10	$15, $25

The above payoff matrix shows the profit associated with the strategic choices of two firms in an oligopolistic market to either collude or cheat. The first entry in each cell is Firm X's profit and the second is Firm Y's profit.

38. Which of the following statements accurately describes the strategies of each firm?
    (A) Firm X's dominant strategy is to cheat while Firm Y's dominant strategy is to collude
    (B) Firm Y's dominant strategy is to cheat while Firm X's dominant strategy is to collude
    (C) Firm X's dominant strategy is to cheat. Firm Y does not have a dominant strategy.
    (D) Firm X's dominant strategy is to collude. Firm Y does not have a dominant strategy.
    (E) Firm Y's dominant strategy is to collude. Firm X does not have a dominant strategy.

39. The fact that a single-price monopoly must lower its price to sell additional units of the good or service it produces is the reason why
    (A) a monopoly is different from monopolistically competitive firms.
    (B) a monopoly is able to maintain market power.
    (C) a monopoly's marginal cost curve is upward sloping.
    (D) a monopoly's marginal revenue curve is below its demand curve.
    (E) a monopoly is rarely regulated by the government.

40. Which of the following accurately describes the relationship between the average product (AP) curve and the marginal product (MP) curve?
    (A) AP rises when MP is above it and falls when MP is below it.
    (B) MP intersects AP at MP's maximum point .
    (C) AP is always rising when MP is rising and falling when MP is falling.
    (D) MP is always above AP.
    (E) AP intersects MP at AP's minimum point.

41. In the short run, the price of a good sold by a firm in a perfectly competitive industry is below its average variable costs. What should this firm do?
    (A) Continue to produce where marginal revenue = marginal cost
    (B) Stay open in the short run, but not in the long run
    (C) Continue to produce where price = average revenue
    (D) Stay open in both the short run and the long run
    (E) Shut down immediately

42. Which of the following is an indicator that two goods are complementary?
    (A) A positive income elasticity
    (B) A price elasticity that is equal to 1
    (C) A negative income elasticity
    (D) A negative cross-price elasticity
    (E) A positive cross-price elasticity

43. The relationship between a monopsony's marginal resource cost curve and the labor supply curve is most similar to which of the following?
    (A) The marginal external cost curve and the marginal private cost curve
    (B) The monopolist's average revenue curve and the market demand curve
    (C) The monopolist's marginal revenue curve and the market demand curve
    (D) The competitive firm's average revenue curve and the market demand curve
    (E) The competitive firm's average revenue curve and the market demand curve

44. The market demand curve for labor will shift to the right when
    (A) the market demand for the good produced by the labor decreases.
    (B) the market demand for the good produced by the labor increases.
    (C) the labor supply curve increases.
    (D) the labor supply curve decreases.
    (E) the workers form a labor union.

45. Education provides benefits to society greater than the benefit to the individual because individuals are more informed voters, more productive workers, and better parents. Based on this information, which of the following is correct?
    (A) Education provides a positive externality to society and should be subsidized.
    (B) Education provides a positive externality to society and should be taxed.
    (C) Education provides decreasing marginal utility and should be subsidized.
    (D) Education provides increasing marginal utility and should be taxed.
    (E) Education provides decreasing marginal utility and should be taxed.

46. Which of the following statements regarding the marginal revenue of a perfectly competitive firm is true?
    (A) It increases as output increases.
    (B) It decreases as output increases.
    (C) It is equal to zero.
    (D) It is constant.
    (E) It exceeds marginal cost at all levels of output.

47. If the demand for apples increases when the price of oranges increases,
    (A) apples are an inferior good and oranges are a superior good.
    (B) apples are a superior good and oranges are an inferior good.
    (C) both apples and oranges are inferior goods.
    (D) apples and oranges are complementary goods.
    (E) apples and oranges are substitute goods.

48. Which of the following must be true if a firm wants to engage in price discrimination?
    I.   The firm must be able to separate the market according to varying buyer demand elasticity.
    II. The firm must be able to prevent arbitrage (the re-sale of its product).
    III. The firm must collude with other firms.
    (A) I only
    (B) II only
    (C) III only
    (D) I and II
    (E) I, II, and III

49. Which of the following firms maximize profit by producing where marginal revenue is equal to marginal cost?
    (A) Monopolies, monopolistically competitive firms, and oligopolies only
    (B) Monopolies and monopolistically competitive firms only
    (C) Perfectly competitive firms only
    (D) Perfectly competitive firms, monopolies, and monopolistically competitive firms only
    (E) Perfectly competitive firms, monopolies, monopolistically competitive firms, and oligopolies

50. Consumer income decreases and the demand for fast food increases. Based on this information, which of the following statements about fast food is correct?
    (A) It is a luxury good.
    (B) It is a normal good.
    (C) It is an inferior good.
    (D) It is a substitute good.
    (E) It should be consumed in greater quantities.

Use the following to answer Questions 51–53:

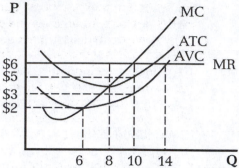

51. Using the above graph for a perfectly competitive firm, what are the firm's total fixed costs at the profit-maximizing level of production?
    (A) $16
    (B) $20
    (C) $28
    (D) $12
    (E) $24

52. Using the above graph, below what price will the firm shut down in the short run?
    (A) $2
    (B) $3
    (C) $5
    (D) $6
    (E) The firm will not shut down in the short run.

53. Using the above graph, at what price will the firm sell its good in the long run?
    (A) $2
    (B) $3
    (C) $5
    (D) $6
    (E) The firm will not remain open in the long run.

54. The short-run supply curve for a perfectly competitive firm is
    (A) its entire marginal cost curve.
    (B) its average total cost curve above the marginal cost curve.
    (C) its marginal cost curve above its average variable cost curve.
    (D) its average variable cost curve above the marginal cost curve.
    (E) its entire average variable cost curve.

55. Which of the following is true if P = MC in a competitive product market?
    (A) The market has achieved productive efficiency.
    (B) The market could increase its revenue by increasing output.
    (C) There is insufficient demand in the market.
    (D) There is a market surplus.
    (E) The market has achieved allocative efficiency.

56. What will happen to the price and quantity of cigarettes if the government places a per-unit tax on cigarette producers?

	Price	Quantity
(A)	Decrease	Decrease
(B)	Decrease	Increase
(C)	Increase	Increase
(D)	Increase	Decrease
(E)	Increase	No change

57. Assume that a monopolistically competitive firm is earning short-run profits. Which of the following accurately describes what will happen to the market equilibrium price and quantity in the long run?
    (A) Firms will enter the market, increasing the market price and quantity sold.
    (B) Firms will enter the market, decreasing the market price and decreasing the quantity sold.
    (C) Firms will enter the market, decreasing the market price and increasing the quantity sold.
    (D) Firms will exit the market, increasing the market price and decreasing the quantity sold.

(E) The number of firms remaining in the market will not change in the long run.

Use the following to answer Question 58:

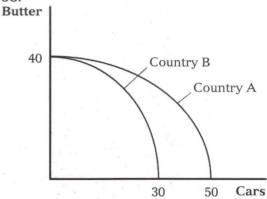

58. Assume that two countries produce only two goods, cars and butter. Using the above production possibilities curve, which of the following is true?
    (A) Country B has the absolute advantage in the production of both goods.
    (B) Country A has the comparative advantage in the production of cars and Country B has the absolute advantage in the production of butter.
    (C) Country A has the comparative advantage in the production of cars, and Country B has the comparative advantage in the production of butter.
    (D) Country B has the comparative advantage in the production of cars, and Country A has the absolute advantage in the production of butter.
    (E) Country A has the absolute disadvantage in the production of both goods.

59. A private market will produce less than is socially optimal when
 (A) the market produces a public good.
 (B) the market privatizes a common resource.
 (C) the production of a good results in a positive externality.
 (D) the production of a good results in a negative externality.
 (E) the production of a good results in higher input costs.

60. A common resource is
 (A) rival and non-excludable.
 (B) non-rival and non-excludable.
 (C) non-rival and excludable.
 (D) rival and excludable.
 (E) most efficiently used when there are no assigned property rights.

STOP
END OF SECTION I
IF YOU FINISH BEFORE TIME IS CALLED, YOU MAY CHECK YOUR WORK ON THIS SECTION. DO NOT GO ON TO SECTION II UNTIL YOU ARE TOLD TO DO SO.

Section II: Free-Response Questions
Planning Time—10 minutes
Writing Time—50 minutes

Directions: You have 50 minutes to answer all three of the following questions. <u>It is suggested that you spend approximately half your time on the first question and divide the remaining time equally between the next two questions.</u> In answering the questions, you should emphasize the line of reasoning that generated your results; it is not enough to list the results of your analysis. Include correctly labeled diagrams, if useful or required, in explaining your answer. A correctly labeled diagram must have all axes and curves clearly labeled and must show directional changes. <u>Use a pen with black or dark blue ink.</u>

FREE-RESPONSE QUESTIONS

1. MedicLab has a drug patent on an effective migraine headache medicine. MedicLab is currently earning an economic profit.
    (a) Draw a correctly labeled graph for MedicLab. In your graph, identify the following.
        (i)   MedicLab's profit-maximizing price and quantity, labeled P_0 and Q_0
        (ii) MedicLab's area of economic profit (area should be shaded in)
    (b) The government is considering new anti-trust legislation and may regulate MedicLab's migraine medicine even though its patent is still valid. Show, on a graph, what price the government may require MedicLab to sell its migraine medication for if it wants MedicLab to produce at the following.
        (i)   The socially optimal level of output, labeled as Q_1 or Q_{so}
        (ii) The fair-return price, labeled as P_2
    (c) If the government decides to regulate MedicLab as in part (b) above, how will this affect the welfare of the consumers who purchase this migraine medication? Use a new graph to identify the consumer surplus for consumers in this market before and after regulation. Specifically, show on your graph and explain the differences in consumer surplus in each of the following situations.
        (i)   Consumer surplus without government regulation
        (ii) Consumer surplus with regulation at the socially optimal output level
        (iii) Consumer surplus with regulation at the fair-return price
    (d) Assume that the government decides against regulating MedicLab's migraine medicine, but that the patent for the drug expires. Explain what happens to the following.
        (i)   MedicLab's profit-maximizing price and quantity
        (ii) MedicLab's profit

2. Assume that the market for unskilled workers is perfectly competitive and that the demand for unskilled workers is relatively elastic. The government imposes a minimum wage in this market.
    (a) Using a correctly labeled graph, show the following.
        (i)   The market wage rate paid to hired unskilled workers
        (ii) The number of unskilled workers hired
        (iii) The number of unskilled workers still looking for employment

(b) Assume that unskilled workers are the primary source of labor in the agricultural industry, strawberries. Use a correctly labeled graph of the strawberry market to explain how the minimum wage law will affect the market for strawberries and identify the following.
   (i) The price of strawberries
   (ii) The quantity of strawberries

3. One approach to the problem of pollution control in a market economy is to sell pollution credits, which are also known as externality rights. The local pollution-control agency has determined that 200 tons of pollutants may be released without harm to the biological ecosystem into the local lake every year. The city has made 200 pollution credits available every year, where each credit owner is allowed to release 1 ton of pollutants into the lake annually.
   (a) Draw a correctly labeled graph illustrating the effect of unregulated pollution in the market for paper and identify the following.
      (i) Marginal private cost
      (ii) Marginal external cost
   (b) Draw a correctly labeled graph for the pollution credits and use your graph to explain how the pollution credits can address the pollution problem in your city.
   (c) Evaluate the effectiveness of pollution credits as a means to control pollution. Specifically, consider the following.
      (i) Costs to consumers, producers, and the general public
      (ii) Benefits to consumers, producers, and the general public

ANSWERS TO MICROECONOMICS PRACTICE TEST 2

SECTION I: MULTIPLE-CHOICE ANSWERS

Using the table below, score your test.
Determine how many questions you answered correctly and how many you answered incorrectly. You will find explanations to the answers on the following pages.

1. D	7. D	13. B	19. C	25. D	31. D	37. A	43. C	49. E	55. E
2. A	8. B	14. D	20. E	26. B	32. C	38. B	44. B	50. C	56. D
3. C	9. B	15. A	21. A	27. E	33. E	39. D	45. A	51. B	57. C
4. E	10. E	16. A	22. B	28. A	34. B	40. A	46. D	52. A	58. C
5. B	11. B	17. E	23. C	29. E	35. E	41. E	47. E	53. B	59. C
6. A	12. C	18. E	24. D	30. C	36. C	42. D	48. D	54. C	60. A

1. **D.** Consumer surplus (CS) is the benefit to consumers who are willing to pay a higher price for a good but end up paying the market equilibrium price. It is the area under the Demand curve and above the market equilibrium price (*Principles of Economics* 5th ed. pages 138–148/6th ed. pages 136–146).

2. **A.** Many economists argue that redistributing a tax on the wealthy to lower income individuals will help to decrease income inequality as long as the tax increase on the wealthy does not make the wealthy poorer than those who the welfare program aims to help. A common example of this type of government action is a subsidy in the form of food stamps. The government uses tax revenue collected from those with higher income to provide the subsidy to those who have lower income. However, some economists also argue that a tax redistribution can create economic inefficiency because the transaction costs incurred from the redistribution detract from overall economic productivity (*Principles of Economics* 5th ed. pages 392–409/6th ed. pages 376–392).

3. **C.** A single-price monopolist produces at a price that is higher and at a quantity that is lower than is socially optimal. The socially optimal level of output is where supply = demand, or in this case, where MC = D, which corresponds with P3 (*Principles of Economics* 5th ed. pages 312–336/6th ed. pages 300–323).

4. **E.** At the socially optimal level of output, the monopoly's ATC is greater than its marginal revenue (MR), and is incurring an economic loss. The monopoly will likely shut down unless the government provides a subsidy to keep the firm in business (*Principles of Economics* 5th ed. pages 312–336/6th ed. pages 300–323).

5. **B.** A monopoly is the sole provider of a good or service and therefore can charge a higher price. In order to maintain its monopoly power, there must be barriers to market entry—if firms

can freely enter/exit as in perfectly competitive markets, the monopoly would lose its market power (*Principles of Economics* 5th ed. pages 312–336/6th ed. pages 300–323).

6. **A.** Labor is a variable input. Since wages increase, the variable costs for the firm increase, which increases the firm's marginal costs, average variable costs, and average total costs since ATC = AVC + AFC. The MC shifts up and to the left, which means that the firm will produce fewer units since MC = MR at a lower output level (*Principles of Economics* 5th ed. pages 290–303/6th ed. pages 280–289).

7. **D.** Since the monopolist is the only seller in the market, its demand curve is the same as the market demand curve, so the monopoly faces a downward sloping demand curve. A perfectly competitive firm faces a perfectly elastic demand curve (*Principles of Economics* 5th ed. pages 312–336/6th ed. pages 300–323).

8. **B.** A perfectly competitive firm does not earn economic profit in the long run, but does earn a normal profit. Firms will enter or exit the industry in the long run, which adjusts the market supply (number of sellers increases/decreases) for the goods/services produced by competitive firms who remain in the industry. This long-run adjustment continues to the point where the firm earns zero economic profit, or where P = ATC = MC = MR (*Principles of Economics* 5th ed. pages 290–303/6th ed. pages 280–289).

9. **B.** Firms selling goods/services in a monopolistically competitive industry must differentiate their product from competitors since their products are usually very similar. One way firms can differentiate their product is to engage in non-price competition, such as advertisement, to create a niche market for their good/service (*Principles of Economics* 5th ed. pages 346–361/6th ed. pages 330–338).

10. **E.** A firm's demand for labor is a derived demand because it depends on the market demand for the firm's product. The labor demand is also the marginal revenue product (MRP), which is determined by the MP of labor and the product price. MRP = MP_L × $P_{product}$ (*Principles of Economics* 5th ed. pages 392–409/6th ed. pages 376–392).

11. **B.** Refer to the section in Chapter 2 on elasticity and total revenue. The elastic portion of the demand curve is where a price decrease leads to an increase in total revenue. In this question, the total revenue increases from $80 to $90 (*Principles of Economics* 5th ed. pages 90–108/6th ed. pages 89–101).

12. **C.** An increase in the price of a good sold in a competitive market will affect the firm's demand for its resources (labor or capital, for example) by increasing its demand for labor MRP = MP_L × $P_{product}$ (*Principles of Economics* 5th ed. pages 392–409/6th ed. pages 376–392).

13. **B.** Since Reilly doesn't pay for the concert tickets, his opportunity cost is just the wage that he gives up in order to attend the concert. He takes 6 hours off from his $10/hour job, so he loses a total of $60 for attending the concert (*Principles of Economics* 5th ed. pages 49–58/6th ed. pages 49–57).

14. **D.** A decrease in the number of unskilled workers shifts the supply of unskilled labor in the competitive labor market to the left. This decreases the quantity of unskilled laborers hired and increases the equilibrium wage paid to any remaining unskilled laborers who are hired (*Principles of Economics* 5th ed. pages 392–409/6th ed. pages 376–392).

15. **A.** When LRATC increases with an increase in output, the firm is no longer producing efficiently and experiences diseconomies of scale (*Principles of Economics* 5th ed. pages 268–281/6th ed. pages 260–272).

16. **A.** Production is efficient at any point along the production possibilities frontier, so points A, C, and E are all possible and efficient resource combinations for production. Point D is unattainable, given the firm's limited resources and point B represents the underutilization of resources (*Principles of Economics* 5th ed. pages 15–24/6th ed. pages 15–24).

17. **E.** Since there is less demand for butter, the nation will devote more of its resources to the production of machines. This decreases the opportunity cost of producing machines (*Principles of Economics* 5th ed. page 25/6th ed. page 26).

18. **E.** Since macaroni and cheese are complementary goods, the decrease in the price of cheese will lead to an increase in the demand for macaroni, which increases its price and quantity sold (*Principles of Economics* 5th ed. pages 66–85/6th ed. pages 67–77).

19. **C.** Consumers' expectations may have changed with the publication of the National Institute of Health's report on bananas. People now know the benefits of eating bananas and so will demand more bananas. The demand for bananas increases, increasing the price and quantity sold in the market (*Principles of Economics* 5th ed. pages 66–85/6th ed. pages 67–77).

20. **E.** An effective price ceiling is one that is set _below_ the market equilibrium price. At this price, the quantity demanded is greater than the quantity supplied and there is a shortage in the market (*Principles of Economics* 5th ed. pages 114–121/6th ed. pages 112–117).

21. **A.** ATC = AFC + AVC = TC/Q (*Principles of Economics* 5th ed. pages 268–281/6th ed. pages 260–272).

22. **B.** A monopolistically competitive firm does not earn an economic profit in the long run, similar to a perfectly competitive firm (*Principles of Economics* 5th ed. pages 346–361/6th ed. pages 330–338).

23. **C.** An oligopoly works only if the few firms can successfully collude to charge a monopoly price at the monopoly's output level. The problem is that a collusive agreement results in an unstable equilibrium because each firm/player knows that if other firms "cheat" and go against the agreement to keep prices high, they will end up losing money, so each firm will consider other firms' decisions when making their pricing or output decisions. Ultimately, firms in an oligopoly will likely end up acting to protect their own self interests and will not be able to maximize collective profits (*Principles of Economics* 5th ed. pages 366–384/6th ed. pages 350–362).

24. **D.** Since firms are price takers, the marginal revenue = price = demand = average revenue for a perfectly competitive firm (*Principles of Economics* 5th ed. pages 290–303/6th ed. pages 280–289).

25. **D.** The marginal product is the additional output produced by an additional worker. The marginal product of the 4th worker is 6 units while the marginal product of the 5th worker is 4 units because of diminishing marginal returns—as the ratio of variable input (labor) to fixed input increases, marginal product decreases (*Principles of Economics* 5th ed. pages 268–281/6th ed. pages 260–272).

26. **B.** If Ed > 0, the demand is elastic and if Ed < 0, the demand is inelastic. In this case, both Goods X and Y are relatively price inelastic, but Good Y is relatively more inelastic than Good X because Ed = −4.0 (vs. Ed = −1.0). The consumers of Good Y bear a larger burden of the tax because their demand is more inelastic relative to Good X *and* its own supply curve (*Principles of Economics* 5th ed. pages 90–108/6th ed. pages 89–101).

27. **E.** Without government intervention, a price above the market equilibrium will result in a decrease in price and quantity to the point of equilibrium. The market "force" of supply and demand will drive the price and quantity back to equilibrium (*Principles of Economics* 5th ed. pages 66–85/6th ed. pages 67–77).

28. **A.** An effective minimum wage is set above the market equilibrium price. The quantity of workers supplied at the minimum wage is greater than the quantity of workers demanded, since the firm's input costs will increase with a minimum wage. This results in a surplus of workers or unemployment (*Principles of Economics* 5th ed. pages 392–409/6th ed. pages 376–392).

29. **E.** A public good is a good that is non-rival and non-excludable. Private firms have little incentive to produce an optimal quantity of public goods because the goods are non-excludable and non-rival.

This is why the government often steps in to provide public goods, such as police security (*Principles of Economics* 5th ed. pages 204–237/6th ed. pages 195–235).

30. **C.** An education subsidy can help low income individuals to gain the skills and interest in higher paying jobs which, in the long run will help to reduce national income inequality (*Principles of Economics* 5th ed. pages 392–409/6th ed. pages 376–392).

31. **D.** A production possibilities curve that is bowed out from the origin reflects increasing opportunity costs and the resources used for the production of the two goods are not perfectly adaptable for switching from the production of one good to the other. Production along any point on the PPF is efficient because limited resources are used to produce any combination of product that society wants (*Principles of Economics* 5th ed. page 25/6th ed. page 26).

32. **C.** Factors of production are the inputs used to produce the goods and services produced and sold in markets. They include: land, labor, capital, and entrepreneurship (*Principles of Economics* 5th ed. pages 392–409/6th ed. pages 376–392).

33. **E.** Economics is the study of how to allocate scarce resources given society's unlimited wants. Where goods/services are made is irrelevant to economics (*Principles of Economics* 5th ed. pages 10–24/6th ed. pages 10–25).

34. **B.** Although the firm has a zero economic profit, the owner of the firm earns a normal profit, which is what he/she would make in his/her next best alternative job and therefore, the firm stays open even with a zero economic profit (*Principles of Economics* 5th ed. pages 290–303/6th ed. pages 280–289).

35. **E.** The least cost rule helps firms to produce at least cost when using more than one input in production. The rule states that firms should hire where $MP_L/P_L = MP_K/P_K$. In this case, $MP_L/P_L = 4$ and the $MP_K/P_K = 3$, so the chocolate factory should hire more labors while decreasing the use of its capital (machinery/equipment) in order to produce at least cost (*Principles of Economics* 5th ed. pages 392–409/6th ed. pages 376–392).

36. **C.** This is an example of a negative externality, where the market produces too much of a good at too low of a price. The marginal social cost is greater than the marginal private cost (*Principles of Economics* 5th ed. pages 204–237/6th ed. pages 195–225).

37. **A.** The cost of cheese is a variable input cost. It is a component of total costs (TC) = total variable cost (TVC) + total fixed cost (TFC) because it is calculated in TVC. It is, therefore, also a component of ATC, AVC, and MC. It is not a fixed cost (*Principles of Economics* 5th ed. pages 268–281/6th ed. pages 260–272).

38. **B.** The two strategy options are to collude or cheat. If Firm Y colludes, it can earn a profit of $5 or $20, depending on what Firm X does and if Firm Y decides to cheat, the profit possibilities are $10 or $25. Regardless of what Firm X does, the profit potential of a cheating strategy will give Firm Y the largest profit so Firm Y's dominant strategy is to cheat. On the other hand, if Firm X colludes, the profit potential is $20 or $25 and if Firm X cheats, the profit potential is $5 or $15, depending on what Firm Y does. Regardless of Firm Y's decision though, Firm X has the greatest profit potential if it colludes, so Firm X's dominant strategy is to collude (*Principles of Economics* 5th ed. pages 366–384/6th ed. pages 350–362).

39. **D.** A monopoly's marginal revenue curve lies below the demand curve because it must lower prices on all additional units sold in order to increase quantity sold (*Principles of Economics* 5th ed. pages 312–336/6th ed. pages 300–323).

40. **A.** The average product (AP) curve intersects the marginal product (MP) curve at its highest point. When the AP is rising, the MP is above the AP; and when the AP is falling, the MP is below the AP. Refer to the graphs in the production costs chapter (*Principles of Economics* 5th ed. pages 268–281/6th ed. pages 260–272).

41. **E.** If P > AVC in the short run, a firm in a perfectly competitive market should still stay open because it can at least cover its variable costs, but since P < AVC in this case, the firm should shut down immediately since it is losing money and unable to cover its variable costs (*Principles of Economics* 5th ed. pages 290–303/6th ed. pages 280–289).

42. **D.** If the cross-price elasticity for two goods is positive (as the price of Good X increases and the quantity of Good Y demanded increases), the two goods are substitutes. If the cross-price elasticity for two goods is negative (as the price of Good X increases, the quantity of Good Y demanded decreases), the two goods are complements (*Principles of Economics* 5th ed. pages 114–121/6th ed. pages 112–117).

43. **C.** A monopolist lowers price in order to sell more units, which is why the MR is below the market demand curve. Similarly, the monopsonist must offer the same wage to all laborers hired and therefore, if the monopsonist wants to hire more workers, it will incur higher marginal resource costs, which is why the MRC is steeper than the labor supply curve (*Principles of Economics* 5th ed. pages 392–409/6th ed. pages 376–392).

44. **B.** Labor demand is a derived demand, dependent on the demand in the product market. When there is greater demand for the product produced by labor, firms' demand for labor will increase (*Principles of Economics* 5th ed. pages 392–409/6th ed. pages 376–392).

45. **A.** This is an example of a positive externality, since the benefits to society are greater than to the individual. Since the market often will not produce an optimal quantity of a good with a positive externality, the government may choose to intervene and provide incentives, such as subsidies, to encourage greater consumption of a good (in this case, higher enrollment in school) (*Principles of Economics* 5th ed. pages 204–237/6th ed. pages 195–225).

46. **D.** Since the perfectly competitive firm is a price taker, it always takes the market price. This means that the firm's marginal revenue is always going to be equal to the market price and is constant (*Principles of Economics* 5th ed. pages 290–303/6th ed. pages 280–289).

47. **E.** Apples are a substitute for oranges because the demand for apples increases when the price of oranges go up. A substitute good is one that is consumed in greater quantities when the price of its alternative increases (*Principles of Economics* 5th ed. pages 66–85/6th ed. pages 67–77).

48. **D.** Price discrimination is when a firm charges different buyers varying prices for the same good. In order to do this, the firm must be able to separate buyers into separate markets in a way that will not negatively affect sales—for example, a firm can separate the market according to age (student vs. senior movie ticket prices) or willingness to pay (first class airline seats vs. coach/economy class). A firm must also be able to prevent the resale of its good in another market (*Principles of Economics* 5th ed. pages 312–336/6th ed. pages 300–323).

49. **E.** All firms maximize profit where MR = MC. This is the profit maximizing rule for all firms producing goods or services sold in free markets (*Principles of Economics* 5th ed. pages 290–303/6th ed. pages 280–289).

50. **C.** When the demand for a product increases when consumer income falls, the good is an inferior good (*Principles of Economics* 5th ed. pages 66–85/6th ed. pages 67–77).

51. **B.** Average fixed costs can be found by taking the difference between average total cost and average variable cost. In this case, average fixed cost is $2/unit ($5 − $3 = $2) produced. The profit-maximizing quantity is 10, so total fixed cost is $20 (*Principles of Economics* 5th ed. pages 268–281/6th ed. pages 260–272).

52. **A.** When P < AVC, the firm will shut down in the short run (*Principles of Economics* 5th ed. pages 290–303/6th ed. pages 280–289).

53. **B.** In the long run, the competitive firm earns zero economic profit and produces at MR = MC = minimum ATC. The ATC intersects the MC at its minimum point, which according to the graph, is $3,

so the firm sells its product for $3 in the long run (*Principles of Economics* 5th ed. pages 290–303/6th ed. pages 280–289).

54. **C.** The portion of the marginal cost curve above the average variable cost curve is the firm's supply curve because, at any point below the average variable cost curve, the firm will shut down in the short run (*Principles of Economics* 5th ed. pages 290–303/6th ed. pages 280–289).

55. **E.** P = MC is also where S = D and where the market is allocatively efficient, or producing what society wants (*Principles of Economics* 5th ed. pages 66–85/6th ed. pages 67–77).

56. **D.** A per-unit tax increases the cost of production and decreases the supply of cigarettes. The price of cigarettes is higher (increases by the amount of the tax) and the quantity sold decreases because the quantity demanded at this higher, tax price falls (*Principles of Economics* 5th ed. pages 123–128/6th ed. pages 121–127).

57. **C.** Short-run economic profits entice new firms to enter the market. This increases the market supply (since the number of sellers has increased) and decreases the demand for the *existing* monopolistically competitive firm's product. This decrease in demand (due to a decrease in the number of buyers) results in a lower price and quantity sold by the existing monopolistically competitive firm, but increases the overall market demand which increases the market price and quantity sold (*Principles of Economics* 5th ed. pages 346–361/6th ed. pages 330–338).

58. **C.** The opportunity cost for Country A to produce butter is 5/4 of a car and 3/4 of a car for Country B. The opportunity cost for Country A to produce a car is 4/5 of a unit of butter (or food) and 4/3 of a unit for Country B. Country A has the lower opportunity cost in the production of cars and Country B has the lower opportunity cost in the production of butter (*Principles of Economics* 5th ed. pages 49–58/6th ed. pages 49–57).

59. **C.** A market will produce too little of a good when there is a positive externality (*Principles of Economics* 5th ed. pages 204–237/6th ed. pages 195–225).

60. **A.** A common resource is something that anyone can use (non-exludable), but one person's use may prevent other people from being able to use it in the future (rival). Review Chapter 7 for examples (*Principles of Economics* 5th ed. pages 90–108/6th ed. pages 89–101).

SECTION II: FREE-RESPONSE ANSWERS

1. (10 points total)
    (a)

    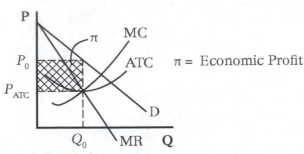

    1 point each for:
    *   Correctly labeled axes, downward sloping D, steeper MR curve
    *   Correctly identified profit-maximizing price and quantity where MR = MC
    *   Correctly labeled area of economic profit

    (b)

    MedicLab

    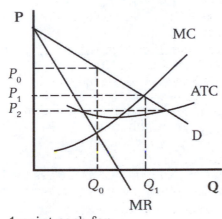

    P_1 = socially optimal

    P_2 = fair-return price

    1 point each for:
    *   Correctly identified the socially optimal level of output (also the perfectly competitive output level) where P = MC
    *   Correctly identified the fair-return price P = ATC (Note that the firm does not earn economic profit if the government chooses to regulate the monopoly at this price, so the government may have to subsidize the firm's production in order for the firm to remain in business.)

(c)

MedicLab

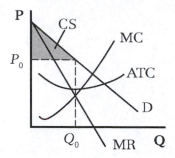

Without Regulation

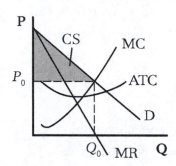

Government regulation
where P = MC
(socially optimal)

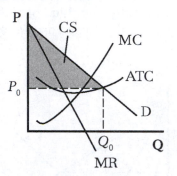

Government regulation
where P = ATC
(fair-return)

1 point each for:
- Correctly identified CS in all 3 scenarios (Note that CS is always the largest when the monopolist produces at the socially optimal or perfectly competitive market quantity.)

(d)

MedicLab

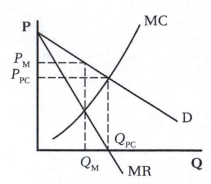

$P_M + Q_M =$ Monopolist's P + Q

$P_{PC} + Q_{PC} =$ Perfectly Competitive Market's P + Q

1 point each for:
- Correctly identified monopoly P and Q vs. competitive P and Q
- Correct explanation: when the patent expires, the monopoly no longer has the barriers to entry so new firms enter and produce the migraine medication as

well. This will lead the monopolist to act like a firm in a competitive market and therefore, will result in a lower price and higher quantity produced/sold. (*Principles of Economics* 5th ed. pages 312–336/6th ed. pages 300–323)

2. (7 points total)
   (a)

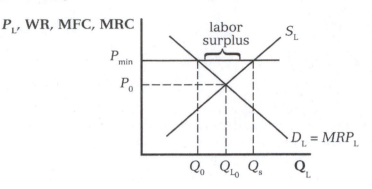

Market for unskilled labor

1 point each for:
- Correctly labeled unskilled labor market graph: Q_L, P_L (or WR, MFC, MRC), upward sloping S_L and downward sloping D_L
- Minimum wage set above the market equilibrium
- The number of unskilled workers hired decreases
- The number of unskilled workers looking for work increases

   (b)

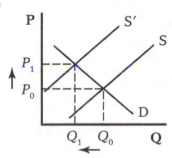

Strawberries

1 point each for:
- Correctly labeled product market graph for strawberries: P, Q, upward sloping S, downward sloping D
- Minimum wage increases input costs and shifts the supply curve to the left (decreases); this increases the price and decreases the quantity of strawberries sold.

(*Principles of Economics* 5th ed. pages 392–409/6th ed. pages 376–392)

3. (8 points total)
   (a)

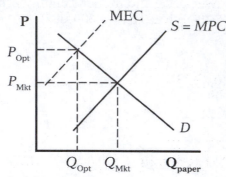

1 point each for:
   - Correctly labeled market graph: P, Q, upward sloping S, downward sloping D
   - Negative externality (MEC > MPC)
   - Identified $Q_{optimal}$ that is lower than Q_{market} and $P_{optimal}$ that is higher than P_{market}

   (b)

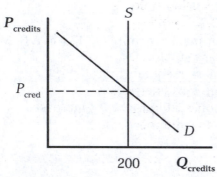

1 point each for:
   - Correctly labeled pollution credit graph: P, Q, perfectly inelastic supply, downward sloping demand
   - S = 200
   - Explanation: The pollution credits can be very expensive, especially if there is an increase in the demand for pollution rights. This is a large input cost for producers and this will encourage them to produce less. (Shift the S = MPC curve to the left so that the producers internalize the cost of pollution.)

   (c) 2 points for:
   - The general public (non-consuming) pays an unintended cost of pollution-emitting production. The producers' marginal private cost is less than the marginal external cost, so a pollution credit system will pass the pollution costs from the general public back onto the producers.

   (*Principles of Economics* 5th ed. pages 204–237/6th ed. pages 195–225)

CALCULATING YOUR SCORE

SECTION I: MULTIPLE-CHOICE QUESTIONS

[_____] × 1.25 = _____
Number Correct   Weighted Section I Score
(out of 60)   (Do not round)

SECTION II: FREE-RESPONSE QUESTIONS

Question 1 _____ × (1.2500) = _____
(out of 10)   (Do not round)

Question 2 _____ × (0.8333) = _____
(out of 7)   (Do not round)

Question 3 _____ × (0.9375) = _____
(out of 8)   (Do not round)

Sum = _____
Weighted Section II Score
(Do not round)

COMPOSITE SCORE

_____ + _____ = _____
Weighted   Weighted   Composite Score
Section I Score   Section II Score   (Round to nearest
whole number)

Composite Score Range	Approximate AP Grade
73–90	5
58–72	4
45–57	3
33–44	2
0–32	1

Practice Test 1: Macroeconomics

This test will give you some indication of how you might score on the AP Macroeconomics Exam. Of course, the exam changes every year, so it is never possible to predict a student's score with certainty. This test will also pinpoint strengths and weaknesses on the key content areas covered by the exam.

AP MACROECONOMICS EXAMINATION
Section I: Multiple-Choice Questions
Time: 70 minutes
60 Questions

Directions: Each of the following questions or incomplete statements is accompanied by five suggested answers or completions. Select the one that best answers the question or completes the statement.

1. Which of the following is generally not considered a macroeconomic goal?
   (A) Economic growth.
   (B) Full employment.
   (C) Low, stable prices.
   (D) Annual increases in real GDP.
   (E) Zero frictional unemployment.

2. Which of the following is consistent with the law of demand?
   (A) A decrease in the price of MP3 players causes an increase in demand for MP3s.
   (B) An increase in the price of tablets leads to an increase in the purchase of tablets.
   (C) An increase in the price of laptops leads to an increase in the demand for personal computers.
   (D) A decrease in the price of mouse pads causes an increase in the amount of mouse pads purchased.
   (E) A decrease in the price of MP3 players leads to an increase in the purchase of headsets.

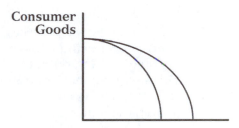

3. The PPC above represents the total amount of capital and consumer goods an economy is capable of producing. What is illustrated by the change shown above?
   (A) An increase in the overall productive capacity of the economy.
   (B) An advancement in technology related to the production of capital goods.
   (C) Decreases in consumer spending due to a recession.
   (D) A reduction in the production of consumer goods.
   (E) Increased wage rates resulting from the increased availability of funds.

GO ON TO NEXT PAGE

4. The study of inflation is a part of
   (A) Microeconomics.
   (B) Macroeconomics.
   (C) Urban economics.
   (D) Labor economics.
   (E) Home economics.

5. The statement "you're better off buying a house than renting" is an example of a(n)
   (A) statement that is always true.
   (B) normative statement.
   (C) objective truth.
   (D) positive statement.
   (E) ceteris paribus condition.

6. GDP in an economy is $4600 billion. Consumer expenditures are $3500 billion, government purchases are $900 billion, and gross private domestic investment is $400 billion. Net exports are
   (A) +$400 billion.
   (B) −$400 billion.
   (C) +$200 billion.
   (D) −$200 billion.
   (E) 0.

7. Which of the following is true if the economy is producing at the full-employment level of output?
   (A) The unemployment rate is zero.
   (B) No person is receiving unemployment compensation from the government.
   (C) There is frictional unemployment.
   (D) The government's budget is balanced.
   (E) The balance of trade is in equilibrium.

8. GDP tends to understate the amount of economic activity in the U.S. because it excludes
   (A) the payments for police protection.
   (B) the expenditure for health care services.
   (C) expenditures for environmental protection.
   (D) foreign demand for U.S. goods abroad.
   (E) the unpaid work performed by homemakers.

9. Which of the following shifts is a consistent response to increases in interest rates?
   (A) An increase in the demand for loanable funds as borrowers seek higher returns.
   (B) A decrease in the supply of money as the central bank seeks to lower unemployment.
   (C) An increase in the short-run Phillips curve illustrating stagflation.
   (D) A decrease in the aggregate demand curve due to lowered levels of consumption and investment spending.
   (E) An increase in the long-run aggregate supply representing long-term economic growth.

10. The consumer price index attempts to measure changes in
    (A) a market basket of consumer goods from month to month.
    (B) the price of all goods and services produced in the U.S.
    (C) prices of intermediate and final goods.
    (D) retail managers annual pricing decisions.
    (E) the behavior of consumers in rural areas.

11. Which of the following transactions would represent an addition to a nation's GDP?
    (A) Mr. Smith purchases a share of stock in an automobile company.
    (B) A retailer increases her stock of imported shoes.
    (C) The government increases its spending on infrastructure repair projects.
    (D) A corporation sells shoes from last year's inventory.
    (E) A mother sells her car to her daughter.

12. A reserve requirement of 20 percent will yield a money multiplier of
    (A) 20.
    (B) 10.
    (C) 5.
    (D) 2.

(E) Not enough information is provided to answer the question.

13. Output increases along the aggregate demand curve as
(A) short-run aggregate supply decreases.
(B) price level decreases.
(C) long-run aggregate supply increases.
(D) income levels increase.
(E) levels of physical capital decrease.

14. How are real GDP and nominal GDP different?
(A) Real GDP is inflated due to the effects of price level changes while nominal GDP does not.
(B) Nominal GDP reflects changes in inflation while real GDP does not.
(C) Nominal GDP measures annual changes in inventory while real GDP does not.
(D) Real GDP has been adjusted for price level changes while nominal GDP has not.
(E) There is no difference between real GDP and nominal GDP; they measure the same thing.

15. The unemployment rate in a country is 10 percent. Total population in the economy is 500 million and the size of the labor force is 300 million. Calculate the number of unemployed workers in this economy.
(A) 270 million
(B) 200 million
(C) 450 million
(D) 50 million
(E) 30 million

16. Which of the following would most likely cause a rightward shift in an economy's short-run aggregate supply curve?
(A) An increase in interest rates.
(B) A tax increase of 50 cents per gallon of gasoline.
(C) An across-the-board reduction of wages in the manufacturing sector.
(D) The passage of legislation mandating a reduction in automobile pollution.

(E) The shutdown of plants and movement of production of goods abroad.

17. The typical result of an adverse supply shock, such as worldwide increase in oil prices, is for
(A) falling output to accompany accelerating deflation.
(B) falling output to accompany accelerating inflation.
(C) rising output to accompany accelerating inflation.
(D) rising output to accompany accelerating deflation.
(E) constant output with accelerating deflation.

18. Under which of the following conditions would a restrictive monetary policy be most appropriate?
(A) High inflation.
(B) High unemployment.
(C) Full employment with stable prices.
(D) Low interest rates.
(E) A budget deficit.

19. If real GDP declines in a given year, nominal GDP
(A) will fall more than real GDP.
(B) will fall less than real GDP.
(C) will always rise.
(D) is unchanged.
(E) may rise or fall.

20. An increase in the interest rates in the United States will have the following effect on U.S. net exports and aggregate demand, ceteris paribus.

	Net Exports	AD
(A)	Increase	Decrease
(B)	Increase	No change
(C)	Decrease	Decrease
(D)	Decrease	Increase
(E)	No change	No change

21. Which of the following would most likely cause an increase in long-run aggregate supply?
(A) Wage rates decrease due to high unemployment.
(B) Consumer incomes increase during an expansionary period.
(C) Business regulation increases.

(D) Technological advances lead to widespread improvements in plant and equipment.
(E) Unemployment benefits receive an extension.

22. The economy experiences a rise in price level accompanied by increases in unemployment. Which of the following may have caused this change?
(A) The price of oil, a major natural resource, increases.
(B) Government spending meant to balance the federal budget decreases.
(C) Businesses purchase new plants and equipment to replace older models.
(D) Foreign purchases of domestic goods decrease due to recessions overseas.
(E) Productivity gains make labor more expendable.

23. This monetary policy has the effect of increasing equilibrium output and price level.
(A) Raising the discount rate
(B) Raising the reserve ratio
(C) Increasing government spending
(D) Lowering income tax rates
(E) Buying bonds on the open market

24. If the marginal propensity to consume in an economy is 0.75, government could eliminate a recessionary gap of $100 billion by increasing spending by:
(A) $25 billion
(B) $50 billion
(C) $100 billion
(D) $150 billion
(E) $200 billion

25. When output levels are below full employment, the intersection of aggregate demand and aggregate supply may be found
(A) to the right of the LRAS curve.
(B) to the left of the LRAS curve.
(C) on the LRAS curve.
(D) at negative price levels.
(E) only by using complicated mathematical formulas.

26. All of the following are components of the money supply in the United States EXCEPT
(A) paper money.
(B) gold.
(C) checkable deposits.
(D) coins.
(E) demand deposits.

27. Open market operations refer to which of the following activities?
(A) The buying and selling of stocks in the New York stock market.
(B) The loans made by the Federal Reserve to member commercial banks.
(C) The buying and selling of government securities by the Federal Reserve.
(D) The government's purchases and sales of municipal bonds.
(E) The government's contributions to net exports.

28. Assume the reserve requirement is 10 percent. If an individual deposits $100 in a commercial bank, what is the initial increase in excess reserves?
(A) $10.
(B) $90.
(C) $100.
(D) $990.
(E) $1000.

29. Which of the following is not one of the functions of money?
(A) Medium of exchange
(B) Unit of account
(C) Store of value
(D) Factor of production
(E) Standard of value

30. If nominal interest rates were to decrease, a response in the money market would be
(A) an increase in the quantity of money demanded.
(B) a decrease in the quantity of money demanded.
(C) an increase in the quantity of money supplied.
(D) an increase in the demand for money.
(E) a decrease in money supply.

31. The Federal Reserve may determine how much money banks must have on reserve by setting the
    (A) federal funds rate.
    (B) discount rate.
    (C) open market operations.
    (D) buying of bonds on the open market.
    (E) reserve requirement.

32. If the price index is 155, then we can determine that
    (A) prices are 155 percent higher than in the previous year.
    (B) prices are 45 percent lower than in the base year.
    (C) prices are 55 percent higher than they were in the base year.
    (D) consumer spending has increased 55 percent.
    (E) consumer spending will decrease in the following month.

33. Which of the following is not a tool of monetary policy?
    (A) Buying government securities on the open market
    (B) Decreasing marginal tax rates
    (C) Increasing the discount rate
    (D) Requiring commercial banks to keep more money on reserve
    (E) Lending money to commercial banks

34. What happens to bank reserves and interest rates when the Federal Reserve buys bonds from commercial banks on the open market?

	Bank Reserves	Interest Rates
(A)	Increase	Increase
(B)	Decrease	Increase
(C)	Increase	Decrease
(D)	Decrease	Decrease
(E)	No change	Increase

35. When commercial banks lend each other money for short-term loans, the rate they charge is called the
    (A) discount rate.
    (B) federal funds rate.
    (C) prime rate.
    (D) reserve ratio.
    (E) commercial rate.

36. Which of the following groups would benefit from unanticipated inflation?
    I.   Savers
    II. Fixed-rate borrowers
    III. Creditors (lenders)
    (A) I only
    (B) II only
    (C) III only
    (D) I and II only
    (E) I and III only

37. The consumer price index (CPI) measures which of the following?
    (A) The change over time of the weighted prices of a particular group of goods and services
    (B) The change over time of the weighted wholesale price index
    (C) The change over time of the difference between the GDP deflator and the wholesale price index
    (D) Inflation corrected for changes in the RGDP
    (E) Inflation corrected for changes in the wholesale price index

38. If the nominal interest rate is 6% and the expected rate of inflation is 4%, the real interest rate is
    (A) 10%.
    (B) 6%.
    (C) 4%.
    (D) 2%.
    (E) −2%.

39. If the marginal propensity to consume is 0.8 and both taxes and government purchases increase by $50 billion, GDP will
    (A) increase by $50 billion.
    (B) decrease by $50 billion.
    (C) increase by $10 billion.
    (D) decrease by $10 billion.
    (E) not increase at all as one offsets the other.

40. If equilibrium income rises by a total of $50 billion in response to an increase in investment of $10 billion, then the marginal propensity to save is
    (A) 0.1.
    (B) 0.2.
    (C) 0.5.
    (D) 0.8.
    (E) 0.9.

41. Assume the federal budget deficit is increasing in the U.S. How will the increased borrowing by government likely affect interest rates and the international value of the dollar, ceteris paribus?

Interest Rates	Int'l Value of the Dollar
(A) Increase	Depreciate
(B) No change	Depreciate
(C) Decrease	No change
(D) Increase	Appreciate
(E) Decrease	Appreciate

42. Positive economic growth can be shown as
    (A) a shift inward of the PPC.
    (B) a rightward shift of the aggregate demand curve.
    (C) simultaneous rightward shifts of aggregate demand and aggregate supply.
    (D) a rightward shift of the long-run aggregate supply curve.
    (E) a leftward shift of the long-run aggregate supply curve.

43. If you received a 1% raise in your salary last year and the CPI increased by 2.5%, then your
    (A) nominal income has decreased
    (B) real income has decreased
    (C) real income has increased
    (D) purchasing power rose
    (E) salary in current dollars has decreased

44. On an AD–AS graph, an increase in government spending is illustrated by
    (A) a rightward shift of aggregate demand.
    (B) a leftward shift of aggregate demand.
    (C) a rightward shift of short-run aggregate supply.
    (D) a leftward shift of short-run aggregate supply.
    (E) a rightward shift of long-run aggregate supply.

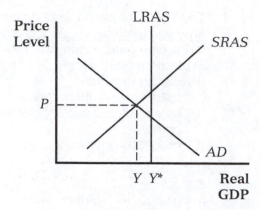

45. Refer to the graph above. What combination of actions would fiscal policymakers recommend for the economy represented?
    I. Decrease government spending
    II. Decrease taxes
    III. Decrease interest rates
    (A) I only
    (B) II only
    (C) III only
    (D) I and II only
    (E) I, II, and III

46. Refer to the graph above. If no policy action is taken, by what mechanism will the economy most likely self-correct?
    (A) A decrease in nominal wage rates
    (B) An increase in consumer spending
    (C) Increases in spending on research and development
    (D) Productivity gains made naturally over time
    (E) Systematic decreases in spending on imported goods

47. Assume the United States has a current account deficit of $200 billion and a capital account surplus of $150 billion. What is the value of the nation's official reserves?
    (A) +$350 billion
    (B) +$200 billion
    (C) +$150 billion
    (D) +$50 billion
    (E) −$50 billion

48. The Federal Reserve can increase the money supply by
    (A) selling gold reserves to the banks.
    (B) selling foreign currency holdings.
    (C) buying government bonds on the open market.
    (D) buying gold from foreign central banks.
    (E) borrowing reserves from foreign governments.

49. Which of the following combinations of monetary and fiscal policies is coordinated to increase output?

	Monetary Policy	Fiscal Policy
(A)	Decrease the reserve requirement	Increase taxes
(B)	Increase the discount rate	Increase spending
(C)	Sell securities	Increase taxes
(D)	Sell securities	Decrease spending
(E)	Purchase securities	Decrease taxes

50. A decrease in an economy's investment in physical capital would
    (A) slow down its rate of economic growth.
    (B) accelerate its rate of economic growth.
    (C) be caused by increases in access to higher education.
    (D) allow inflation to cool.
    (E) cause net exports to increase.

51. Assume trade is balanced on the U.S. current account. The United States will experience a trade deficit if
    (A) prices in the U.S. are higher relative to other nation's prices.
    (B) other nations reduce trade barriers against the U.S.
    (C) the dollar becomes stronger (appreciates) against foreign currencies.
    (D) the U.S. economic growth is slower than other nations.
    (E) imported products are relatively expensive.

52. If the government simultaneously engages in expansionary monetary and fiscal policies, which of the following is the likely effect on interest rates and unemployment?

	Interest Rates	Unemployment
(A)	Increase	Either increase or decrease
(B)	Increase	Decrease
(C)	Decrease	Decrease
(D)	Either increase or decrease	Increase
(E)	Either increase or decrease	Decrease

53. Which of the following is an example of an automatic stabilizer?
    (A) Congress passes a bill to reduce the marginal tax rates.
    (B) Congress authorizes government spending on military defense projects.
    (C) The President promises a child tax refund of $1,000 for taxpayers.
    (D) The federal government attempts to balance the budget.
    (E) Unemployment compensation increases as workers lose their jobs.

54. Crowding out due to government borrowing occurs when
    (A) lower interest rates increase private sector investment.
    (B) lower interest rates decrease private sector investment.
    (C) a smaller money supply increases private sector investment.
    (D) a smaller money supply decreases private sector investment.
    (E) higher interest rates decrease private sector investment.

55. According to Keynesian theory, decreasing taxes and increasing government spending will most likely change consumption expenditures and unemployment in which of the following ways?

	Consumption	Unemployment
(A)	Decrease	Increase
(B)	Decrease	No change
(C)	Increase	Decrease
(D)	Increase	Increase
(E)	No change	Decrease

56. Positive shocks in short-run aggregate supply will
    (A) shift the short-run Phillips curve to the right.
    (B) shift the short-run Phillips curve to the left.
    (C) move upwards along the long-run Phillips curve.
    (D) shift the long-run Phillips curve to the right.
    (E) shift the long-run Phillips curve to the left.

57. If an economy improves technology, what can be expected to happen to price levels and real GDP, ceteris paribus?

	Price Level	Real GDP
(A)	Rise	Rise
(B)	Rise	Fall
(C)	Fall	Fall
(D)	Fall	Rise
(E)	No change	Rise

58. Economic growth is best defined as
    (A) annual increases in nominal output.
    (B) increased production levels from one month to the next.
    (C) gains in potential GDP brought about due to increased levels of technology and capital stock.
    (D) rightward shifts of aggregate demand.
    (E) rightward shifts of the long-run Phillips curve.

59. The intersection of the aggregate supply curve and the aggregate demand curve occurs at the economy's equilibrium level of
    (A) real investment and the interest rate.
    (B) real disposable income and unemployment.
    (C) real national output and the price level.
    (D) government expenditures and taxes.
    (E) imports and exports.

60. Economics is a(n)
    (A) natural science.
    (B) social science.
    (C) managerial science.
    (D) business science.
    (E) arithmetical science.

STOP
END OF SECTION I
IF YOU FINISH BEFORE TIME IS CALLED, YOU MAY CHECK YOUR WORK ON THIS SECTION. DO NOT GO ON TO SECTION II UNTIL YOU ARE TOLD TO DO SO.

Section II: Free-Response Questions
Planning Time—10 minutes
Writing Time—50 minutes

Directions: You have 50 minutes to answer all three of the following questions. It is suggested that you spend approximately half your time on the first question and divide the remaining time equally between the next two questions. In answering the questions, you should emphasize the line of reasoning that generated your results; it is not enough to list the results of your analysis. Include correctly labeled diagrams, if useful or required, in explaining your answer. A correctly labeled diagram must have all axes and curves clearly labeled and must show directional changes. Use a pen with black or dark blue ink.

1. Assume unemployment is high and is a major problem in the United States.
    (a) In an effort to get unemployment back to its natural rate, the Federal Reserve enacts an expansionary monetary policy by purchasing $10 million in U.S. Treasury bonds.
        (i) If the reserve ratio is 10 percent, what is the maximum increase in money supply that may occur as a result of the Fed's open market operation?
        (ii) Give one reason why money supply may not increase by the amount given in part (a)(i)?
    (b) Using a correctly labeled aggregate demand and aggregate supply graph, identify each of the following.
        (i)   The natural rate of output, labeled Y_f.
        (ii) The equilibrium output and price level prior to the Fed policy action, labeled Y_1 and PL_1, respectively.
        (iii) The new equilibrium output and price level after the Fed policy action, labeled Y_2 and PL_2, respectively.
    (c) Fiscal policymakers also attempt to decrease unemployment by increasing government spending by $50 million. Given a marginal propensity to consume of 0.75, calculate the expected increase in output that will occur due to the increase in government spending.
    (d) Congress also decides to decrease corporate tax rates. Explain the effect of the tax cut on the following.
        (i) Private investment. Explain.
        (ii) Long-term economic growth
    (e) Due to the now lowered corporate tax rates, foreign firms begin purchasing land in America.
        (i) This is a credit to which of the two balance of payments subaccounts?
        (ii) Illustrate on a correctly labeled graph of the loanable funds market how this capital inflow will affect real interest rates in the United States.

2. Two related long-term concepts are those of economic growth and the natural rate of unemployment. Frequently, policymakers target these well-known indicators.
    (a) Explain how the following policy actions affect the rate of economic growth.
        (i)   Investment tax credits encourage firms to increase spending on research and development.
        (ii) Marginal tax cuts combined with increased government spending cause the federal budget deficit to rise.
        (iii) Increased access to government grants allow greater access to higher education and vocational training.

(b) Identify how the following policy actions affect the long-run Phillips curve and the natural rate of unemployment.
    (i) Unemployment benefits are extended from 27 to 54 weeks.
    (ii) Frictional and structural unemployment decrease due to federal work programs.

3. The table below lists the maximum combination of automobiles and toy cars produced in a month by Germany and China, respectively.

	Automobiles	Toy Cars
Germany	5,000	10,000
China	3,000	12,000

(a) If the two nations were to specialize and trade, which nation should produce each product, according to the theory of comparative advantage? Explain.
(b) Assume China imposes quotas limiting the number of automobiles imported from German manufacturers. Describe the effect of the quota on Germany's GDP.
(c) Using a correctly labeled graph of the foreign exchange market for the euro, illustrate the change in the value of the German currency, the euro, in terms of the Chinese currency, the yuan, as a result of the quota. Be certain to indicate the following.
    (i) The new demand of euros on the market.
    (ii) The original and new exchange rates, labeled e and e_1, respectively.

ANSWERS TO MACROECONOMICS PRACTICE TEST 1

SECTION I: MULTIPLE-CHOICE ANSWERS

Using the table below, score your test.

Determine how many questions you answered correctly and how many you answered incorrectly. You will find explanations to the answers on the following pages.

1. E	11. C	21. D	31. E	41. D	51. C
2. D	12. C	22. A	32. C	42. D	52. E
3. B	13. B	23. E	33. B	43. B	53. E
4. B	14. D	24. A	34. C	44. A	54. E
5. B	15. E	25. B	35. B	45. B	55. C
6. D	16. C	26. B	36. B	46. A	56. B
7. C	17. B	27. C	37. A	47. D	57. D
8. E	18. A	28. B	38. D	48. C	58. C
9. D	19. E	29. D	39. A	49. E	59. C
10. A	20. C	30. A	40. B	50. A	60. B

1. **E.** Frictional unemployment is understood to be present in any economy, no matter how well the economy is functioning. Even at full employment, people tend to find themselves between jobs (*Principles of Economics* 5th ed. pages 617–623/6th ed. pages 596–602).

2. **D.** The law of demand states that price and quantity demanded are inversely related; when price goes up, quantity demanded goes down; and when price goes down, quantity demanded goes up (*Principles of Economics* 5th ed. page 67/6th ed. page 67).

3. **B.** While the economy is now able to produce more capital goods, the amount of consumer goods that may be produced has not changed. As a result, the PPC illustrates an increase in potential capital goods by shifting outward along its capital goods axis (*Principles of Economics* 5th ed. pages 25–28/6th ed. pages 26–28).

4. **B.** Macroeconomics is the study of the economy as a whole; inflation is a rise in price level for an economy. Only changes in the price of individual goods would be studied under microeconomics; the other options are too specialized to include inflation (*Principles of Economics* 5th ed. pages 28–30/6th ed. page 29).

5. **B.** The statement is best described as a normative one. Normative statements include some degree of judgment or opinion; positive statements are objective and include only proven facts (*Principles of Economics* 5th ed. pages 30–31/6th ed. pages 30–31).

6. **D.** GDP is the sum of consumption, investment, government spending, and net exports. The sum of C + I + G in this question is $4,800 billion, therefore net exports must be −$200 billion to get GDP to its final figure of $4600 billion. A negative net export figure implies that imports are greater than exports because net exports equals exports minus imports (*Principles of Economics* 5th ed. pages 512–515/6th ed. pages 496–499).

7. **C.** Even at the full employment level of output, we can assume that both frictional and structural unemployment are present. None of the other assumptions may be made (*Principles of Economics* 5th ed. pages 617–623/6th ed. pages 596–602).

8. **E.** GDP is intended to be an indicator of productive activity that takes place in an economy. As there is no practical way to include unpaid work, even if it is productive activity, GDP inevitably understates economic activity (*Principles of Economics* 5th ed. pages 512–515/6th ed. pages 496–499).

9. **D.** The aggregate demand (AD) curve will shift left when interest rates rise. This is because interest-sensitive consumption (C) and investment (I) spending are both inversely related to interest rates; as rates rise, C and I fall, causing AD to shift left (*Principles of Economics* 5th ed. pages 739–771/6th ed. pages 719–752).

10. **A.** The consumer price index is intended to be a monthly measure of prices consumers pay on goods (*Principles of Economics* 5th ed. pages 530–537/6th ed. pages 514–521).

11. **C.** Government spending on infrastructure counts as one of the four components of GDP while the purchase of stock (A), sale of a previous year's inventory (D), and non–market activity (E) do not. The purchase of imported goods (B) would actually decrease GDP (*Principles of Economics* 5th ed. pages 512–515/6th ed. pages 496–499).

12. **C.** The money multiplier is found by dividing one by the reserve requirement. In this case, 1/0.2 equals 5 (*Principles of Economics* 5th ed. pages 651–653/6th ed. pages 630–631).

13. **B.** As price level decreases, output demanded increases. This is why the aggregate demand curve is downward sloping (*Principles of Economics* 5th ed. pages 746–748/6th ed. pages 726–728).

14. **D.** Real GDP has been adjusted for the effects of price level changes and gives a more accurate picture of output changes from year to year (*Principles of Economics* 5th ed. pages 516–518/6th ed. pages 500–502).

15. **E.** Unemployment measures the number of people out of the labor force not working. In this case, 10 percent of the 300 million people in the labor force are not working; this comes to 30 million

unemployed workers (*Principles of Economics* 5th ed. pages 614–616/6th ed. pages 594–596).

16. **C.** Wages are the payment for labor, an input price. Decreases in input prices cause short-run aggregate supply to shift outward (*Principles of Economics* 5th ed. pages 755–761/6th ed. pages 734–740).

17. **B.** As aggregate supply shifts left, equilibrium moves up the aggregate demand curve. With this movement, output falls and price level rises (*Principles of Economics* 5th ed. pages 739–771/6th ed. pages 719–752).

18. **A.** Restrictive (or contractionary) monetary policy decreases money supply and is intended to reduce the effects of high inflation (*Principles of Economics* 5th ed. pages 778–787/6th ed. pages 758–767).

19. **E.** Whether nominal GDP rises or falls is dependent upon price level and may not be determined solely on fluctuations of real GDP (*Principles of Economics* 5th ed. pages 516–518/6th ed. pages 500–502).

20. **C.** All other things held equal, as interest rates rise, the dollar appreciates on the foreign exchange market. With a higher valued dollar, imports increase and exports decrease, leading to a decrease in both net exports and aggregate demand (*Principles of Economics* 5th ed. pages 716–721/6th ed. pages 696–701).

21. **D.** Improvements in technology and capital stock lead to more efficient production processes and increases in productivity, which is the cause of rightward shifts of the LRAS curve (*Principles of Economics* 5th ed. pages 752–756/6th ed. pages 732–735).

22. **A.** Increases in input prices, such as oil, cause the short-run aggregate supply curve to shift left. With no change in aggregate demand, the leftward shift of the SRAS curve will increase price level while decreasing output, causing unemployment to rise (*Principles of Economics* 5th ed. pages 739–771/6th ed. pages 719–752).

23. **E.** By buying bonds, the central bank increases bank reserves and decreases interest rates. The decrease in interest rates causes investment and consumption spending to increase, shifting the AD curve to the right, increasing output and price level. While increasing government spending and lowering taxes are expansionary, they are fiscal, not monetary, policies (*Principles of Economics* 5th ed. pages 778–787/6th ed. pages 758–767).

24. **A.** With an MPC of 0.75 and an MPS of 0.25, the spending multiplier will be 4. Any increase in government spending will be multiplied by 4. Therefore, a $25 billion increase in government

spending would increase GDP by $100 billion (*Principles of Economics* 5th ed. pages 788–790/6th ed. pages 769–770).

25. **B.** Output levels to the left of the LRAS curve indicate production below full employment; this is where equilibrium would be found on the AD–AS curve in this scenario (*Principles of Economics* 5th ed. pages 739–771/6th ed. pages 719–752).

26. **B.** Gold is not considered money while the other options are all counted as part of the M1 money supply (*Principles of Economics* 5th ed. pages 642–646/6th ed. pages 620–625).

27. **C.** In order to manipulate money supply, the Fed enters the open market for U.S. Treasury securities (*Principles of Economics* 5th ed. pages 653–656/6th ed. pages 633–635).

28. **B.** Excess reserves will increase by 90 percent of the deposit, in this case, $90. The other $10 will be kept as required reserves (*Principles of Economics* 5th ed. pages 651–653/6th ed. pages 630–631).

29. **D.** Money does not serve as a factor of production (*Principles of Economics* 5th ed. pages 642–646/6th ed. pages 620–625).

30. **A.** Changes in interest rates cause movement up or down the money demand curve, not shifts of the curve. Therefore, if interest rates were to fall, the quantity of money demanded would increase, but money demand itself would not change (*Principles of Economics* 5th ed. pages 779–781/6th ed. pages 759–761).

31. **E.** The reserve requirement mandates how much money banks must keep in reserves either at the bank vault or deposited at the Federal Reserve (*Principles of Economics* 5th ed. pages 653–656/6th ed. pages 633–635).

32. **C.** The base year for a price index always has a value of 100. Therefore, when compared to the base year, a price index of 155 indicates a 55 percent increase in prices (*Principles of Economics* 5th ed. pages 530–537/6th ed. pages 514–521).

33. **B.** Adjustments to marginal tax rates are considered fiscal policy, not monetary (*Principles of Economics* 5th ed. pages 787–790/6th ed. pages 767–770).

34. **C.** When the Fed buys securities, it pays by writing a check to the bank that was the previous owner. As this money is deposited in a commercial bank, bank reserves increase, causing interest rates to decrease (*Principles of Economics* 5th ed. pages 778–787/6th ed. pages 758–767).

35. **B.** The federal funds rate is the rate charged among commercial banks on overnight loans (*Principles of Economics* 5th ed. pages 653–656/6th ed. pages 633–635).

36. **B.** Borrowers at a fixed-rate gain from unanticipated inflation because the money they pay back to lenders is worth less than that the money they borrowed. In this case, lenders (including savers) are hurt by the inflation (*Principles of Economics* 5th ed. page 682/6th ed. pages 661–662).

37. **A.** The CPI is the measure of a market basket of consumer goods from month to month. It can be used as an indicator of inflation, but is not inherently a measurement of inflation (*Principles of Economics* 5th ed. pages 530–537/6th ed. pages 514–521).

38. **D.** The Fisher equation explains that nominal interest rates equal real interest rates plus inflation. With the nominal rate at 6 percent and the expected inflation at 4 percent, the real interest rate must be 2 percent (6 − 4 = 2) (*Principles of Economics* 5th ed. pages 674–676/6th ed. pages 655–656).

39. **A.** Due to the balanced budget multiplier (which is always one), when taxes and government purchases are changed by the same amount (in this case, $50 billion), the change in GDP will be that amount (*Principles of Economics* 5th ed. pages 788–790/6th ed. pages 769–770).

40. **B.** The spending multiplier equals 1/MPS. If a $10 billion increase in investment caused a $50 billion increase in output, the multiplier must be 5. Therefore, 5 equals 1/MPS and MPS equals 0.2 (*Principles of Economics* 5th ed. pages 788–790/6th ed. pages 769–770).

41. **D.** In theory, increased borrowing by government causes interest rates to rise. On the foreign exchange market, high interest rates cause demand for the dollar to increase, making the dollar appreciate internationally (*Principles of Economics* 5th ed. pages 791–793/6th ed. pages 771–773).

42. **D.** The LRAS curve represents the natural rate of output. Economic growth indicates an increase in the natural rate of output, thus a rightward shift of the LRAS curve (*Principles of Economics* 5th ed. pages 752–756/6th ed. pages 732–735).

43. **B.** Real variables consider the effects of inflation. When your salary rises 1%, your nominal income has risen 1%. Because prices rose by an amount greater than your salary, your real income actually fell (*Principles of Economics* 5th ed. page 669/6th ed. page 649).

44. **A.** Government spending is a shifter of aggregate demand; as government purchases increases, the AD curve shifts to the right (*Principles of Economics* 5th ed. pages 746–748/6th ed. pages 726–728).

45. **B.** Fiscal policymakers would attempt to stimulate spending and get output back to full employment levels by cutting taxes. Decreasing spending would have the opposite effect; fiscal policymakers have no direct control over interest rates (*Principles of Economics* 5th ed. pages 787–790/6th ed. pages 767–770).

46. **A.** Nominal wages will likely fall if the economy is left alone as workers are willing to accept pay cuts in order to acquire or maintain employment in a weak economy (*Principles of Economics* 5th ed. page 763/6th ed. page 742).

47. **D.** Official reserves are used to offset any imbalances between the current and capital account. Because the current account deficit was $50 billion greater than the capital account surplus, a credit of $50 billion had to be made to the official reserves (*Principles of Economics* 5th ed. pages 692–693/6th ed. pages 672–673).

48. **C.** Buying bonds on the open market will increase bank reserves and money supply (*Principles of Economics* 5th ed. pages 653–656/6th ed. pages 633–635).

49. **E.** To increase output, policies would have to be expansionary. Purchasing securities and cutting taxes accomplishes this goal (*Principles of Economics* 5th ed. pages 778–790/6th ed. pages 758–770).

50. **A.** Productivity gains create economic growth and come, in part, due to investment in the capital stock; if productivity were to falter due to lower investment levels, so too would economic growth rates (*Principles of Economics* 5th ed. pages 752–756/6th ed. pages 732–735).

51. **C.** A strong dollar encourages increased imports and decreased exports (*Principles of Economics* 5th ed. pages 716–721/6th ed. pages 696–701).

52. **E.** While both expansionary fiscal and monetary policies will likely reduce unemployment, their effects on interest rates are less consistent. Expansionary fiscal policies tend to result in increased interest rates (the root cause of crowding out) while expansionary monetary policies decrease interest rates (*Principles of Economics* 5th ed. pages 778–790/6th ed. pages 758–770).

53. **E.** Automatic stabilizers require no new legislation as they are already written into law; unemployment compensation is an example of this (*Principles of Economics* 5th ed. page 797/6th ed. pages 777–778).

54. **E.** Crowding out occurs because government borrowing drives interest rates up which in turn causes private investment to decrease (*Principles of Economics* 5th ed. pages 791–793/6th ed. pages 771–773).

55. **C.** Decreased taxes and increased spending combine to make an expansionary fiscal policy; it is intended to increase levels of

consumer spending and output, causing unemployment to fall (*Principles of Economics* 5th ed. pages 787–790/6th ed. pages 767–770).

56. **B.** A rightward shift of the SRAS curve will cause the price level to fall and output to rise; a leftward shift of the SRPC will illustrate lower inflation rates and lower levels of unemployment (*Principles of Economics* 5th ed. pages 755–761, 802–816/6th ed. pages 734–740, 786–798).

57. **D.** Improved technology will shift the aggregate supply curve to the right, resulting in decreased price level and increased output (*Principles of Economics* 5th ed. pages 755–761/6th ed. pages 734–740).

58. **C.** The term economic growth implies that an economy can produce more from the same amount of resources. This is not the same as increases in nominal output or aggregate demand. Economic growth is synonymous with increases in potential, or full employment, GDP (*Principles of Economics* 5th ed. pages 752–756/6th ed. pages 732–735).

59. **C.** The AD–AS model illustrates an economy's current output and price level at that point where aggregate demand and aggregate supply intersect (*Principles of Economics* 5th ed. pages 739–771/6th ed. pages 719–752).

60. **B.** Economics is a social science as it analyzes decisions made by rational people (*Principles of Economics* 5th ed. page 4/6th ed. page 4).

Section II: Free-Response Answers

1. **(13 points total)**
   (a) 2 points
      (i) $100 million
      (ii) Either of the following: banks do not lend all of their excess reserves, borrowers do not redeposit loans into the banking system (hold some as cash)
   (b) 4 points

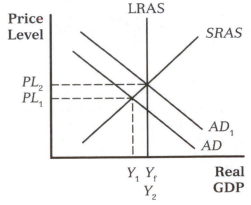

   (i) See graph, Y_f.
   (ii) See graph, Y_1, PL_1.
   (iii) See graph, Y_2, PL_2.

(c) 1 point
Output would increase $200 million

(d) 3 points
(i) Private investment will increase. A decrease in corporate tax rates will increase expected rates of return, causing firms to increase levels of investment spending, leading to a higher level of capital stock.
(ii) Long-term economic growth will increase.

(e) 3 points
(i) Capital Account

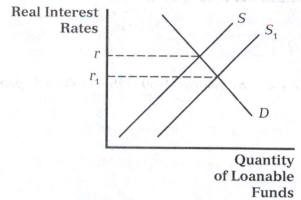

(ii) See graph, real interest rates will fall.

(*Principles of Economics* 5th ed. pages 613–635, 692–693, 739–771, 778–790/6th ed. pages 593–613, 672–673 719–752, 758–770)

2. **(5 points total)**
(a) 3 points
(i) The rate of economic growth will increase due to gains in the level of technology.
(ii) The rate of economic growth will slow/decrease due to the crowding out effect; public borrowing crowds out private investment.
(iii) The rate of economic growth will increase as a result of increased levels of human capital.
(b) 2 points
(i) The long-run Phillips curve will shift to the right, and the natural rate of unemployment increases.
(ii) The long-run Phillips curve will shift to the left, and the natural rate of unemployment decreases.

(*Principles of Economics* 5th ed. pages 752–756, 802–816/6th ed. pages 732–735, 786–798)

3. **(7 points total)**
(a) 2 points
Germany should produce automobiles and China should produce toy cars. Germany has comparative advantage in producing automobiles due to its lower opportunity cost (2 toy cars vs. 4 toy cars) for each automobile produced. Likewise, China has a lower opportunity cost for producing toy cars (1/4 of an automobile vs. 1/2 of an automobile).
(b) 1 point
Germany's GDP will decrease due to a decrease in net exports.
(c) 4 points

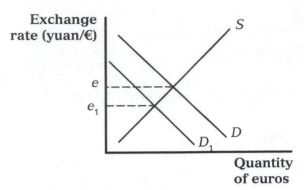

(i) See graph, D_1.
(ii) See graph, e_1.

(*Principles of Economics* 5th ed. pages 54–59, 716–721/6th ed. pages 54–59, 696–701)

CALCULATING YOUR SCORE

SECTION I: MULTIPLE-CHOICE QUESTIONS

[_____] × 1.25 = _____
Number Correct   Weighted Section I Score
(out of 60)   (Do not round)

SECTION II: FREE-RESPONSE QUESTIONS

Question 1 _____ × (1.2500) = _____
(out of 13)   (Do not round)
Question 2 _____ × (0.8333) = _____
(out of 5)   (Do not round)
Question 3 _____ × (0.9375) = _____
(out of 7)   (Do not round)

Sum = _____
Weighted Section II Score
(Do not round)

COMPOSITE SCORE

_____ + _____ = _____
Weighted   Weighted   Composite Score
Section I Score   Section II Score   (Round to nearest
whole number)

Composite Score Range	Approximate AP Grade
73–90	5
58–72	4
45–57	3
33–44	2
0–32	1

Practice Test 2: Macroeconomics

This test will give you some indication of how you might score on the AP Macroeconomics Exam. Of course, the exam changes every year, so it is never possible to predict a student's score with certainty. This test will also pinpoint strengths and weaknesses on the key content areas covered by the exam.

AP MACROECONOMICS EXAMINATION
Section I: Multiple-Choice Questions
Time: 70 minutes
60 Questions

Directions: Each of the following questions or incomplete statements is accompanied by five suggested answers or completions. Select the one that best answers the question or completes the statement.

1. If the maximum combination of consumer and capital goods potentially produced by an economy has increased over time, which of the following is true?
   (A) Marginal tax rates have increased due to contractionary fiscal policy.
   (B) Keynesian policy initiatives have allowed for increased consumption of both consumer and capital goods.
   (C) New physical capital has been introduced to firms throughout the economy.
   (D) Resources are being utilized inefficiently at this combination of goods and services.
   (E) Monetary policy authorities have effectively decreased bank reserves through open market operations.

2. Unemployment is studied as a part of
   (A) macroeconomics.
   (B) microeconomics.
   (C) labor economics.
   (D) urban economics.
   (E) home economics.

3. The law of supply indicates that producers
   (A) decrease production levels when prices rise.
   (B) will produce more of a good when markets dictate a higher price.
   (C) make production decisions based solely on forecasts of demand.
   (D) are dependent on surveys when pricing their products.
   (E) increase the price of their goods when competing firms increase production.

4. Which of the following is a positive economic statement?
   (A) Three percent annual growth is a strong rate of growth for any economy.
   (B) Unemployment should stay within the 4-6 percent range.
   (C) Prices of new homes decreased 2 percent last month.
   (D) Inflationary pressure is the worst of all economic problems.
   (E) The U.S. economy is poised for a strong recovery.

GO ON TO NEXT PAGE

5. If the price of hot dogs goes up, we can expect the demand for mustard to
   (A) increase because hot dogs and mustard are complementary goods.
   (B) decrease because hot dogs and mustard are complementary goods.
   (C) increase because hot dogs and mustard are substitute goods.
   (D) decrease because hot dogs and mustard are substitute goods.
   (E) remain constant because hot dogs and mustard are not related.

6. GDP is an indicator of a nation's production of goods and services in a given year. Which of the following would cause an increase in a nation's GDP?
   (A) The purchase of foreign oil.
   (B) Sales of used automobiles increase dramatically.
   (C) A carpenter builds a dining room table for his daughter's apartment.
   (D) Fees earned by a broker for the purchase of financial assets for her clients.
   (E) A mechanic restores a vintage automobile.

7. The best example of cyclical unemployment is
   (A) a worker loses his/her job during a recession.
   (B) companies move workers from full time to part time.
   (C) a new college graduate is searching for her first job.
   (D) new technology makes workers' jobs obsolete.
   (E) an individual leaves his job to find more satisfying employment in another city.

8. Consider a nation with an adult population of 100 million. If the unemployment rate is 10 percent and 6 million adults are considered unemployed, how many are employed?
   (A) 94 million.
   (B) 60 million.
   (C) 54 million.

   (D) 4 million.
   (E) Not enough information is provided to accurately answer the question.

9. Part-time workers
   (A) are not counted in the official calculation of the unemployment rate.
   (B) count as unemployed in calculating the unemployment rate because they are not full time.
   (C) count the same as full-time workers when calculating the unemployment rate.
   (D) do not count as part of the labor force, but do count towards the unemployment rate.
   (E) count as 1/2 of an employed person when calculating unemployment rate.

10. The consumer price index was 100 one year and 104.5 the next. What was the inflation rate that year?
   (A) 104.5 percent.
   (B) 10.45 percent.
   (C) 1.045 percent.
   (D) 0.45 percent.
   (E) 4.5 percent.

11. What function is money serving when you purchase food at the grocery store?
   (A) Medium of exchange
   (B) Store of value
   (C) Standard of value
   (D) Unit of account
   (E) Factor of production

12. Which of the following would be considered an addition to the United States GDP for a given year?
   (A) Purchases of foreign made automobiles increase.
   (B) An automobile manufacturer purchases tires from a wholesaler to put on a new model hybrid sedan.
   (C) A monthly Social Security payment is made to a retired couple.
   (D) A local retailer sees annual inventories increase $10,000.
   (E) Strong market returns lead to high levels of trading on Wall Street.

GO ON TO NEXT PAGE

13. Price level rises and unemployment falls. Which of the following events may have been a cause of this?
    (A) Production costs increase due to a shortage of a major natural resource.
    (B) Government spending is reduced in an effort to balance the federal budget.
    (C) Interest rates fall in response to easy money policies at the central bank.
    (D) Capital stock increases after years of research.
    (E) New restrictions severely limit trade with foreign partners.

14. In a given year, real GDP in Country Y was $1,000 billion. Government spending totaled $150 billion, investment was $200 billion and a $150 billion trade deficit existed. How much consumption spending occurred that year?
    (A) $1,000.
    (B) $800.
    (C) $500.
    (D) $100
    (E) Cannot be determined.

15. With fixed rates of interest, unanticipated inflation
    (A) hurts borrowers but helps lenders.
    (B) hurts lenders but helps borrower.
    (C) hurts lenders and borrowers.
    (D) helps lenders and borrowers.
    (E) causes rates of economic growth to increase.

16. Which of the following is best described as a certificate of indebtedness?
    (A) Stocks.
    (B) Bonds.
    (C) Currency.
    (D) Checkable deposits.
    (E) Traveler's checks.

17. The short-run aggregate supply curve is likely to shift to the left when there is an increase in
    (A) the cost of productive resources.
    (B) productivity.
    (C) the money supply.

(D) the federal budget deficit.
(E) imports.

18. More than one person can have a claim on each dollar in a commercial bank. This fact is representative of the
    (A) fractional reserve system.
    (B) Federal Reserve system.
    (C) balance of payments system.
    (D) real balances effect.
    (E) wealth effect.

19. An increase in marginal income tax rates will shift
    (A) aggregate demand to the right due to higher levels of government revenue.
    (B) long-run aggregate supply to the left due to decreased productivity.
    (C) short-run aggregate supply to the left due to increased production costs.
    (D) money supply to the right due to increased bank reserves.
    (E) aggregate demand to the left due to decreased levels of consumer spending.

20. Assume the stock market experiences relatively high gains and consumer wealth increases. According to the aggregate demand-aggregate supply model, what will happen to price level and output?

	Price Level	Output
(A)	Increase	Increase
(B)	Increase	Decrease
(C)	Decrease	No change
(D)	Decrease	Increase
(E)	No change	Decrease

21. Which of the following would cause the level of output demanded to increase along the aggregate demand curve?
    (A) Increase in the price level.
    (B) Decrease in the price level.
    (C) Increase in marginal tax rates.
    (D) Decrease in interest rates.
    (E) Increase in the money supply.

GO ON TO NEXT PAGE

22. If the U.S. dollar were to appreciate relative to foreign currencies, one may expect net exports and price level to change in which of the following ways?

	Net Exports	Price Level
(A)	Increase	Decrease
(B)	Decrease	Increase
(C)	No change	Increase
(D)	Increase	Increase
(E)	Decrease	Decrease

23. An individual deposits $1,000 into a commercial bank. If the required reserve ratio is 10 percent, what is the maximum increase in money supply that may occur as a result of this deposit?
    (A) $10,000.
    (B) $9,000.
    (C) $1,000.
    (D) $900.
    (E) $0.

24. When increased levels of total spending drive prices up, we call it this:
    (A) Unanticipated inflation.
    (B) Hyperinflation.
    (C) Cost-push inflation.
    (D) Demand-pull inflation.
    (E) Disinflation.

25. Assume a prolonged recession increases excess capacity of businesses throughout the country. As a result,
    (A) aggregate supply will increase to fill the extra warehouse space.
    (B) aggregate demand will decrease as a result of declining levels of investment.
    (C) the short-run Phillips curve will decrease.
    (D) aggregate demand will increase due to new found capacity to work with.
    (E) aggregate supply will decrease due to declining price levels.

26. The central bank announces that it expects inflation to be relatively low while unemployment rises in the following months. What would be an expected monetary policy action as a result of this forecast?
    (A) Increase government spending.
    (B) Decrease the discount rate.
    (C) Increase the reserve ratio.
    (D) Sell bonds on the open market.
    (E) Decrease marginal income tax rates.

27. Consumers expect to see their income rise significantly in the near future. This will cause
    (A) aggregate demand to increase.
    (B) aggregate supply to increase.
    (C) aggregate demand to decrease.
    (D) aggregate supply to decrease.
    (E) both aggregate demand and aggregate supply to increase.

28. Monetary policy decisions are ultimately made by the
    (A) President.
    (B) Senate.
    (C) Federal Open Market Committee (FOMC).
    (D) U.S. Treasury.
    (E) Council of Economic Advisors.

29. A decrease in short-run aggregate supply will likely cause which of the following?
    (A) An increase in price level
    (B) A decrease in output
    (C) An increase in employment
    (D) Both A and B
    (E) A, B, and C

30. Assume the Federal Reserve enacts an expansionary policy intended to increase money supply and encourage banks to lend. What affect would this have on the graph for the loanable funds market?
    (A) Increase supply of loanable funds.
    (B) Decrease supply of loanable funds..
    (C) Increase demand for loanable funds.
    (D) Decrease demand for loanable funds.

GO ON TO NEXT PAGE

(E) It would have no effect on loanable funds

31. Which of the following may be a reason why the maximum increase in money supply predicted by the money multiplier may not happen?
    I.   Borrowers do not redeposit loans.
    II. Some borrowed money is kept as cash.
    III. Banks do not lend their entire excess reserves.
    (A) I only.
    (B) II only.
    (C) III only.
    (D) I and II only.
    (E) I, II, and III.

32. Congress passes new legislation which decreases marginal tax rates at all levels of income. What type of fiscal policy is this?
    (A) Automatic, expansionary.
    (B) Discretionary, expansionary.
    (C) Automatic, contractionary.
    (D) Discretionary, contractionary.
    (E) Discretionary, regressive.

33. Lending by commercial banks
    (A) creates money.
    (B) destroys money.
    (C) keeps money supply constant.
    (D) creates jobs.
    (E) lowers inflationary pressure.

34. Assume commercial banks have been buying government bonds from the Federal Reserve on the open market. What affect will this have on the graph for the money market?
    (A) Increase money demand and interest rates.
    (B) Decrease money demand and interest rates.
    (C) Decrease money supply and increase interest rates.
    (D) Increase money supply and decrease interest rates.
    (E) Decrease interest rates and increase the quantity of money demanded.

35. A major advantage of automatic stabilizers in fiscal policy is that they
    (A) reduce the public debt.
    (B) increase the possibility of a balanced budget.
    (C) stabilize the unemployment rate.
    (D) go into effect without passage of new legislation.
    (E) automatically reduce the inflation rate.

36. Assume expansionary fiscal policies have led to high federal deficits and crowding out. Which of the following would be considered an accommodative policy action by the Federal Reserve?
    (A) Raising the discount rate
    (B) Cutting corporate income tax rates
    (C) Lowering government spending on entitlements
    (D) Purchasing Treasury securities on the open market
    (E) Raising the reserve ratio

37. Assume no taxes. If the MPC is 0.8, assuming the full multiplier effect, the result of an increase in autonomous investment spending of $200 billion should be an increase in real output of
    (A) $1,000 billion.
    (B) more than $200 and less than $1,000 billion.
    (C) $200 billion.
    (D) less than $200 billion but more than zero.
    (E) zero.

38. Required reserves of a commercial bank must be kept in one of two places: as cash in that bank's vault or deposited at
    (A) the U.S. Treasury.
    (B) the Federal Deposit Insurance Corporation (FDIC).
    (C) the Internal Revenue Service (IRS).
    (D) that bank's district Federal Reserve bank.
    (E) the Board of Governors.

GO ON TO NEXT PAGE

39. Which of the following fiscal policy measures is designed to increase aggregate demand?
    I. Decrease of personal income taxes
    II. Increase of excise taxes (e.g., cigarette, alcohol, gasoline)
    III. Decrease government expenditures
    (A) I only
    (B) II only
    (C) III only
    (D) I and III only
    (E) I, II, and III

40. Which of the following describes where commercial banks borrow money from the Federal Reserve?
    (A) The open market.
    (B) The discount window.
    (C) The premium window.
    (D) The markdown window.
    (E) Wall Street.

41. Assume inflation expectations have become a problem in the economy. How might the Federal Reserve combat the problem?
    (A) Lower the reserve ratio in order to decrease the demand for money.
    (B) Buy securities on the open market, which will decrease the demand for loanable funds.
    (C) Sell securities on the open market, causing a decrease in money supply.
    (D) Raise marginal tax rates so that disposable income decreases
    (E) Lower the discount rate and encourage banks to lend more money.

42. Unemployment is high but so is inflation. What set of policy actions by Congress and the Fed would have offsetting affects on the economy due to misaligned intentions?
    (A) Increased government spending and decreased discount rate.
    (B) Decreased taxes and selling securities on the open market.
    (C) Decreased taxes and buying securities on the open market.

(D) Increased taxes and raising the discount rate.
(E) Increased government spending and lowering the reserve ratio.

43. A Federal Open Market Committee press release states that policymakers intend to "increase the target for the Federal Funds rate." Based on that statement, what does the Fed consider to be the most pressing economic problem at the time?
    (A) Unemployment.
    (B) The Federal deficit.
    (C) The trade deficit.
    (D) Inflation.
    (E) Deflation.

44. Which of the following policy combinations is most likely to be associated with a decrease in exported goods?
    (A) Expansionary fiscal and expansionary monetary policy.
    (B) Expansionary fiscal and contractionary monetary policy.
    (C) Contractionary fiscal and contractionary monetary policy.
    (D) Contractionary fiscal and expansionary monetary policy.
    (E) Lifting of trade sanctions.

45. Productivity is best described as
    (A) average output per unit of labor.
    (B) average input per unit of labor.
    (C) average output per unit of currency.
    (D) average output per capita.
    (E) average input per square foot.

46. Congressional action aimed at achieving full employment by manipulating government spending and taxation is called
    (A) domestic policy.
    (B) economic policy.
    (C) financial policy.
    (D) fiscal policy.
    (E) monetary policy.

GO ON TO NEXT PAGE

47. Assume a new tax is designed which automatically increases as an individual's income level increases. What kind of tax is this?
    (A) Progressive.
    (B) Proportional.
    (C) Regressive.
    (D) Negative.
    (E) Voluntary.

48. The nation Maritime is capable of producing 25 naval ships per month while its neighbor Terracotta produces only 15. From this information we can conclude
    (A) Terracotta has a more diverse and stable economy.
    (B) Maritime is more economically stable than Terracotta.
    (C) Terracotta has comparative advantage in producing naval ships.
    (D) Maritime has comparative advantage in producing naval ships.
    (E) Maritime has absolute advantage in producing naval ships.

49. A contractionary fiscal policy is illustrated by a(n)
    (A) decrease in the supply of loanable funds.
    (B) increase in money supply.
    (C) increase in aggregate demand.
    (D) decrease in aggregate supply.
    (E) decrease in aggregate demand.

50. Assume policymakers desire a $10 billion increase in output. Holding taxes constant, by how much would government spending have to increase in order to create such a change if the marginal propensity to consume is 0.9?
    (A) $1 billion.
    (B) $2 billion.
    (C) $5 billion.
    (D) $9 billion.
    (E) $10 billion.

51. The most commonly used measure for standard of living comparisons between economies is an increase in the
    (A) aggregate demand.
    (B) real GDP per capita.
    (C) real GDP per worker.
    (D) real GDP per dollar of capital stock.
    (E) value of the dollar.

52. Which of the following would count as a debit to the capital account on the United States balance of payments?
    (A) A farmer in Nebraska purchases a tractor manufactured in South Korea.
    (B) A German businessman acquires a majority share of stock in an American company.
    (C) A Canadian entrepreneur enters into a contract with a supplier located in Ohio.
    (D) An American clothing manufacturer builds a factory in Mexico.
    (E) An American investor receives rental payments on a house she owns in Spain.

53. Which of the following is not generally considered a factor in determining economic growth?
    (A) Physical capital per worker
    (B) Human capital per worker
    (C) Natural resources per worker
    (D) Technological advances
    (E) Increasing levels of disposable income

54. When the aggregate demand–aggregate supply model indicates increased price levels and decreased output, the following change will occur on the graph of the Phillips curve.
    (A) Movement up the short-run Phillips curve.
    (B) Leftward shift of the long-run Phillips curve.
    (C) Leftward shift of the short-run Phillips curve.
    (D) Rightward shift of the short-run Phillips curve.
    (E) Movement down along the short-run Phillips curve.

GO ON TO NEXT PAGE

55. What is the anticipated inflation rate when banks decide to charge 7 percent on loans with the intention of receiving a 3 percent real return?
(A) 21 percent.
(B) 10 percent.
(C) 4 percent.
(D) −4 percent.
(E) 1 percent.

56. The Federal Reserve decides to implement a policy of buying securities on the open market while the Bank of England maintains their current monetary policy. Based on the expected change in interest rates that will occur, what will be the change in exchange rates of the U.S. dollar versus the British pound?

	Dollar	Pound
(A)	Appreciate	Depreciate
(B)	Depreciate	Appreciate
(C)	No change	Depreciate
(D)	Depreciate	No change
(E)	Appreciate	Appreciate

57. Inflation and unemployment are both rising. Which of the following may have caused this scenario?
(A) Natural gas prices have fallen.
(B) Average levels of human capital have increased.
(C) Consumption spending declines severely during a prolonged recession.
(D) Tax revenue increases following a tax hike.
(E) Subsidies in major industries have been reduced or entirely eliminated.

58. A government intending to protect infant industry from foreign competition will likely consider which of the following actions?
(A) Reducing export subsidies for related industries
(B) Eliminating any outstanding import quotas
(C) Enforcing tariffs on related products from foreign producers
(D) Manipulating foreign exchange markets in order to strengthen the domestic currency abroad
(E) Promoting the merits of free trade through a nationwide campaign

59. Economic growth is best illustrated by which of the following:

I. Rightward shift of the long-run aggregate supply curve

II. Outward expansion of the production possibilities curve

III. Rightward shift of the aggregate demand curve
(A) I only
(B) II only
(C) III only
(D) I and II only
(E) I, II, and III

60. One nation has comparative advantage in producing dress shoes relative to a major trade partner. This means the nation with comparative advantage
(A) is capable of producing dress shoes at a lower opportunity cost than its trade partner.
(B) has a larger population than its trade partner.
(C) should exploit its trade partner for valuable natural resources.
(D) can produce more dress shoes than its trade partner.
(E) should not trade dress shoes with this particular partner anymore.

STOP
END OF SECTION I
IF YOU FINISH BEFORE TIME IS CALLED, YOU MAY CHECK YOUR WORK ON THIS SECTION. DO NOT GO ON TO SECTION II UNTIL YOU ARE TOLD TO DO SO.

GO ON TO NEXT PAGE

Section II: Free-Response Questions
Planning Time—10 minutes
Writing Time—50 minutes

Directions: You have 50 minutes to answer all three of the following questions. It is suggested that you spend approximately half your time on the first question and divide the remaining time equally between the next two questions. In answering the questions, you should emphasize the line of reasoning that generated your results; it is not enough to list the results of your analysis. Include correctly labeled diagrams, if useful or required, in explaining your answer. A correctly labeled diagram must have all axes and curves clearly labeled and must show directional changes. Use a pen with black or dark blue ink.

FREE-RESPONSE QUESTIONS

1. Assume the U.S. economy has been operating at output levels beyond full employment.
    (a) Draw a correctly labeled graph of aggregate demand and aggregate supply and show each of the following.
        (i) The long-run aggregate supply curve
        (ii) The current equilibrium output and price levels, labeled Y_e and PL_e, respectively.
    (b) Assume that no policy action is taken.
        (i) Show on your graph from part (a) the change in short-run aggregate supply that will return the economy to the natural rate of output. Explain why this happens.
        (ii) Label the new equilibrium output, Y_2, and price levels, PL_2.
    (c) Monetary policy authorities will respond to the change in price level that occurred in part (b). How might the central bank respond to the change you described in part (b)?
    (d) Draw a correctly labeled graph of the money market.
        (i)   Label the equilibrium interest rate.
        (ii) Show on your graph the change in money supply that will occur due to the monetary policy described in part (c).
        (iii) Show on your graph the change in interest rates that will occur due to the monetary policy described in part (c).
    (e) At the same time, assume that policymakers at the Bank of England enforce an expansionary monetary policy.
        (i) Using a correctly labeled graph of the foreign exchange market for the U.S. dollar, show how the relative change in interest rates between the U.S. and England will affect the value of the dollar versus the pound. Explain.
        (ii) What affect will this fluctuation have on net exports in the United States?

2. A production possibilities curve (PPC) represents the maximum amount of two goods or services produced by manufacturers in an economy.
    (a) Draw a correctly labeled PPC for U.S. production of consumer and capital goods.
    (b) Policy makers enact an investment tax credit for firms that finance technological research and development. Assuming producers of both consumer and capital goods are affected, illustrate on your PPC the long-term effects of this tax credit.
    (c) Using a correctly labeled graph of the long-run aggregate supply curve, show how the natural rate of output would respond to the tax credit in the long run. Explain.
    (d) How are the PPC and long-run aggregate supply curve similar?

3. Assume the United States has a trade surplus with Brazil and imposes new tariffs on Brazilian coffee, a major export to the United States.
   (a) Describe the effect of the tariff on the equilibrium price and quantity of coffee in the United States.
   (b) What affect will the tariff have on the current account balance in the United States? Explain.
   (c) Brazil responds by imposing their own tariff on U.S. made agricultural machinery.
      (i) The Brazilian purchase of U.S. agricultural machinery is a debit to which subaccount of the Brazilian balance of payments?
      (ii) What will happen to the quantity of agricultural machinery produced by Brazilian manufacturers?

ANSWERS TO MACROECONOMICS PRACTICE TEST 2

SECTION I: MULTIPLE-CHOICE ANSWERS

Using the table below, score your test.

Determine how many questions you answered correctly and how many you answered incorrectly. You will find explanations to the answers on the following pages.

1. C	11. A	21. B	31. E	41. C	51. B
2. A	12. D	22. E	32. B	42. B	52. D
3. B	13. C	23. B	33. A	43. D	53. E
4. C	14. B	24. D	34. C	44. B	54. D
5. B	15. B	25. B	35. D	45. A	55. C
6. D	16. B	26. B	36. D	46. D	56. B
7. A	17. A	27. A	37. A	47. A	57. E
8. C	18. A	28. C	38. D	48. E	58. C
9. C	19. E	29. D	39. A	49. E	59. D
10. E	20. A	30. A	40. B	50. A	60. A

1. **C.** An increase in the maximum amount of goods produced by an economy equates to an increase in economic growth. Increases in physical capital lead to economic growth (*Principles of Economics* 5th ed. pages 25–28, 752–756/6th ed. pages 26–28, 732–735).

2. **A.** Unemployment is a concept that applies to the economy as a whole; hence, it is studied as part of macroeconomics (*Principles of Economics* 5th ed. pages 28–30/6th ed. page 29).

3. **B.** Price and quantity supplied are positively related; as prices in a market go up, producers are motivated to produce more than before (*Principles of Economics* 5th ed. page 73/6th ed. page 73).

4. **C.** Positive statements include no judgment; they are statements of fact. Only option C regarding the percent change in home prices qualifies as a positive statement (*Principles of Economics* 5th ed. pages 30–31/6th ed. pages 30–31).

5. **B.** Hot dogs and mustard are considered complementary goods; enough people purchase them together to assume they are related. Therefore, if the price of hot dogs goes up, the quantity of hot dogs purchased goes down, leading to a decrease in the demand for mustard (*Principles of Economics* 5th ed. page 70/6th ed. page 70).

6. **D.** Broker fees are a form of commission; commissions are payments for services rendered which counts as consumption

spending (*Principles of Economics* 5th ed. pages 512–515/6th ed. pages 496–499).

7. **A.** Cyclical unemployment is defined as that unemployment that occurs due to downturns in the business cycle; loss of jobs during a recession amounts to cyclical unemployment (*Principles of Economics* 5th ed. pages 617–623/6th ed. pages 596–602).

8. **C.** Unemployment represents the percent of the labor force (employed + unemployed) currently not working. Although the total adult population is 100 million, not all are included in the labor force. With 10 percent unemployment equaling 6 million people, the labor force must equal 60 million; therefore, 54 million people are employed (*Principles of Economics* 5th ed. pages 614–616/6th ed. pages 594–596).

9. **C.** The unemployment rate counts full-time and part-time workers the same way; it is a figure which represents the percentage of the labor force currently employed (*Principles of Economics* 5th ed. pages 613–635/6th ed. pages 593–613).

10. **E.** The percent change in CPI represents the inflation rate; in this case, CPI has increased 4.5 percent (*Principles of Economics* 5th ed. pages 530–537/6th ed. pages 514–521).

11. **A.** Money is used to exchange ownership of private property; in this context, it is a medium of exchange and successfully eliminates the need for barter (*Principles of Economics* 5th ed. pages 642–646/6th ed. pages 620–625).

12. **D.** Additions to inventory are counted as investment spending in the calculation of GDP (*Principles of Economics* 5th ed. pages 512–515/6th ed. pages 496–499).

13. **C.** Decreased interest rates will lead to an increase in investment spending and shift the aggregate demand curve to the right. Price level will rise, output will rise and unemployment will fall (*Principles of Economics* 5th ed. pages 739–771/6th ed. pages 719–752).

14. **B.** GDP is the sum of consumption (C), investment (I), government spending (G) and net exports (NX). Here, the question states that G = $150 billion, I = $200 billion, and NX = −$150 billion; these three component sum to $200 billion. Therefore, the remainder of GDP ($800 billion) is consumption spending (*Principles of Economics* 5th ed. pages 512–515/6th ed. pages 496–499).

15. **B.** Due to the unanticipated inflation, borrowers will be paying back loans with money worth less than that they borrowed. Lenders receive a smaller real return than anticipated (*Principles of Economics* 5th ed. page 682/6th ed. pages 661–662).

16. **B.** Bonds are IOUs; when purchasing a bond, an individual is essentially lending their money to the issuer who must later pay that bond holder back, plus interest (*Principles of Economics* 5th ed. pages 576–577/6th ed. pages 556–557).

17. **A.** Input prices are a determinant of short-run aggregate supply. When they increase, the SRAS curve shifts to the left, or decreases, because the overall cost of production has increased (*Principles of Economics* 5th ed. pages 755–761/6th ed. pages 734–740).

18. **A.** The fractional reserve system allows banks to lend money to borrowers from excess reserves; excess reserves come from depositors who still have a claim to them. For this reason, money is created whenever banks make loans (*Principles of Economics* 5th ed. pages 650–651/6th ed. pages 628–629).

19. **E.** Increased income tax rates will decrease disposable income, causing a decline in consumption spending (*Principles of Economics* 5th ed. pages 746–748/6th ed. pages 726–728).

20. **A.** An increase in consumer wealth will cause consumption spending to increase, shifting the aggregate demand curve to the right and increasing both price level and real output (*Principles of Economics* 5th ed. pages 746–748/6th ed. pages 726–728).

21. **B.** Movement along the aggregate demand curve occurs due to changes in the overall price level; because of the negative slope of AD, decreasing price levels will cause the output demanded to increase (*Principles of Economics* 5th ed. pages 746–748/6th ed. pages 726–728).

22. **E.** A strong currency causes exported goods to be more expensive for foreigners while imported goods become cheaper. Therefore, net exports decrease, causing aggregate demand to decrease and price level to fall (*Principles of Economics* 5th ed. pages 716–721/6th ed. pages 696–701).

23. **B.** The maximum increase in money supply is determined by multiplying the addition to excess reserves ($900) by the money multiplier (10). 900 × 10 = 9,000 (*Principles of Economics* 5th ed. pages 651–653/6th ed. pages 629–631).

24. **D.** Increases in total spending cause aggregate demand to shift to the right, pulling up price levels with it (*Principles of Economics* 5th ed. pages 739–771/6th ed. pages 719–752).

25. **B.** Excess capacity essentially refers to the amount of room a firm has to expand. With more room to expand, the incentive to invest decreases, as does aggregate demand (*Principles of Economics* 5th ed. pages 746–748/6th ed. pages 726–728).

26. **B.** Decreasing the discount rate encourages banks to borrow money from the Fed at the discount window and, in turn, increase

lending throughout the economy. This is a form of expansionary monetary policy intended to increase output and decrease unemployment (*Principles of Economics* 5th ed. pages 778–787/6th ed. pages 758–767).

27. **A.** With the expectation of greater income, consumers will feel free to spend more money; consumption will increase and aggregate demand will shift to the right (*Principles of Economics* 5th ed. pages 746–748/6th ed. pages 726–728).

28. **C.** The FOMC, as part of the Federal Reserve system, determines the direction of monetary policy. It is designed to be independent of the political process to allow policymakers to be objective in their decision making (*Principles of Economics* 5th ed. pages 648–649/6th ed. pages 638–639).

29. **D.** As the SRAS curve shifts left, equilibrium moves up the aggregate demand curve, causing price level to rise and output to fall (*Principles of Economics* 5th ed. pages 739–771/6th ed. pages 719–752).

30. **A.** Expansionary monetary policies have the effect of increasing bank reserves; this causes an increase in the supply of loanable funds (*Principles of Economics* 5th ed. pages 583–591/6th ed. pages 564–572).

31. **E.** All three options are reasons why the money multiplier may overestimate the amount of money created at any given time (*Principles of Economics* 5th ed. pages 651–653/6th ed. pages 630–631).

32. **B.** The policy is discretionary because new legislation was required and it is expansionary as it is intended to encourage growth by shifting AD to the right (*Principles of Economics* 5th ed. pages 787–790/6th ed. pages 767–770).

33. **A.** The money creation process actually takes place through the commercial banking system (*Principles of Economics* 5th ed. pages 651–653/6th ed. pages 630–631).

34. **C.** When commercial banks purchase bonds from the Fed, bank reserves actually decrease, causing money supply to decrease and drive up interest rates (*Principles of Economics* 5th ed. pages 779–781/6th ed. pages 759–761).

35. **D.** Automatic stabilizers function without explicit legislation actions needed to put them into effect, as opposed to discretionary stabilization policy (*Principles of Economics* 5th ed. page 797/6th ed. pages 777–778).

36. **D.** An accommodative policy would be one that is consistent with the intentions of the fiscal policy in place. Buying bonds on the open market is one form of expansionary monetary policy; it will

likely lower interest rates while limiting the effects of crowding out (*Principles of Economics* 5th ed. pages 778–787/6th ed. pages 758–767).

37. **A.** With an MPC of 0.8, the spending multiplier is 5 (1/0.2). Therefore, the maximum change in output equals the multiplier (5) times the change in spending ($200 billion) (*Principles of Economics* 5th ed. pages 788–790/6th ed. pages 769–770).

38. **D.** The alternative to keeping required reserves as cash would be to deposit the money at the district Federal Reserve bank that has jurisdiction over that particular commercial bank (*Principles of Economics* 5th ed. pages 653–656/6th ed. pages 633–635).

39. **A.** Cutting personal income taxes should have the effect of increasing disposable income and consumer spending, causing an increase in aggregate demand. Increasing excise taxes and/or decreasing government spending would cause a decrease in aggregate demand (*Principles of Economics* 5th ed. pages 787–790/6th ed. pages 767–770).

40. **B.** Commercial banks may borrow money from the Federal Reserve at the discount window. The interest rate charged on these loans is called the discount rate (*Principles of Economics* 5th ed. pages 653–656/6th ed. pages 633–635).

41. **C.** To combat inflation, the Fed must implement a contractionary monetary policy and drive interest rates up. Selling bonds on the open market is one way this may be done (*Principles of Economics* 5th ed. pages 778–787/6th ed. pages 758–767).

42. **B.** Decreasing taxes is an expansionary fiscal policy aimed at lowering unemployment; selling securities is a contractionary monetary policy intended to lower inflation (*Principles of Economics* 5th ed. pages 778–790/6th ed. pages 758–770).

43. **D.** The Fed will raise the federal funds rate by selling securities; this is a contractionary policy intended to decrease inflationary pressure (*Principles of Economics* 5th ed. pages 778–787/6th ed. pages 758–767).

44. **B.** High interest rates increase the demand for a currency on the foreign exchange market and causes the currency to appreciate. An appreciated currency leads to a decrease in exports as goods are relatively more expensive. The combination of expansionary fiscal and contractionary monetary policies will cause interest rates to rise (*Principles of Economics* 5th ed. pages 716–721, 778–790/6th ed. pages 696–701, 758–770).

45. **A.** Productivity refers to the amount of output produced by each unit of input, primarily labor (*Principles of Economics* 5th ed. page 555/6th ed. page 537).

46. **D.** The name given to Congressional stabilization policy is fiscal (*Principles of Economics* 5th ed. pages 787–790/6th ed. pages 767–770).

47. **A.** A tax that increases as income increases is called progressive. If it were to decrease as income increases, it would be regressive; proportional taxes do not change when income changes (*Principles of Economics* 5th ed. page 255/6th ed. page 247).

48. **E.** The only thing we know is that Maritime can produce more ships than Terracotta, which means they have absolute advantage in ship-building. There is not enough information presented to make any other conclusions (*Principles of Economics* 5th ed. pages 54–59/6th ed. pages 54–59).

49. **E.** Contractionary fiscal policies cause the aggregate demand curve to decrease due to decreases in consumption (by increased taxes) and/or decreases in government spending (*Principles of Economics* 5th ed. pages 787–790/6th ed. pages 767–770).

50. **A.** With an MPC of 0.9, the spending multiplier is 10 (1/0.1). To determine the proper amount of spending, divide the desired output change (10 billion) by the multiplier (10). The answer is 1 billion (*Principles of Economics* 5th ed. pages 788–790/6th ed. pages 769–770).

51. **B.** Dividing real GDP by the population gives an indication of how much a nation produces per person. While GDP per capita does not explicitly illustrate a nation's standard of living, it is often used as such because living standards frequently fluctuate with it (*Principles of Economics* 5th ed. pages 12–13/6th ed. pages 13–14).

52. **D.** The building of a factory is considered foreign direct investment and is counted on the capital account; it is a debit because money is leaving the American economy (*Principles of Economics* 5th ed. pages 692–693/6th ed. pages 672–673).

53. **E.** Increasing levels of disposable income will cause increases in consumption and aggregate demand. These are associated with increased production, but not economic growth, a long-run concept (*Principles of Economics* 5th ed. pages 752–756/6th ed. pages 732–735).

54. **D.** Leftward shifts of the aggregate supply curve may be associated with increased price levels and decreased output; this would appear on the graph of the Phillips curve as a rightward shift of the short-run curve (*Principles of Economics* 5th ed. pages 802–816/6th ed. pages 786–798).

55. **C.** According to the Fisher equation, nominal interest rates (those charged by banks) equal real interest rates (the real return over time) plus the anticipated inflation rate. Therefore, the 7 percent charged by banks was determined by adding the 3 percent desired

return by the anticipated inflation rate of 4 percent (*Principles of Economics* 5th ed. pages 674–676/6th ed. pages 655–656).

56. **B.** Demand for a currency on the foreign exchange market is directly proportional to domestic interest rates; as the Fed's expansionary policy causes interest rates to fall relative to those in England, we can expect English demand for the dollar to decrease. As a result, the dollar depreciates versus the pound and the pound appreciates relative to the dollar (*Principles of Economics* 5th ed. pages 716–721/6th ed. pages 696–701).

57. **E.** A reduction or elimination of subsidies would have a negative effect on the short-run aggregate supply curve, causing price level to rise, output to fall, and unemployment to rise (*Principles of Economics* 5th ed. pages 755–761/6th ed. pages 734–740).

58. **C.** Tariffs are protectionist measures meant to restrict foreign competition and protect domestic producers (*Principles of Economics* 5th ed. pages 177–195/6th ed. pages 171–187).

59. **D.** Both the LRAS and PPC are representative of full employment output levels. An outward shift of either illustrates long-term economic growth; increases in AD do not necessarily indicate economic growth has occurred (*Principles of Economics* 5th ed. pages 752–756/6th ed. pages 732–735).

60. **A.** Comparative advantage is defined as being able to produce a good at a lower relative opportunity cost than another producer (*Principles of Economics* 5th ed. pages 54–59/6th ed. pages 54–59).

SECTION II: FREE-RESPONSE ANSWERS

1. **(14 points total)**

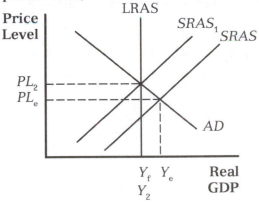

a. 2 points
   See graph, Y_e, PL_e.
b. 3 points
   i. See graph, $SRAS_1$. At output levels beyond full employment, workers will recognize that their real wages have fallen and demand higher nominal wages. When firms respond by raising nominal wages, the SRAS curve will shift left due to the increase in input prices.
   ii. See graph, Y_2, PL_2.

c. 1 point
Any of the following: Sell securities, raise the discount rate, or raise the reserve ratio

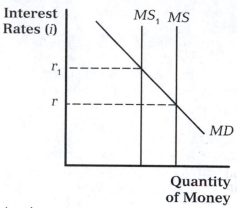

d. 4 points
i.   See graph, r.
ii. See graph, MS$_1$.
iii. See graph, r$_1$.

e. 4 points

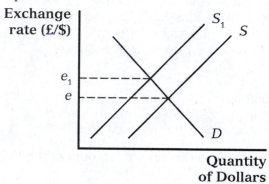

i.   See graph, e$_1$. The dollar will appreciate relative to the pound due to relatively higher interest rates.
ii. Net exports in the United States will decrease.

(*Principles of Economics* 5th ed. pages 716–721, 739–771, 778–787/6th ed. pages 696–701, 719–752, 758–767)

2. **(5 points total)**

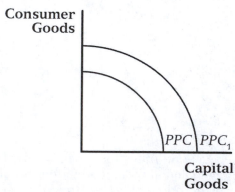

a. 1 point
See graph.

b. 1 point
See graph, PPC₁.

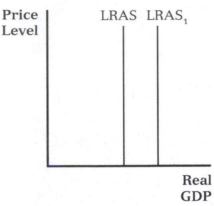

c. 2 points
See graph, LRAS₁. The investment tax credit will encourage firms to spend more on research and development, increasing future levels of both physical and human capital, as well as the overall level of technology. This increase in productivity shifts LRAS to the right.
d. 1 point
Both the PPC and LRAS curve illustrate an economy's full employment rate of output.
(*Principles of Economics* 5th ed. pages 54–59, 752–756/6th ed. pages 54–59, 732–735)

3. **(5 points total)**
a. 1 point
Equilibrium price of coffee will increase; output will decrease.
b. 2 points
The tariff will increase the surplus on the current account of the U.S. This is because imports will decrease.
c. 2 points
i. Current account
ii. They will produce more machinery; quantity will increase.
(*Principles of Economics* 5th ed. pages 177–195, 692–693/6th ed. pages 171–187, 672–673)

CALCULATING YOUR SCORE

SECTION I: MULTIPLE-CHOICE QUESTIONS

[_____] × 1.25 = _____
Number Correct   Weighted Section I Score
(out of 60)   (Do not round)

SECTION II: FREE-RESPONSE QUESTIONS

Question 1 _____ × (1.2500) = _____
          (out of 14)   (Do not round)
Question 2 _____ × (0.8333) = _____
          (out of 5)   (Do not round)
Question 3 _____ × (0.9375) = _____
          (out of 5)   (Do not round)
                        Sum = _____
                        Weighted Section II Score
                        (Do not round)

COMPOSITE SCORE

_____ + _____ = _____
Weighted   Weighted   Composite Score
Section I Score   Section II Score (Round to nearest
                                    whole number)

Composite Score Range	Approximate AP Grade
73–90	5
58–72	4
45–57	3
33–44	2
0–32	1